Ebbets Field

McFarland Historic Ballparks

1. *Forbes Field: Essays and Memories of the Pirates' Historic Ballpark, 1909–1971.* Edited by David Cicotello and Angelo J. Louisa. 2007

2. *Ebbets Field: Essays and Memories of Brooklyn's Historic Ballpark, 1913–1960.* Edited by John G. Zinn and Paul G. Zinn. Series Editors David Cicotello and Angelo J. Louisa. 2012

Ebbets Field

Essays and Memories of Brooklyn's Historic Ballpark, 1913–1960

Edited by John G. Zinn *and*
Paul G. Zinn

McFarland Historic Ballparks, 2

Series Editors David Cicotello *and* Angelo J. Louisa

McFarland & Company, Inc., Publishers
Jefferson, North Carolina, and London

Library of Congress Cataloguing-in-Publication Data

Ebbets Field : essays and memories of Brooklyn's historic ballpark,
1913–1960 / edited by John G. Zinn and Paul G. Zinn.
p. cm. — (McFarland historic ballparks)
David Cicotello and Angelo J. Louisa, series editors.
Includes bibliographical references and index.

ISBN 978-0-7864-4827-2
softcover : acid free paper ∞

1. Ebbets Field (New York, N.Y.)—History. 2. Brooklyn Dodgers
(Baseball team)—History. I. Zinn, John G., 1946– II. Zinn, Paul G.
GV417.E23 2013 796.35709747'23—dc23 2012042011

British Library cataloguing data are available

On the cover: Ebbets Field in its inaugural year of 1913

Manufactured in the United States of America

McFarland & Company, Inc., Publishers
Box 611, Jefferson, North Carolina 28640
www.mcfarlandpub.com

As this work neared publication, the Zinn-Kaufman family was blessed with our newest baseball fan — Sophie Ann Zinn, born on May 17, 2012. It is a pleasure to dedicate this book to her.

Table of Contents

Preface and Acknowledgments 1

I — History and Background

Charles Ebbets: Builder of Ballparks, Ballclubs and More JOHN G. ZINN 8

A Ballpark and Its "City": Ebbets Field, Brooklyn and Changing Times
ELLEN M. SNYDER-GRENIER 31

The Alpha and the Omega: First and Last Dodger Games at Ebbets Field
JOHN G. ZINN 48

History, Tragedy and Comedy: The Dodgers at Ebbets Field
PAUL G. ZINN *and* JOHN G. ZINN 58

Before Jackie: Black Baseball at Ebbets Field JAMES OVERMYER 83

Ebbets Field: Sporting Venue and Community Center PAUL G. ZINN 101

Ebbets Field by the Numbers RONALD M. SELTER 123

II — Memories of Ebbets Field

Visiting Players Reminisce About the Brooklyn Ballpark 140

The Home Team: Recollections of the Brooklyn Dodgers 163

Vox Populi: The People Remember Ebbets Field 176

Appendices
A: Play-by-Play and Box Scores for Ebbets Field's Two 1913 Openers 223
B: Play-by-Play and Box Score for the Last Dodger Game at Ebbets Field 227
C: Music Played at the First and Last Games at Ebbets Field 229

Bibliography 231

About the Contributors 233

Index 235

"Ebbets Field, which bears the same relation to
Brooklyn as the Academy of Music does to arts and sciences...."
— Edward J. McKeever, *Brooklyn Daily Eagle*, July 11, 1921

Preface and Acknowledgments

John G. Zinn

Roger Kahn, renowned author of *The Boys of Summer*, wrote that "summarizing the 1951 [National League pennant] race is akin to summarizing *King Lear*. Before anything else, your effort will diminish majesty."[1] Analyzing the relationship between Brooklyn, Ebbets Field, and the Dodgers runs much the same risk. All historic ballparks created important relationships, but Ebbets Field is special in its own way.

The first two decades of the twentieth century witnessed a new generation of ballparks, with nearly every major league team either building a new facility or substantially renovating an old one. For the next 50 years or more those facilities were "cathedrals," where countless people had unforgettable experiences, including their first game, special family memories, and moments of excitement, joy, and heartbreak. When it came time to replace those ballparks, however, the closing of the old one almost always meant the opening of the new. Forbes Field, Sportsman's Park, and Crosley Field died, but the Pirates, Cardinals, and Reds continued the next chapter of their franchises in new venues that also served as a connector to the old park.

Brooklyn's experience was, of course, radically different, since neither the team nor the ballpark survived. By 1960, no tangible evidence remained of 45 years of memorable baseball and personal history. To be sure, Brooklyn was not alone in losing both ballpark and ballclub, but in the other cases, lack of success on the field and at the box office meant only a small, though passionate, group of caring fans was left behind. Yet today, more than 50 years after the last game at Ebbets Field, programs about the Dodgers continue to draw capacity crowds at venues like the Brooklyn Historical Society.

While risking "diminishing majesty," this book attempts to analyze the phenomena of Ebbets Field and to simultaneously preserve some of the memories of fans and players. One important conclusion of the collective research is that the special relationship between the Dodgers, Brooklyn, and Ebbets Field is in large measure due to how Charles Ebbets built a solid connection between the borough, ballclub, and ballpark. This is not to suggest the Brooklyn owner was a disinterested civic saint. Ebbets was in baseball to make money, but he gradually learned his interests and those of the borough were interrelated.

Ebbets Field was significant to Brooklyn not just because of the Dodgers. Like all ballparks, since there have been ballparks, Ebbets Field did its owners little good when it stood vacant. At the same time, Brooklyn needed a facility to host major sporting events, as well as important local contests. What is significant to note is Brooklynites did not just watch, but they also participated on this hallowed ground. Stretched over 40-plus years, these experiences strengthened the connection between the borough and ballpark.

At its heart, however, the relationship between Brooklyn and Ebbets Field depended on the Dodgers. The excitement and pride of the 1913 opening and the heartbreak of the 1957 closing, described in the third chapter, illustrate the three-part relationship of borough, ballpark and ball club. Although the chapter discusses the wake-like atmosphere of that sad September night, the book itself does not focus on the Dodgers' departure. That story has been told and analyzed many times in recent years and regardless of whether the Dodgers left Brooklyn or not, the club's days at Ebbets Field were numbered. This book focuses on the special place that Ebbets was and continues to be in the collective memory.

In between the opening and closing were 45 years of memorable baseball, some exciting and historic, some heartbreaking, with plenty of comedy thrown in for good measure. Many of the moments described here, ranging from the well known to those "picked from the worm-holes of long-vanished days,"[2] are supplemented by firsthand accounts of players and fans in the second half of the text. Whether the memories of Dodger players, their fans, or opponents, these stories testify to the importance of what happened on Bedford Avenue over almost half a century.

Rounding out the story of Ebbets Field are essays by three primary contributors. Ronald M. Selter drew on his award-winning *Ballparks of the Deadball Era: A Comprehensive Study of Their Dimensions, Configurations and Effects on Batting, 1901–1919*, to provide quality and detailed analysis of hitting at the Brooklyn ballpark. While Ebbets Field was, of course, the place where the color line was broken, African Americans played baseball there long before 1947. Jim Overmyer's background as the author of a book about Effa Manley and the Newark Eagles, as well as his many years of Negro League research, made him the ideal person to tell this story. The history of any ballpark, particularly its opening and closing, needs to be placed into the context of its host community — none more so than Ebbets Field. From the outset I believed the person best qualified to provide that context is Ellen M. Snyder-Grenier, former chief curator of the Brooklyn Historical Society and author of *Brooklyn! An Illustrated History*. Since Ellen is a fellow New Jerseyan, I also had the benefit of several in-depth conversations with her about Brooklyn and Ebbets Field. Paul and I are immensely grateful to all three contributing authors for being part of this project.

Although it was not through Ellen's participation, the Brooklyn Historical Society (BHS) also played an important part in this book. In a grace-filled moment, the BHS decided to focus its 2010 Exhibition Laboratory (Ex Lab) project on Ebbets Field and the Dodgers. Ex Lab is a wonderful program where local high school students create an exhibit primarily from the Society's collections. Fortunately for this book, I was asked to serve as lead historian on the project. In addition to working with an extraordinary group of young people and the dedicated BHS staff, this role opened the door to many of those whose memories are part of this volume. I am particularly grateful to Kate Fermoile, Andrea Del Valle, Keara Duggan, and Sady Sullivan for this opportunity. At the BHS, I also met Ron Schweiger, Brooklyn's borough historian, who kindly showed me his collection of Dodger memorabilia and shared his memories of Ebbets Field.

Another grace-filled moment was an interview with John Sexton, president of New York University. John told me of his own experiences at the Brooklyn ballpark, and then introduced me to Tom Oliphant, retired *Boston Globe* columnist and author of *Praying for Gil Hodges*. After sharing his memories, Tom introduced me to Doris Kearns Goodwin, who subsequently reminisced with me about Ebbets Field. That occurred because John Sexton generously invited me to a class where Doris and Tom discussed the Dodgers with a highly engaged group of college students. Thank you to John, Tom, and Doris for their assistance and participation.

Seeking out those with memories of Ebbets Field was challenging, surprising, and almost always rewarding. While I was never fortunate enough to go to Ebbets Field, I was pleasantly surprised to find that longtime friends such as Bill Bess, Dick Denby, Stuart Grant, and George Saltsman not only had been there, but were very willing to talk about it. Others I met through this book had fascinating stories, such as Susan Horowitz's two memorable encounters with the Ebbets Field cornerstone. It was also a special pleasure to speak with *New York Times* columnist Dave Anderson and Pulitzer Prize–winning author Robert Caro.

Utilizing his prior experience as a sports journalist, Paul Zinn undertook most of the player interviews, with me pinch-hitting as necessary. Two I particularly enjoyed were lengthy telephone conversations with Dick Groat and Carl Erskine. I always admired Dick Groat as a player, and I was glad to connect with him through his son-in-law, Lou Goetz, who is also my college classmate. Anyone who has had the opportunity to speak with Carl Erskine knows it is an unforgettable experience. I had the pleasure of speaking for over an hour with this articulate gentleman, who wondered if he was "taking too much of my time"— there was not a chance of that! One of the sad aspects of the player interview process was seeing the "Boys of Summer" and their opponents pass on. At least three former players have died since Paul spoke with them. But we are very pleased to have been able to preserve their last memories of Ebbets Field. It is unfortunate there are not more memories of former Dodger players in this book, but many of the survivors have been interviewed so often they were reluctant to participate. Paul and I understand and respect their position.

One of the biggest challenges to this project was finding pictures and illustrations, especially of non–Dodger events. Ultimately, Paul and I are pleased with the final product and particularly want to thank those who went out of their way to help us. This group includes Roger Godin, who provided pictures of the Brooklyn Football Dodgers, and Charles Lamb of the University of Notre Dame Archives, who supplied the fascinating picture of the 1923 Notre Dame–Army game at Ebbets Field. Erika Gorder at Rutgers University's Special Collections helped us with the picture of Paul Robeson in action at Ebbets Field. We are also grateful to the staff of the Brooklyn Public Library, the Los Angeles Dodgers, and the National Baseball Hall of Fame Library, particularly John Horne from the latter institution. My niece, Andrea Magno, took time from a fulltime job and two children under the age of five to organize the collage of advertisements from the Ebbets Field opening. My Civil War historian colleague, Henry F. Ballone, generously scanned and cleaned up the line drawings and cartoons that appear throughout the text, with one exception: the Gene Mack cartoon of Ebbets Field, which was supplied by the National Baseball Hall of Fame Library. We are especially grateful to Joseph Duggan, the copyright owner, for his prompt approval of our request.

As usual, libraries were invaluable sources of information. The newspaper collections at the New York Public Library greatly facilitated the complete and convenient review of all New York and Brooklyn newspapers. The August "Garry" Gold Mine Herrmann papers at the National Baseball Hall of Fame Library in Cooperstown are a gold mine for anyone interested in baseball ownership during the Deadball Era. Thank you to Freddy Berowski and the rest of the staff at the A. Bartlett Giamatti Research Center at the Hall of Fame. Bill Trafton of the Verona Public Library was very helpful with interlibrary loans, as he has been on countless other research projects.

As in previous books, I want to say a special word of thanks and praise to the Alexander Library at my alma mater, Rutgers University. I spent many happy and productive hours poring over the library's complete run of the *Brooklyn Daily Eagle.* While not a library, an inestimable debt of gratitude is due to Dave Smith and the Retrosheet team. The information there makes source checking nearly painless. Thanks also to Paul's college classmate and close friend, Asad Butt, who produced our website, www.ebbetsfieldmemories.com, which generated a number of valuable fan memories. Series editors Angelo Louisa and David Cicotello were supportive throughout the process and always ready to help solve problems and remove obstacles.

John Milton once wrote, "They also serve who only stand and wait."[3] In this case, that group is made up of friends who offered encouragement and support since the inception of this project. Included are my running friends: Margo DiStefano, Vince Dahmen, James J. McDonald, and Mark Zablow. Also very supportive were friends and neighbors who generously listen to me now that I am retired. Butch Ceccacci and Gary Kistner shared my excitement of speaking to players we remembered from our youth, while Diane Ceccacci and Cathy Ward provided words of support and encouragement.

This book was a true partnership between Paul and me. As with our first joint book, *The Major League Pennant Races of 1916: "The Most Maddening Baseball Melee in History,"* we divided up the tasks, filled in for one another, and worked together to finish the project. I am especially grateful to Paul for his willingness to do the bulk of the player interviews and for his editing skills, two areas where I am sorely lacking. John Sexton said to me, "The important thing about your book is that you are doing it with your son." Mr. Sexton is a very wise man!

Our final thanks go to our wives, Sarah Kaufman and Carol Zinn, who continue to be very supportive of our writing efforts. This time they had to put up with not only endless photocopies of old newspaper articles, but also long phone calls, many with individuals they had never heard of. It is impossible to find words to express how much they mean to us, but it is clear that this book, and much else in our lives, would never have been completed without their support. Unconditional love is a rare commodity, and we are both extremely fortunate to have spouses who willingly provide it.

With the birth of Sarah and Paul's daughter, Sophie Ann Zinn, all of us in the Zinn-Kaufman family are adapting to new roles and responsibilities. Sophie has already been to Fenway Park twice and it's safe to say she will make many trips to historic ballparks.

Whether our efforts will "diminish majesty" is for others to judge. Ultimately, the passage of time will end the oral tradition of Ebbets Field. Books like this one, which collect stories that would otherwise be lost, preserve that history. Paul and I are grateful to have the opportunity to do this and hope those who examine the ensuing pages will enjoy learning of a special place that, although gone forever, will never die.

Notes

1. Roger Kahn, *The Era 1947–1957: When the Yankees, the Giants and the Dodgers Ruled the World* (New York: Ticknor & Fields, 1993), 268.
2. William Shakespeare, *Henry V*, 2.4.86.
3. John Milton, "On His Blindness."

I — History and Background

EBBETS FIELD AS IT WILL APPEAR WHEN COMPLETED

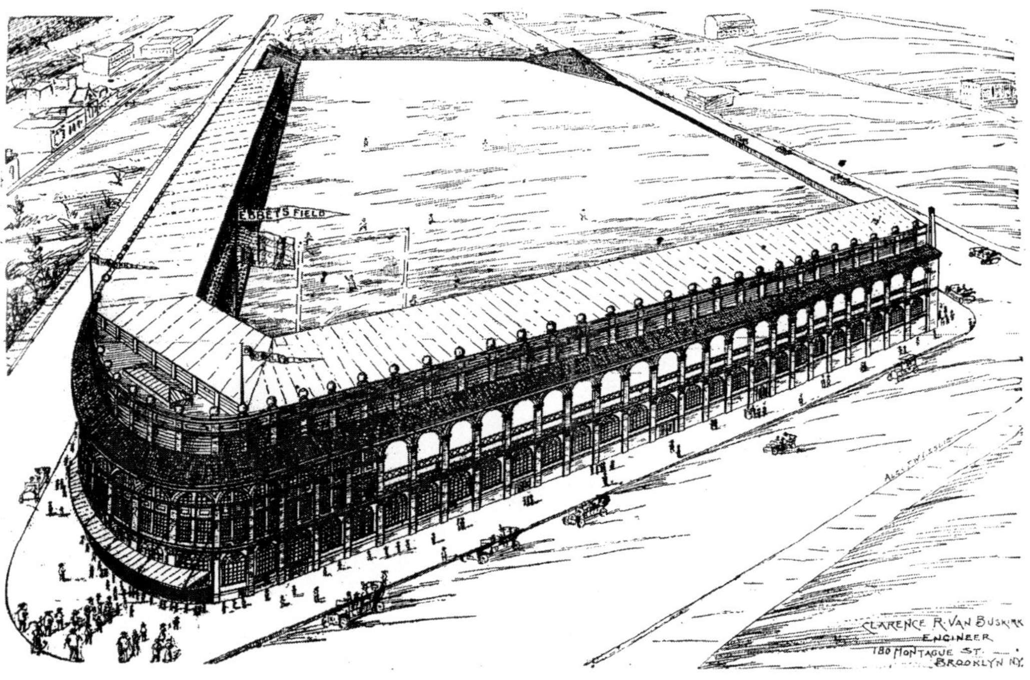

Architect Clarence R. Van Buskirk's drawing illustrates Charles Ebbets' vision of Brooklyn's new ballpark (*Brooklyn Daily Eagle*, April 6, 1912).

Charles Ebbets

Builder of Ballparks, Ballclubs and More

John G. Zinn

Charles Ebbets died early on the morning of April 18, 1925, the day of the first Dodger–Giant game that season. The game was played as scheduled at the ballpark Ebbets built, and which bore his name, because as Wilbert Robinson reportedly said, "Charlie wouldn't want anybody to miss a Giant–Brooklyn series just because he died." The next day was Sunday, and the two teams played again — something legal largely through Ebbets' leadership. Two days later, all National League games were postponed as an estimated 2,000 mourners, including most of Ebbets' fellow club owners, attended the funeral in Brooklyn. Games in New York that day would have been rained out anyway, causing ticket holders to use their rain checks — another Ebbets innovation. In fact, the 154-game schedule was also largely the design of the Brooklyn owner. In a career that spanned more than four decades, Charles Ebbets was a major contributor to the game he loved.[1]

According to Ebbets, his over 40-year baseball career began the same day the Brooklyn baseball club played its first home game: May 12, 1883. Many years later, he described his role as a "sort of assistant secretary and handyman." Since the club was a small startup operation, Ebbets probably did everything from selling scorecards to arranging road trips. Over the next 15 years, while the club played at three different facilities in three different leagues, Ebbets gradually was given more responsibility, so that he was effectively in "full charge" by the late 1890s. While Ebbets may have been running the club, he had neither the appropriate title, nor a significant ownership interest. It must, therefore, have seemed like a dream come true when he took control of the Dodgers at the end of 1897 through the combination of a stock purchase and an option agreement that would make him majority owner.[2]

Charles Ebbets in his prime, about 1910 (Library of Congress, Prints & Photographs Division, Bain Collection [LC-DIG-ggbain-05526]).

Ebbets would have been excused, however, for wondering whether it was a dream or a nightmare. The 38-year-old president took over a team that was unsuccessful on the field and at the box office. Part of the revenue problems were due to a home field that was inconvenient and unpopular. And if that was not enough, new and formidable competition loomed on the horizon, both in New York and nationally. To make matters worse, solutions to these challenges required money Ebbets did not have. Although he ultimately transformed the Dodgers into a successful and profitable franchise embedded in the DNA of Brooklyn, it took almost 20 years and the construction of one of the most legendary ballparks in baseball history.

Foremost among the challenges facing Ebbets in 1898 was the ballpark, a by-product of the 1890 Players' League war. Frustrated by their inability to negotiate higher salaries, players formed a third league that competed with the National League and the American Association during the 1890 season. Although the new league folded after that opening campaign, George Chauncey, the owner of the Players' League Brooklyn franchise and a real estate developer, purchased a share of the Brooklyn Dodgers and the two teams merged. As part of the negotiations, Chauncey convinced his new partners, Charles Byrne, Ferdinand Abell, and Joseph Doyle, to move the team from south Brooklyn to Eastern Park in the East New York section of Brooklyn, beginning with the 1891 season.[3]

Looking back many years later, Ebbets claimed the move "cost Messer's Byrne, Abell, and Doyle a barrel of money," because it was motivated, not by the interests of the team and its fans, but by "development of real estate situated on the Kings County elevated" railroad. Ebbets claimed the site was "comparatively inaccessible," and fans would not go there even to see a successful team. The truth of the latter assertion was hard to prove since the club consistently finished in the middle of a 12-team league. While the surviving records do not indicate attendance was that bad, there was consensus the financial results were poor. Ebbets himself contended the club had been a financial failure since the move.[4]

In confronting these challenges, Ebbets was further hampered by his lack of money. Unlike many of his peers, Ebbets could not rely on money from outside of baseball, family, or otherwise. Reportedly, the new owner had to borrow $25,000 for his 1897 stock purchase and ultimately could not afford the option he held on Ferdinand Abell's shares, which would have given Ebbets majority ownership. That left Ebbets in charge of day-to-day operations, but dependent on Abell for larger sums of money, funds Abell was increasingly reluctant to provide. The situation was further complicated because the club was $56,000 in debt ($1.5 million today). Since Ebbets had 15 years of baseball experience, he knew full well the only real source of baseball revenue was ticket sales, so solving the ballpark problem had to be the first priority. Attracting fans through a new and more convenient facility was less complicated than the complexities of building a team and then hoping it would be successful against the other 11 clubs.[5]

In addition to money, time was also a problem. Almost immediately after Ebbets took over the team, the *Brooklyn Daily Eagle* emphasized that a decision about the venue for the 1898 season "requires more hurry than any other feature." Further confirming the club's financial woes, the paper also claimed the inability to come up with $4,000 had prevented a move back to south Brooklyn the previous year. Although multiple locations were supposedly under consideration, Ebbets was most likely inclined all along toward the club's historic roots in south Brooklyn, near the original Washington Park, the club's home between 1883 and 1890. On March 14, 1898, with only about six weeks until the home opener, Ebbets announced a 10-year lease for construction of a new Washington Park, adjacent to the site of the old one. Even more important than the close proximity to the club's original home field was the location near multiple public transit lines, which in addition to offering convenient fan access, gave local transportation companies incentive to help with the financing. In the end, the new park cost between $60 and $100,000, with the streetcar companies paying a portion. Since the stands would be made of wood and the ground was "almost perfectly level," with only two "obstructions," the short time frame was not a problem. In fact, while construction did not begin until March 24, the park was ready for the April 30 opener. The magnitude of Ebbets' achievement was recognized early in 1899, when the *Eagle* claimed "no other man" could have exchanged the "white elephant" at Eastern Park for such a good location, built at little expense to the club and its stockholders.[6]

A new, accessible facility in a proven location would attract fans, but getting them to return was dependent upon the quality of play on the field. This started with the manager, and in Ebbets' case he inherited Bill Barnie, who had "led" the club to an 1897 sixth-place finish, with a below .500 record. Barnie had prior managerial experience but not much success. Although Ebbets would prove to be loyal to his managers, perhaps to

Bill Dahlen was one of the star players imported for Brooklyn's championship teams of 1899 and 1900. A decade later, he became the club's manager (Library of Congress, Prints & Photographs Division, Bain Collection [LC-DIG-ggbain-04615]).

a fault, when action was required, he took it. Such was the case with Barnie. Not even two months into the 1898 season, the media reported the team was not in shape, suffered from cliques, and had a manager, Barnie, who was playing favorites. On June 3, the *Eagle* said Ebbets needed to act, and within a week Barnie's tenure was over.[7]

In his place, Ebbets installed team captain Mike Griffin, one of the club's best players. After three defeats in four games, Griffin wasted no time giving back the managerial reins, supposedly to focus on playing. At this point, there were probably few alternatives, so Ebbets himself stepped in and managed the team for the rest of the season. As part of this merry-go-round, Ebbets may have recognized the 1898 season was going to be a disaster, both on and off the field. In spite of the new and more convenient ballpark, attendance fell by almost 100,000, a drop of 45 percent. The major factor in the decline was, no doubt, the club's 10th-place finish, 46 games out of first, but attendance was poor throughout the league, reportedly due to the Spanish-American war. Since Ebbets had observed earlier in the season that "we are not in baseball for our health [something he would say more than once] and the money invested here demands that the team must win games," the situation had to change. Ebbets was probably well aware that quick fixes were few and far between. This was one time however, when such a solution appeared to be at hand — a fix that would resolve both the managerial and talent issues and perhaps the financial problems. However, if a nagging internal voice told Ebbets this was too good to be true, he would have been well advised to listen.[8]

The 1899 quick fix took a form incomprehensible today — syndicate baseball. Simply put, syndicate baseball was the ownership of multiple teams by one group of owners, enabling them to concentrate the best players on one team. Such syndicates or trusts were popular in business during this period, so it was only natural the concept would spread to the sporting world. In this case, the syndicate brought together Brooklyn and one of the great teams of the 1890s, the Baltimore Orioles. In spite of their on-field success, the Orioles had never been a big draw at the box office, and a possible Baltimore–Brooklyn combination was not a new idea. Brooklyn owner and primary financial backer Ferdinand Abell had reportedly proposed the idea in 1896 but was rejected. Now, however, Baltimore was losing money, so owner Harry von der Horst and his manager, Ned Hanlon, were more amenable. The economics, as one historian noted, were "unassailable." Brooklyn's population was twice the size of Baltimore's, not to mention the market potential in the rest of greater New York. Accounts in the *Eagle* conservatively estimated that average home attendance of 4,000 per game would yield an annual bottom line profit of $70,000 (almost $1.9 million today), while 5,000 to 6,000 would generate $100,000 (almost $2.7 million today), assuming in either case the team broke even on the road. Under the syndicate arrangement, the Baltimore (von der Horst and Hanlon) and Brooklyn (Ebbets and Abell) owners would own 50 percent of each team. Although Ebbets would continue as Brooklyn team president, he directly owned no more than 10 percent of the stock.[9]

The first payoff for Ebbets was Ned Hanlon as a manager — a future Hall of Famer who had led the Orioles to three National League pennants and two second-place finishes in the last five years. Hanlon did not come to Brooklyn empty-handed either, bringing half of his starting lineup and three 20-game winning pitchers with him. Included in the group were future Hall of Famers Willie Keeler, Joe Kelley, and Hughie Jennings. When

Hanlon acquired Bill Dahlen, one of the best shortstops in the game, Brooklyn quickly became a prohibitive favorite to win the 1899 National League pennant. And the team did just that, moving into first place on May 22 and remaining there the rest of the way. Nicknamed the Superbas after a popular vaudeville act called Hanlon's Superbas, Brooklyn won 101 games, finishing an incredible 84 games ahead of the worst team in major league history, the Cleveland Spiders (20–134). Brooklyn also had no local competition, or at least not on the field, as the 10th-place Giants finished 42 games behind Brooklyn.[10]

Ominously, however, the on-field dominance did not produce anything close to the projected levels of financial success. Attendance did double that of the prior year but was only fourth best in the National League. More significantly, the average home attendance was under 3,000, less than the conservative estimate of 4,000 per game and well below the upper estimates of 5,000 to 6,000. As a result, profits were not in the $70 to 100,000 range, but more in the "neighborhood of $50,000." All of this did not auger well for the future, and impending changes in major league baseball made things even more problematic. After the 1899 season, National League owners finally accepted that a 12-team circuit was too big. The number of clubs was reduced from 12 to eight, where it would remain for more than 60 years. There were also rumblings about a new, rival major league, raising the specter of the second baseball war within a decade. Although Ebbets proudly proclaimed he had achieved his three major goals — putting baseball in Brooklyn on a "business basis," building a centrally located park, and putting together a championship team — he had to be concerned about the future.[11]

Contraction to eight teams ended the Baltimore part of the syndicate, leaving Hanlon, von der Horst, Abbell and Ebbets with one team — the defending champion Superbas — as well as the rights to the Oriole players. The change also meant all of the talent could be moved to one team. As a result, six more former Oriole players came to Brooklyn, including two who were making a return trip. Highlighting the group was future Hall of Famer Joe McGinnity, who along with fellow hurler Frank Kitson, combined for 50 wins in 1899. While there may have been expectations the Brooklyn team would be even more dominant in 1900, such was not the case. Since there were only eight major league teams, even the weakest club had more talent, almost guaranteeing a more competitive race. Though Brooklyn was still good enough to repeat, it was not easy as they led by only one game on September 25, before finally pulling away from second-place Pittsburgh. Brooklyn topped off its regular season title by defeating the Pirates in a best of five postseason series, every game of which was played in Pittsburgh.[12]

The lack of postseason games in Brooklyn was all the evidence necessary that things had not gone well at the box office. Attendance actually fell by almost one-third from the previous season, putting Brooklyn next to last in admissions. Moreover, the pennant-winning Superbas lost money at home because the average Washington Park attendance of 2,500 was far below the "conservative" estimates that had made the economic logic of the syndicate "unassailable." However, Ebbets and his partners were not the only ones worried about the situation. As early as June, concern about Brooklyn's low attendance was expressed throughout the National League, reviving 1899 rumors that Ebbets and Abell planned to relocate the team to Washington D.C. A furious Ebbets claimed he would keep the team in Brooklyn, even if he could make twice as much in D.C., because

Brooklyn "is my home" and because of his pride in "keeping baseball alive in Brooklyn." Although competition from horse racing and boxing were suggested as factors in the poor attendance, Ebbets felt the major cause was the lack of really tight pennant races, since it seemed a team that won the pennant without much competition lost "patronage almost as speedily as a tail end team." Ironically, road attendance, which was only counted on to cover traveling expenses, produced a profit, otherwise "losses would have been large." Although rejecting moving the club, Ebbets was open to selling "if we can get a fair price."[13]

Ebbets was never specific about the definition of a fair price, but had he known what lay ahead, his minimum figure might have dropped considerably. Unlike other National League owners, when war broke out with the new American League in 1901, Ebbets received not one, but three blows to his "financial chin." Simply surviving the carnage may have been one of Ebbets' greatest achievements as owner. First came the player raids, which saw 70 to 100 National Leaguers join American League clubs. The impact, however, was not equally distributed. Pittsburgh, for example, lost only one regular, while no team "was hit harder than Brooklyn." It was not as if Ebbets did not know how to fight player raids, since in the 1890 Brotherhood War he saw how Charles Byrne paid "top salaries" to keep the Brooklyn club "virtually intact." Years later it was claimed the defections could have been prevented, but Ferdinand Abell, the man with the money, "refused outright."[14]

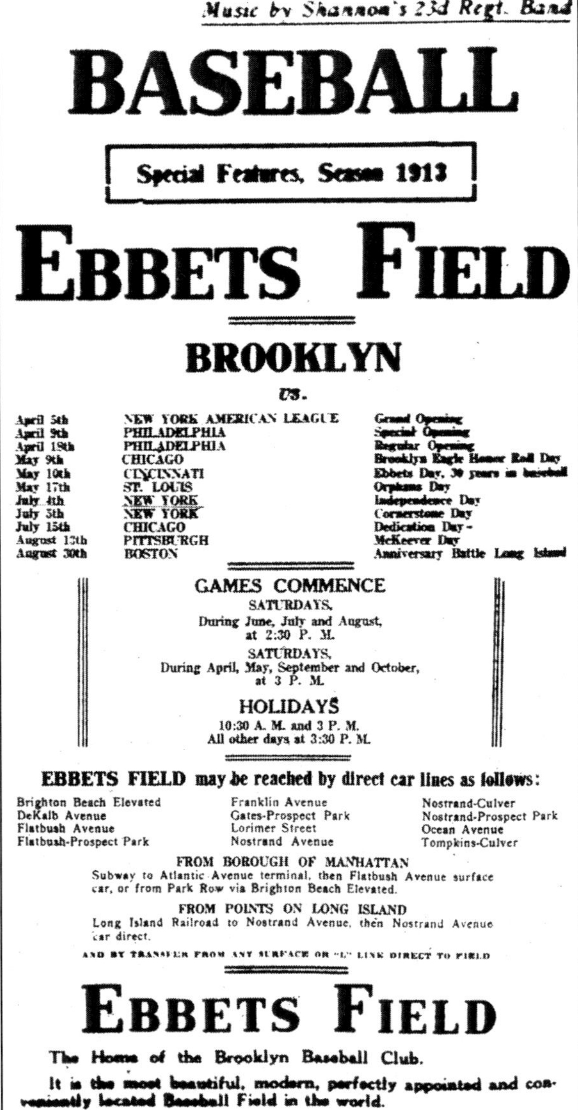

Special events were one of the methods Ebbets used to build attendance during the dark days at Washington Park. The opening of his new ballpark in 1913 enabled him to take full advantage of the idea (*Brooklyn Daily Eagle*, April 5, 1913).

The player losses themselves were bad enough, but the advent of the American League also provided second and third blows by introducing new local competition and facilitating a major change in the existing National League competition. After the 1902 season, the American League moved a team into New York that would become permanent after the 1903 peace agreement. While the first championship Yankee teams were two decades away, the American League club was competitive from 1904 to 1906, drawing crowds that exceeded those seen at Washington Park by 100,000 or more per year. Far worse, however, was the resurrection that took place in upper Manhattan. The New York American League team had originally played in Baltimore under the leadership of the fiery John McGraw, and to no one's surprise, McGraw's massive ego could not co-exist with that of American League founder Ban Johnson. During 1902, McGraw bolted to the New York Giants through a ploy that enabled him to bring four of his players with him. Suddenly, the team known as "the sick man of the National League" had a new manager, new players, and a new owner in John T. Brush, reportedly "the hardest man in baseball, its wiliest politician." By 1905, the Giants had won two straight National League pennants and were World Series champions.[15]

The newfound success at the Polo Grounds was mirrored by a corresponding decline at Washington Park. After finishing third in 1901 and a distant second the following year, Charles Ebbets' club fell into the second division, where it would remain for more than a decade. The decline on the field obviously did not help at the box office, as 1901 and 1902 attendance was seventh and sixth, respectively, among National League clubs. Although admissions improved somewhat through 1908, Brooklyn remained at the bottom of the league in attendance, even worse than the on-field results. In contrast, the Giants enjoyed an increase of 276,000 spectators in attendance between 1902 and 1903, a figure greater than Brooklyn's total 1903 attendance. For the next five years, the Giants averaged almost 603,000 in annual admissions, more than double that of Brooklyn, and ultimately reached the almost absurd ratio of 910,000/275,600 for the epic 1908 season. These and other figures suggest the Giants' profits were consistently three times those of Brooklyn, at a time when McGraw's team already had better personnel. The *Eagle* clearly understood the meaning of the figures, commenting during the 1905 season, that without new revenue sources such as Sunday baseball, Ebbets could not afford "the enormous outlay necessary to put the club in the first division."[16]

Hanlon's grasp of the financial realities most likely contributed to the appearance that the Brooklyn manager was "sour on his job." This was probably no surprise since prior to the start of the season, Ebbets attempted to cut Hanlon's salary from $12,500 to $6,000, before compromising between $7,500 and 8,000. Unlike Ebbets, Hanlon had an easy way out of the situation, leaving Brooklyn to become the new Cincinnati manager for the 1906 season. Although no longer on the scene, Hanlon could not be forgotten since he was still part owner of the Brooklyn club. He had already tried to buy von der Horst's shares, gain control of the club, and possibly move it to Baltimore. Although Ebbets lacked the funds to buy the shares, he outmaneuvered Hanlon by arranging for his friend, Harry Medicus, to buy out von der Horst. However, Hanlon and to some degree, Ferdinand Abell, were not finished, as a year later they sued Ebbets to recover $30,000 the defunct Orioles organization had lent to the Brooklyn club. Once again, Ebbets lacked the necessary funds and considered selling his two best players, Harry Lumley and Tim Jordan, to the archrival Giants. In the end, though, he declined the offer. Somehow Ebbets ultimately convinced Abell to accept $20,000 in notes and bought out

Hanlon, in exchange for their shares and all claims against the Brooklyn club. Fighting with little or nothing in the way of weapons (money), Ebbets not only eliminated the last challenge to his control of the ball club, but also strengthened community support by not selling Brooklyn's best players.[17]

Unfortunately, internal problems were not the only owner-related challenges Ebbets faced during this difficult period. In 1901, John Brush (owner of the Reds at the time), along with then Giant owner, Andrew Freedman, pushed a trust plan that could have been disastrous for Brooklyn. Claiming the end of the 10-year agreement binding the National League teams together required a new structure, the duo, along with Frank Robison of St. Louis and Arthur Soden of Boston, proposed a trust agreement that would control all eight franchises and assign players to the teams. Especially sinister was the proposed ownership percentages, where the proposers would have two-thirds of the shares, while two-time defending champion Brooklyn would own only 6 percent. Fortunately, the four owners could not get their plan approved, and the argument that the National League was "a perpetual organization" carried the day.[18]

While fighting on multiple fronts, Ebbets looked for more permanent solutions to his financial woes. Short of finding more investors, the only significant source of new revenue was higher ticket sales. While the number of games could not be increased (although Ebbets periodically advocated unsuccessfully for a 168-game schedule), and improving the on-field product would take time, Sunday home games would significantly expand the potential market of paying customers. Although charging admission to baseball games on Sunday was illegal in New York, Ebbets tried to play Sunday games from 1904 to 1906 by using various ploys, such as free admission with a mandatory scorecard purchase. Each attempt was ruled illegal, forcing Ebbets and other interested parties to go the legislative route, which took more than ten years. When Sunday baseball finally became legal in New York in 1919, it was a financial windfall, and the wisdom of Ebbets' strategy was proven once and for all. However, there was also a cautionary note from the 1904–06 experience. In the first two seasons that Ebbets experimented with Sunday games, attendance started high but fell off in direct relationship to the Superbas' poor play. Clearly there would be no sustained increase in paying customers without a better team.[19]

Upgrading the on-field performance meant finding good players and managing them effectively. Much of this responsibility rested with the manager. With Hanlon's departure, Ebbets faced his first managerial hiring decision. Managerial hiring is never a sure thing, but during the early Deadball Era it had its own unique difficulties. Playing managers like Frank Chance of the Cubs were still popular, but that meant identifying candidates on a major league roster and then acquiring them. Since the Superbas had been gutted by defections to the American League, there was little or no material that could be traded for an aspiring player-manager. Additionally, Brooklyn's weak financial condition made purchasing these types of candidates difficult at best. With the player-manager possibilities limited, if not nonexistent, Ebbets had to consider unemployed managers with experience or retired players without managerial experience. While there were former managers with experience, little was of a winning variety since a number of the pennant-winning managers between 1901 and 1913 were still with those clubs.[20]

For the 1906 season, Ebbets hired Patsy Donovan, a very successful player (lifetime

.300 hitter) who also had six years of major league managing experience, finishing as high as fourth. Although the move was praised by the press, Donovan was unsuccessful, finishing fifth twice and seventh once in three years with Brooklyn. When he was let go after the 1908 season, there were claims that Ebbets did not give Donovan a "free hand," but at least one sportswriter said the "truth" was that the only hand Donovan lacked was a firm one with his players. Of course, no manager would be successful without talent, and from 1904 to 1907, the only effective players acquired by Ebbets were Lumley, Jordan, and star pitcher Nap Rucker, which was hardly enough. The ballclub hit rock bottom in 1908 when the Superbas lost 101 games and finished seventh.[21]

As difficult as it is to determine the turning point in a game or even a season, it is even harder to define the turning point for a franchise. After the horrible 1908 season, Ebbets, the Superbas, and their fans still had five more losing campaigns ahead of them, but there were positive signs. In spite of the woeful 1908 record, it was the third consecutive year the club at least broke even financially. If nothing else, this meant Ebbets could begin investing in his ball club and his ballpark. To that end, he signed a five-year extension on the Washington Park lease early in 1908. Interestingly, the statement in the *Eagle* that "no option was available for 1913, but the club entertains no fear of being compelled to move," did not lead to any significant media speculation.[22]

Although Ebbets claimed the decision to fire Patsy Donovan was the "hardest task" in his 26-year career, he did it, which meant choosing a new manager for the 1909 season. As in 1905, there were no managerial candidates with proven track records available, and to make matters worse, a number of other clubs were also looking for a new skipper. If, however, Ebbets could not get a proven major league manager, another possibility was someone who had learned from the best. Using that criteria, there could not have been a better candidate than Bill Dahlen, currently playing for the Boston Braves. A star shortstop, who had played for future Hall of Fame managers Cap Anson, Ned Hanlon, and John McGraw, Dahlen had an excellent pedigree. Since he had been part of the Brooklyn National League championship teams of 1899 and 1900, Dahlen was also a known commodity.[23]

Unfortunately, however, Dahlen was the property of the Boston Braves and their owner George Dovey. Although Dovey said he would not "stand in the way of Dahlen's advancement," when it came time to formalize the arrangement, he wanted either money, which Ebbets could not or would not pay, or players the Brooklyn owner would not release. By the time it was clear the Dahlen option was dead, at least for 1909, Ebbets had even fewer choices. The result was hiring star outfielder Harry Lumley, clearly a mistake when the decision was made. Unlike Ebbets' other managerial hiring decisions, this one was panned at the time — around the league, in the media, and in Brooklyn. The problem was if Donovan was fired "for being too friendly with his players," Lumley was "far more friendly in the way that got Donovan into trouble." It was even suggested Lumley would not make it to season's end. While he survived the campaign, this was one managerial firing that was not hard for Ebbets.[24]

Although there was little progress evident in a 98-loss, sixth-place finish in 1909, the roster was changing. Even if Lumley was too easygoing to be a successful manager, he was not reluctant to shake up the roster, releasing 13 players. Cleaning out deadwood was important, but the real challenge was finding better players. Like most owners of the period, Ebbets did a lot of his own scouting, but by 1909, he had "decided to go systematically about securing new players" and hired Larry Sutton as his primary scout. It certainly was not an obvious choice, as Sutton had not been a player himself. He did, however, know talent, which he demonstrated by signing first baseman Jake Daubert and outfielder Hy Myers, two members of Brooklyn's 1916 World Series team. In fact, Sutton signed that team's starting outfield, along with half of the infield. Equally important given Ebbets limited financial resources, Sutton did so at a relatively low cost. The scout later recalled that the total acquisition cost for the 1916 club was just over $15,000.[25]

After firing Lumley, Ebbets was finally able to hire Bill Dahlen. Although Dahlen had no managerial experience, he seemed to fit the profile of successful Deadball Era managers—"experience, knowledge of inside tactics and pugnacity." Unfortunately while the choice made sense, the decision did not work out. During Dahlen's four-year tenure, Brooklyn never won more than 64 games and finished no higher than sixth. As with Donovan, Ebbets was loyal to Dahlen, which was probably why he kept his job after the 1912 season. Even when 1913 saw only slight improvement, Ebbets still wanted to retain Dahlen, but the contrary opinions of the McKeever brothers prevailed. Ebbets called the firing the "most unpleasant duty of his career in baseball," apparently topping the "hardest task" of firing Donovan in 1908. Although there was no improvement in the standings, Dahlen had finished cleaning house and developed a much-improved lineup. In fact, sportswriter Abe Yager claimed that having put together "a real ball club," Dahlen apparently "didn't know what to do with it." In reality, the roster, while improved, still needed upgrading, something carried out by Ebbets' final managerial hire. That manager would be working in a new ballpark.[26]

Although the media did not pick up on it, Ebbets' decision to extend his Washington Park lease for a limited period of time could have been interpreted as part of a plan to secure a new home for the Dodgers. With the newly-expanded Washington Park facility locked in for five years, the Brooklyn owner was positioned to evaluate how best to proceed in an era of new ballpark construction. Technological advances had made it possible to build baseball facilities out of steel and cement at a reasonable cost, which significantly reduced the danger and costs of fire. Probably even more important to Ebbets, who was struggling financially, was the expanded seating capacities of the new generation of ballparks.

Between 1909 and 1915 almost every major league team built a new ballpark or renovated an old one. To fairly evaluate Ebbets' performance in building the facility that bore his name, it is necessary to compare his record with that of his peers. Since the challenges faced by owners who secured and built on a new site were different than those involved in building or renovating at an existing location, the best comparison is with the first group. The chart below summarizes this group of owners and their new ballparks:

Owner	*Park*	*Year Opened*	*Length of Construction*
Mack/Shibe	Shibe Park	1909	12 Months
Barney Dreyfuss	Forbes Field	1909	6 Months
Charles Comiskey	Comiskey Park	1910	4½ Months
John Taylor	Fenway Park	1912	7 Months
Charles Ebbets	Ebbets Field	1913	13 Months
Charles Weeghman	Wrigley Field	1914	7 Weeks
James Gaffney	Braves Field	1915	5 Months

Building a new ballpark at a new site requires successful management of site acquisition, site preparation, construction, and finance. Regarding site acquisition, Ebbets' experience was far different and more complicated than his peers, with the exception of Philadelphia A's owners Connie Mack and Ben Shibe. Other owners mainly dealt with one parcel of land. For example, James Gaffney of the Boston Braves even purchased a

DIAGRAM FOR GRADING EBBETS FIELD.

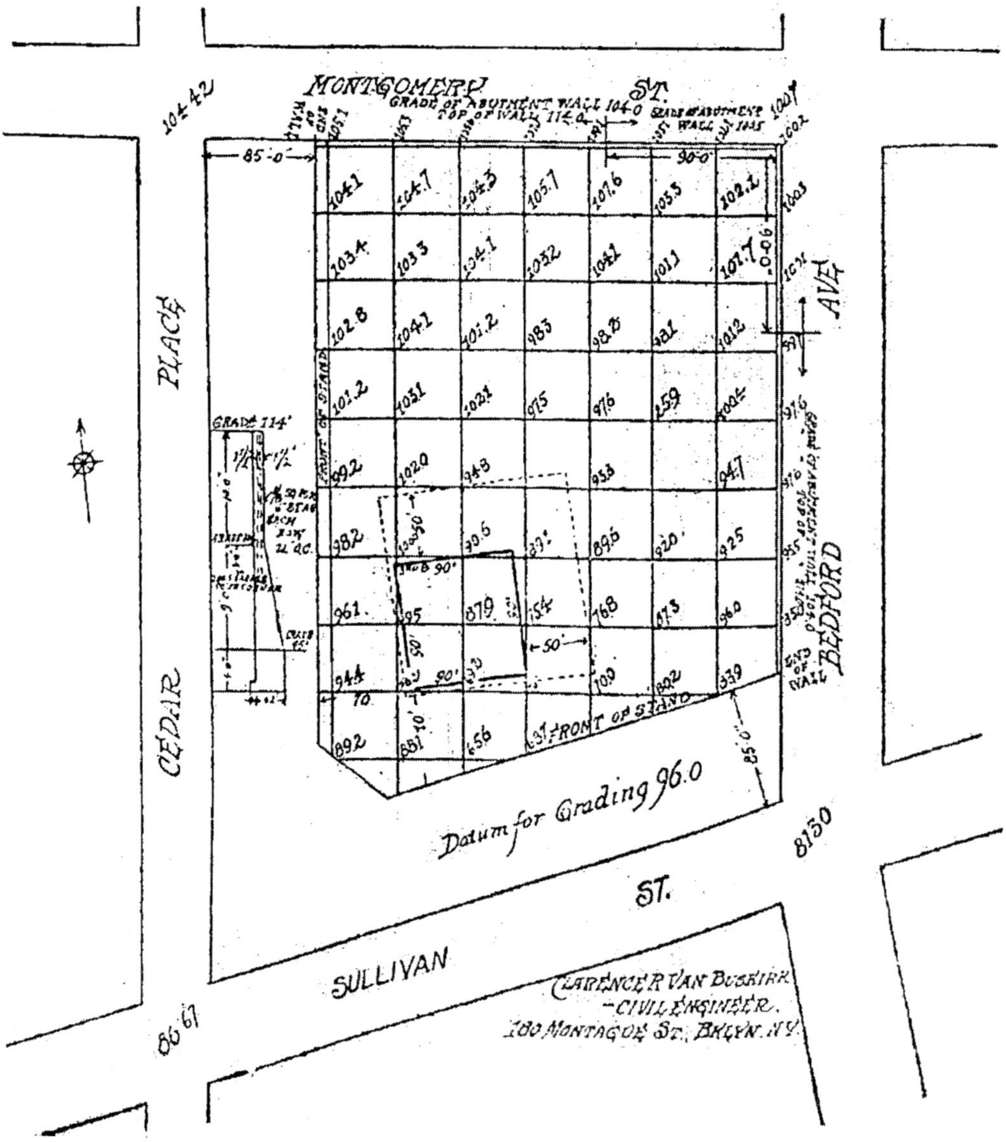

Clarence R. Van Buskirk's drawing of the site work required before Ebbets Field could be built. One side had to be elevated eight feet, another excavated eight feet (*The [Brooklyn] Standard Union*, February 1, 1912).

larger parcel than he needed and sold off part at a profit, while his Boston American League counterparts, the Taylors, "in effect, ... sold themselves a chunk of cheap land." The only "complicated series of transactions" was the Shibe and Mack purchase of seven lots from three owners.[27]

No matter how "complicated" the Philadelphia transaction was, Ebbets would gladly have changed places. Exactly when Ebbets identified the Dodgers' future home is not clear, but he began purchasing the land in September of 1908. Using a "dummy" corporation to keep prices affordable, it took Ebbets over three years to purchase 30 parcels of land, over four times the number acquired by the Athletics owners. One particular accomplishment was the purchase of "Old Clove Road" from the city, without attracting the notice of speculators. The *Eagle* felt Ebbets' right-hand man and attorney, Barney York, "must be some sort of a wizard" to have accomplished this feat. Ominously, the total cost for the land was roughly $200,000 and about half of it was financed by mortgages taken back by the sellers. These debts were still outstanding in May of 1912 after construction had actually begun.[28]

Unfortunately for Ebbets, site acquisition was not the only area where he had more problems than his contemporaries. The general surprise at the proposed site was partially due to Ebbets being one of the few who could visualize it as a baseball field. After Tom Rice of the *Brooklyn Daily Eagle* explored it, he advised future tourists to wear hip boots and take a walking stick. The "mud and more mud" was one thing, but the "miniature Grand Canyon," was a greater concern. The problem was recognized almost immediately by the *Brooklyn Daily Times*, which called the project a work "of such a stupendous nature," that the hoped for opening date of June 14 would probably have to be pushed back to August 27 (the anniversary of the Battle of Brooklyn). Ebbets informed Cincinnati Reds owner August Herrmann he was "building an entire new field which is on the side of a hill," requiring "an eight foot cut at one end and an eight foot fill at another." Of the other six owners building from scratch, only Barney Dreyfuss in Pittsburgh had a similar problem.[29]

However, Dreyfuss was more fortunate than Ebbets in one area that no one could control: the weather. Site work at both parks was to take place during January and February, but in 1909, the winter weather in Pittsburgh was not a problem, and the work was finished in time for construction to begin on March 1. Ebbets was not even close to being that lucky as brutal cold froze tugboats in New York Harbor. Efforts to begin site work on February 3, 1912, found the ground frozen to 38 inches. Further February attempts were futile, so the filling and excavation did not begin until March 4, also the day of the groundbreaking. By this point, the weather-related delays had effectively destroyed any hope of opening the new ballpark in 1912. Given the "stupendous" nature of the site work, it was not surprising the excavating and filling were not completed until May. Since in construction, time equals money, the length of the construction period is always a concern, but in the case of a ballpark, the timing in relationship to the season is also important. The shorter time frames for construction of the other ballparks allowed them to open for at least part of their first seasons. This was the case with Forbes Field, which was open for one-half of the season and the World Series. With the Superbas once again headed nowhere on the field, a 1912 opening could have generated some badly needed revenue, but it was not to be.[30]

Frozen firefighting equipment in Brooklyn in January 1912 was indicative of the cold weather that delayed the site work at Ebbets Field (Library of Congress, Prints & Photographs Division, Bain Collection [LC-DIG-ggbain-10066]).

Although Ebbets was not responsible for the weather, his decision to act as general contractor was a mistake. While Ebbets had an architectural background, trying to manage a construction project on a tight budget and timeline, in addition to running a ball club, was far more than any one person could do effectively. This would have been the case even if everything went smoothly, but problems with sewers, municipal approvals, labor woes, and steel deliveries hampered construction even more. Looking back after the park opened in 1913, Ebbets admitted to reporters he had "bitten off more than he could chew." If the other owners building new parks had similar problems, they were not documented, and the short construction periods suggest this was not the case.[31]

Finance, however, was the area where Ebbets had a significantly more difficult time than any of his peers. Each of the other owners had outside sources of funding, profitable ball clubs, or in the case of Connie Mack and the Shibes, both. Dreyfuss borrowed from his family, the Taylors owned the *Boston Globe* as well as the Red Sox, Chicago's Charles Weeghman was rich from the restaurant business, and Braves owner James Gaffney owned a very successful construction business. While Charles Comiskey may not have enjoyed any outside funding sources, the White Sox reportedly realized net profits of $700,000 between 1901 and 1911. Ebbets, on the other hand, had accumulated $125,000 for the project, but beyond that had no ready source of outside funding, and while his ball club was at least breaking even, it did not produce the money needed to finance a new ballpark. Ideally, a major real estate project is funded through a combination of equity (the owner's money) and mortgage debt (loans paid off over the long term). If the estimated $200,000 land acquisition cost is accurate, Ebbets' $125,000 was long gone, and there were still $99,250 in purchase-money mortgages to be paid. The prudent way to finance such a project is to arrange all the financing before construction begins. Construction is then financed, first with equity (no interest cost), and then a construction loan, which is replaced by the long-term debt or mortgage. The key is obtaining commitments for the equity and debt before starting the construction. It appears Ebbets either could not, or did not, do this. His letter to August Herrmann in May of 1912, which speculates about financing construction through $275,000 in bonds, $100,000 in loans, and a 1912 profit of $50,000, confirms the proposed financing was not in place more than two months after construction had already begun.[32]

Further confirmation of Ebbets' poor financial planning was provided in August when the Brooklyn owner visited Julius Fleischmann, part owner of the Reds, looking for money. Reporting on Ebbets' visit, Fleischmann told Herrmann it appeared Ebbets "is in a mighty bad fix regarding his finances," and Fleischmann did not see "how he is going to get out of it." The problem was Ebbets "went right along and let his contracts, without arranging the financial end of his business." Fleischmann made it clear he had no intention of bailing Ebbets out, nor would he suggest the Reds or the National League do so. Given the inside knowledge of Ebbets' plight in Cincinnati, it was not surprising rumors surfaced of unnamed investors from that city buying out the Brooklyn owner. In the end, Ebbets found the money he needed, not in Ohio, but right in Brooklyn by selling 50 percent of the club to Steve and Ed McKeever. Estimates of how much the brothers invested range from $100,000 to $500,000. In any event, the money, as well as the McKeever's construction experience, enabled the new partners to finish Ebbets Field in time for Opening Day in 1913.[33]

Ebbets Field playing surface being prepared for the ballpark's grand opening (Library of Congress, Prints & Photographs Division, Bain Collection [LC-DIG-ggbain-11612]).

In the final analysis, Ebbets' poor handling of the project's finances, as well as any other mistakes, should not obscure the magnitude of his accomplishment. Facing greater challenges than his peers and working with far less money, the Brooklyn owner gave Brooklyn a state-of-the-art ballpark. The significance and difficulty of Ebbets' achievement was recognized by National League Secretary, John Heydler, in April of 1912, when he pointed out it was unusual for a second-division club to take on such a project. Charles Ebbets frequently expressed the belief Brooklyn was worthy of major league baseball, and he put that belief into the most tangible form possible. It is no surprise that by August of 1915, the *Brooklyn Daily Eagle* called home plate at Ebbets Field, "the heart of Brooklyn."[34]

Although the on-field results did not improve in 1913, the new ballpark was enough of an attraction that attendance rose by over 100,000 spectators—a 43 percent increase from 1912. If, however, Ebbets had any illusions his financial problems were over, he was disabused of the notion by the third baseball war of his career. Formed in 1913, the new Federal League tried to go head-to-head with the two established leagues. Unlike Ebbets' last experience, however, this time the competition was not just for players but for Brooklyn itself. Owned by Robert Ward, a prominent Brooklyn businessman, the Tip-Tops or Brooklyn Feds had money behind them, as witnessed by the construction of a new steel and cement Washington Park on the same site as the old facility. While the Superbas finally began to show improvement on the field in 1914, things went in the opposite direction at the box office. Having risen by over 40 percent in 1913, attendance the following year fell by 224,000 spectators or an incredible 65 percent. It was no wonder, therefore, that by September of 1914, Ebbets was begging fellow owner August Herrmann to renew debts due to the Cincinnati club, since Brooklyn was "straining every condition to close [the] season." Plaintively, the Brooklyn owner pleaded, "please do not fail me." It must have been bitterly frustrating for Ebbets to have overcome all of the obstacles to build his new ballpark, and then once again be on the brink of financial disaster. The impact of the plummeting attendance at the new ballpark was magnified because Ebbets was paying the price necessary to survive a baseball war. Anticipating what was coming early in 1914, Ebbets traveled the country to sign his best players to multi-year contracts. Expensive as it was, Ebbets did not lose any of his leading players, and Brooklyn maintained its competitive position.[35]

The on-field improvement was largely due to Charles Ebbets' final managerial hiring decision. Wilbert Robinson, better known as "Uncle Robby" or just "Robby," took over the club for the 1914 campaign. Since, as in the past, there were few proven candidates available, Ebbets and the McKeevers again relied on pedigree. Like Bill Dahlen, Robinson played for Ned Hanlon (serving as team captain), and both played with and coached for John McGraw. "Robby" brought with him a reputation for developing pitchers, a major Brooklyn weakness. In his first year, the Dodgers won ten more games than the prior season, finishing only four games below .500. Improvement continued in 1915 as Brooklyn contended for the pennant through September, finishing above .500 and in third place. Although Robinson's hiring was considered a surprise choice, it was generally well received. The job was also more attractive because, as sportswriter Sid Mercer commented, seldom does a manager get to take over "so good a team." Another alleged issue disappeared with Robinson's hiring. Deserved or not, Ebbets had a reputation of interfering with his manager or at least limiting their authority. All of this ceased with Robinson. According to Robby's biographers, Ebbets and Robinson were "a strong and compatible combination," and "there never seemed to be friction between them." It took Charles Ebbets a long time to find the right manager, but when he did, he was smart enough to keep him.[36]

Since Robinson's strength was developing pitchers, overhauling Brooklyn's staff became a priority, which climaxed in 1915 when the Dodgers made three major pitching acquisitions. Trading for three-time, 20-game winner Larry Cheney was straightforward, but Robinson and Ebbets went out on a limb with former greats Jack Coombs and Rube Marquard. Coombs had major health issues that threatened his life, not just his career, while Marquard's performance with the archrival Giants had fallen off dramatically. *Brooklyn Eagle* writer Tom Rice called the Coombs signing "a sheer baseball gamble" that could prove to be a "useless expense." Any team could have had Marquard, but all except the Dodgers were apparently scared off by his $7,500 salary. Although Cheney and Marquard were acquired too late in 1915 to help much, the team's pitching had dramatically improved.[37]

Brooklyn's on-field resurgence coincided with an end to National League dominance by a few teams. When Boston won the pennant in 1914, it marked the first time since 1900 that a club other than the Giants, Pirates, or Cubs finished first. Philadelphia then broke through the following year, and the stage was set for Brooklyn in 1916. The Superbas did not disappoint, winning a close race they led nearly from beginning to end. The second place Phillies had even won one more game than in their pennant-winning season, showing that Brooklyn's 14-game improvement was primarily based on their new pitching acquisitions. Although the Dodgers lost the World Series to the powerful Boston Red Sox, there was a real sense of pride and satisfaction throughout Brooklyn. Over a four-year period, Ebbets had given the borough a new ballpark, a new manager, and now a National League pennant.[38]

With three starters and four regulars over the age of 30, the pennant-winning Superbas had been built to win in 1916, which became abundantly clear when Brooklyn crashed back to earth in 1917, finishing seventh. Things did not improve over the next two years as the club and its fans suffered through two more below–.500 finishes, while World War I wreaked havoc with baseball. However, Ebbets and Robinson were in the process of gradually building another pennant winner. Once again pitching was the key, especially a 1918 trade of Casey Stengel and George Cutshaw to Pittsburgh for Burleigh Grimes, Al Mamaux, and a third player. Like Marquard, Mamaux had been a 20-game winner whose performance had fallen off significantly. While the acquisition of Grimes, a future Hall of Famer, looks like a steal in retrospect, his career record at the time was 5–19. The duo, along with 1916 holdovers Jeff Pfeffer and Marquard, anchored a pitching staff that brought another pennant to Brooklyn in 1920, followed by another World Series defeat, this time at the hands of Cleveland. For the remaining four years of Ebbets' life, Brooklyn typically

Workers putting the finishing touches on the left field bleachers (Library of Congress, Prints & Photographs Division, Bain Collection [LC-DIG-ggbain-11611]).

finished about .500 in a league dominated by the Giants. In 1924, however, Brooklyn came close to the top, finishing only 1½ games behind the heavily-favored Giants.[39]

In Ebbets' 25-plus year tenure as Brooklyn president, only during the last ten years did he have the right manager, a state of the art ballpark, and the money to put a good team on the field. Unfortunately, the same period saw the Giants win five pennants, including four in a row from 1921 to 1924. Brooklyn, however, did win the National League flag twice (1916 and 1920), doubling Chicago, Philadelphia, and Cincinnati, while the Braves, Cards, and Pirates failed to win a single pennant. Throughout these years, Ebbets and Robinson used a combination of trades and new talent to build two pennant-winning teams and one second-place finisher. The return of Larry Sutton toward the end of 1919, following a two-year hiatus with the Reds, also helped Ebbets and Robinson find new talent, the most prominent of which was another future Hall of Famer, Dazzy Vance. Given the overlapping executive responsibilities of the era, it is hard to know what part of the success was directly due to Ebbets. However, he put the team together and had to be involved at some level with all major roster decisions, at least from the financial end.[40]

The new ballpark and pennant-winning teams clearly contributed to Ebbets' improved financial prospects. Another key factor was ultimate victory in the struggle to legalize Sunday baseball. Since various ploys failed to circumvent the existing laws, the only option was to pass a new one. However, control of the New York State Legislature by rural upstate interests with a strong "anti–New York City bloc," doomed earlier efforts to pass new legislation. By 1918, however, Sunday baseball had gained significant support, facilitated by leaving the final decision to local option. Finally on April 19, 1919, Governor Al Smith signed into law the Walker Act, and 10 days later, the New York Board of Alderman followed suit. Ebbets wasted no time taking advantage of the new law, and a crowd of 22,000 saw the first legal Sunday baseball game at Ebbets Field on May 4, 1919. The legalization of Sunday baseball in New York provided Brooklyn with added competitive advantages beyond making games available to an expanded market. Since the "blue laws" in Pennsylvania and Massachusetts remained unchanged, the Phillies, Pirates, and Braves still could not play at home on Sunday, giving Brooklyn even more Sunday home dates. This was further facilitated by the relatively close proximity of Philadelphia and Boston, and to some extent Pittsburgh, which allowed for one-day "home stands." The Dodgers also had an advantage over the Yankees and Giants through 1922 because the two teams shared a park for their Sunday dates. By 1922, the Dodgers were averaging at least 20,000 a game on Sunday, well over the average daily attendance.[41]

Sunday baseball, the new ballpark, and competitive teams transformed Brooklyn's (and therefore Ebbets') financial fortunes to the point that by 1923 the *Eagle* labeled the ball club "a mint." Attendance, which had fallen to 83,831 in the war-shortened 1918 season, increased more than fourfold in 1919 (first season of Sunday baseball) and almost tenfold in the 1920 pennant-winning season. Although attendance fell off the next three years, it topped 800,000 again during the near miss in 1924. And despite the drop in attendance, from 1919 through 1924 Brooklyn consistently finished in the top four in National League attendance. In a May 1923 article, the *Eagle* analyzed the club's finances in detail and concluded Brooklyn's share of the gate receipts for 19 Sunday home games, in addition to one or two holiday matchups, covered all of the team's expenses. If that was correct, all of the remaining receipts from 13 Saturday contests, 44 weekday games, and their share of 77 road matchups went straight to the bottom line. Based on this, the paper projected net profits of just over $335,000 or $4.2 million today. Ebbets himself more or less confirmed the figures, calling them "slightly exaggerated, but not so much. Let it go at that." It also appears from 1920 through 1922 all of the profits remained invested in the ball club. For the last two years of Ebbets' ownership, the Dodgers paid $120,000 of dividends, but this was out of profits of roughly $357,000. At the time of his death in 1925, Ebbets was investing his newfound financial resources back into the ball club. To claims of his supposed statement that "I got mine," Ebbets responded he did, but it was in real estate, or in this case, the ballpark. This is confirmed to some degree by Ebbets' estate, which had a net appraised value of just over $1,115,000, of which $833,000 was his Dodger stock.[42]

Charles Ebbets once reportedly said he wanted to die at a ballgame. While it did not come to that, Ebbets was certainly active in baseball right up until his death in April of 1925. At the National League meetings in December of 1924, Ebbets proposed a 2–3–2 format for the World Series. Approved by his fellow magnates and confirmed by the American League owners, this arrangement has continued ever since. Working for the benefit of the game was not just a deathbed experience for Ebbets. He did so even when it cost him money. For example, although the visitor's dressing room at Washington Park did not have "shower baths and other luxuries," in late 1906, he proposed such facilities be required at every National League ballpark. At the same meeting, Ebbets also recommended the establishment of set pregame practice times, another reform adopted by his fellow owners.[43]

Another Ebbets innovation was probably only appreciated when it was needed — the combination ticket/rain check. Prior to this change, fans surrendered their tickets at the gate, and if the game was rained out, had to wait in line for a rain check, a "very slow and unsatisfactory" process. Ebbets introduced a two-part ticket with the fan retaining the rain check portion. Ultimately, owners in both leagues adopted this "invention of Charles Ebbets." Of far more significance, not just to baseball but all of sports, was the major reform Ebbets fought for in the player draft. Hard as it may seem to believe, at the time, draft order was determined by lot, limiting unsuccessful teams' chances to rebuild. Ebbets argued long and hard that the teams with the worst record should have the first choices in the following year's draft. Ultimately this idea was adopted, not just by baseball, but every professional sport.[44]

While umpires are probably the most unpopular group in baseball, owners come in a close second, and the importance of their role is even less understood. The average fan wants to see a successful team in a comfortable venue at the lowest possible cost. He or she has little interest in the owner's need for financial return, and more importantly, the role profits play in providing comfortable venues and successful teams. This makes for a complicated relationship between owners and fans, even more so during the pre-television era when almost all revenue came from spectators. To Charles Ebbets' credit, he made the relationship work, so that Brooklyn came to identify with the Dodgers and vice versa.

The connection between Brooklyn and the team was facilitated because Ebbets took over the Dodgers at literally the same time Brooklyn lost its municipal independence and needed new forms of identity. Ebbets began well by building a new ballpark that was more accessible for the fans. Then in that first season, when he had to be concerned about losing money he did not have, Ebbets started to build and strengthen his club's connections to Brooklyn. On at least two occasions, the Dodgers owner publicly stated he would not move games from Brooklyn to other sites "no matter how big the [financial] inducements," including the possibility of moving a Labor Day game to the much larger Polo Grounds. In publicly declining, Ebbets emphatically stated he would not do so "even if the New York Club gave him the entire receipts and he did not receive a dollar at Washington Park." Unfortunately, Ebbets then made one of his biggest mistakes, thinking the quick fix of syndicate baseball would give him a good team, championships, and, therefore, solid fan support. While the transfer of Ned Hanlon and the Baltimore stars to Brooklyn accomplished the first two, it failed miserably at the last one. As one historian put it, "This was not Brooklyn's team, and the cranks knew it," so they did not support it.[45]

When defections to the American League tore apart that artificially-constructed team, Ebbets started over and while it took a long time, he succeeded in the end. Intentionally or not, the owner established a rock-solid connection between his ball club and Brooklyn by the teams he developed, the managers he hired, and the ballpark he built. The National League championship teams of 1916 and 1920 consisted primarily of home-grown talent and players looking to rebuild their careers. The likes of Casey Stengel, Zack Wheat, and Jake Daubert began their major league careers in Brooklyn, developing a closer relationship with fans who "knew" them when they were just starting out. Outsiders like Jack Coombs and Rube Marquard were acceptable because they were trying to come back from injury or poor performances, a scenario any fan could identify with, even though in Marquard's case, he arrived from the hated New York Giants. In Wilbert Robinson, Ebbets found a manager who knew baseball but also had a personality the community could relate to. Readers of Tom Rice's constant references to Robinson as "your uncle" in the *Brooklyn Daily Eagle* could not escape feeling some kind of personal relationship with the manager and the team.

Perhaps most important was the building of Ebbets Field. The Dodgers' home field tends to be viewed nostalgically as a small, intimate ballpark of a bygone age. That was not, however, how it was viewed when it was built. Like the rest of the facilities built during the Deadball Era, Ebbets Field was seen as a new, state-of-the-art ballpark, enabling Brooklyn, even though only a borough, to keep pace with other major league cities. Since it was a physical

A rain check from a 1916 Dodger game. Ebbets introduced a new form of rain check that was widely adopted throughout both leagues (National Baseball Hall of Fame Library, Cooperstown, New York).

structure, the ballpark outlived Charles Ebbets, his manager, and his teams. Ebbets' death in 1925, followed shortly thereafter by Ed McKeever's demise, led to a long 15 years in the baseball wilderness when the feuding of the Ebbets and McKeever heirs almost destroyed the ball club. When the resurgence came in the late 1930s, however, Charles Ebbets' ballpark was tangible evidence of Brooklyn's identification with the Dodgers — a solid foundation for the glory days of the 1940s and '50s.[46]

As strong as that community connection was, it could not withstand the pressures that took the Dodgers to Los Angeles in 1958. In discussing that tragedy, Michael Shapiro wrote that Walter O'Malley was not a bad person, rather he was "a limited man," who "should have never owned a baseball team because he could not see what he had." For all his own foibles, limitations, and weaknesses, no one could ever say that about Charles Ebbets. He knew what he had and valued it. Historian Burt Solomon wrote Ebbets "was a businessman only to a point. He believed in Brooklyn. The borough was the biggest thing he put his faith in." It was a faith well justified and well rewarded.[47]

Notes

1. Frank Graham, *The Brooklyn Dodgers: An Informal History* (New York: G.P. Putnam's Sons, 1945), 95; Burton A. Boxerman and Benita W. Boxerman, *Ebbets to Veeck to Busch: Eight Owners Who Shaped Baseball* (Jefferson, N.C., McFarland, 2003), 11, 26–27.

2. *Brooklyn Daily Eagle*, January 2, 1898, January 7, 1898, January 18, 1913.

3. Bob McGee, *The Greatest Ballpark Ever: Ebbets Field and the Story of the Brooklyn Dodgers* (New Brunswick, N.J.: Rutgers University Press, 2005), 29–30.

4. www.ballparksofbaseball.com; *Brooklyn Daily Eagle*, January 2, 1898, February 21, 1913.

5. Andy McCue, "A History of Dodger Ownership," *The National Pastime: A Review of Baseball History* no. 13 (1993): 37; *Brooklyn Daily Eagle*, February 2, 1898; www.measuringworth.com.

6. *Brooklyn Daily Eagle*, January 7, 1898, March 15, 1898, March 16, 1898, March, 25, 1898, January 21, 1899; Ronald M. Selter, *Ballparks of the Deadball Era: A Comprehensive Study of Their Dimensions, Configurations and Effects on Batting, 1901–1919* (Jefferson, N.C.: McFarland, 2008), 38.

7. *Brooklyn Daily Eagle*, June 3, 1898, June 7, 1898; *Sporting Life*, June 11, 1898; www.retrosheet.org.

8. Richard Goldstein, *Superstars and Screwballs: 100 Years of Brooklyn Baseball* (New York: Penguin, 1992), 72; www.ballparksofbaseball.com; McGee, 35; *Brooklyn Daily Eagle*, June 7, 1898.

9. McCue, 37; Burt Solomon, *Where They Ain't: The Fabled Life and Untimely Death of the Original Baltimore Orioles, The Team That Gave Birth to Modern Baseball* (New York: Doubleday, 1999), 142, 145–146; *Brooklyn Daily Eagle*, December 21, 1898, February 7, 1899; www.measuringworth.com.

10. Solomon, 156, 175; www.retrosheet.org.

11. *Brooklyn Daily Eagle*, September 18, 1899, January 3, 1900; www.ballparksofbaseball.com.

12. Lyle Spatz, *Bad Bill Dahlen* (Jefferson, N.C.: McFarland, 2004), 72, 78, 80, 86; Harold Seymour, *Baseball: The Early Years* (New York: Oxford University Press, 1960), 305.

13. www.ballparksofbaseball.com; *Brooklyn Daily Eagle*, January 3, 1900, June 10, 1900, June 16, 1900, September 2, 1900, October 13, 1900.

14. Seymour, *Baseball: The Early Years*, 314; Solomon, 202, 205; Goldstein, 54; *Brooklyn Daily Eagle*, June 14, 1905; Spatz, 94.

15. www.ballparksofbaseball.com; Seymour, *Baseball: The Early Years*, 302, 321; Solomon, 227–231; Charles Alexander, *John McGraw* (Lincoln: University of Nebraska Press, 1988), 90–91, 95.

16. *Brooklyn Daily Eagle*, June 14, 1905; *Organized Baseball*, Hearings Before the Subcommittee on [the] Study of Monopoly Power of the Committee on the Judiciary, House of Representatives, 82nd Congress, 1st Session, Serial No. 1, Part 6 (Washington, DC: Government Printing Office, 1952), 1617.

17. *Brooklyn Daily Eagle*, March 20, 1905, March 21, 1905, June 14, 1905, December 14, 1905; *New York Times*, January 21, 1912; Solomon, 245–246, 250–252.

18. *Brooklyn Daily Eagle*, December 11, 1901; Seymour, *Baseball: The Early Years*, 317–319.

19. Charles Bevis, *Sunday Baseball: The Major League's Struggle to Play Baseball on the Lord's Day, 1876–1934* (Jefferson, N.C.: McFarland, 2003), 152–163, 194.

20. www.retrosheet.org.

21. *The Sporting News*, December 23, 1905; *Sporting Life*, December 23, 1905; *Evening World*, November 12, 1908.

22. *Brooklyn Daily Eagle*, December 8, 1906, October 27, 1907, January 5, 1908, November 11, 1908.

23. *The Sporting News*, October 29, 1908, November 19, 1908.

24. *The Sporting News*, December 3, 1908, December 24, 1908, January 14, 1909; *Sporting Life*, January 16, 1909, January 23, 1909; *Evening World*, January 9, 1909.

25. Tom Simon, ed., *Deadball Stars of the National League* (Dulles, Virginia: Brassey's, Inc., 2004), 280; *Brooklyn Daily Eagle*, September 18, 1910; Larry Sutton and Hugh Bradley, "I Have Bought $1,000,000 Worth of Men," *American Magazine* 115, no. 2 (February 1933): 100, *New York Times*, June 23, 1944.

26. *The Sun*, October 29, 1909, November 18, 1913; Spatz, 170, 192–193; *The Sporting News*, October 30, 1913, November 13, 1913; *Sporting Life*, October 25, 1913; *Brooklyn Daily Eagle*, October 14, 1912, October 25, 1912.

27. Sam Bernstein, "Barney Dreyfuss and the Legacy of Forbes Field," in *Forbes Field: Essays and Memories of the Pirates' Historic Ballpark, 1909–1971*, ed. David Cicotello and Angelo J. Louisa (Jefferson, N.C.: McFarland, 2007), 15–17; Bruce Kuklick, *To Everything a Season: Shibe Park and Urban Philadelphia, 1909–1976* (Princeton: Princeton University Press, 1991), 24–25, 29–30; Michael Ian Borer, *Faithful to Fenway: Believing in Boston, Baseball and American's Most Beloved Ballpark* (New York: New York University Press, 2008), 40; Lawrence Ritter, *Lost Ballparks: A Celebration of Baseball's Legendary Fields* (New York: Viking Studio Books, 1992), 30; Raymond D. Kush, "The Building of Chicago's Wrigley Field," *Baseball Research Journal* 10 (1981), 10–15; Bill Price, "Braves Field," *Baseball Research Journal* 7 (1978), 1–6.

28. McGee, 43, 45, 47; *Brooklyn Daily Eagle*, January 3, 1912; Ebbets to Herrmann, May 5, 1912, August "Garry" Herrmann Papers, BA MSS 12, National Baseball Hall of Fame Library, Cooperstown, New York.

29. *Brooklyn Daily Eagle*, January 3, 1912, January 4, 1912; *Brooklyn Daily Times*, January 3, 1912; Ebbets to Herrmann, February 3, 1912, August "Garry" Herrmann Papers, BA MSS 12, National Baseball Hall of Fame Library, Cooperstown, New York; Donald G. Lancaster, "Forbes Field Praised as a Gem When It Opened," *Baseball Research Journal* 15 (1986), 26.

30. Lancaster, 26–27; *Brooklyn Daily Eagle*, January 5, 1912, January 6, 1912, January 14, 1912, February 4, 1912. February 10, 1912, February 19, 1912, March 5, 1912; *Standard Union*, May 2, 1912; *Brooklyn Citizen, May 2, 1912.*

31. *Brooklyn Daily Eagle*, March 20, 1912, April 5, 1912, April 29, 1913; *Standard Union*, April 18, 1912; *Brooklyn Citizen*, August 16, 1912; *Brooklyn Daily Times*, August 14, 1912.

32. Norman L. Macht, *Connie Mack and the Early Years of Baseball* (Lincoln: University of Nebraska Press, 2007), 198; Kuklick, 17; Harold Seymour, *Baseball: The Golden Age* (New York: Oxford University Press, 1971), 71; Borer, 40; McGee, 38, 47; Ebbets to Herrmann, May 12, 1912, August "Garry" Herrmann Papers, BA MSS 12, National Baseball Hall of Fame Library, Cooperstown, New York; Bernstein, 13–15.

33. *Standard Union*, August 20, 1912; Fleischmann to Herrmann, August 3, 1912, August "Garry" Herrmann Papers, BA MSS 12, National Baseball Hall of Fame Library, Cooperstown, New York; McCue, 39.

34. *Brooklyn Daily Times*, April 18, 1912; *Brooklyn Daily Eagle*, August 13, 1915.

35. *Organized Baseball*, Hearings Before the Subcommittee on [the] Study of Monopoly Power of the Committee on the Judiciary, House of Representatives, 82nd Congress, 1st Session, Serial No. 1, Part 6 (Washington, DC: Government Printing Office, 1952), 1617; Goldstein, 105–106, 115; Ebbets to Herrmann, September 17, 1914, September 20, 1914, August "Garry" Herrmann Papers, BA MSS 12, National Baseball Hall of Fame Library, Cooperstown, New York.

36. *The World*, November 19, 1913; *Globe and Commercial Advertiser*, November 18, 1913, November 19, 1913; Jack Kavanagh and Norman Macht, *Uncle Robbie* (Cleveland, Ohio: SABR, 1999), 59; Spatz, 170, 178; *Sporting Life*, December 23, 1905.

37. www.retrosheet.org; *Brooklyn Daily Eagle*, January 19, 1915, August 29, 1915, August 30, 1915.

38. Paul Zinn and John Zinn, *The Major League Pennant Races of 1916: "The Most Maddening Baseball Melee in History"* (Jefferson, N.C.: McFarland, 2009), 237.

39. www.retrosheet.org; Zinn and Zinn, 10.

40. *Brooklyn Daily Eagle*, November 30, 1919; *New York Times*, June 23, 1944.

41. Bevis, 174, 180–181, 188, 190, 193–194; *Brooklyn Daily Eagle*, May 2, 1923; February 11, 1925; *Organized Baseball*, Hearings Before the Subcommittee on [the] Study of Monopoly Power of the Committee on the Judiciary, House of Representatives, 82nd Congress, 1st Session, Serial No. 1, Part 6 (Washington, DC: Government Printing Office, 1952), 1617.

42. *Brooklyn Daily Eagle*, May 2, 1923, May 4, 1923; *Organized Baseball*, Hearings Before the Subcommittee on [the] Study of Monopoly Power of the Committee on the Judiciary, House of Representatives, 82nd Congress, 1st Session, Serial No. 1, Part 6 (Washington, DC: Government Printing Office, 1952), 1600–01, 1617; *New York Times*, December 12, 1928.

43. *Brooklyn Daily Eagle*, January 3, 1907, December 11, 1924, February 4, 1925; Boxerman and Boxerman, 11; *The Sporting News*, December 18, 1924.

44. *Brooklyn Daily Eagle*, August 16, 1905, February 26, 1907, January 4, 1911, September 21, 1912, September 16, 1913, September 17, 1913; *Sporting Life*, September 27, 1913, December 20, 1913; Boxerman and Boxerman, 11–12.

45. *Brooklyn Daily Eagle*, August 10, 1898, September 3, 1898; Solomon, 196.

46. Bernstein, 25.

47. Michael Shapiro, *The Last Good Season: Brooklyn, the Dodgers, and Their Final Pennant Race Together* (New York: Doubleday, 2003), 324; Solomon, 216.

48. *New York Herald*, April 5, 1913.

49. *New York Times*, September 25, 1957; *New York Herald Tribune*, September 25, 1957; *Newark Evening News*, September 25, 1957; *New York Journal American*, September 25, 1957.

A Ballpark and Its "City"

Ebbets Field, Brooklyn and Changing Times

Ellen M. Snyder-Grenier

On March 4, 1912, the *New York Times* reported, a crowd of "more than 500 enthusiastic baseball fans, with their wives and children" gathered in Flatbush, Brooklyn. They were there to celebrate the groundbreaking for a new, modern ballpark for the Dodger baseball team.

To the unknowing eye, the place where they assembled was little more than a desolate lot. The *Times* described it as "a howling wilderness ... [with] several old houses and shanties and goats." In fact, the site had a rich past and a complicated future. Native Americans had once hunted there. Dutch farmers had once tilled the soil. Nearby, during the Revolutionary War, American troops and forces of the Crown had fought the Battle of Brooklyn — a bloody engagement that ended in a British victory and the occupation of New York City. (Some had even proposed that the ballpark "be named after General Montgomery or General Sullivan, American officers who figured conspicuously in the Battle of Brooklyn, which raged over the ground where the baseball war will be fought...").[1] So, although at first glance the land seemed to have little to recommend it, it was actually fitting that an important chapter in Brooklyn's history would unfold on the site.

In the middle of the largely barren expanse stood a bunting and flag-draped platform. On it sat Charles Ebbets, president of the Brooklyn Baseball Club, and Alfred E. Steers, Brooklyn's borough president. Steers' presence was an indicator of the occasion's significance. In addition, as a lifelong Flatbush resident, he brought the perspective of someone who had seen the immense changes taking place in Brooklyn as it evolved from a handful of suburbs and country villages into a great city and, eventually, became a borough in an even greater city.

Steers had been born in Flatbush in 1860, at a time when it was still one of the six original towns of the City of Brooklyn. Back then, recalled *The Realm of Light and Air: Flatbush of To-Day*, Flatbush had just three north-south streets: "Clove Road, Hunterfly Road and the Flatbush Turnpike; the only two cross streets were Fulton Street and Kings Highway."[2] By the time of Ebbets Field's groundbreaking, Flatbush was a modern suburb. "Few people who used to drive through the corn fields of the Flatbush of yesterday could have dreamed of the transformations which have changed the old Dutch farms into the City Beautiful of to-day," observed *The Realm of Light and Air*. "The lanes have changed into boulevards, the gable-roofed, broad-shingled houses into villas, the cabbage and potato fields into places of habitation. The milk wagons and market carts have been exchanged for swift moving autos, the old Erasmus into the stately structure, thronged with happy children...."[3]

"Site of the New Field of the Brooklyn Baseball Club," "This Picture," reads the caption for this image in the *Eagle*, "Shows a Panorama of the Field Chosen by the Brooklyn Baseball Club as the Location for its New Diamond." Spectators at the groundbreaking could only imagine what the jumble of homes and open fields would become (*Brooklyn Daily Eagle*, January 4, 1912. Collection of the Brooklyn Historical Society).

Fittingly, as Steers rose to address the crowd, he used language that drew upon both past and present, recalling one of Brooklyn's early baseball teams — the Atlantics — and the ball field upon which they played. He reminisced, said the *Times*, "about way back in 1870, when the Atlantics and the Cincinnati Red Stockings were playing at the old Capitoline grounds," when he watched the baseball game "through a knothole in the fence." To loud cheers from the crowd, Steers spoke about the bright future that lay ahead for Brooklyn baseball:

> It is not only because I deem it a pleasure to be with Mr. Ebbets on this occasion that I come here ... but also because I deem it my duty as Borough President. Mr. Ebbets is doing a fine thing for Brooklyn in giving the city one of the greatest ball parks in the world. I was born in this neighborhood, and every bit of the ground is dear to me, and it gives me much pleasure to be here, fans and ladies and gentlemen, and see the start of this proposed magnificent ball grounds. I tell you what I want to see, and I know you all want to see it, too, and that is for Brooklyn to proudly take her place at the top of the baseball world ... as she did in the old days when I was a boy and used to peek through the holes in the fence.[4]

When he had finished speaking, Steers accompanied Ebbets down the steps of the platform. The two men stood before the enthusiastic crowd. Ebbets drew forth a gift from the Castle Brothers, contractors for the new ball field: a solid silver shovel with an ebony handle. Then, the *Times* noted, "Mr. Ebbets, standing with the Borough President, faced the brigade of snapshotters and turned a spadeful of earth. When the posing was over, a "party of citizens from Italy, with regular picks and shovels, settled down to real work," said the paper. It was the start of "work on the new home for the Trolley Dodgers near Prospect Park."[5]

A little more than a year later, the ballpark was open for business. Just as real estate developers had transformed Flatbush farmland into a neighborhood in step with modern ideas about suburban life, a baseball mogul had transformed a desolate patch of land into a modern entertainment center in step with new ideas about professional baseball. Ebbets' namesake ballpark was very different from the flimsy wooden stands that had earlier served Brooklyn baseball fans. Made from concrete and steel, Ebbets Field was a monument to permanence. The new ballpark, one of many modern, new stadiums being built throughout the United States, symbolized a commitment to baseball and to the new borough. "We had a frame structure in an unsightly neighborhood.... We were forever being urged to get out and build decent grounds in a better class section, and to furnish the innumerable comforts and conveniences that amusement patrons must have," observed Charles Ebbets in the March 15, 1913, *Brooklyn Daily Eagle*. "We have responded by building Ebbets Field." Ebbets' investment in the "concrete plant" was so big — so daring — said the *Eagle*, that "it should last forever, or until destroyed by a cataclysm."[6]

A little less than 50 years later, the scene at Ebbets Field was radically different. There were no celebratory speeches, no platform, and no bunting to welcome the relatively small group that gathered in 1960 to witness the beginning of the ballpark's final days. (Only two years earlier, just after the end of the 1957 season, the Brooklyn Dodgers had left to play in California.) Over the decades, the desolate lot described at the 1912 groundbreaking had been radically transformed. It was now packed with buildings and asphalt streets crowded with cars and buses. Subway lines rumbled beneath the sidewalks. The ballpark, no longer a domineering presence in an unfinished landscape, seemed to be shoehorned into an absurdly small area.

"Yesterday," noted the February 24, 1960, *New York Times*, "about two hundred people saw the walls of Ebbets Field in Brooklyn crumbling before the pounding of a wrecker's ball.... On the half-acre site at Flatbush and Bedford Avenues where the Dodger faithfuls cheered a victory or groaned at defeat, a 1,317-family housing project will be built, the largest of its kind in the five boroughs."[7]

In many ways, these two strikingly different scenes define the massive transformations that took place in Brooklyn in the first half of the twentieth century, as a growing population, rising industry, and wide-scale development gave way to job loss, the departure of the urban middle class for the suburbs and stagnating development. These changes were not unique to Brooklyn; in fact, they were also playing out in other northeastern, urban industrial areas, just as elsewhere, ball teams were leaving cities for newer, more lucrative pastures.

What was striking about the demise of Ebbets Field and the departure of the Brooklyn Dodgers for the West Coast was the way in which it seemed to strike at the heart of Brooklyn's identity. The team was a high-profile vestige of Brooklyn as an independent city before it became one of New York City's five boroughs in 1898. The demolition of the famous ballpark eradicated a distinctive, city-defining feature in a place that in many ways held tightly to its past. With the demise of the venerable *Brooklyn Daily Eagle* in 1955, the end of Brooklyn's renowned trolleys on its streets in 1956, the closing of Coney Island's famous Steeplechase Park in 1964, and the decommissioning of the massive Brooklyn Navy Yard in 1966, the borough seemed to have lost many of the things which, at the beginning of the twentieth century, had given it a distinct identity.

Looking more closely at Brooklyn at the time of Ebbets Field's construction suggests why the ballpark served as one of a number of enduring symbols of a *city*—even after Brooklyn had become a borough of New York City—and how its demolition in 1960 was all the more poignant as a symbol of changing times.

Brooklyn at the Birth of Ebbets Field

At the March 1912 groundbreaking for Ebbets Fields, Borough President Steers praised Charles Ebbets. "Mr. Ebbets is doing a fine thing for Brooklyn," he enthused, "in giving the city one of the greatest ball parks in the world."[8]

Steers' use of the word "city" to describe the *borough* of Brooklyn is interesting. Perhaps it was merely a slip of the tongue, but it was telling. Just 14 years earlier, Brooklyn had relinquished its long-time role as an independent city—and its status as the fourth largest city in the United States—when it was annexed by Greater New York, joining Manhattan ("old" New York), along with Staten Island, the Bronx, and Queens. The

"Brooklyn Bridge—looking from Brooklyn toward old New York, U.S.A," ca. 1901. The Brooklyn Bridge did physically in 1883 what consolidation would do in 1898: join two cities. The caption for this image—published shortly after the fact—refers to Manhattan as "old" New York, a nod to the days before the uneasy union (Library of Congress, Prints & Photographs Division, Stereograph Cards Collection [LC-USZ62-134655]).

annexation, which followed the lead of cities like Philadelphia and Chicago, exponentially increased the physical size and population of New York City.[9] The bold move had been spurred on by several Progressive politicians, chief among them Andrew Haswell Green, a New York City lawyer, planner, and preservationist.[10]

While Manhattanites were largely proconsolidation, Brooklynites had been fairly equally divided. Although some in Brooklyn saw the merger as a way to benefit from Manhattan's tax base, others saw it as an attack on local rule and the core of their community.[11] In a speech delivered on the eve of consolidation, *Brooklyn Daily Eagle* editor St. Clair McKelway, a decided Brooklyn loyalist, reminded all those present that although Brooklyn faced a new chapter as just one of the five boroughs in New York City, it was imperative that it maintain its unique identity:

> Brooklyn is emphatically a city with those urban characteristics which justify confidence in the people, if that confidence is anywhere to be justified. Brooklyn has repeatedly shown herself to be the most independent urban community in the world.... Brooklyn can best do that by maintaining her individuality in the partnership, while collecting her dues under it. That individuality can be maintained by loyal adherence to Brooklyn interests, to Brooklyn organizations, to Brooklyn names, and to Brooklyn ideas. Let us be no branch office. Let our institutes be Brooklyn institutes, our banks Brooklyn banks, our libraries Brooklyn libraries, our churches Brooklyn churches, our journals Brooklyn newspapers, our colleges Brooklyn colleges, our schools and academies Brooklyn schools and academies, our streets and our homes Brooklyn streets and Brooklyn homes, our stores and our offices Brooklyn offices and Brooklyn stores, and our boys and our girls Brooklyn boys and Brooklyn girls.[12]

Moreover, he might just as well have added, let our baseball teams and ballparks be Brooklyn baseball teams and ballparks. For clearly, although Brooklyn had undergone a major political transformation in 1898, for many of its citizens it remained its own entity, a city in feel if not technically one, and one worthy of its own institutions and icons.

With the completion of Ebbets Field just a little more than a decade after consolidation, Brooklyn had something uniquely its own: a modern facility that could rival the many others rising in concrete and steel around the country. As the *New York Times* reported about an almost-complete Ebbets Field in February 1913, "The new park embraces all the improvements of the recently constructed stands in other cities and contains several innovations heretofore unthought of in grand stand construction."[13] Charles Ebbets himself had paid homage to the Brooklyn officials who "realized that the new ball field is, in a way, a civic enterprise, and that the quality of the ball park furnished a major league team these days is something to be praised or deprecated by the citizens at large as much as that of the appearance of the courthouse or city hall."[14]

Therefore, in many ways, the modern ballpark was a powerful symbol of a city on the rise. As an administration representative pointed out in a speech given on "Brooklyn Day" at the 1904 Louisiana Purchase Exposition (the only day, according to a New York State Commission report, "formally set apart by the Exposition management in honor of a political division less than a municipality"),

> Brooklyn herself has awakened from her sleep of almost ten years, and the sound of the hammer and the saw and the ring of the trowel are heard on every hand. Owing to the enterprise, energy and self-sacrificing efforts of many of the men who are with us to-day, she is astonishing the country by the wonderful increase in population. Brooklyn can no

longer be regarded as the bedroom of Manhattan, for Manhattan is rapidly becoming only the workshop of Brooklyn; we can no longer be regarded as the little brother of Manhattan, for we are rapidly becoming a very big brother.[15]

One had merely to tour Brooklyn's waterfront and factories to see the changes that were taking place. By 1890, the then-city was ranked fourth among American cities for the value of goods it produced: $269 million.[16] In a feature on Brooklyn in the April 1893 issue of *Harper's New Monthly Magazine*, Julian Ralph described its industrial demeanor in a passage that bordered on the poetic:

> There is a view of Brooklyn which gives it the appearance of a smoky seat of manufactures. It is obtained from the east side of New York, looking over at the great sugar-refineries which tower like Rhenish castles beside the swift East River. Brooklyn really has great manufacturing interests, and many of the goods that the people of the country buy as of New York make are really made in Brooklyn. The census reports 10,560 manufacturing establishments in 229 different lines of industry. These employ nearly 104,000 hands. Very large hat-works, chemical-works, foundries and iron-works, candy factories, coffee and spice mills, and boot and shoe factories are notable among the industrial establishments of the place. It will be news to most persons, I think, that thirty lines of steamships (all but two or three of them transatlantic) dock at Brooklyn wharves, and use 231 steamers in their regular service. The city has fourteen dry docks, upon which 2000 vessels are docked every year, and thirteen grain-elevators are upon its waterfront.[17]

Brooklyn was also home to the massive Brooklyn Navy Yard, located on Wallabout Bay. The yard had a history of building and outfitting ships that dated back to the early 1800s. In 1895, it launched the massive battleship *Maine*; later, during World War II, it became the United States' biggest naval construction facility.[18]

As befit an urban economic powerhouse, Brooklyn firms helped to build and outfit Ebbets Field, as the *Brooklyn Daily Eagle* reported in April 1913.

> The lumber used in the construction was furnished by Johnson Brothers and Louis Bossert & Sons of Brooklyn.... Ernest Capelle, of Brooklyn, received the contract for the steel flagpole placed on the walls

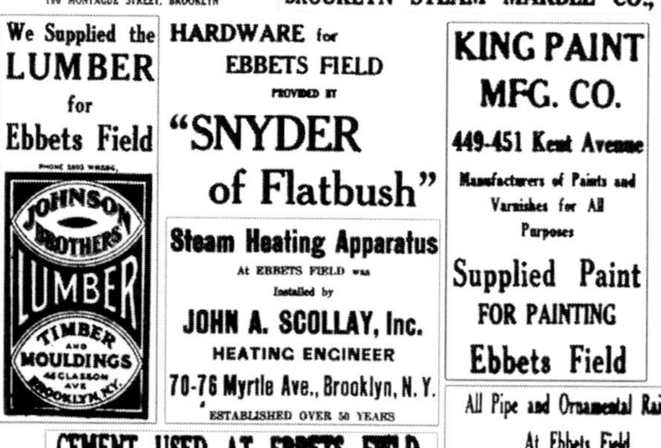

Brooklyn's diverse workforce and manufactories helped to build Ebbets Field, as these advertisements show ("Ebbets Field Ads," collage by Andrea Magno. Source *Brooklyn Daily Eagle*, April 9, 1913).

> surrounding the field.... The marble used in the main entrance and on all portions of the grandstand was supplied by the Brooklyn Steam Marble Company.... The floor tiling in reception rooms, offices and other apartments was furnished by Henry Miles & Son of Brooklyn.... J.G. Carlin of Brooklyn had far more brickwork and plastering to do than the casual observer might think in speaking of a steel and concrete plant.... Another side angle was the cement, for which the John Morton's Sons Company of Brooklyn had the contract.... Apart from the ironwork, there was the hardware, and it was no small item, as the club found when it let the contract to "Snyder of Flatbush."[19]

The rise of industrial Brooklyn was aided by the arrival of increasing numbers of newcomers, many of whom supplied the skilled and unskilled labor necessary in factories. Brooklyn was, by the mid–1800s, already a city of immigrants, with nearly 50 percent foreign-born in a city of 138,882. Most were from Germany and Ireland; they would later be joined by massive numbers of newcomers from Southern and Eastern Europe. By 1910, of the 1,634,351 people living in the borough, 21 percent were born in Russia (or had parents born there), 20.5 percent in Germany, 18.1 percent in Ireland and 13.6 percent in Italy.[20]

Brooklyn's overall growth at the turn of the 20th century was also due, in part, to advances in its transportation system, which was far-reaching. In 1883, the Brooklyn Bridge — a famous symbol of the then-city — had opened to great acclaim; connecting Brooklyn and Manhattan, it would eventually spell the end of ferry travel, which had operated at the mercy of tides and weather. In 1885, the first elevated train line in Brooklyn made its debut, carrying commuters high above congested thoroughfares. By the 1890s, elevated lines were extending far into Brooklyn. In 1890, the electric trolley — at a cost of five cents per ride, affordable to most — debuted on Brooklyn streets, and by the mid–1890s had all but replaced the much slower horsecars.[21]

"But a matter of even greater importance was accomplished by the Brooklyn Rapid transit management," noted the *Brooklyn Daily Eagle Almanac*, when

> in 1898 — the same year that saw Brooklyn and New York consolidated into a single city — through surface car operation was begun across the Brooklyn [B]ridge to Park [R]ow and the extra three-cent toll demanded of all Brooklyn passengers on all routes across the bridge [was] abandoned. That one liberal step on the part of the Brooklyn system contributed many millions of dollars to the value of realty in the borough.[22]

Ten years later, in 1908, the subway opened in Brooklyn. One account noted that the "neighbourhood of the Borough Hall was brightly illuminated," and on the "front of the Temple Bar Building a mammoth electric sign read: 'Welcome subway.'"[23] It would eventually reach far into the borough, bringing ever-greater numbers of residents to newly developing neighborhoods.

Transportation was, of course, crucial to the development of Ebbets Field as an entertainment venue. The ballpark was conveniently located within reach of any of a number of mass transit lines. "Ebbets Field is located in the center of a population approximating 4,000,000," noted the *Brooklyn Daily Eagle*. "The geographical center of Greater New York is only half a mile away. Twelve lines of surface cars and elevated trains are within two minutes' walk, and these twelve transfer to eighteen more."[24] As a 1913 real estate advertisement observed, these lines would help to bring patrons to games (and, once there,

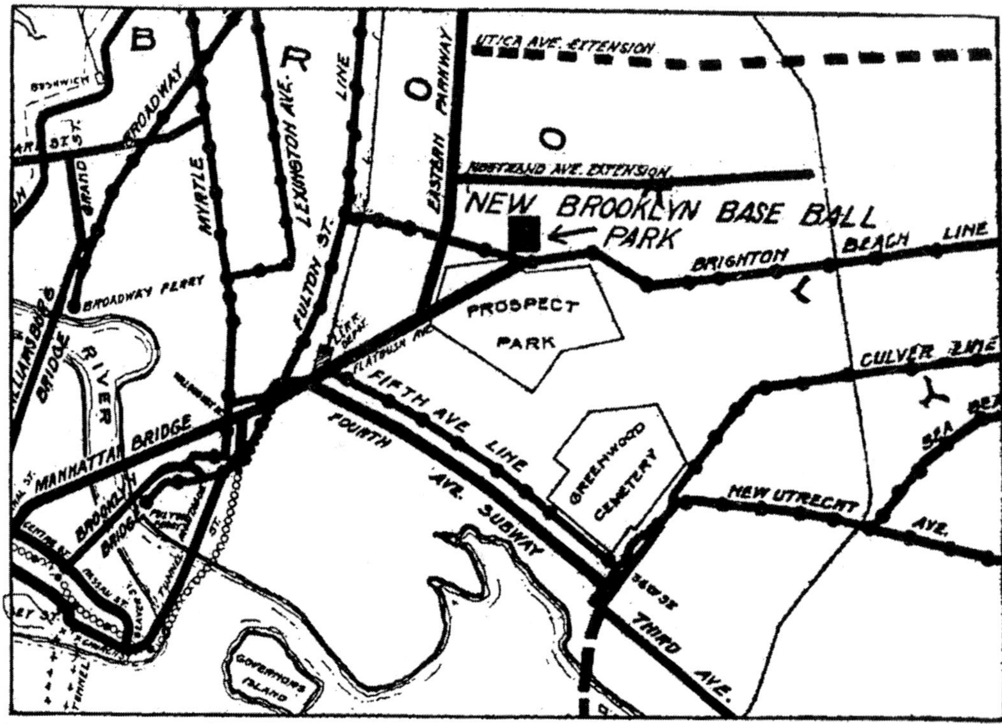

This Shows the Location of the Ball Park and the Transit Lines Leading to It.

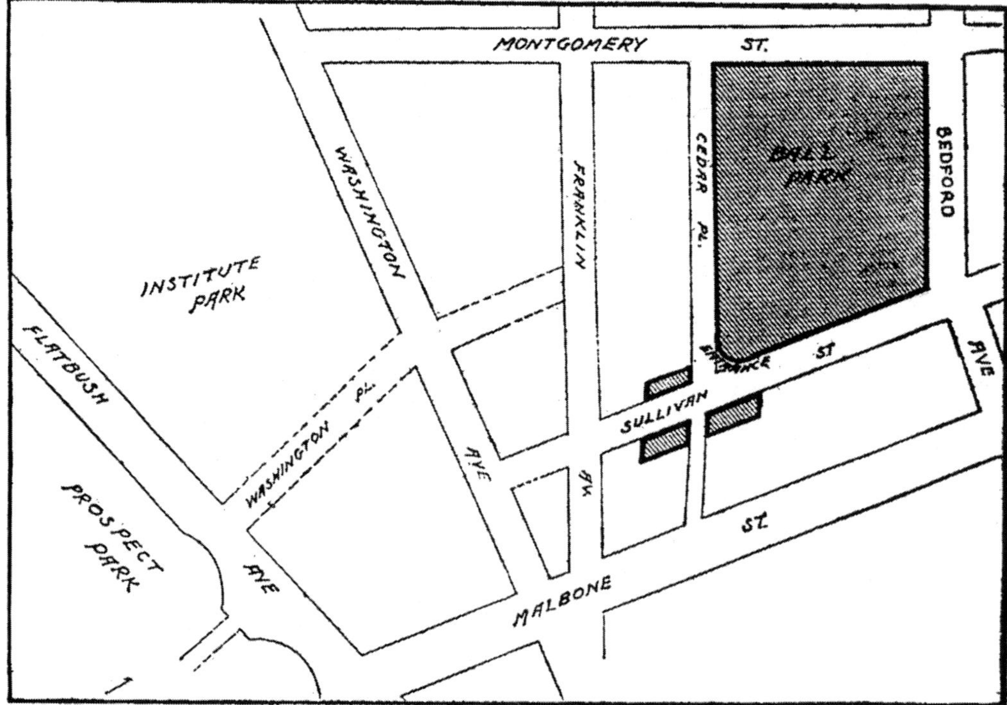

Tint Shows Property in Flatbush Bought by the Owners of the Brooklyn Baseball Club for the Erection of a Great New Ball Park.

possibly consider moving to Brooklyn). "After the Ball Game Take a Look Around! Thousands of Manhattanites will come to Flatbush for the first time at the opening of the Ball Grounds," it admonished. "They will be surprised to see so fine a locality, fifteen minutes from Manhattan."[25]

The same transportation routes that made it possible for patrons to travel to Dodgers games also made it possible for them to travel to participate in other forms of commercial entertainment. Brooklyn was home to a rising—even renowned—world of commercial leisure that rivaled neighboring Manhattan. At the turn of the century, amusement parks, dance halls, beer gardens, saloons, vaudeville theaters, nickelodeons, movie theaters, and more flourished, as people with less work hours, more money, and the time to spend it sought out new amusements. One pleasure ground stood out: Coney Island.

Like Ebbets Field, Coney Island was a symbol of Brooklyn identity. Located at Brooklyn's southern tip, it had drawn beachgoers and pleasure seekers throughout much of the 19th century. It was not until the late 1800s, though, that it emerged as a major

Luna Park, Coney Island, ca. 1905. Luna Park was a fantastic mixture of pleasure, entertainment, spectacle, and education, a place where urban dwellers from all over New York City rubbed shoulders in the pursuit of a good time (Library of Congress, Prints & Photographs Division, Bain Collection [LC-DIG-ggbain-09490]).

Opposite: **A diagram showing the location of Ebbets Field and local transit lines. As the diagram illustrates, the proposed ballpark was at the crossroads of a number of transit lines, including the relatively new subway (*Brooklyn Daily Eagle*, January 3, 1912).**

entertainment destination. Beginning with Steeplechase Park in 1897, entrepreneurs built fantastic, enclosed theme parks — Luna Park in 1903 and Dreamland in 1904 — that provided different brands of over-the-top fun for their city patrons, from topsy turvy mechanical rides to "educational" depictions of far-away lands.

Coney Island's entertainment was live-action and fast-paced (and may have provided

THE BROOKLYN DAILY EAGLE. NEW YORK. FRIDAY, AUGUST 13.

HOME RULE FIGHT ON IN CONVENTION; LOW EXPLAINS BILL

Says It Is Necessary to Relieve Legislature of Local Measures.

WOULD LESSEN CITY BILLS

Morgan J. O'Brien, Democratic Minority Leader, Offers Substitute Proposal.

(Special to The Eagle.)

Albany, August 13—The home rule fight on the floor of the Constitutional Convention opened this morning. According to the schedule now arranged by George W. Wickersham, floor leader of the Republican majority, it is to continue all day today and tomorrow, and may possibly be carried over into next week. Mr. Wickersham declared today that he considered the subject so important that he would allow all the time wanted for debate, and that a vote would not be taken on the Low home rule bill, around which the fight centers, until everybody who desired had been heard fully. He said that it was quite possible that the convention would not be ready for the question before Monday or Tuesday of next week.

Seth Low, chairman of the Cities Committee, in his argument, called the attention of the convention to the fact that the cities have little more home rule now than they had in 1870, forty-five years ago. He pointed out that it had become necessary to relieve the Legislature of the detail local legislation asked for by cities because of the growing amount of real State-wide legislation which he said had tended to lessen the careful consideration of city bills and had resulted in much of it being passed without thorough scrutiny. As an example of this he called attention to the revision of the Greater New York Charter in 1901, which he said had been passed so hastily at the end of the session that the term of every official was reduced from four to two years save that of Coroner, which was left at four years, contrary to the purpose and intention of the Legislature.

In summing up, he said:

"I confidently submit to the judgment of this convention that the amendment proposed by your Cities Committee does four things essential to any plan which is to solve the problem with which this convention is called upon to deal. 1. It grants adequate and exclusive power to the cities to deal at home with their own local affairs. 2. It provides the means by which cities may currently adjust the machinery by which they conduct their business to the changing needs of the hour. 3. It prevents the Legislature from interfering in the details of the city action, so far as the city is acting in relation to its own affairs only. The Legislature naturally cannot pass any law within the field of the city's exclusive power. Under the Cities Committee amendment it cannot initiate any charter amendment, and, therefore, it will secure jurisdiction over such amendments only at the request of the cities; and lastly, in the twilight zone, where the cities act as the agent of the State, ... [illegible]

THE HEART OF BROOKLYN

BUILD RACERS HERE TO WAR ON U-BOATS

"Unhittable" Speed Boats, Tried Out at Sag Harbor, Will Patrol for Allies.

500 ARE BEING BUILT HERE

Craft Has Only Thirty-Inch Draft and High Speed Makes Her Almost Unhittable.

(Special to The Eagle.)

Sag Harbor, L. I., August 13—Successful trial runs of a 60-foot light draught boat, said to be one of a lot of 500 in course of construction in this country for the Allies and to be used to combat the German submarines, were held yesterday over a measured course in Noyack Bay. The boat which was used in the tests is one of a dozen constructed by the Greenport Basin and Construction Company.

The boats are of a new type designed especially to meet the attacks of submarines. Their light draught of less than 30 inches makes it very difficult to strike them with a torpedo and their high speed makes them an uncertain target. They will be used to patrol the coasts of the Allies and repel submarine attacks by the Germans.

In the trials yesterday the boat developed a speed of 28 7-10 miles, although the specifications call for a speed of only 27 miles. The builders, however, will receive a large bonus for the extra speed. The boat also made a five-hour endurance run with great success.

An inspector, who spoke with a Russian accent and had a distinctly Russian appearance, attended the trials and, it is said, represented the Allies. He appeared much elated at the success of the boat in meeting all the conditions set down in the specifications.

The boats have a cruising radius of 1,000 miles and are provided with quarters for eight men. Three engines, almost noiseless, develop 450-horsepower. The Greenport Company is turning out a boat each week and expects to bid for another order as soon as it completes its present contract. The trials yesterday were made over a measured mile course in Noyack Bay, loaned for the occasion by the E. W. Bliss Company of Brooklyn, which has a torpedo-proving range in the bay.

OBITUARY

George H. Westfall.

George H. Westfall of 1814 Union street, who died suddenly yesterday at 132 New York avenue, was secretary and treasurer of the Kentucky Warehouse and Distilleries Company for sixteen years. He was born in Brooklyn, August 23, 1876, and had lived here all his life. He is survived by his parents, John H. and Christina Westfall; his wife, Edith Moller Westfall, and two brothers, Edward A. and Diedrick W. Westfall. Funeral services will be held tomorrow evening at [illegible] o'clock at 132 New York avenue. The interment will be private.

James Kilcoyne.

James Kilcoyne, 55, of 173 Stuyvesant avenue, died yesterday of complications. He was born in Castlebar, County Mayo, Ireland, was a journeyman mason and lived thirty years in Brooklyn. He leaves his wife, Mary Lawless, and a stepson, James Lawless. His funeral will be held tomorrow afternoon, with interment in Holy Cross Cemetery.

Mrs. Mary Helena McGettrick.

[illegible]

Mrs. Rebecca Augusta Lloyd.

[illegible]

'Jimmie' Smith's SpyGlass Stirs Tiny Patients' Envy

Every Youngster in the Kings County Hospital Wants "Some Nice Lady" to Bring Him Something, but Small-Sized "Admiral" Has His Glass and He Is Happy.

Ever since the world was let into the secret that "Jimmie Smith," in the Tubercular Ward for Children at the Kings County Hospital, wanted a spyglass so that he could see the ships go by, there has been such a to-do among the small patients in the ward as never was seen there before. ... [illegible]

"The Heart of Brooklyn" (*Brooklyn Daily Eagle*, August 13, 1915).

some competition to the ballpark, at least for the time that their seasons overlapped). "By the end of the week," noted the May 12, 1913, *New York Times*, "New Yorkers will find the amusement park season in full swing, most of the managers of large outdoor entertainment places having announced their intention of throwing open the gates. The sounds of hammering and the smell of paint will give way to feminine shrieks and the odor of roasted corn and hot frankfurters."

They would come across, said the story, huge crowds and attractions ranging from vaudeville to mammoth spectacles, a dizzying array of fantastic attractions. "George C. Tilyou's Steeplechase Park at Coney Island started the ball rolling by opening its season yesterday," noted the paper. "The fair weather brought 75,000 persons to Coney, and Steeplechase got its share of the visitors. The New Brighton Theatre also opens for the season to-day at Brighton Beach" and offered, the article noted, dancing, bands, acrobats, musicians, ventriloquists, and more. "Fred Thompson will open Luna Park on Wednesday for its tenth season," it added, and the place would feature spectacles with such provocative names as "Fire and Sword" (showing, as it put it, the "destruction of a Turkish city in the war of the Balkan allies on the Ottoman Empire"), "Crazy Town," "Tornado and Flood," and "Fairyland," along with an "exhibition by diving girls," and other "novelties, including a ride on handcars."[26]

This signature resort — along with thriving industries, a burgeoning population, a well-oiled transportation system, and more — was yet another indicator of Brooklyn as a metropolis on the ascent. Together, these successful markers of city growth all seemed to point toward a similarly bright future for Ebbets Field, which would look to Brooklyn for its patrons. In a speech he gave at a tribute to Charles Ebbets shortly after Ebbets Field opened to the public, Brooklyn Public Works commissioner Lewis H. Pounds, who served as toastmaster, alluded to this bright future. "It has been said that Brooklyn could not support such a magnificent field," he observed, "but Ebbets believed it could, and the tremendous attendance drawn to every game thus far played is proof that he is right. Moreover, Brooklyn is increasing in population at a rate of 178 persons per day, and that certainly inspires confidence that she will never be less able to support ... the American game."[27]

It could, and it did. On August 13, 1915, the *Brooklyn Daily Eagle* featured a telling editorial cartoon, run in the paper at a point in the season when the Dodgers were establishing themselves as serious contenders for the National League pennant. In the simple image, "Home Plate Ebbets Field" is centered under the poignant title, "The Heart of Brooklyn."

Brooklyn at the Death of Ebbets Field

Just as Ebbets Field's construction mirrored the borough's rise as a modern urban entity, its demise and abandonment by the Dodgers mirrored a downturn in Brooklyn at mid-century. In 1947, Ebbets Field saw its highest attendance in a single season: 1,807,526.[28] Enthusiastic fans not only thrilled to the crack of the bat but laughed at the antics of the Sym-Phony (a ragtag band of five musicians who regaled the fans, players,

Crystal Motors, 5901 Bay Parkway, Brooklyn. Automobile ownership rose dramatically in the years of postwar prosperity following World War II, and this is just one of many car dealerships that appealed to Brooklynites' wallets. Along with the rise in cars came a rise in the construction of highways, which took people through, and out of, cities. "But what is Brooklyn to the highway engineer," asked critic and philosopher Lewis Mumford in the November 14, 1959, *New Yorker*, "except a place to go through quickly, at whatever necessary sacrifice of peace and amenity by its inhabitants?" (Library of Congress, Prints and Photographs Division, Gottscho-Schleisner Collection [LC-G613-T-56585]).

and the umpires), hummed to the organ playing of Gladys Goodding, held their ears when fan Hilda Chester rang her brass cowbells, and witnessed the end of segregated ball as Jackie Robinson took to the field on April 15. Many patrons recall, throughout it all, an almost indescribable sense of closeness, intimacy, and community that drew them together around a common love — Dodger baseball.[29] In 1950, Brooklyn's population peaked at 2.7 million.

But there were changes afoot. For one, the automobile was remaking the American landscape and transforming cities. Federal policies in the 1940s encouraged highway construction, making it increasingly easy for residents to move to new suburbs in New Jersey, Long Island, and, especially with the construction of the Verrazano-Narrows Bridge in 1964, Staten Island. The rise of the automobile had a direct impact on Ebbets Field. The stadium, designed in an era of elevated trains and electric trolleys, only had parking for 700 cars. In the age of the automobile, it was antiquated, unable to accommodate a growing population of car owners. For Dodger owner Walter O'Malley, the number also spelled low profits; he wanted to be able to feature more parking so that he could rake in more proceeds.[30]

The automobile also helped to take urban dwellers out of Brooklyn. Increasingly, the middle class left in search of single-family homes with yards — often, after World War II, made more affordable by low-cost GI loans. Between 1950 and 1957, Brooklyn's population dropped by more than 135,000.[31] At the same time, the borough saw the beginning of a process that would result in a dramatic loss of jobs.[32] Manufacturing employment peaked in 1954 and remained at about the same level into the 1960s. Waterfront jobs also peaked — and then they declined. When in 1966, the Brooklyn Navy Yard closed, it was a symbol of dramatic changes in the industrial workplace, not just in Brooklyn but also throughout other northeastern industrial cities, as many businesses left, their decision fueled by government policies that made it more economical for them to move to New Jersey and the American South.

On the waterfront, shipping began to relocate to New Jersey's larger, more modern facilities. The increasing use of containers meant that goods that had once been packed in crates or sacks were now being packed into metal containers and loaded onto vehicles. With automation, the army of longshoremen who had once loaded and unloaded ships could now be dismissed. Thousands of jobs were lost; the new containerized waterfront required only one-sixth the workforce of the old one.[33]

Walter O'Malley, ca. 1950. This photograph was taken around the time that Walter O'Malley became president of the Brooklyn Dodgers. His choice of the Fort Greene meat market as a site for a new ballpark took into account its easy access to subway lines and the Long Island Railroad. But one of his major detractors, city parks commissioner Robert Moses, was not interested in supporting a project that favored public transportation over a rising automobile culture (National Baseball Hall of Fame Library, Cooperstown, New York).

Along with changes in work came changes in leisure. Ebbets Field faced new competition in television. Visitors no longer needed to travel to the ballpark to see the Dodgers play. Ironically, television viewing of major league baseball games first took place at Ebbets Field when the Dodgers hosted the Cincinnati Reds for a doubleheader on August 26, 1939. As the *New York Times* reported, owners of television sets "as far away as fifty miles" could, over the "video-sound channels" of station W2XBS, view "the action" and hear "the roar of the crowd."[34]

Although few people had television sets in their homes to watch the game at the time — the first television sets appeared in bars and restaurants where people enjoyed them in public — in the 1950s, television ownership rose dramatically, becoming part of American domestic life and remaking the entertainment landscape. Even Coney Island felt the impact, as the little screen — along with movies and increased ease of travel — meant potential patrons did not need to travel to the edge of Brooklyn to see or experience "far-away lands."

In short, Brooklyn in the 1950s was undergoing enormous upheaval. As people and industries left, they left behind aging buildings and a worn urban infrastructure. Those who moved in did not find the same first step up on the economic ladder that earlier newcomers had. The largely African American working class population that looked to find a home in the borough met with blatant discrimination in housing, home ownership loans and jobs. Neighborhoods and city services began to decline.[35]

All of these changes, along with the limitations of Ebbets Field, led club president Walter O'Malley to seek a new Brooklyn home for his ball club. Ultimately O'Malley found what he felt was the ideal site, the Fort Greene meat market, which offered the necessary land plus easy access to the Long Island Railroad. However, the Dodger owner insisted that he needed help from government in assembling the land. But municipal leaders, especially Robert Moses, rebuffed him. Blocked in Brooklyn, O'Malley declined to consider local options, such as moving the Dodgers to Queens, and began considering an even more drastic move — to Los Angeles, California.

Ebbets Field — like the *Brooklyn Daily Eagle*, the beloved trolleys, the Brooklyn Navy Yard, and Coney Island — was about to become a casualty of changing times. By July 1957, it was clear that its days were numbered. "It is claimed that Brooklyn would not be Brooklyn without the beloved Bums," observed *Sports Illustrated*. "The same thing was said about the *Brooklyn Eagle*, which nevertheless folded. That was a damn shame and so, in some respects, would be the departure of the Dodgers...."[36]

In an October 9, 1957, article about the end in sight, *New York Times* writer Joseph M. Sheehan called upon the same sense of city and identity that *Brooklyn Daily Eagle* editor St. Clair McKelway had conjured up years before:

> In deserting Brooklyn for Los Angeles, the Dodgers will leave an aching void in the Borough of Churches. Few baseball clubs have had greater identity with, and greater impact on, their communities than the Dodgers have had on Brooklyn.
>
> A mention of New York seldom evokes a chain-of-idea response of "Giants" or "Yankees" such as Brooklyn does of "Dodgers."
>
> Brooklyn basically had always been the city's dormitory and for sixty-odd years its major league ball club has been its principal claim to public attention.
>
> Perhaps because of this situation, Brooklynites generally have raised louder hosannahs at Dodger successes and have taken Dodger failures harder than baseball fans in other cities.
>
> It is peculiarly expressive of the Dodger fan's fierce devotion that he could scream from the Ebbets Field stands — and mean it — "Ya, bums, ya," without surrendering one iota of loyalty.[37]

At the March 1912 groundbreaking for Ebbets Field, people had cheered, the *New York Times* reported, "and fond mothers held their children on their shoulders so that they could see the impressive sight and remember it in after years." On the fateful day in February 1960, as a wrecking ball smashed into the ballpark stands and brought Ebbets Field crumbling to the ground, one wonders if any of those small children — now middle-aged men and women — came to watch, each remembering, in his or her mind's-eye, a much different day. "The end of Ebbets Field marks a period in the past of professional baseball," remarked the *Times*, "but though the iron ball can demolish the ball park it cannot touch the memories that baseball fans will always have of their pleasant afternoons and evenings spent at Ebbets Field."[38]

Almost two years later, an apartment complex stood on the site. "A new chapter in

Opening the Ebbets Field cornerstone, April 1960. Just months after Ebbets Field was demolished by a wrecking ball, one of the wreckers, according to the caption for this UPI photo, took a "whack at the old cornerstone of Ebbets Field during an auction sale at the old stamping grounds of the Brooklyn Dodgers.... Balls, bats, and other diamond bric-a-brac dear to the hearts of the Flatbush Faithful were sold at auction." Contents reportedly included a 1912 calendar and letters from President William Howard Taft and New York City's mayor, William J. Gaynor. The ephemera were a tangible reminder of the time when the ballpark was a modern innovation that symbolized a Brooklyn on the rise (National Baseball Hall of Fame Library, Cooperstown, New York).

the history of Ebbets Field will open late this month, when the first tenants are scheduled to move into the middle-income housing project nearing completion on the former playing field of the Brooklyn Dodgers, now the Los Angeles Dodgers," reported the *Times*. "The tan brick-faced structure, the largest single apartment house of its kind in the five boroughs, was started eighteen months ago. Since then, all traces of the bandbox-sized ballpark, where the Dodgers held sway for forty-five seasons, from 1913 to 1957, have vanished."[39]

Times had changed in Brooklyn. Heralded in one era as a modern monument and a proud feature of a city on the rise, Ebbets Field in the mid–20th century was a casualty of changing times and of larger urban forces: of the rise of the automobile and of television, the decline of industry and jobs, and the lure of the suburbs. Located in a crowded borough that could not accommodate its owner's desires, home to a team with a dwindling audience, the outdated structure gave way to new needs. For many, though, the concrete structure bounded by Bedford Avenue, Sullivan Place, McKeever Place, and Montgomery Street, would forever be an enduring symbol of a "city."

Notes

1. "Ebbets Field Is Chosen as Name of New Ball Park," *Brooklyn Daily Eagle,* January 5, 1912.
2. Herbert Foster Gunnison, *The Realm of Light and Air: Flatbush of To-Day* (Brooklyn: n.p., 1908), 136, Google Books, http://books.google.com/books?id=EtsTAAAAYAAJ&pg=PA136&lpg=PA136&dq=Alfred+A.+Steers&source=bl&ots=Z4nRMTVR2o&sig=n8aqNJ4VqFzRTTvYoCk7-MTBksk&hl=en&ei=zIufTN_hCoSKlweLv7jxCQ&sa=X&oi=book_result&ct=result&resnum=7&ved=0CCgQ6AEwBg#v=onepage&q=Alfred%20A.%20Steers&f=false.
3. Gunnison, 16. "Erasmus" refers to Erasmus Hall High School, founded by Dutch settlers in 1786 as a private academy. In 1896, the school became part of the public school system. Kenneth T. Jackson, ed., *The Encyclopedia of New York City* (New Haven: Yale University Press; New York: New-York Historical Society, 1995), 381–382.
4. "Dirt Flies in New Brooklyn Ball Park," *New York Times,* March 5, 1912.
5. Ibid.
6. "Ebbets Field Is Chosen as Name of New Ball Park," *Brooklyn Daily Eagle,* January 5, 1912.
7. "End of a Ballpark," *New York Times,* February 24, 1960.
8. "Dirt Flies in New Brooklyn Ball Park," *New York Times,* March 5, 1912.
9. Kenneth T. Jackson, *Crabgrass Frontier: The Suburbanization of the United States* (New York: Oxford University Press, 1987), 142–143.
10. Jackson, *The Encyclopedia of New York City,* 504.
11. Andrew Sancton, *Merger Mania: The Assault on Local Government* (Montreal: McGill-Queens University Press, 2000), 32.
12. "Ceremonies in Brooklyn: Union Quietly Observed by a Reception in City Hall by the Mayor and ex–Mayors. Orators Praise the Old City," *New York Times,* January 1, 1898; also see Edwin G. Burrows and Mike Wallace, *Gotham: A History of New York City to 1898* (New York: Oxford University Press, 2000), 1233.
13. "Brooklyn Ball Park Nearly Completed," *New York Times,* February 21, 1913.
14. "Ebbets Confident New Park Will Be Opened This Season," *Brooklyn Daily Eagle,* April 5, 1912.
15. *New York at the Louisiana Purchase Exposition, St. Louis, 1904: Report of the New York State Commission.* Prepared and compiled by Delancey M. Ellis (Albany: J. B. Lyon, 1907), 165–168, Google Books, http://books.google.com/books?id=bUoWAAAAYAAJ&pg=PA168&dq=Brooklyn+as+Manhattan%27s+bedroom&hl=en&ei=d9urTJeSBIG88gbBr7WZCA&sa=X&oi=book_result&ct=result&resnum=2&ved=0CDgQ6AEwAQ#v=onepage&q&f=false.
16. Joshua Brown and David Ment, *Factories, Foundries, and Refineries: A History of Five Brooklyn Industries* (Brooklyn: Brooklyn Educational & Cultural Alliance, 1980), 5.
17. Julian Ralph, "The City of Brooklyn," Harper's New Monthly Magazine, 86 (April 1893): 664–665.
18. Jackson, *The Encyclopedia of New York City,* 159–160.
19. "Construction of Ebbets Field Interested Many Concerns," *Brooklyn Daily Eagle,* April 9, 1913.
20. Ron Miller, Rita Seiden Miller, and Stephen Karp, "The Fourth Largest City in America — A Sociological History of Brooklyn," in Rita Seiden Miller, *Brooklyn USA: The Fourth Largest City in America* (New York: Brooklyn College Press, 1979), 18; *Thirteenth Census of the United States, Taken in 1910,* 3 (Washington, D.C.: GPO, 1913): 188, 217.
21. See Ellen M. Snyder-Grenier, *Brooklyn! An Illustrated History* (Philadelphia: Temple University Press, 1996).
22. *Brooklyn Daily Eagle Almanac 1910,* 25 (January 1910): 445; Jackson, *The Encyclopedia of New York City,* 151.
23. "Brooklyn Subway Opened," *The Summary,* 30 (January 11, 1908): 1, Google Books, http://books.google.com/books?id=pwFLAAAAYAAJ&pg=PA8-IA1&dq=opening+of+the+brooklyn+subway+1908&hl=en&ei=ehSgTMSLAsb_lgez093sAg&sa=X&oi=book_result&ct=result&resnum=5&ved=0CEMQ6AEwBA#v=onepage&q=opening%20of%20the%20brooklyn%20subway%201908&f=false.
24. "Most Modern of Baseball Parks Soon to Be Home of Superbas," *Brooklyn Daily Eagle,* April 6, 1912.
25. *Brooklyn Daily Eagle,* April 9, 1913.
26. "Amusement Parks to Open This Week," *New York Times,* May 12, 1913.
27. "Brooklyn Baseball Enthusiasts' Tribute to Ebbets," *Brooklyn Daily Eagle,* May 11, 1913.
28. Jackson, *The Encyclopedia of New York City,* 358.
29. See Peter Golenbock, *Bums: An Oral History of the Brooklyn Dodgers* (New York: Putnam, 1984).
30. Andrew Paul Mele, "Why Did the Dodgers Leave Brooklyn?" Brooklyn Eagle online, August 6, 2007, http://www.brooklyneagle.com/categories/category.php?category_id=27&id=14608.
31. James Rubin, "The Brooklyn Dodgers and Ebbets Field — Their Departure," in Miller, *Brooklyn*

USA, 167. Rubin cites statistics from Brooklyn Communities, *Population Characteristics and Neighborhood Social Resources*, 2 vols. (New York: Bureau of Community Statistical Services, Community Council of Greater New York, 1959): xvi.

32. Jackson, *The Encyclopedia of New York City,* 152.

33. Snyder-Grenier, 159–162.

34. "Games Are Televised," *New York Times*, August 27, 1939.

35. Snyder-Grenier, 255.

36. "Robert Moses on the Battle of Brooklyn: New York's Outspoken Park Commissioner, Accusing the Dodgers' O'Malley of Bad Faith, Presents a Plan for a National League Site in N.Y.," *Sports Illustrated*, July 22, 1957.

37. "Fans Added Zest to Lore of 'Bums,'" *New York Times,* October 9, 1957.

38. "End of a Ball Park," *New York Times,* February 24, 1960.

39. "New Chapter for Ebbets Field: Apartments Open This Month," *New York Times*, September 2, 1962.

The Alpha and the Omega

First and Last Dodger Games at Ebbets Field

John G. Zinn

Although most ballparks have only one first game, Ebbets Field had five, scheduled over two years. Three were planned in 1912, only to be cancelled due to construction delays, followed by two actual 1913 openings. At the gala January 2, 1912, dinner where Ebbets announced plans for his new ballpark, the opening was projected to take place less than six months later, on Flag Day, June 14. Even at the time, the date was thought to be unrealistic, with August 27 (the anniversary of the Battle of Brooklyn) considered to be more feasible. As construction lagged over the summer of 1912, there was speculation about various September dates, but the opening was ultimately put off until 1913.

It might have been expected that the exact date and circumstances of the 1913 opening would be worked out as part of major league baseball's routine schedule making. Such expectations did not, however, take into account the resourcefulness of Tom Rice from the *Brooklyn Daily Eagle.* Rice took advantage of a National League schedule committee meeting in December of 1912 to campaign for a special opening day for Ebbets Field. Since the Superbas were supposed to begin the 1913 campaign in Philadelphia on April 10, Rice suggested opening Ebbets Field a day earlier, preferably against the Giants, or even the Phillies, if hosting Brooklyn's cross town rivals was not possible. While favorable to the idea, Ebbets reportedly was reluctant to fight for it because he was sensitive to complaints regarding how "plums" in the schedule were awarded. Ultimately, there was opposition to the Giants being part of a special date, but not the Phillies, so the game was set for April 9, a day earlier than the rest of the league started play. It took until February to confirm the date, but finally on February 20, 1913, Ebbets publicly announced the April 9 opener at a luncheon for sportswriters at Henry Pohlmeyer's restaurant. Understandably, the *Eagle* quickly took credit for the special opening, confidently predicting "it surely looks like a big day *The Eagle* got for the fans and we cannot be blamed even if we do swell up a little over our getting the deal through."[1]

The prediction that the Ebbets Field opening would be a big day was correct, but not quite how the *Eagle* had envisioned it. In addition to negotiating the special opening, Ebbets also arranged for two exhibition games against the New York Yankees, prior to April 9. Whether through design, accident, or some combination of the two, the first contest, on Saturday, April 5, became the gala opening. Part of the excitement was due to the opposition, more specifically the opposition's manager. While the New York American League club had not enjoyed much real success in their first 10 years of existence, there was a great deal of interest in the team's new manager, Frank Chance, the former "peerless leader" of the great Cub teams of the prior decade and a future Hall of Famer. The April 5 exhibition game would mark Yankee fans' first chance to see their new leader in action and many would take advantage of the opportunity.[2]

The combination of a new ballpark for the Brooklyn club and a new manager for the Yankees, along with the normal excitement of a new baseball season, guaranteed a big crowd as long as the weather cooperated. Given all the weather-related problems Ebbets encountered in building his new facility, he deserved a break in this department and, probably to his surprise, he got one. Overnight rain did not augur well for the big day, but it cleared by 5:00 A.M., and it turned out to be "one of the nicest little spring days the oldest inhabitants of Flatbush could remember." The "glorious sunshine," along with the "huge stadium's" ability to absorb or block the wind, ensured the fans "were not a bit uncomfortable."[3]

Right to left: Edward and Jennie McKeever with Charles Ebbets at the grand opening on April 5, 1913 (Library of Congress, Prints & Photographs Division, Bain Collection [LC-DIG-ggbain-12682]).

In promoting his new venture, Ebbets had cited easy access by public transportation from almost any place in Manhattan and Brooklyn. On the day of the park's opening, this premise was tested and proved to be well founded. The subways from Manhattan were so crowded the riders were "bruised and bumped on the cars to a fare-ye-well," as an estimated 10,000 men, women, and children made their way across the East River. Mass transit in Brooklyn also got a workout since the elevated trains on the Fulton Street and Brighton Beach lines "fairly groaned with the crowds." Closer to the ground, trolleys on Flatbush, Franklin, Nostrand, and Ocean Avenues also carried "their share of eager fans." While spectators were clearly taking full advantage of the 12 direct public transit routes and the approximately 40 means of access via transfer, even in 1913 there were those determined to travel by automobile and carriages. It was reported to be the "most elaborate motor display ever seen on this side of the river," as the number of vehicles on Bedford Avenue and Eastern Parkway led Flatbush residents to claim "there ain't that many machines made."[4]

After dropping off their passengers near the entrance, many drivers parked on Malbone Street and joined the crowd who "poured almost like water through a sieve" from "an almost endless procession of trolley cars," as well as the "steady volume" flowing out of Consumer's Park Station. "Hurrying, chatty and happy" the crowds converged "on the gates which open into the handsome lobby of the stadium." While not everyone in Brooklyn was present, it may have seemed that way since "the business of the city was summarily set aside shortly after noon." Some arrived as early as 10:00 A.M. even though the gates did not open until noon, by which time thousands were awaiting entrance. Overseeing the scene were Inspector Henry Cohen and Captain Bernard Gallagher, in charge of 50 men, some on horseback and others on bikes, with the balance on foot. Witnessing the growing sea of humanity, the captain and inspector called for 100 reinforcements, but fortunately there were few problems. When the gates did open, however, there was a real bottleneck at the ticket windows in the rotunda. The police solved the problem by opening and closing the gates to the rotunda, gradually admitting the crowd. Tickets in hand, fans moved through turnstiles, which were functioning "like sluice gates of a dam," onto the "gentle approaches" of ramps, which were favorably compared to the more standard stairs. Once at the top of the ramps, spectators had their first view of the new ballpark. Setting the standard for thousands who would never forget this experience, "there were

Jennie McKeever raises the stars and stripes over Brooklyn's new ballpark (Library of Congress, Prints & Photographs Division, Bain Collection [LC-DIG-ggbain-50205]).

shouts of hearty approval from the big audience as it drew its first sweeping glance of Ebbets great new plant." Quickly it was proclaimed "a wonder, and no mistake."[5]

Estimates of those in the ballpark ranged from twenty-four to thirty thousand. Not so fortunate were another five to ten thousand fans, who were turned away. Some tried alternative sites, particularly a "small hillock" behind the left-center field wall. Space on what was reportedly the site of "the famous Crow Hill Penitentiary," was free, and some "'deadheads,' who had never got a decision over Ebbets before were in their element." Nearby, entrepreneurs built a stand where "300 or more" paid for the privilege of risking "breaking their necks to get a peek at the players from a distance of two city blocks." Others watched from "houses, barns, trees and telegraph poles," so all the "high points" were "black with people and the few trees bent under the loads of boys and men."[6]

Finally at about 1:30, Brooklyn took the field for batting practice, which was followed by a "snappy" fielding practice. However, as soon as Frank Chance made his first appearance, the Dodgers were forgotten in "the roar of welcome." Grantland Rice reported even though the crowd was divided in its allegiances, there was "no division in the welcome boomed to" Chance, and "no manager ever drew such a tumultuous reception upon a visiting field." Although the game was scheduled to start at 3:00, it was later when Ebbets and Mr. and Mrs. Ed McKeever walked to the flagpole in center field followed by the Dodger players. Resplendent in a "stunning coat of green," with a matching green hat and a white skirt, Mrs. McKeever was to raise the American flag, but there was a slight delay since the banner had been forgotten and needed to be retrieved. As Mrs. McKeever

Genevieve Ebbets, daughter of Charles Ebbets, in a "wide black hat and ostrich plume" throws out the first pitch (Library of Congress, Prints & Photographs Division, Bain Collection [LC-DIG-ggbain-12681]).

did the honors, Shannon's 23rd Regimental Band played the "Star Spangled Banner," while "everybody stood up and remained standing till Old Glory stretched full length in the Flatbush breezes." According to the writer, "it was a picture the thirty thousand will have in their minds as long as they live." Ebbets and the McKeevers then led a parade of the Dodger players to the stands where Ebbets' daughter, Genevieve, equally resplendent, in a "wide black hat with ostrich plume and a ceries waist," threw out the first pitch.[7]

When all the formalities were over, it was past 3:30, and the game itself finally began. Ace Brooklyn lefthander, Nap Rucker, took the mound to face Bert Daniels of the Yankees. According to Tom Rice of the *Eagle*, the "throngs sat motionless, " while "every eye was glued on the great 'Nap,'" who uncorked "one of those lazy fadeaways that put a dent in so many, many batting averages." Daniels let the first pitch go with "a look of withering scorn," but it "snaked" back over the plate, bringing a mighty roar when umpire Tim Hurst called it a strike. With that, major league baseball at Ebbets Field was underway, and Rucker proceeded to set down the American Leaguers. Brooklyn second baseman George Cutshaw got the first hit at Ebbets Field in the bottom of the inning, and the Superbas took a 2–0 lead into the ninth behind inside-the-park home runs by Casey Stengel and Jake Daubert. Unfortunately for the Brooklyn faithful, a bad throw by pitcher Frank Allen allowed the Yankees to tie the game up in the ninth. The net result, however, was merely to give Brooklyn the opportunity for a dramatic win in the bottom of the inning, which the Superbas supplied when J. Carlisle Smith singled in Zack Wheat with the winning run. Although only an exhibition game, Rice felt it was well worthy of the

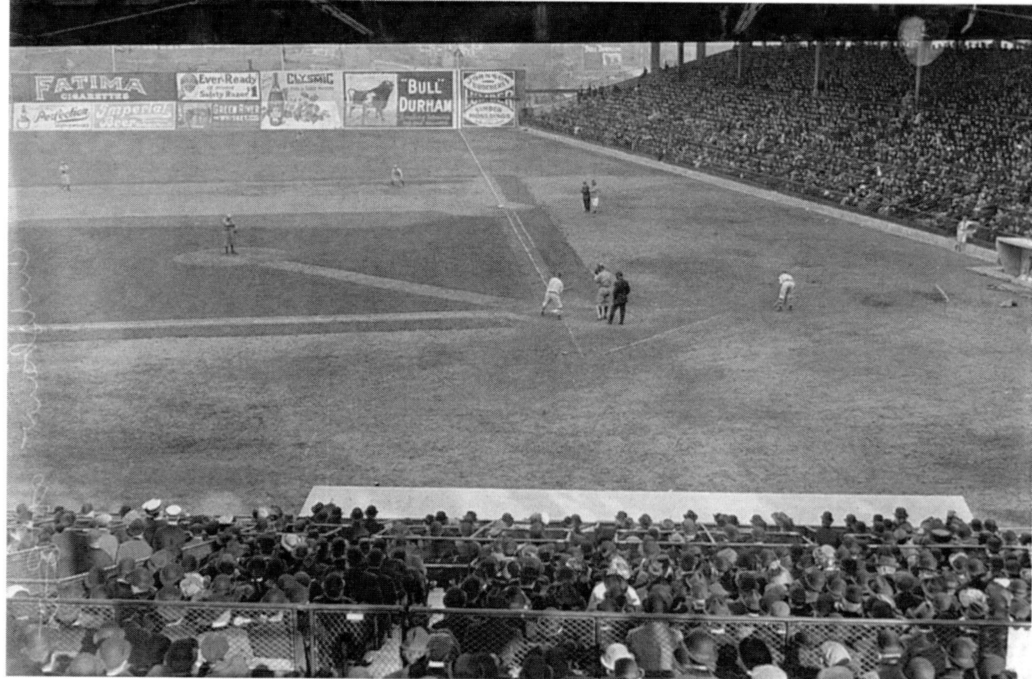

Game action between the Dodgers and the New York Yankees on April 5, 1913 (Library of Congress, Prints & Photographs Division, Bain Collection [LC-DIG-ggbain-12804]).

occasion, calling it "an unparalleled performance of unlimited variety and under circumstances that may never be repeated in this generation of fans."[8]

The exciting ending was followed by "no little commotion" when fans filled the aisles, and then realized they did not know the way out. Eventually, however, the private policemen and firemen began providing directions, and spectators found their way to the exits. The Brooklyn fans were, of course, "frenzied with victory," and the Yankee rooters were "chagrined at defeat," but there was clear agreement that "Ebbets Field is the realization of a dream, something almost too good to be hoped for." Multiple sources concurred the crowd had to be the largest ever at an exhibition game. While there were a few glitches, there was consensus the event "went along with the smoothness and éclat of a real championship opening." Similarly, although there were issues to be resolved, like the overcrowding in the rotunda before the game, there was universal praise for the "great stand of steel and concrete," a facility worthy to "be classed with America's greatest baseball plants." Charles Ebbets, of course, was well aware of the financial implications from $20,000 in estimated gate receipts for an exhibition game, especially as he thought of the lean days and years at Washington Park. But Ebbets also fully understood the larger significance of the building that bore his name. In a piece published in the *Brooklyn Daily Times* on the day of the opening, the Brooklyn owner wrote Ebbets Field was "built for Brooklynites, by Brooklynites: is essentially a Brooklyn institution."[9]

The only downside of the grand opening on April 5 was the little likelihood of a repeat performance during the April 9 special opening Ebbets (or the *Eagle)* had secured from the powers that be. A severe drop in temperature all the way to 37 degrees turned the likelihood into a certainty. Despite the expectation of a big crowd, the actual attendance was estimated at 10,000, "large" as one paper noted, given the weather, but "small" for a special opening. At least one writer felt the "edge" had been taken "off the regular opening" by the gala opening against the Yankees. Perhaps anticipating this to some degree, Ebbets scheduled opening ceremonies that were "short and simple," including Borough President Steers throwing out the first pitch.[10]

Those in attendance were no doubt grateful for the short ceremonies, and even more pleased the game lasted only 1 hour and 33 minutes. Even through there was bright sunshine, its rays could not "temper" the "chilly, raw winds" that "swirled through the open places," causing many to stand, stamping their feet and clapping their hands in an effort to keep warm. In spite of the harsh conditions, few left what became a low-scoring pitcher's duel. As happened so many times in his Brooklyn career, Nap Rucker was masterful, only to be betrayed by a lack of support. Rucker allowed just an unearned run on eight hits, but his teammates managed only six singles and were shut out. As with the game against the Yankees, George Cutshaw had the honor of making the first Brooklyn hit. Even though it was a loss (and one that counted), Ebbets could take some satisfaction that his new ballpark had pleased more visitors. The *Philadelphia Inquirer* gave the facility high praise, calling it "a model ballyard" with "awe inspiring grandstand" and "an athletic enclosure second to none."[11]

After the April 9, 1913, "special opener," the Brooklyn Dodgers played more than 3,300 regular season games, two playoff games, and 28 World Series games at Ebbets Field, not to mention countless exhibition contests. It all came to an end, however, on the evening of Tuesday, September 24, 1957, against the Pittsburgh Pirates. While there had not yet been a public announcement, there was little doubt in the media or the 6,702 fans who showed up that this was the last hurrah or, perhaps more appropriately, the last stand. The 1957 season was the year age finally caught up with the "Boys of Summer," and they finished a distant third, 11 games behind Milwaukee. Just as Walter O'Malley feared, the younger Braves, supported by sellout crowds at their new home in Milwaukee, would go on to the World Series.

The Dodgers last home stand in Brooklyn was a brief four-game affair with three contests against the Phillies and the finale with the Pirates. There was little fan interest for the last game, and it was not much different for the three weekend games with Philadelphia, where only one crowd topped the small turnout against Pittsburgh, by all of 47 people. As well as a lack of energy and nostalgia, there also seemed to be little in the way of protests. The only reported demonstration was a futile effort by three young men to hang a "paper stuffed dummy of O'Malley from the upper first base stands" during the Saturday game on September 21.[12]

By the time Tuesday night rolled around, it was clear Dodger management just wanted to get things over with, and the few fans wanted to mourn, not protest. Unlike the Giants, who took time at their last home game a few days later to commemorate the team's years in New York, the Dodgers took no official notice of the occasion. Many years later, Dave Anderson, who covered the game for the *Journal American*, said this was intentional on Walter O'Malley's part because the vote of National League owners was still pending. Anticipating the general attitude would be more of sorrow than anger, John Hennigan of the *New York Mirror* predicted a wake-like atmosphere where "Death — as it must to all — will come to Ebbets Field tonight."[13]

Although no official notice was taken of the occasion, one Dodger employee, longtime organist Gladys Goodding, took it upon herself to highlight the sad event with a full repertoire of appropriate songs. Either not knowing or not caring about any restrictions, Goodding made it impossible to ignore what was happening. Dave Anderson of the *Journal American* wrote Goodding's performance turned the game into a "Name That Tune" contest. According to Bill Roeder of the *World Telegram and Sun*, there was one song the press could not identify, so they called Goodding for the name. Upon learning it was "Don't Ask Me Why I Am Leaving," everyone in the press box agreed "it was a swell song." Anderson labeled it the "most sarcastic song" of the night. As these comments suggest, the members of the fourth estate knew exactly what was going on and were not pleased. When it was announced that 1957 attendance marked 13 straight years of over one million total spectators, a wisecrack over the press box public address system noted the Dodgers were the only team "to leave after doing it." Equally sarcastic was the suggestion that public address announcer Tex Rickard's standard "use any exit that leads to the street" announcement should have been modified to "any exit that leads to Chavez Ravine." All of this apparently wore down "hard shelled" press box staffer Benny Weinrig, who broke down after the game. Weinrig also had his own take on the event, observing that it reminded him "of the night they closed the old Star burlesque House in Brooklyn — for the last time that is."[14]

Gladys Goodding's farewell concert also had its effects in the stands, and Sid Gray of

Nap Rucker, star lefthander, started both of the 1913 openers. He lost the April 9 National League opener, 1–0, symbolic of his hard-luck career (Library of Congress, Prints & Photographs Division, Bain Collection [LC-DIG-ggbain-25542]).

Opened by one lefthander, Ebbets Field was closed by another on September 24, 1957, as Danny McDevitt shut out Pittsburgh, 2–0 (National Baseball Hall of Fame Library, Cooperstown, New York).

the *New York Herald Tribune* commented, "if there was a dry eye in the house at the finish, nobody can say she didn't try." Certainly shedding tears was a widely shared behavior that night with one man wailing, "don't leave us Walter," near O'Malley's box. Most of the weepers were, however, females, particularly young girls from the different fan clubs, such as two teenage members of the Duke Snider fan club, who sat behind home plate and cried "all through the game." Equally upset were a group of girls who hung out by the clubhouse entrance, including a "little redhead," who was so "hysterical" she had to be "walked up and down" by friends. Although there were no reports of their emotions, another group that had to have heavy hearts were the Dodger office personnel, many of whom were there for a "last look." As Gus Steiger noted in the *New York Mirror*, "They're the ones who deserve your sympathy." Perhaps feeling their irreverent approach would be out of place at a wake, the Sym-Phony band was absent.[15]

It would not, of course, be Ebbets Field without one last "rock" or moment of "daffiness," which in this case was supplied by a gatekeeper, who was "as dense as any Dodger of the daffiness days of Uncle Robbie." The employee, who most likely was not invited to go to Los Angeles, denied admission to Mrs. Jim Mulvey, the daughter of former owner Steve McKeever and the wife of a current co-owner. Hopefully, Mrs. Mulvey was not delayed too long, or she might have missed the first Dodger run when Elmer Valo drove in Junior Gilliam. The Dodgers scored again in the third when Gil Hodges drove in Gino Cimoli with the last run ever scored at Ebbets Field. Hodges also recorded the last putout, on a throw from Don Zimmer, who also had the honor of making the last Dodger hit in Brooklyn. As with the first game 44 years earlier, the Dodgers had a lefthander on the mound, Danny McDevitt, who shut the Pirates out on five hits in just two hours and three minutes. Dodger players were, for the most part, measured in their comments after the game, probably reflecting some combination of uncertainty and self-preservation. Perhaps not surprisingly, much more outspoken and critical was Carl Furillo, who bemoaned the impact on "thousands of knotholers." Rhetorically, but poignantly, he asked what will these kids "do next Summer when there's no baseball game to go to."[16]

Scoreboard at the end of the last game (National Baseball Hall of Fame Library, Cooperstown, New York).

Once the game ended, the police stopped some fans from attempting to run the bases, and the grounds crew went through their standard routine as if preparing for the next game. There were no reports of fans trying to take souvenirs, but a crowd did gather around the Dodger dugout to watch the batboy put away "the lumber" for the last time. Joe Pignatano remembered he was the last player to leave, with manager Walter Alston right behind him. Finally, "a lone woman came out of the stands. She walked out behind second base, picked up some grass and placed it tenderly in a cup."[17]

Notes

1. *Brooklyn Daily Eagle*, December 28, 1912, December 30, 1912, December 31, 1912, February 21, 1913.
2. *New York Times*, April 6, 1913.
3. *New York Times*, April 6, 1913; *The Sun*, April 6, 1913; *Morning Telegraph*, April 6, 1913.
4. *New York American*, April 6, 1913; *Brooklyn Daily Times*, April 3, 1913; *Standard Union*, April 6, 1913.
5. *Standard Union*, April 6, 1913; *Brooklyn Daily Eagle*, April 5, 6, 1913; *Evening Mail*, April 5, 1913; *Brooklyn Daily Times*, April 5, 1913; *New York Times*, April 6, 1913.
6. *Evening Mail*, April 5, 1913; *New York Times*, April 6, 1913; *New York Herald*, April 6, 1913; *Standard Union*, April 6, 1913; *The Sun*, April 6, 1913; *New York American*, April 6, 1913; *Morning Telegraph*, April 6, 1913; *Brooklyn Daily Eagle*, April 6, 1913.
7. *Evening Mail*, April 5, 1913; *Standard Union*, April 6, 1913; *Morning Telegraph*, April 6, 1913; *New York Tribune*, April 6, 1913; *New York Times*, April 6, 1913; *New York Herald*, April 6, 1913; *New York American*, April 6, 1913.
8. *Standard Union*, April 6, 1913; *Brooklyn Daily Eagle*, April 6, 1913.
9. *Brooklyn Daily Eagle*, April 6, 1913; *Standard Union*, April 6, 1913; *The World*, April 6, 1913; *The New York Times*, April 6, 1913; *Morning Telegraph*, April 5, 1913; *New York American*, April 1, 1913; *The Sun*, April 6, 1913; *Brooklyn Daily Times*, April 5, 1913.
10. *Standard Union*, April 10, 1913; *Philadelphia Inquirer*, April 10, 1913; *New York Herald*, April 10, 1913; *Brooklyn Daily Times*, April 10, 1913; *The Sun*, April 10, 1913; *New York Evening Journal*, April 9, 1913.
11. *Brooklyn Daily Times*, April 10, 1913; *The Sun*, April 10, 1913; *Standard Union*, April 10, 1913; *Philadelphia Inquirer*, April 10, 1913; *Evening Mail*, April 9, 1913.
12. www.retrosheet.org; *New York Journal American*, September 22, 1957.
13. *The New York Mirror, September 24, 1957;* Dave Anderson, telephone interview by John G. Zinn, March 11, 2010.
14. *New York Journal American*, September 25, 1957; *World Telegram and Sun*, September 25, 1957; *New York Times,* September 25, 1957; *New York Herald Tribune*, September 25, 1957; *New York Post*, September 25, 1957.
15. *New York Herald Tribune*, September 25, 1957; *New York Post*, September 25, 1957; *New York Mirror*, September 25, 1957; *World Telegram and Sun*, September 25, 1957.
16. *New York Post*, September 25, 1957; *Newark Evening News*, September 25, 1957; *New York Mirror*, September 25, 1957.
17. *New York Times*, September 25, 1957; *New York Post*, September 25, 1957; *World Telegram and Sun*, September 25, 1957; *New York Daily News*, September 25, 1957; *New York Mirror*, September 25, 1957; Joe Pignatano, telephone interview by Paul G. Zinn, June 30, 2010.

History, Tragedy and Comedy

The Dodgers at Ebbets Field

Paul G. Zinn *and* John G. Zinn

If, as William Shakespeare wrote, "All the world's a stage, and all the men and women merely players," Ebbets Field was just such a stage for baseball drama. Some of the following are better known than others, but like Shakespeare's plays, all have elements of comedy, history, and tragedy. What follows are some of the most memorable moments from 45 seasons of Brooklyn Dodger baseball at Ebbets Field.

April 26, 1913—After losing four straight games at their new home, the Dodgers broke the jinx with their first Ebbets Field win. The victory was even sweeter because it was over the archrival New York Giants, who were making their first appearance at Brooklyn's new park. Casey Stengel broke a 3–3 seventh inning tie with a two-run, inside-the-park home run to the flagpole in deep center field. Before today's game, Brooklyn had scored only once in four straight defeats to the Phillies, losing 1–0 three times and 2–1 once.

New York	***AB***	***R***	***H***	***BB***	***SO***	***PO***	***A***	***E***
Snodgrass, cf	3	0	1	1	1	4	0	0
Shafer, ss	4	0	1	0	0	2	0	0
Burns, rf	4	0	0	0	0	1	0	0
Doyle, 2b	4	1	1	0	0	3	0	1
Murray, lf	4	0	1	0	0	1	0	0
Merkle, 1b	4	0	2	0	0	10	0	0
Herzog, 3b	4	1	1	0	0	0	2	0
Meyers, c	2	0	1	1	0	3	3	0
Wilson, c	0	0	0	0	0	0	1	0
Wiltse, p	2	0	0	0	0	0	5	0
Crandall, p	0	0	0	0	0	0	0	0
*McCormick	1	0	1	0	0	0	0	0
**Devore		1	0	0	0	0	0	0
Total	32	3	9	2	1	24	11	1

Brooklyn	***AB***	***R***	***H***	***BB***	***SO***	***PO***	***A***	***E***
Stengel, cf	4	1	2	0	0	5	1	0
Cutshaw, 2b	4	1	1	0	0	4	3	1
Hummel, rf	4	0	2	0	0	1	0	0
Wheat, lf	3	0	0	1	1	2	0	0
Daubert, 1b	4	0	1	0	0	9	2	0
Smith, 3b	3	1	1	0	0	2	3	0
Fisher, ss	3	1	1	0	0	1	1	1
Miller, c	3	0	0	0	0	3	1	0
Ragan, p	3	1	1	0	1	0	5	0
Rucker, p	0	0	0	0	0	0	0	0
	31	5	9	1	2	27	16	2

	1	***2***	***3***	***4***	***5***	***6***	***7***	***8***	***9***	
Brooklyn	0	0	0	1	2	0	2	0	x	5
New York	0	0	0	0	0	0	3	0	0	3

*Batted for Wiltse in the seventh inning. **Ran for Meyers in the seventh. Three base hits—Hummel, Fisher, McCormick. Home run—Stengel, Stolen Bases—Stengel, Merkle, Herzog. First base on error—New York, 1. Left on bases, Brooklyn, 3; New York, 4. Double plays—Ragan, Fisher and Daubert; Fisher and Daubert. Struck out—By Ragan, 1; Wiltse, 2. Bases on balls—Off Ragan, 2; Crandall, 1. Hits—Off Ragan, 9 in seven innings, (at bat 26:) off Rucker, 0 in 2 innings, (at bat 6:) off Wiltse, 7 in six innings, (at bat, 24:) off Crandall, 2 in two innings, (at bat, 7:) Umpires—Messers Klem and Byron. Time of Game—One hour and twenty-two minutes. Editors' Note: Brooklyn was the home team but was listed first in the box score.

August 28, 1913—Having already made the first Brooklyn hit at Ebbets Field, second baseman George Cutshaw put on a fielding clinic, handling 13 chances and taking part in five double plays while playing errorless ball in a 5–1 win over Boston.

August 15, 1914—Although he was suffering from an ankle injury, Jake Daubert still played both games of a doubleheader against Philadelphia. Unable to run, the resourceful Brooklyn first baseman laid down six sacrifice bunts as the Dodgers swept the twin bill.

Casey Stengel's home run on April 26, 1913, against the archrival New York Giants, drove in the winning runs in the Dodgers' first victory at Ebbets Field (Library of Congress, Prints & Photographs Division, Bain Collection [LC-DIG-ppmsca-18466]).

September 9, 1915—In a game marked by minimal offense, the Dodgers defeated the Boston Braves, 1–0, on a scratch hit of the comic variety. Attempting to make a force play at second, Boston's first baseman Butch Schmidt hit the runner in the back with the throw. Since the scorer felt the ball could not have been fielded, he gave Brooklyn's Gus Getz a single. The Braves were not much better, registering only two cheap hits of their own in a game that briefly revived Brooklyn's pennant chances.

May 6, 1916—In a moment of drama with comic overtones, Brooklyn second baseman George Cutshaw broke up a 2–2 eleventh inning tie with "the freakest home run ever hit at Ebbets Field, or any other field east of the Elysian Fields." Cutshaw hit a line drive down the right field line that struck a hard spot inside the foul line and bounced over the wall for what, under the rules of the day, was a walk-off home run. Supposedly Cutshaw's arrival at home plate was greeted by "a storm of laughter" that included that of umpire Lord Byron.[1]

September 30, 1916—On this cold September day, the Dodgers had a half-game lead on the Phillies as the two teams played a doubleheader at Ebbets Field. After Philadelphia's easy win in the first game, the outlook was bleak for Brooklyn since 33 game-winner Grover Cleveland Alexander was pitching for the Phillies. However, Casey Stengel "fell upon" an Alexander pitch that "fell upon the pavement outside the right field wall," a home run which broke a 1–1 tie. Brooklyn went on to an easy 6–1 victory, reclaiming first place in the process.[2]

George Cutshaw's bizarre walk-off home run in early 1916 was an omen that it was going to be Brooklyn's year (Library of Congress, Prints & Photographs Division, Bain Collection [LC-DIG-ggbain-16219]).

October 3, 1916 — Just three days later, the Dodgers made history by clinching the first of their nine pennants while playing at Ebbets Field. In a back and forth affair, Brooklyn came from behind to defeat the archrival Giants, 9–6. Incredibly, the Dodger victory and the pennant was almost eclipsed by the postgame controversy surrounding John McGraw's storming off the field while complaining his team was not trying to win. Although there was much debate, nothing came of a situation that foreshadowed the 1919 scandal.

October 10, 1916 — After dropping the first two games of the World Series in Boston, Brooklyn won the first Fall Classic game ever played at Ebbets Field. The Dodgers took a 4–0 lead and then held on behind the pitching of Jack Coombs and Jeff Pfeffer. Unfortunately, it was to be Brooklyn's only victory of the Series.

Brooklyn

	AB	*R*	*H*	*PO*	*A*	*E*	*2b*	*3b*	*HR*	*TB*	*SB*	*SH*	*BB*	*SO*
Myers, cf	3	0	0	3	0	0	0	0	0	0	0	1	0	1
Daubert, 1b	4	1	3	8	0	0	0	1	0	5	0	0	0	0
Stengel, rf	3	0	1	2	1	0	0	0	0	1	0	1	0	0
Wheat, lf	2	1	1	4	0	0	0	0	0	1	1	0	2	0
Cutshaw, 2b	4	0	1	4	0	0	0	0	0	1	0	0	0	0
Mowrey, 3b	3	1	0	2	0	0	0	0	0	0	0	0	1	1
Olson, ss	4	1	2	1	2	0	0	1	0	4	0	0	0	0
Miller, c	3	0	0	3	2	0	0	0	0	0	0	1	0	1
Coombs, p	3	0	1	0	2	0	0	0	0	1	0	0	0	0
Pfeffer, p	1	0	1	0	1	0	0	0	0	1	0	0	0	0
Total	30	4	10	27	8	0	0	2	0	14	1	3	3	3

Boston

	AB	R	H	PO	A	E	2b	3b	HR	TB	SB	SH	BB	SO
Hooper, rf	4	1	2	1	0	0	0	1	0	4	0	0	0	0
Janvrin, 2b	4	0	0	1	0	0	0	0	0	0	0	0	0	1
Shorten, cf	4	0	3	0	0	0	0	0	0	3	0	0	0	0
Hoblitzel, 1b	4	0	1	12	2	0	0	0	0	1	0	0	0	0
Lewis, lf	4	0	0	1	1	0	0	0	0	0	0	0	0	0
Gardner, 3b	3	1	1	2	0	1	0	0	1	4	0	0	0	0
Scott, ss	3	0	0	1	7	0	0	0	0	0	0	0	0	0
Thomas, c	3	0	0	5	0	0	0	0	0	0	0	0	0	1
Mays, p	1	0	0	0	4	0	0	0	0	0	0	0	0	1
a Henrickson	0	1	0	0	0	0	0	0	0	0	0	0	1	0
Foster, pl	1	0	0	1	2	0	0	0	0	0	0	0	0	1
Total	31	3	7	24	16	1	0	1	1	12	0	0	1	4

a Batted for Mays in sixth.

Score By Innings

Brooklyn	0	0	1	1	2	0	0	0	x–4
Boston	0	0	0	0	0	2	1	0	0–3

Hits and earned runs — Off Mays 7 hits and 3 runs in 5 innings; off Foster, 3 hits and 0 runs in 3 innings; off Coombs 7 hits and 3 runs in 6⅓ innings; off Pfeffer, no hits and no runs in 2⅓ innings. First base on error — Brooklyn 1. Left on bases — Brooklyn 9; Boston 2. Struck out — By Coombs, 1; by Pfeffer, 3; by Mays, 2 by Foster, 1. Bases on balls — Off Coombs 1; off Mays 3. Hit by pitcher — by Mays, (Myers). Wild pitch — Foster. Umpires — Mr. O'Day, plate: Mr. Connolly, bases; Mr. Quigley, left field; Mr. Dineen, right field. Time of game — Two hours and one minute. Editors' Note: Brooklyn was the home team but was listed first in the box score.

August 22, 1917 — In what was scheduled to be the first game of a doubleheader, the Dodgers and Pirates made National League history, playing in what was then the longest contest in the 41-year history of the senior circuit. After Pittsburgh tied the score in the seventh, the two teams played 14 scoreless innings before Brooklyn put across the winning run in the 22nd frame. Ironically, Rube Marquard was the winning pitcher, just as he had been in the previous longest game, a 21-inning Giant–Pirate matchup in 1914.

Brooklyn	*AB*	*R*	*H*	*PO*	*A*	***Pittsburgh***	*AB*	*R*	*H*	*PO*	*A*
Olson, ss	9	1	3	4	11	Jackson, rf	3	0	0	0	0
Daubert, 1b	9	0	1	27	4	King, rf	7	1	1	7	0
Myers, of, 2b	10	1	5	6	0	Bigbee, lf	11	0	6	6	0
Stengel, rf	8	1	4	4	1	Carey, cf	8	0	1	7	1
Johnston, 2b	4	0	1	1	7	Boeckel, 3b	5	0	2	2	2
S. Smith, cf	0	0	0	0	0	Debus, 3b	3	0	0	0	2
M. Wheat, cf	8	0	0	0	0	Ward, ss	9	1	2	4	8
Hickman, lf	9	2	5	7	0	R. Miller, 1b	8	0	1	17	1
O'Rourke, 3b	9	0	3	1	4	Pitler, 2b	9	2	3	15	4
O. Miller, c	9	0	4	13	1	W. Wagner, c	7	1	2	7	5
Cadore, p	4	1	1	2	3	Schmidt, c	2	0	0	0	1
Cheney, p	4	0	1	1	6	Cooper, p	3	0	1	0	2
Marquard, p	0	0	0	0	1	Jacobs, p	6	0	0	0	6
b Wheat	0	0	0	0	0	a. J. Wagner	1	0	0	0	0
c. Krueger	0	0	0	0	0						
Total	83	6	28	66	38		82	5	19	65	32

a Batted for Boeckel in the thirteenth. b Ran for Johnston in the twelfth. c Batted for Smith in the thirteenth. *Two out when the winning run was scored. Errors — Olson, Myers, Johnston, O. Miller, Cadore, Debus, Ward, (2), W. Wagner.

Brooklyn	1	2	2	0	0	0	0	0	0	0	0	0	0	0	0	0	0	0	0	0	0	1–6
Pittsburgh	0	0	1	0	0	2	2	0	0	0	0	0	0	0	0	0	0	0	0	0	0	0–5

Two-base hits — Cooper, Pitler, R. Miller, Olson, Myers, Hickman. Stolen base — Stengel. Sacrifice hits — Daubert, O'Rourke, Johnston, (2) O. Miller, Olson, Cheney, Carey, R. Miller. Double plays — Jacobs, Wagner, and R. Miller; Ward and R. Miller. Left on bases — Pittsburgh, 22; Brooklyn 18. First base on errors — Pittsburgh, 3 Brooklyn, 2. Bases on balls — Off Cooper, 1; Jacobs, 3; Cadore, 4; Cheney, 1; Marquard, 1. Hits and earned runs — Off Cooper, 11 hits and 5 runs in 5 innings; Jacobs, 17 and 1 in 17; Cadore, 9 and 5 in 7; Cheney, 9 and 0 in 13; Marquard, 1 and 0 in 2. Hit by pitcher — By Cadore. (W. Wagner, Carey, Boeckel.) Struck out by — By Jacobs, 1; Cadore, 1; Cheney, 7; Marquard, 2. Passed ball — W. Wagner. Time — 4 hours 15 minutes. Umpires — Klem and Emslie. Editors' Note: Brooklyn was the home team, but was listed first in the box score.

June 3, 1918 — In one of the first, but certainly not the last, bizarre moments at Ebbets Field, the protest of a game by the Dodgers was upheld by National League President John Tener. During the sixth inning of a game against St. Louis, Cardinals base runner Doug Baird went from second to third on a line drive to center field. After touching third base and fearing that Brooklyn left fielder Jim Hickman might catch the ball, Baird retreated toward second base, touching third again in the process. However between second and third, Baird realized Hickman had not made the catch. Apparently thinking there was no need to touch third again, Baird took a direct path to home plate. Incredibly, umpire Cy Rigler ruled Baird safe, and the Cardinals went on to win the game, 15–12, in 12 innings, but which should have been a 12–11 loss in nine. The game was made up as part of a July 27 doubleheader. To further add to the absurdity, St. Louis won the replay by a football-like score of 22–7.

May 4, 1919 — Charles Ebbets realized a longtime dream as the Dodgers played the first legal major league Sunday game in Brooklyn. Ebbets estimated the capacity crowd at 25,000, reportedly the largest by far for a regular season game at Ebbets Field. The Dodgers celebrated what would prove to be a major new source of revenue with a 6–2 win over Boston.

May 15, 1919 — A scoreless pitcher's duel between Hod Eller of Cincinnati and Al Mamaux of Brooklyn came to an absurd and comic end when the Reds scored 10 times in the top of the 13th. Even though he had kept Cincinnati off the scoreboard until then, Mamaux had struggled with his control all afternoon. Fifteen Reds came to bat in the disastrous 13th as the Dodger right-hander surrendered seven straight hits.

May 25, 1919 — In a comic moment that became part of the legend of Casey Stengel, the former Dodger outfielder, now a Pittsburgh Pirate, doffed his cap in response to an ovation from the Ebbets Field crowd only to release a sparrow. The event prompted great laughter from the fans and also umpire Cy Rigler. Supposedly, Stengel had obtained the bird from Leon Cadore when he stopped off at the Dodger bullpen en route to the Pirate dugout from right field.

September 10, 1920—Clinging to first place in a tight pennant race, the Dodgers staged two dramatic late inning rallies to defeat the Cardinals. Trailing 5–3 in the bottom of the ninth, Brooklyn scored twice to force extra innings. However, St. Louis scored three times in the top of the 11th to once again put the Dodgers' backs against the wall. Brooklyn responded, though, with two more in the bottom of the inning but still trailed by one run with two out and nobody on base. The Robins were not finished, however, as three hits and a Cardinal miscue plated the tying and winning runs in "the greatest fight that Brooklyn fans have gazed upon this year."[3]

Brooklyn (N)	*AB*	*R*	*H*	*PO*	*A*	*St. Louis (N)*	*AB*	*R*	*H*	*PO*	*A*
Olson, ss	6	0	3	1	5	Schultz, rf	6	1	3	4	0
Johnston, 3b	5	1	1	2	2	Fournier	6	1	1	11	0
Nets, rf	5	1	3	5	0	Stock, 3b	5	0	1	0	2
Wheat, lf	5	2	1	3	0	Hornsby, 2b	5	1	2	4	5
Myers, cf	5	2	3	1	0	McHenry, lf	5	0	0	2	0
Konetchy, 1b	5	0	0	8	3	Lavan, ss	5	1	2	2	2
Kilduff, 2b	4	1	1	3	3	Heathcote, cf	4	2	2	4	0
Miller, c	5	1	1	10	1	Clement, c	5	0	1	5	0
Marquard, p	2	0	0	0	1	Dilhoefer, c	0	1	0	0	0
Smith, p	0	0	0	0	1	Schupp, p	3	1	0	0	3
Pfeffer, p	1	0	1	0	0	Sherdel, p	0	0	0	0	0
a. Krueger	1	0	0	0	0	Knode	0	0	0	0	0
b. Schmandt	1	0	1	0	0						
c Lamar	0	0	0	0	0						
d McCabe	0	1	0	0	0						
Total	45	9	15	33	16	0	44	8	12	32	12

*Two out when winning run scored. a Batted for Marquard in seventh. b Batted for Smith in ninth. c Ran for Schmandt in ninth. d Ran for Pfeffer in eleventh. e Batted for Schupp in eleventh. Errors—Olson, Kilduff, Schultz, Fournier.

Brooklyn	3	0	0	0	0	0	0	0	2	0	4–9
St. Louis	0	1	0	0	0	0	4	0	0	0	3–8

Two-base hits—Johnston, Miller. Three-base hits—Schultz, Myers. Home run-Fournier, Hornsby. Sacrifices—Johnston, Wheat. Left on bases—St. Louis 6, Brooklyn 9. Bases on balls—Off Marquard 2, Pfeffer, 1, Schupp 3. Hits—off Marquard 6 in 7 innings, Pfeffer 5 in 2, Smith 1 in 2, Schupp 10 in 10, Sherdel 5 in 1. Struck out—By Marquard 6, Smith 1, Pfeffer 2, Schupp 4. Wild pitch—Schupp. Winning pitcher—Pfeffer. Losing pitcher—Sherdel. Umpires—Klem and Emslie. Time of game—2:22. Editors' Note: Brooklyn was the home team but was listed first in the box score.

September 26, 1920—In the closing days of the pennant race, Rube Marquard held off his former teammates, and Brooklyn broke a 1–1 tie in the eighth inning to defeat the archrival and second place Giants. A "frenzied" overflow crowd of 25,000 saw Brooklyn move within one game of clinching the National League pennant.

October 6, 1920—Behind the shutout pitching of Burleigh Grimes, Brooklyn defeated Cleveland, 3–0, to tie the 1920 World Series at a game apiece. Another brilliant pitching performance the next day by Sherrod Smith gave the Dodgers a 2–1 series lead. Unfortunately, when the scene shifted to Cleveland, the Indians won four straight to take the World Series, five games to two.

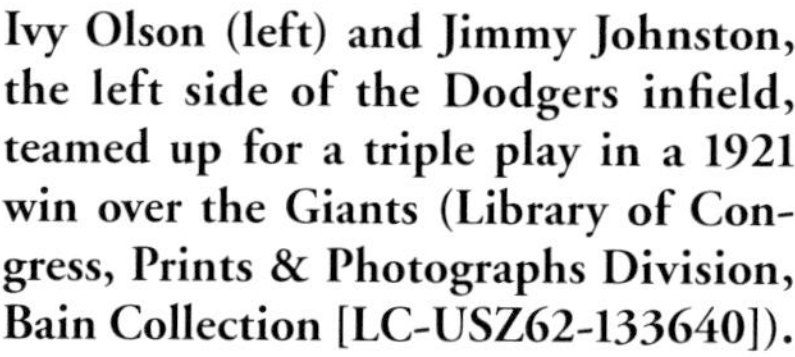

Ivy Olson (left) and Jimmy Johnston, the left side of the Dodgers infield, teamed up for a triple play in a 1921 win over the Giants (Library of Congress, Prints & Photographs Division, Bain Collection [LC-USZ62-133640]).

September 1, 1921—Brooklyn third baseman Jimmy Johnston and shortstop Ivy Olson teamed up on a triple play in a 5–1 win over the Giants. The contest marked Brooklyn's 11th win in 17 games against the soon to be World Series champion Giants.

August 1, 1924 — On his way to pitching a three-hit shutout against the Chicago Cubs, future Hall of Famer Dazzy Vance made history by striking out 14 batters, including a record-tying seven straight. Vance began his streak by fanning another future Hall of Famer, Gabby Hartnett, to end the first, and then struck out the side in the second and

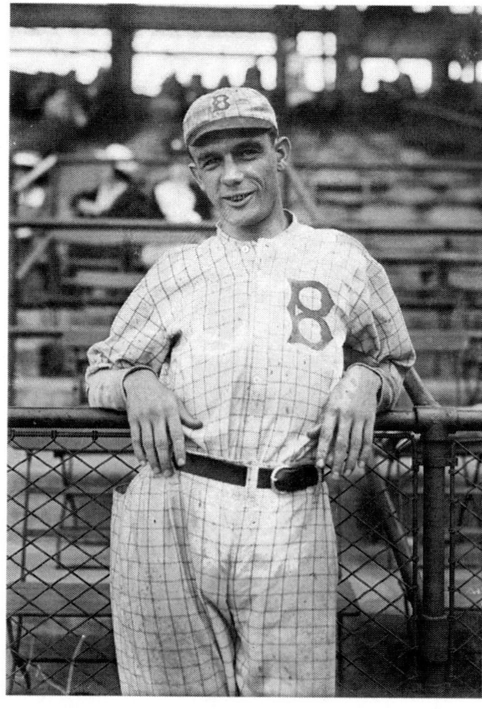

On September 26, 1920, future Hall of Famer Rube Marquard defeated his old team, the New York Giants, to move the Dodgers within one game of their second World Series (Library of Congress, Prints & Photographs Division, Bain Collection [LC-DIG-ggbain-22462]).

third innings. The Dodger hurler tied the record set by Hooks Wiltse of the Giants in 1906. The current record of 10 straight strikeouts is held by another Hall of Famer, Tom Seaver. Vance's performance was part of a dominant season, as he went 28–6 with a league leading 262 strikeouts.[4]

Brooklyn	***AB***	***R***	***H***	***PO***	***A***	***E***	***Chicago***	***AB***	***R***	***H***	***PO***	***A***	***E***
High, 2B	3	1	1	2	1	0	Statz, cf	4	0	0	2	1	0
Mitchell, ss	3	0	0	1	0	0	Hollocher, ss	3	0	2	4	3	0
Wheat, lf	2	0	0	2	0	0	Adams, 2b	3	0	0	4	3	0
Fournier, 1b	3	0	1	3	0	0	Hartnett, c	4	0	0	2	1	2
Brown, cf	3	0	2	2	0	0	Friberg, 3b	3	0	0	0	2	0
Stock, 3b	3	1	1	0	0	0	Grigsby, lf	3	0	0	4	1	0
Griffith, rf	3	1	1	2	0	0	Heathcote, rf	3	0	0	2	0	0
Berry, c	2	1	1	15	0	0	Barret, 1b	3	0	1	6	0	1
Vance, p	2	0	0	0	2	0	Aldridge, p	2	0	0	0	1	0
							*Grantham	1	0	0	0	0	0
							Milstead p	0	0	0	0	0	0
Totals	24	4	7	27	3	0		29	0	3	24	12	3

*Batted for Aldridge in the eighth inning

Chicago	0	0	0	0	0	0	0	0	0–0
Brooklyn	0	0	0	0	0	0	2	2	x–4

Two-base hits — Brown, Griffith, Three-base hits — Hollocher. Sacrifices — Adams, Brown, High, Vance. Sacrifice Flies — Mitchell, DeBerry. Left on bases — Chicago, 4; Brooklyn, 3. First base on balls — Off Vance, 1; off Aldridge, 6; of Milstead, 1. Struck out — By Vance, 14; by Aldridge, 1. Hits — Off Aldridge, 6 in 7 innings, off Millstead, 1 in 1 inning. Passed ball — Hartnett. Losing pitcher — Aldridge. Umpires — Klem and Wilson. Time 1:35

September 7, 1924 — As the pennant race heated up, the Dodgers and Giants played a back-and-forth affair at Ebbets Field. Trailing 8–4 in the bottom of the ninth, Brooklyn rallied for three runs, only to see pinch hitter Dutch Ruether strike out to end the game with the tying and winning runs on base. The scene at Ebbets Field was as much the story as the game itself since some 32,000 were inside the ballpark, while an estimated 15,000 were turned away. Some fans climbed the outfield walls to watch from a precarious perch, while others broke down the left field gate. To further add to the mayhem, fans ringed the field, frequently interfering with play.

September 16, 1924 — Brooklyn's pennant hopes took a major hit when they were routed, 17–3, by the Cardinals. St. Louis first baseman Jim Bottomley was a one-man wrecking crew as his six hits drove in 12 Cardinal runs, setting a major league record for RBIs in the process. To make it even more painful, the previous record was held by Brooklyn manager Wilbert Robinson.

September 13, 1925 — Having just missed pitching the first no-hitter in Ebbets Field history several days earlier, Dazzy Vance took no chances with his second opportunity. On September 8 in the first game of a doubleheader against Philadelphia, Vance had allowed only one hit while facing the minimum 27 batters. Although this time he gave up a walk and an unearned run, Vance held the Phillies hitless in an easy 10–1 victory, once again in the first game of a twin bill. All told, Vance allowed only one hit over 18 innings and pitched 16 consecutive hitless frames.

Brooklyn (N)	*AB*	*R*	*H*	*PO*	*A*
J. Mitchell, ss	5	2	3	1	2
Stock, 2b	4	3	2	1	2
Johnston, lf	4	2	3	3	0
Cox, rf	5	1	4	2	0
Brown, cf	4	0	0	3	0
H'gre'v's, 1b	4	1	1	6	2
Tierney, 3b	3	0	1	0	0
DeBerry, c	3	1	1	9	0
Vance, p	4	0	0	2	1
Total	36	10	15	27	7

Philadelphia (N)	*AB*	*R*	*H*	*PO*	*A*
Sand, ss	1	0	0	2	1
a. Wri'tst'ne	1	0	0	0	0
Metz, ss	0	0	0	1	1
b. Kimmick	1	0	0	0	0
Leach, cf	4	0	0	3	0
Williams, rf	3	0	0	2	0
Harper, lf	3	0	0	3	0
Hawks, 1b	3	1	0	3	0
Huber, 3b	3	0	0	1	2
Friberg, 2b	2	0	0	4	0
Wilson, c	2	0	0	0	0
Wendell, c	1	0	0	5	2
C. Mitch'll, p	0	0	0	0	0
Decatur, p	1	0	0	0	0
Betts, p	1	0	0	0	1
c. Fonseca	1	0	0	0	0
	27	1	0	24	7

Errors — Philadelphia 2 (Sand, Friberg), Brooklyn 3 (Johnston 2, Hargreaves 1). a Batted for Sand in sixth. b Batted for Metz in ninth. c Batted for Betts in ninth.

Brooklyn	4	0	0	4	0	1	1	0	0–10
Philadelphia	0	1	0	0	0	0	0	0	0–1

Two-base hits — J. Mitchell, Cox. Three-base hit — Johnston. Stolen bases — J. Mitchell, Stock, Johnston, Cox, Hargreaves. Sacrifices — Friberg, DeBerry. Double plays — Huber and Sand; Wendell and Friberg. Left on bases — Philadelphia 1, Brooklyn 6. Bases on balls — Off Decatur, 2 Betts, 1, Vance, 1. Struck out — By Betts, 4, Vance, 9. Passed balls — DeBerry, Wilson. Hits — Off C. Mitchell 3 (none out in first inning), Decatur, 7 in 4, Betts 5 in 4. Losing pitcher. C. Mitchell. Umpires — Pfirman, Wilson and O'Day. Time of Game — 1:45. Editors' Note: Brooklyn was the home team but was listed first in the box score.

June 14, 1926 — Future Hall of Famer Rabbit Maranville turned a Ray Blades line drive into a triple play, tossing the ball to second baseman Chick Fewster, who caught one Cardinal runner coming to the bag and the other returning to it. The heroics helped Brooklyn to an 8–5 victory.

August 15, 1926 — Babe Herman was at the heart of the most famous comic event in Brooklyn Dodger lore when the club put three men on third base at the same time.

Future Hall of Famer Dazzy Vance pitched the first no-hitter in Ebbets Field history on September 13, 1925, against Philadelphia (National Baseball Hall of Fame Library, Cooperstown, New York).

With the bases loaded in the seventh inning of a tie game against the Boston Braves, Herman hit a line drive off the right field wall. As reported by the *New York Times*, "Vance (on second base) was satisfied to advance one base on the blow, Fewster (on first base) thought he ought to take two and Herman insisted on making three." The ruling on the play was that Fewster and Herman were out, ending the inning. Lost in all the excitement was that Herman's hit drove in what proved to be the winning run, and Brooklyn won the game, 4–1.[5]

September 15, 1930—Once again Babe Herman was involved in a moment of base-running comedy. In the first inning of a contest against Cincinnati, Herman was on first when Glenn Wright hit a high fly ball to center field. While Herman was waiting to see if the ball would be caught, Wright passed him on his way to third. Eventually both runners ended up on third on what should have been a two-run home run. Instead, Wright was out for passing a base runner, and his home run, statistically speaking, became a single. As with the incident involving three men on one base, the blunder overshadowed a 13–5 Brooklyn victory, their 11th straight, giving them a one-game lead over second place St. Louis. The Dodgers would ultimately finish fourth, six games off the pace.

September 16, 1930—The very next day some 30,000 fans packed Ebbets Field for a classic contest during the heat of the pennant race. Having won 11 straight and leading the Cardinals by one game, Brooklyn sent ace Dazzy Vance to the mound against the Cardinal's hurler Bill Hallahan. The St. Louis lefthander was brilliant, pitching a no-hitter into the eighth. Both teams had chances to score in regulation, with Brooklyn missing out on a first-and-second-and-one-out opportunity in the ninth when St. Louis turned an attempted sacrifice into a double play. St. Louis lost its chance in a bizarre turn of events in the sixth when Sparky Adams' steal of home was negated because Vance's pitch hit the batter, producing a dead ball. After the Cardinals finally got a run in the top of the tenth, Brooklyn loaded the bases with one out in the bottom of the inning. Al Lopez then hit a hard grounder that initially got away from Adams, the Cardinal shortstop, bringing the crowd to its feet. Unfortunately for Brooklyn, Adams quickly recovered and started a game-ending double play. The 1–0 defeat knocked Brooklyn out of first place and started a seven-game losing streak as the Dodgers fell out of the race, finally finishing fourth.

Babe Herman's exploits as part of Dodger daffiness tend to obscure his .324 lifetime batting average (National Baseball Hall of Fame Library, Cooperstown, New York).

September 27, 1931—In a fitting ending to his 19-year managerial career in Brooklyn, Wilbert Robinson's last game as Brooklyn skipper was against John McGraw and the Giants. While the Giant skipper won more pennants over the period, the two managers almost broke even in head-to-head competition with McGraw holding a 197–190 edge. As 25,000 looked on, Brooklyn triumphed 12–3, helping the long-time Dodger manager to go out in style.[6]

September 12, 1932 — Brooklyn's Johnny Frederick made history with a record-setting sixth pinch-hit home run in one season. Trailing the Cubs 3–2 in the bottom of the ninth, Frederick followed Glenn Wright's double with a walk-off two-run home run. Ironically the blow came off former Dodger hurler and future Brooklyn manager, Burleigh Grimes. The record stood until 2000, and is now held by Dave Hansen and Craig Wilson with seven apiece.[7]

May 14, 1933 — In another dramatic pinch-hitting moment at Ebbets Field, Hack Wilson hit a ninth-inning grand slam home run to send Brooklyn to an 8–6 victory over Philadelphia. Wilson's achievement was even more impressive since it came in a pouring rain that threatened to wash out the game.

September 21, 1934 — A day after his older brother referred to him as "no-hit Dean," Paul Dean made the prediction come true no-hitting Brooklyn, 3–0, in the second game of a doubleheader at Ebbets Field. Dean allowed only one walk as the doubleheader sweep brought St. Louis to within three games of first-place New York. In that same prophecy, Dizzy Dean referred to himself as "one-hit Dean." He was not too far off on that one either, giving up just three hits in a 13–0 Cardinal victory in the first game of the twin bill.[8]

August 27, 1937 — Although he kept the Reds hitless, Fred Frankhouse's bid for a place in baseball history was thwarted by the weather. Frankhouse had a no-hitter for 7⅔'s innings when the rain turned Ebbets Field into a lake. Frankhouse was, however, far from perfect, giving up six walks, so that the Reds left six men on base in a game where they got no hits.

June 15, 1938 — The 38,748 in attendance witnessed multiple historic moments at the first night game ever played at Ebbets Field. As part of marking the occasion, four-time Olympic gold medal winner Jesse Owens ran a 100-yard dash with members of both teams before the game. The contest itself was even more historic as

It was a doubleheader dominated by Deans as the St. Louis Cardinal pitchers won both ends of a September 21, 1934, twin bill, with Dizzy (on the left) pitching a three-hit shutout and Daffy (on the right) pitching a no-hitter (National Baseball Hall of Fame Library, Cooperstown, New York).

the Reds' Johnny Vander Meer pitched his second consecutive no-hitter, despite wildness that included eight walks, and loading up the bases in the ninth inning.

Cincinnati (N)	*AB*	*R*	*H*	*PO*	*A*	*E*	*Brooklyn (N)*	*AB*	*R*	*H*	*PO*	*A*	*E*
Frey, 2b	5	0	1	2	2	0	Cuyler, rf	2	0	0	1	0	0
Berger, lf	5	1	3	1	0	0	Coscarart, 2b	2	0	0	1	2	0
Goodman, rf	3	2	1	3	0	0	a Brack	1	0	0	0	0	0
McCor'mick, 1b	5	1	1	9	1	0	Hudson, 2b	1	0	0	1	0	0
Lombardi, c	3	1	0	9	0	0	Hassett, lf	4	0	0	3	0	0
Craft, cf	5	0	3	1	0	0	Phelps, c	3	0	0	9	0	0
Riggs, 3b	4	0	1	0	3	0	b Rosen	0	0	0	0	0	0
Myers, ss	4	0	0	0	1	0	Lavagetto, 3b	2	0	0	0	2	2
V. Meer, p	4	1	1	2	4	0	Camilli, 1b	1	0	0	7	0	0
							Koy, cf	4	0	0	4	0	0
							Durocher, ss	4	0	0	1	2	0
							Butcher, p	0	0	0	0	1	0
							Pressnell, p	2	0	0	0	0	0
							Hamlin, p	0	0	0	0	1	0
							c English	1	0	0	0	0	0
							Tamulis, p	0	0	0	0	0	0
Total	38	6	11	27	11	0		27	0	0	27	8	2

a Batted for Coscarart in sixth. b Ran for Phelps in ninth. c Batted for Hamlin in eighth.

Cincinnati	0	0	4	0	0	0	1	1	0–6
Brooklyn	0	0	0	0	0	0	0	0	0–0

Runs batted in — McCormick 3, Riggs, Craft, Berger. Two-base hit — Berger. Three-base hit — Berger. Home run — McCormick. Stolen base — Goodman. Left on bases — Cincinnati 9, Brooklyn 8. Bases on balls — Off Butcher 3, Vander Meer 8, Hamlin 1. Struck out — By Butcher 1, Pressnell 3, Vander Meer 7, Hamlin 3. Hits — Off Butcher 5 in 2⅔, Hamlin 2 in 1⅓, Presnell 4 in 3⅔, Tamulis 0 in 1. Losing pitcher — Butcher. Umpires — Stewart, Stark and Barr. Time of game — 2:22.

June 1, 1939 — After the first two Cubs reached in the twelfth inning of a 2–2 game, the Dodgers turned a triple play to end the threat. Then, with the bases loaded and Leo Durocher at bat in the 14th, rookie catcher Bob Garback dropped Charlie Root's pitch, and by the time he got it, Gene Moore had scored the winning run.

August 26, 1939 — For the first time in its history, the action at Ebbets Field was seen beyond the ballpark itself. Television and baseball history was made as NBC showed the first live television baseball broadcast, the Reds and Dodgers splitting a doubleheader.

August 24, 1941— In front of a huge gathering of 31,253 with a "World Series air in Flatbush," the Dodgers and Cardinals split a doubleheader, and Brooklyn remained 1½ games ahead of the Cardinals. St. Louis won easily in the opener, but Whitlow Wyatt's single in the ninth drove home Pee Wee Reese with the winning run in the "nightcap" to salvage a split. The day also saw a moment that was both historic and comic, what seems to have been the first media recognition of "The Brooklyn Sym-Phony." The next day, the *New York Times* wrote, "The group of musicians (?) which is in evidence at Ebbets Field on important days was on hand. The boys, led by a top-hatted maestro, entertained (?) the customers."[9]

In the first game under the lights at Ebbets Field on June 15, 1938, Johnny Vander Meer pitched the second half of his back-to-back no-hitters (courtesy Los Angeles Dodgers).

October 5, 1941— In what was undoubtedly the most tragic moment in Ebbets Field long history, Dodger catcher Mickey Owen dropped Hugh Casey's third-strike pitch to Tommy Heinrich of the Yankees. A win would have evened the World Series at two games each. With an extra life, the Yankees rallied to win the contest and closed out the World Series the next day. Owen's efforts to retrieve the ball may have been hampered by police, who thinking the Dodgers had won, were trying to control the crowd. Owen manfully took responsibility for the error and received a rousing ovation from the Brooklyn fans in the fifth game.[10]

June 15, 1942 — Cubs' pitcher Claude Passeau was dominant in a five-hit, 6–0 shutout in a contest that marked the first twilight night game at Ebbets Field. The first three innings were played in natural light, the middle innings during dusk (the lights were on but had little effect), and only the final two innings under ordinary night-game conditions with the lights fully effective. The attendance was 16,549, including Giants' President Horace Stoneham, who liked the idea and planned to follow suit. The crowd was reportedly double the typical Monday day game attendance. In an odd twist, the *Brooklyn Eagle* reported no inning would have started after 9:05 P.M., and the game would have been stopped at 9:24 P.M. Fortunately, the 7:00 P.M. matchup took just two hours and seven minutes and beat the deadline.[11]

August 6, 1944 — In a day of wartime comic relief, some 15,605 fans saw Brooklyn lose both ends of a twin bill to the Boston Braves. In the top of the seventh of the second game, the crowd saw an unlikely triple play. Boston had the bases loaded with none out when Eddie Stanky took Butch Nieman's one-hop ground ball and threw to Mickey

Owen for a force out at home. Owen quickly tossed to first for the second out of what appeared to be the end of a fairly routine double play. However, Chuck Workman of the Braves was somehow stuck between first and second. A throw to shortstop Bobby Bragan nailed Workman for the last leg of the triple killing, due in large measure to "daffy" base running, for once not by the Dodgers. Earlier in the game, Workman hit a "priority" home run — so called because it went right through an opening in the right field screen. War-time restrictions, or "priorities," had prevented Brooklyn ownership from obtaining the materials to repair the damage.[12]

August 20, 1945 — In an 11–1 loss to the Pirates, 17-year-old Tommy Brown became the youngest player ever to hit a home run. The seventh-inning blow was described by the *New York Times* as "an incredible wallop" into the "upper leftfield section."[13]

April 23, 1946 — Dodger pitcher Ed Head made his return from World War II service a memorable one by tossing a no-hitter against the Boston Braves. In defeating Boston, 5–0, the hurler walked three, and one Brave reached base on an error. Originally a left-hander, Head learned to pitch with his right arm after fracturing the left one in a 1935 bus accident. But to pitch his masterpiece, he also had to overcome a service injury to his right arm. Unfortunately, Head went only 2–2 the remainder of the season — his last in the major leagues.[14]

August 14, 1946 — Some historic moments at Ebbets Field were accompanied by debate. A rainout on the night of the 13th led to what was claimed to be the first day-night doubleheader in baseball history. Previously morning and afternoon contests had been played on holidays, but this was the first time an evening start time was used. The *Eagle* claimed this was the first day-night doubleheader in history, but the *New York Times* disagreed, saying it had been done in St. Louis. Regardless, the first contest began at 2:30 P.M., the second at 8:30 P.M., and the fans responded, with at least 57,000 in total attendance. Those who came to the first game got to see Pete Reiser steal home at the front end of a triple steal. It was Reiser's sixth theft of home that season on the way to a National League record of seven. To add to the great day at the box office, Brooklyn beat the archrival Giants twice, putting the Dodgers 1½ games ahead of the second-place Cardinals.[15]

After a highly successful season with Montreal, it would take more than a sign to keep Jackie Robinson out of the Dodger locker room (National Baseball Hall of Fame Library, Cooperstown, New York).

September 11, 1946 — After 19 scoreless innings, an important game in the pennant race between the Dodgers and Reds was declared a tie. The game was the longest scoreless tie in major league history, and the teams came within one inning of tying the record for most scoreless innings, which was set in 1918 between the Pirates and the Braves. Hal Gregg started for the Dodgers and pitched the first 10 frames, while Johnny Vander Meer was dominant for the Reds, hurling the first 15 innings and striking out 14 while increasing his consecutive scoreless innings streak against the Dodgers to 26. Two Reds were thrown out at the plate during the game. Fortunately for Brooklyn, it won the replay of the matchup later that month, finally breaking through against Vander Meer after 28 consecutive scoreless innings.[16]

October 3, 1946 — Sadly the first National League playoff and the first playoff game at Ebbets Field ended with the Dodgers being eliminated by the Cardinals, 8–4. Down 8–1 in the ninth, Brooklyn rallied for three runs and had the bases loaded when Harry Brecheen of the Cardinals struck out the last two Dodger hitters.

April 15, 1947 — Both baseball and American history were made this day as Jackie Robinson broke the color barrier, becoming the first African American to play major league baseball in the 20th century. Despite the historic overtones and Robinson's scoring the winning run after reaching first on a rushed throw during a sacrifice bunt, Arthur Daley of the *New York Times* called the debut "quite uneventful," and the *Brooklyn Daily Eagle* took no special notice of the event. The crowd of 25,623 fell short of a sellout.[17]

Boston (N)	***AB***	***R***	***H***	***PO***	***A***	***E***	***Brooklyn (N)***	***AB***	***R***	***H***	***PO***	***A***	***E***
Culler, ss	3	0	0	0	2	0	Stanky, 2b	3	1	0	0	3	0
b Holmes	1	0	0	0	0	0	Robin'n, 1b	3	1	0	11	0	0
Sisti, ss	0	0	0	0	0	0	Schultz, 1b	0	0	0	1	0	0
Hopp, cf	5	0	1	2	0	0	Reiser, cf	2	3	2	2	0	0
McComick, rf	4	0	3	2	0	0	Walker, rf	3	0	1	0	0	0
R. Elliott, 3b	2	0	1	0	2	0	Tatum, rf	0	0	0	0	0	0
Litwhiler, lf	3	1	0	1	0	0	e Vaughan	1	0	0	0	0	0
Rowell, lf	1	0	0	0	0	0	Furillo, rf	0	0	0	0	0	0
Torge'n, 1b	4	1	0	10	1	1	Herm'ski, lf	4	0	1	3	0	0
Masi, c	3	0	0	4	0	0	Edwards, c	2	0	0	2	0	1
Ryan, 2b	4	1	3	4	7	0	d Rackley	0	0	0	0	0	0
Sain, p	1	0	0	0	1	0	Bragan, c	1	0	0	3	0	0
Cooper, p	0	0	0	1	0	0	Jorg'son, 3b	3	0	0	0	4	0
a Neill	0	0	0	0	0	0	Reese, ss	3	0	1	3	2	0
Lanfranconi, p	0	0	0	0	0	0	Hatten, p	2	0	1	1	1	0
							c Stevens	1	0	0	0	0	0
							Gregg, p	1	0	0	1	0	0
							Casey, p	0	0	0	0	0	0
Total	31	3	8	24	13	1		29	5	6	27	10	1

a Hit by pitcher batting for Cooper in eighth. b Flied out for Culler in eighth. c Struck out for Hatten in sixth. d Ran for Edwards in sixth. e Grounded out for Tatum in seventh.

Boston	0	0	0	0	1	2	0	0	0–3
Brooklyn	0	0	0	1	0	1	3	0	x–5

Runs batted in — Edwards, Hopp, Ryan 2, Jorgenson, Reiser, 2, Hermanski. Two-base hits — Reese, Reiser. Sacrifices — Sain 2, Culler, Masi, Robinson. Double plays — Stanky, Reese and Robinson; Culler, Ryan and Torgeson.

Left on bases — Boston 12, Brooklyn 7. Bases on balls — Off Hatten 3, Sain 5, Gregg 2. Strike outs — Hatten 2, Sain 1, Gregg 2, Lanfranconi 2, Casey 1. Hits-Off Sain 6 in 6 innings; Cooper 0 in 1; Lanfranconi 0 in 1; Hatten 6 in 6; Gregg 2 in 2⅓; Casey 0 in ⅔. Hit by pitcher — By Hatten (Litwhiler); Sain (Edwards) Gregg (Neill). Wild pitch — Hatten. Winning pitcher — Gregg. Losing pitcher — Sain. Umpires — Pinelli, Barlick and Gore. Attendance — 26,623. Time of game — 2:26.

October 3, 1947 — It could not have been any more dramatic as the Dodgers evened up the World Series with the Yankees at two games apiece in front of 33,443, some of whom stormed the field afterward. New York pitcher Bill Bevens had a 2–1 lead and a no-hitter with two out in the ninth when pinch-hitter Cookie Lavagetto hit a two-run double for a 3–2 victory. Bevens could have made history with the first ever World Series no-hitter, but his failure was in part due to a historic accomplishment of the negative variety. The Yankees right-hander established a World Series record by issuing 10 free passes, including walking the eventual tying and winning runs in the ninth, the latter intentionally.

NY Yankees	*AB*	*R*	*H*	*PO*	*A*	*E*	*Brooklyn Dodgers*	*AB*	*R*	*H*	*PO*	*A*	*E*
Stirnweiss, 2b	4	1	2	2	1	0	Stanky, 2b	1	0	0	2	3	0
Henrich, rf	5	0	1	2	0	0	e Lavagetto	1	0	1	0	0	0
Berra, c	4	0	0	6	1	1	Reese, ss	4	0	0	3	5	1
DiMaggio, cf	2	0	0	2	0	0	Robinson, 1b	4	0	0	11	1	0
McQuinn	4	0	1	7	0	0	Walker, rf	2	0	0	0	1	0
Johnson, 3b	4	1	1	3	2	0	Hermanski, lf	4	0	0	2	0	0
Lindell, lf	3	0	2	3	0	0	Edwards, c	4	0	0	7	1	1
Rizzuto, ss	4	0	1	1	2	0	Furillo, cf	3	0	0	2	0	0
Bevens, p	3	0	0	0	1	0	b Gionfriddo	0	1	0	0	0	0
							Jorgensen, 3b	2	1	0	0	1	1
							Taylor, p	0	0	0	0	0	0
							Gregg, p	1	0	0	0	1	0
							a Vaughan	0	0	0	0	0	0
							Behrman, p	0	0	0	0	1	0
							Casey, p	0	0	0	0	1	0
							c Reiser	0	0	0	0	0	0
							d Miksis	0	1	0	0	0	0
Total	33	2	8	26*	7	1		26	3	1	27	15	3

*Two out when winning run scored. a Walked for Gregg in seventh. b Ran for Furillo in ninth. c Walked for Casey in ninth. d Ran for Reiser in ninth. e Doubled for Stanky in ninth.

New York	1	0	0	1	0	0	0	0	0–2
Brooklyn	0	0	0	0	1	0	0	0	2–3

Runs batted in — DiMaggio, Lindell, Reese, Lavagetto 2. Two-base hits — Lindell, Lavagetto. Three-base hit — Johnson. Stolen bases — Rizzuto, Reese, Gionfriddo. Sacrifices — Stanky, Bevens. Double plays — Reese, Stanky and Robinson; Gregg, Reese and Robinson; Casey, Edwards and Robinson. Earned runs — New York 1, Brooklyn 3. Left on bases — New York 9, Brooklyn 8. Bases on balls — Off Taylor 1 (DiMaggio), Gregg 3 (DiMaggio, Lindell, Stirnweiss), Bevens 10 (Stanky 2, Walker 2, Jorgensen 2, Gregg, Vaughn, Furillo, Reiser). Struck out — by Gregg 5 (Stirnweiss 2, Henrich, Mcquinn, Bevens), Bevens 5 (Edwards 3, Gregg, Robinson).

Pitching summary — Off Taylor 1 run, 2 hits in 0 innings (none out in first);Gregg 1 run, 4 hits in 7; Behrman 0 runs, 2 hits in 1⅓; Casey 0 runs, 0 hits in ⅔. Wild pitch — Bevens. Winning pitcher — Casey. Umpires — Goetz (NL), plate; McGowan (AL), first base; Pinelli (NL) second base; Rommel (AL), third base; Boyer (AL), left field; Magerkurth (NL), right field. Time of game 2:20. Attendance — 33,443.

July 4, 1948 — While it had no impact on the pennant race, the Dodgers and Giants put on a holiday classic at Ebbets Field. A total of 37 players saw action, and the Dodgers twice rallied from multiple run deficits to finally prevail, 13–12. Trailing 8–4, Brooklyn scored twice in the seventh and three times in the eighth to lead, 9–8, heading to the ninth. In what should have been a warning for the future, Ralph Branca imploded in relief, allowing two Giant home runs that gave New York a 12–9 advantage. Brooklyn was far from done, however, as the Dodgers scored four times without an out being recorded in their last at bat to win.

August 22, 1948 — Although the Dodgers missed a chance to pass the Braves in the standings, they did steal eight bases, including five in one inning. The five thefts in the fifth were highlighted by a triple steal that featured Jackie Robinson swiping home plate for the fourth time that season.

April 26, 1949 — Inserted into the lineup in place of Cal Abrams, Gene Hermanski not only hit a home run, but made "an extraordinary catch" to start a triple play. Just like five years ago, the trick was turned against Boston who had first and second occupied with no one out in the third. Alvin Dark hit a "twisting fly ball" into short left field and Hermanski made a shoestring catch. Both runners assumed the ball would not be caught

As the tying and winning runs head towards home, Cookie Lavagetto's game-winning hit in game four of the 1947 World Series bounces off the short right field wall (courtesy Los Angeles Dodgers).

and were easy outs. Ironically Eddie Stanky, who started the 1944 triple play, was one of the victims this time.[18]

July 12, 1949 — Ebbets Field hosted its first and only All-Star Game in front of 32,577, becoming the last current major league park to hold one. With every team now having had the opportunity to host the event, there was some speculation that the mid-summer's classic might be terminated. After allowing four unearned runs in the first inning, the National League rallied but never evened the score. Locally, the highlight was Jackie Robinson (a double, with three runs scored), who along with Don Newcombe, Roy Campanella, and Larry Doby, became one of four African Americans to play in the Midsummer Classic for the first time.[19]

American League	*AB*	*R*	*H*	*PO*	*A*	*E*
D. DiMag, Bost, rf-cf	5	2	2	2	0	0
Rashci, N.Y. p	1	0	0	0	1	0
Kell, Detroit, 3b	3	2	2	0	1	0
Dillinger, St. L., 3b	1	2	1	0	2	0
Williams, Boston, lf	2	1	0	1	0	0
Mitchell, Cleve., lf	1	0	1	1	0	1
J. DiMaggio N.Y., cf	4	1	2	0	0	0
Doby, Cleve., rf-cf	1	0	0	2	0	0
Joost, Phila., ss	2	1	1	2	2	0
Stephens, Boston, ss	2	0	0	2	0	0
E. Rbinson, Wash.,1b	5	1	1	8	0	0
Goodman, Bost., 1b	0	0	0	1	1	0
Michaels, Chic., 2b	2	0	0	1	3	0
J. Gordon, Cleve., 2b	2	1	1	3	3	0
Tebbets, Boston, c	2	0	2	2	0	0
Berra, N.Y. c	3	0	0	2	1	0
Parnell, Boston, p	1	0	0	0	1	0
Trucks, Detroit, p	1	0	0	0	0	0
Brissle, Phila p	1	0	0	0	0	0
Wertz, Detroit, rf	2	0	0	0	0	0
Total	41	11	13	27	15	1

National League	*AB*	*R*	*H*	*PO*	*A*	*E*
Reese, Brooklyn, ss	5	0	0	3	3	1
J. Rbinson, Bklyn, 2b	4	3	1	1	1	0
Musial, St. L., cf-rf	4	1	3	2	0	0
Kiner, Pittsburg, lf	5	1	1	3	0	0
Mize, N.Y. 1b	2	0	1	1	0	0
Hodges, B'klyn. 1b	3	1	1	8	2	0
Marshall, N.Y. rf	1	1	0	1	0	1
Bickford, Boston, p	0	0	0	0	0	0
b Thomson, N.Y.	1	0	0	0	0	0
Pollet, St. Louis, p	0	0	0	1	0	0
Blackwell, Cinc.i, p	0	0	0	0	0	0
Slaughter, St. L.., rf	1	0	0	0	0	0
Roe, Brooklyn, p	0	0	0	0	0	0
Kazak, St. Louis, 3b	2	0	2	0	0	1
S. Gordon, N.Y. 3b	2	0	1	0	4	0
Seminick, Phila, c	1	0	0	3	0	1
Campanella, B'klyn, c	2	0	0	2	0	1
Spahn, Boston, p	0	0	0	0	0	0
Newcombe, B'klyn, p	1	0	0	0	0	0
a Schoendsnt, St. L	1	0	1	0	0	0
Munger, St. Louis, p	0	0	0	0	0	0
Pafko, Chicago, cf	2	0	1	2	0	0
Total	37	7	12	27	10	5

a Singled to center for Newcombe in the fourth. b Flied out for Bickford in Sixth.

Amer. League	4	0	0	2	0	2	3	0	0–11
Nat'l League	2	1	2	0	0	2	0	0	0–7

Earned runs — American League 7, National League 7. Runs batted in — J. DiMaggio 3, E. Robinson, Tebbetts, Musial 2, Newcombe, Kazak, Joost 2, Kiner, 2 D DiMaggio, Dillinger, Mitchell. Two-base hits — J. Robinson, Tebbets, Gordon, D. DiMaggio, J. DiMaggio, J. Gordon, Mitchell. Home runs — Musial, Kiner. Stolen base — Kell. Double plays — Michaels, Joost, and E. Robinson; Joost, Michaels and E. Robinson; J. Robinson, Reese and Hodges. Left on bases — American League 8, National League 12. Bases on balls — Off Spahn 2, (Joost, Williams), Parnell (Marshall), Newcombe (Williams), Trucks 2 (J. Robinson, Marshall), Munger (Michaels), Bickford (Kell), Brissie 2 (Campanella, Reese), Raschi 3 (S. Gordon, Pafko, Musial). Struck out — By Spahn 3 (D. DiMaggio, Williams, Parnell), Parnell (Mize), Brissie (Pafko), Blackwell 2 (J. Gordon, Stephens), Raschi (Campanella).

Pitching Summary — Off Spahn 4 hits and 4 runs in 1⅓ innings, Parnell 3 and 3 in 1 (none out in 2nd), Newcome 3 and 2 in 2⅔, Trucks 3 and 2 in 2, Munger 0 and 0 in 1, Bickford 2 and 2 in 1, Brissie 5 and 2 in 3, Pollet 4 and 3 in 1, Blackwell 0 and 0 in 1, Roe 0 and 0 in 1, Raschi 1 and 0 in 3. Hit by pitcher — By Parnell (Seminick). Winner — Trucks. Loser — Newcombe. Umpires — Barlick (N) plate, Hubbard (A) 1b, Gore (N) 2b, Summers (A) 3b, Ballanfant (N) LF, Grieve (A) RF. Time of game — 3:04. Attendance — 32,577 (paid). Receipts — $79,225.02

August 31, 1950 — Home run history was made when Gil Hodges highlighted a 19–3 rout of Boston by hitting four home runs to become the second major leaguer and first National Leaguer to hit that many in a nine-inning game. In all, Hodges hit for 17 total bases (which also tied a record) and drove in nine runs, all of them coming on the round-trippers. The first baseman became the third Dodger to hit three or more home runs in a game that season, and his fourth four-base knock helped the Dodgers set a new club record for home runs in a season.[20]

October 1, 1950 — After a memorable September run that saw the Dodgers make up eight games in the standings in less than two weeks, Brooklyn was unable to catch the Phillies on the final day of the season. Philadelphia won, 4–1, in 10 innings on Dick Sisler's three-run homer off Don Newcombe. Robin Roberts was dominant for the Phillies in his 20th win of the season. The Dodgers lone run came on an odd homer from Pee Wee Reese that was declared gone when it became lodged in the screen at the top of the wall. If the ball had fallen back into the field, it may very well have been ruled in play as there were no ground rules covering that possibility. As late as September 19, Brooklyn had been in third place, nine games out of first.

In a scene repeated four times in one game on August 31, 1950, Gil Hodges crosses home plate after hitting a home run (National Baseball Hall of Fame Library, Cooperstown, New York).

May 31, 1951 — In a vivid illustration of his base running prowess, Jackie Robinson escaped a run down between third and home, while six Phillies vainly tried to retire him. The run proved to be the winning tally in a 4–3 Dodger victory that also featured three hits by pitcher Carl Erskine.

August 13, 1951 — Although few may have thought Walter O'Malley had a sense of humor or was the type to give away free admissions, the Brooklyn owner admitted fans free if they brought an instrument and played in honor of the Brooklyn Sym-Phony. The popular

Brooklyn "musical" group was in a dispute with the Local 802 of the American Federation of Musicians, which for a time tried to stop them from playing at Dodger games. The event was supposed to be called "Music Appreciation Night," but ended up being called "Music Depreciation Night," which was "remarkably apt" according to Milton Bracker of the *New York Times*. In all, 2,426 spectators were admitted free, and numerous politicians joined them, including Mayor Vincent Impellitteri and Borough President John Cashmore. Milton Bracker's description of the occasion does justice to the event. "There was nothing pallid about the reinforcements who were drummed up. Clad in blue-jeans, Charlie Chaplin outfits, sunsuits, dirndls, uniforms and smocks, they tooted, fiddled, banged, boomed, squeaked, tinkled and clanged on violins, accordions, ocarinas, trumpets, saxophones, cymbals and at least one trick trombone, only nine inches long."[21]

Momentarily preserving Brooklyn's 1950 pennant hopes, Pee Wee Reese's home run sticks in the right field screen. It would be to no avail as Dick Sisler's three-run homer in the 10th would win the game and the pennant for Philadelphia (Brooklyn Public Library — Brooklyn Collection).

August 27, 1951—The legendary throwing ability of Dodger right fielder Carl Furillo was immortalized this day as some 32,561 fans saw him throw out the Pirates' Mel Queen at first base on what appeared to be a clean single to right field in the

Music, or a facsimile thereof, filled the air on August 13, 1951, as fans with instruments were given free admission on what came to be known as "music depreciation night" (Brooklyn Public Library — Brooklyn Collection).

third inning. Interestingly, the play preserved a no-hitter that Ralph Branca took into the ninth inning before allowing two hits in what would ultimately be a 5–0 shutout.

May 21, 1952 — Brooklyn set six modern Major League records by scoring 15 runs in the first inning on its way to a 19–1 victory over the Reds. Remarkably, the first batter of the inning made an out, and 12 runs scored after two men were retired. The records included runs scored in one inning, most men at bat in one inning, most runs scored after two were out, most runs in the first inning, most runs batted in, and most batters to reach safely in a row. The half inning took about an hour, and Cincinnati used four pitchers. Every Dodger starter except Gil Hodges (two walks) had a hit in the inning, and all nine scored and drove in a run. Reds outfielder Bob Borkowski later recalled that he wished he was wearing armor. While that half inning lasted 59 minutes, amazingly, the entire game took only two hours and 26 minutes.

Cincinnati (N)	*AB*	*R*	*H*	*PO*	*A*	*Brooklyn (N)*	*AB*	*R*	*H*	*PO*	*A*
Hatton, 2b	1	0	0	0	0	Cox, 3b	2	1	1	0	0
Temple, 2b	3	0	0	1	3	Morgan, 3b	3	2	2	1	3
Adams, 3b	1	0	0	2	1	Reese, ss	3	2	2	0	3
Kazak, 3b	3	0	0	0	0	Snider, cf	4	2	2	2	0
Kl'sz'ski, 1b	1	0	0	1	0	Williams, cf	1	0	0	1	0
Wyrostek, 1b	3	0	1	8	0	Robinson, 2b	1	2	1	0	0
Adcock, lf	4	0	0	1	0	Bridges, 2b	3	0	0	3	3
Westlake, cf	3	0	1	2	0	Pafko, rf	4	1	1	1	0
Borkowski, rf	3	0	0	2	0	Furillo, rf	1	0	0	0	0
Howell, c	3	1	2	4	2	Shuba, lf	5	2	2	4	0
McMillan, ss	1	0	1	0	0	Hodges, 1b	2	2	0	9	0
Pellagrini, ss	2	0	0	3	2	Walker, c	5	2	2	6	0
Blackwell, p	0	0	0	0	0	Van Cuyk, p	5	3	4	0	2
Byerly, p	0	0	0	0	0						
Wehmeier, p	0	0	0	0	0						
Smith, p	1	0	0	0	1						
a Post	1	0	0	0	1						
Nuxhall, p	1	0	0	0	1						
Total	31	1	5	24	11		39	19	17	27	11

a Struck out for Smith in sixth.

Cincinnati	0	0	0	0	1	0	0	0	0–1
Brooklyn	(15)	0	2	0	2	0	0	0	x–19

Error — Pafko. Runs batted in — Cox, Morgan 4, Reese 2, Snider 2, Robinson, Pafko 2, Shuba, Hodges, Walker 3, Van Cuyk 2, Howell. Two-base hits — Robinson, Shuba, Reese. Home runs — Snider, Morgan 2, Howell. Double plays — Reese, Bridges and Hodges; Pellagrini, Temple and Wyrostek; Morgan, Bridges and Hodges. Left on bases — Cincinnati 3, Brooklyn 8. Bases on balls — Off Blackwell 2, Byerly 1, Wehmeier 1, Smith 6. Struck out — By Smith 2, Nuxhall, 3 Van Cuyk 5. Hits — Off Blackwell 3 in ⅓ innings, Byerly 4 in ⅓, Wehmeier 1 in 0, Smith 8 in 4⅓, Nuxhall 1 in 3. Runs and earned runs — Off Blackwell 4 and 4 Byerly 5 and 5, Wehmeier 3 and 3, Smith 7 and 7, Nuxhall 0 and 0. Van Cuyk 1 and 1. Hit by pitcher — By Wehmeier (Robinson), by Smith (Cox). Winning pitcher — Van Cuyk (3–2). Losing pitcher — Blackwell (1–6). Umpires — Goetz, Dascoli, Secory and Warneke. Time of game 2:26. Attendance —11,850.

June 19, 1952 — Twenty-five-year-old Carl Erskine tossed a no-hitter and received a $500 check from Walter O'Malley, who also provided a case of champagne for the postgame celebration. The only blemish was a third-inning walk to Cubs' pitcher Willie Ramsdell on four pitches. Erskine allowed just five balls to be hit to the outfield even though he struck out just one Cub batter.

October 1, 1952 — Joe Black became the first African American pitcher to win a World Series game as Brooklyn defeated the New York Yankees, 4–2, in Game One of the Fall Classic.

October 7, 1952 — Although not as tragic as Mickey Owen's dropped third strike, Billy Martin's shoestring catch in the bottom of the seventh of the seventh game of the World Series broke hearts in Brooklyn. The play cut off the Dodgers last rally as Brooklyn came close but still failed to win is first World Series.

October 2, 1953 — In a must-win situation, Dodgers' pitcher Carl Erskine struck out a Fall Classic record 14 to cut the Yankees' Series lead to 2–1. It was a major turnaround from the first game when Erskine allowed four runs in the first inning. He was dominant on this day, striking out Mickey Mantle and Joe Collins four times. The mark of 14 broke the previous record of 13 by Howard Ehmke, set in 1929. Roy Campanella, who nearly did not play because of a hand injury, hit a tiebreaking home run in the eighth inning. A record World Series crowd of 35,270 witnessed the drama.

NY Yankees	*AB*	*R*	*H*	*PO*	*A*	*Brooklyn Dodgers*	*AB*	*R*	*H*	*PO*	*A*
McDougald, 3b	4	0	1	2	3	Gilliam, 2b	4	0	1	1	2
c Noren	0	0	0	0	0	Reese, ss	4	0	1	1	4
Collins, 1b	5	0	0	8	0	Snider, cf	3	1	1	0	0
Bauer, rf	4	1	1	1	0	Hodges, 1b	2	0	1	8	1
Berra, c	1	0	1	4	1	Campanella, c	4	1	1	14	0
Mantle, cf	4	0	0	2	0	Furillo, rf	4	0	0	1	0
Woodling, lf	4	0	1	0	0	Robinson, lf	4	1	3	1	0
Martin, 2b	3	1	1	3	4	Thompson, lf	0	0	0	0	0
Rizzuto, ss	3	0	1	3	3	Cox, 3b	3	0	0	0	1
a Bollweg	1	0	0	0	0	Erskine, P	3	0	0	0	2
Raschi, p	2	0	0	1	1						
b Mize	1	0	0	0	0						
Total	32	2	6	24	12		31	3	8	26	10

a Struck out for Rizzuto in ninth. b Struck out for Raschi in ninth. c Walked for McDougald in ninth.

Yankees	0	0	0	0	1	0	0	1	0–2
Dodgers	0	0	0	0	1	1	0	1	x–3

Errors — None. Runs batted in — McDougald, Cox, Robinson, Woodling, Campanella. Two-base hit — Robinson. Home run — Campanella. Sacrifices — Raschi, Cox. Double play — Rizzuto, Martin and Collins. Left on bases — Yankees 9, Dodgers 8. Bases on balls — Off Erskine 3 (Berra, Martin, Noren), Raschi, 3 (Snider, Hodges 2). Struck out — By Erskine 14 (McDougald, Collins 4, Mantle 4, Rizzuto, Raschi, Woodling, Bollweg, Mize) Raschi 4 (Reese, Campanella, Furillo, Cox). Runs and earned runs — Off Erskine 2 and 2, Raschi 3 and 3. Hit by pitcher — By Erskine (Berra 2). Wild pitch — Erskine. Balk — Raschi. Umpires — Hurley (A.L.), plate; Gore (N. L.), first base; Grieve (A.L.), second base; (Stewart (N.L.), third base; Soar (A.L.), left-field foul line; Dascoli (N.L.), right-field foul line. Time of game — 3:00. Paid Attendance — 35,270.

July 31, 1954 — Milwaukee won its ninth straight, but the story was Joe Adcock of the Braves, who put on a one-man offensive show, hitting four home runs and a double for seven RBIs. Adcock set the record for total bases in one game with 18 and also tied the mark of five for extra-base hits in a nine-inning contest. Ironically, Adcock had hit a home run the previous night but also broke his bat that evening and had to use Charley White's the next day, which was supposedly the heaviest on the team. The five home runs in two straight games also tied a mark, and both teams combined to hit 10 in the game, which evened a National League record.[22]

April 21, 1955 — Keyed by the relief pitching of Joe Black and a four-for-four performance by Don Zimmer, Brooklyn defeated the Phillies, 14–4, to set a new major league record with its 10th straight win to start the season. That mark had previously been held by the Giants (1918), Brooklyn itself (1940), and the St. Louis Browns (1944), all with nine. Of the three, only the Browns would ultimately win the pennant, as would Brooklyn in 1955. Just 3,874 fans witnessed the event, but Dodger President Walter O'Malley promised each attendee a "suitable memento," which turned out to be a commemorative coaster.[23]

May 12, 1956 — Two walks were the only blemishes on Carl Erskine's line, as he became just the ninth pitcher and the third in the National League to hurl two no-hitters since 1900. The contest was CBS' "Game of the Week" and was most likely seen by more fans than any other no-hitter to that time. Erskine also made history as the only pitcher to throw two no-hitters at Ebbets Field.

Carl Erskine was the only pitcher to throw two no-hitters at Ebbets Field (National Baseball Hall of Fame Library, Cooperstown, New York).

June 17, 1956 — Joe Adcock hit another historic home run, the first one to clear the left field roof at Ebbets Field.[24]

June 29, 1956 — Trailing 5–2 to the Phillies heading to the bottom of the ninth, Brooklyn erupted for three consecutive home runs for a 6–5 come-from-behind victory. With a runner on first and one out, Duke Snider, Randy Jackson, and Gil Hodges all homered, with Hodges accounting for the winning run. Randy Jackson cited this as the best memory of his time in Brooklyn.

September 25, 1956 — With his team's back to the wall in the closing days of the pennant race, Sal Maglie pitched a no-hitter, defeating the Phillies, 5–0. The feat put an exclamation point on the irony of a former bitter enemy playing a major role in Brooklyn's final National League flag. The contest also marked Pee Wee Reese's 2,000th game in a Dodger uniform, which tied him with Zack Wheat as the only players to do so for Brooklyn.[25]

September 30, 1956 — On the final day of the season, Don Newcombe recorded his 27th victory, and Duke Snider hit two home runs and made a great catch to help the Dodgers win their final pennant in Brooklyn. The Dodgers had rallied to overtake Milwaukee late, and then held them off by sweeping Pittsburgh after losing three of four to the Pirates the previous weekend. It was Brooklyn's ninth pennant during the Modern Era, and 31,983 celebrated by rushing the field. The Dodgers' hit five home runs, and Snider's two helped him set the club record (43) and win the National League crown. Now Brooklyn would have the chance to defend its only World Series championship, and nothing negative was on anyone's mind, as "real progress" was being made toward a new park.[26]

Pittsburgh (N)	*AB*	*R*	*H*	*PO*	*A*
Clemente, rf	5	0	2	1	1
Virdon, cf	5	0	2	1	0
Skinner, 1b	4	0	0	8	0
Friend, p	0	0	0	0	0
f Foiles	1	0	0	0	0
Thomas, 3b	4	0	1	0	0
Walls, lf	4	1	2	5	0
Groat, ss	4	1	2	2	3
e E. O'Brien, ss	0	0	0	0	0
Mazeroski, 2b	3	1	1	2	6
d Freese, 2b	1	0	0	0	0
Shepard, c	4	2	3	3	0
Law, p	0	0	0	0	0
Face, p	0	0	0	0	1
a Cole	0	1	0	0	0
Purkey, p	0	0	0	0	0
b Powers	1	0	0	0	0
Kline, p	0	0	0	0	0
c Long, 1b	2	0	0	2	0
Total	38	6	13	24	11

Brooklyn (N)	*AB*	*R*	*H*	*PO*	*A*
Gilliam, 2b	4	1	0	6	2
Reese, ss	3	1	2	6	8
Snider, cf	4	2	2	3	0
Robinson, 2b	4	1	1	0	1
Amoros, lf	4	2	2	1	0
Hodges, 1b	4	0	2	6	0
Furillo, rf	4	0	0	1	0
Campanella, c	3	0	1	4	0
Newcombe, p	3	1	1	0	3
Bessent, p	1	0	1	0	0
Total	34	8	12	27	14

a Walked for Face in third. b Grounded into double play for Purkey in fifth. c Popped up for Kline in seventh. d Reached first on error for Mazeroski in eighth. e Ran for Groat in eighth. f Struck out for Friend in ninth.

Pittsburgh	0	0	2	0	0	0	3	1	0–6
Brooklyn	3	0	1	0	2	1	0	1	x–8

Error — Robinson. Runs batted in — Snider 4, Clemente 2, Robinson, Reese, Amoros 2, Virdon 3, Walls. Two-base hits — Newcombe, Groat, Virdon. Three-base hit — Walls. Home run — Snider 2, Robinson, Amoros 2, Walls. Sacrifice fly — Reese. Double play — Newcombe, Reese and Hodges; Robinson, Reese and Hodges; Gilliam, Reese and Hodges. Left on bases — Pittsburgh 6, Brooklyn 5. Bases on balls — Off Law 1, Kline, 1, Newcombe 1. Struck out — By Kline, 2 Newcombe 2, Bessent 2. Hits — Off Law 3 in ⅔ inning, Face 0 in 1⅓, Purkey 1 in 2, Kline 3 in 2 Friend 5 in 3, Newcombe 11 in 7⅓, Bessent 2 in 1⅓. Runs and earned runs — Law 3 and 3, Purkey 1 and 1, Kline, 3 and 3, Friend 1 and 1, Newcombe 6 and 6. Wild pitch — Newcombe. Winning pitcher — Newcombe (27–7), Losing pitcher — Law

(8–16). Umpires Jackowski, Belmore, Conland and Landes. Time of game—2:30. Attendance 31,953.

October 9, 1956—Jackie Robinson's two-out single to left field drove home Junior Gilliam with the winning run, allowing the Dodgers to play another day and force a Game 7 against the Yankees. Clem Labine, usually a reliever, went the distance for the 1–0 win and was outstanding, while Bob Turley was the hard-luck loser, allowing just four hits (Labine gave up seven) and setting a Yankee World Series strikeout record with 11. Labine got the win though, just his second complete-game victory of the season, both occurring at critical times.

Notes

1. *Brooklyn Daily Eagle*, May 7, 1916; *New York Times*, May 7, 1916.
2. *Brooklyn Daily Eagle*, October 1, 1916.
3. *New York Times*, September 11, 1920.
4. http://www.baseball-almanac.com
5. *New York Times*, August 16, 1926.
6. www.retrosheet.org
7. http://www.baseball-almanac.com
8. *New York Times*, September 22, 1934.
9. *New York Times*, August 25, 1941.
10. Bob McGee, *The Greatest Ballpark Ever: Ebbets Field and the Story of the Brooklyn Dodgers*, (New Brunswick, N.J.: Rutgers University Press, 2005), 57–58; *Brooklyn Daily Eagle*, October 6, 1941.
11. *Brooklyn Daily Eagle*, June 16, 1942.
12. *New York Times*, August 7, 1944.
13. http://www.baseball-almanac.com; *New York Times*, August 21, 1945.
14. *New York Times*, April 24, 1946
15. *Brooklyn Daily Eagle*, August 14, 1946, August 15, 1946; *New York Times*, August 14, 1946, August 15, 1946; http://www.baseball-almanac.com.
16. *Brooklyn Daily Eagle*, September 12, 1946; *New York Times*, September 12, 1946, September 21, 1946.
17. *Brooklyn Daily Eagle*, April 16, 1947; *New York Times*, April 16, 1947.
18. *New York Times*, April 27, 1949.
19. *Brooklyn Daily Eagle*, July 13, 1949.
20. *Brooklyn Daily Eagle*, September 1, 1950.
21. *New York Times*, August 14, 1951.
22. *New York Times*, August 1, 1954; *Brooklyn Daily Eagle*, August 1, 1954.
23. *New York Times*, April 22, 1955.
24. *New York Times*, June 18, 1956.
25. *New York Times*, September 26, 1956.
26. *New York Times*, October 1, 1956.

Before Jackie

Black Baseball at Ebbets Field

James Overmyer

The Brooklyn team in the National League had played 507 official games at modern Ebbets Field when a team of black guys took the field for a 1919 series against a team of white professionals and local stars. The black team, the Bacharach Giants, has the honor of being the first African Americans to play at Charles Ebbets' new park and more than held their own against the whites.

But that series, a small step toward the eventual reintegration of professional baseball, also meant something important at the time. The Bacharachs' very presence in Ebbets Field challenged the white-dominated power structure then running black baseball in New York City. The Giants made Brooklyn their home into the 1920s, and in each succeeding decade until the Dodgers led the daring reintegration of the major leagues in 1947, there were further distinctive African American contributions at Ebbets Field.

In 1935, a husband and wife team, rank newcomers to sports ownership, started a franchise in Brooklyn and launched themselves on distinguished careers that would land one of them in the Baseball Hall of Fame. In 1945, a new Negro team took the field. Today, its wins and losses are not important. But what went on in its front office was fascinating — baseball was being pushed rapidly toward integration in Brooklyn, even if many did not realize it at the time.

Among the things essential for a successful baseball game is a place to play. Real estate is not everything in the sport, but it matters a lot. No black team in New York City owned its own park — few black teams anywhere did — and the availability of Ebbets Field to these three black baseball ventures was crucial.

The story of black baseball at Ebbets Field began in the spring of 1916 when the nucleus of the Duval Giants of Jacksonville, Florida, were lured to Atlantic City, becoming one of the best semiprofessional teams in Southern New Jersey and Philadelphia. Atlantic City was turning from a sandy island into a crowded resort city as fast as streets and buildings could be built. The city had an African American population of more than 11,000, a quarter of the permanent residents, and the Giants fit right in.[1] Almost immediately, the two local men who brought the team north, Thomas Jackson and Henry Tucker, named it the Bacharach Giants, after the city's mayor, Harry Bacharach.

Why name the Bacharachs after somebody who had little or nothing directly to do with the team? Simply put, the owners needed municipal cooperation and good honest publicity could not hurt the mayor or the team. It is not clear if naming the team after Bacharach was a gambit to entice the mayor's support or an honor for a good deed already done. But it is surely no pure coincidence that Jackson, listed in the 1918 Atlantic City directory as a "laborer," had by the 1920 edition become an "assistant rubbish inspector" for the city health bureau.[2]

Atlantic City attracted vacationers to its famous Boardwalk, hotels, and beaches by giving them more than sun and sand. There was also liquor and Sunday entertainment, Prohibition and Blue Laws be damned, as part of the political leaders' economic development strategy. Several of them (not Mayor Harry, who avoided major scandal and gained a reputation as a progressive politician) went to jail for the corruption that inevitably accompanied this behavior.

No one has ever connected the Bacharach Giants with the graft and corruption, just with giving the popular Mayor Bacharach his free advertising. However, the players quickly became part of the city's highly politicized life. "Some of 'em come in here and got into politics and went from there," recalled first baseman Napoleon "Chance" Cummings, who himself wound up working for the local prosecutor's office. "We were only here a few days before we got registered to vote."[3] The Bacharach Giants were a staple of summer entertainment in the city, but apparently did not produce enough revenue to cover expenses, possibly because of the fierce competition for the leisure dollar in Atlantic City. In 1919, Tucker and Jackson teamed up with new partners, a pair of New Yorkers with substantial reputations in the sporting world.

One new partner was John R. Connor, a black restaurant owner who had migrated to Brooklyn from Portsmouth, Virginia, after service in the Navy in the Spanish-American War. Shortly after the turn of the 20th century he had a place in Brooklyn, the Royal Café. Connor also had a keen interest in baseball. In 1905, he launched his own club, the Brooklyn Royal Giants, who soon became an Eastern Seaboard powerhouse. But Connor lost out in a power struggle over the very thing that made professional baseball possible, an enclosed ballpark. As semiprofessional ball grew ever more popular in the New York area, the business part became better organized to help set up games in a predictable way that would draw fans to the best teams. This was done through "booking" organizations, which would secure the rights to ball fields, match up opponents, and charge a percentage of admission revenues.

The booking agents provided a valuable service to the understaffed part-time teams. But after a time, control swung to just a few agents who had locked up rights to many parks, and dictated their terms to just about every team. The leading agent was Nathaniel C. "Nat" Strong, a former sporting goods salesman and a commercial building owner in Manhattan, described as "strong willed and dictatorial."[4] Connor himself was no pushover. He refused to do business with Strong, a white man trying to make money off a black enterprise. Connor shut Strong out of the Royal Giants' business affairs, but Strong shut Connor out of the best local bookings. Later, Connor wound up selling the team to Strong, probably at a distressed price.

The other new New York City partner in the Bacharach Giants was another nightlife entrepreneur. Barron D. Wilkins was a flamboyant rule breaker who ran several popular nightspots, the last being the Exclusive Club in Harlem. He made a lot of money, much of it from white patrons, and gave much of it away to the destitute in the black community. Even before Prohibition he was a target of police surveillance and raids.

So Connor and Wilkins, with help from Henry Tucker of the original ownership, had a good team, and enough money to support it. However, there seemed few acceptable options for a park other than going back to Nat Strong. In the end, Connor eluded Strong's grip on ballparks and dealt directly with the Brooklyn Robins, for the rental of Ebbets Field. The deal was good for both organizations, since a professional ballpark on a day without a game is basically a money incinerator. No tickets are being sold, but the players, the property taxes, the basic upkeep, and the mortgage, if any, still have to be paid. So, finding other revenue generating uses for the park contributed to the park owner's bottom line.

After splitting the 1919 season between Inlet Park in Atlantic City and the Dyckman Oval in Harlem, the Bacharachs first played at Ebbets Field in October 1919 against the International Stars, a team that included two major leaguers, veteran Dick Rudolph and youngster Johnny Enzmann, as the core of its pitching staff. The Bacharach Giants played five games against the All-Stars at Ebbets and won three of them, sweeping the last two decisively on November 2.

Connor and Wilkins came back to Ebbets Field in 1920, although it could be said that they had three "home fields": Inlet Park in Atlantic City, Dyckman Oval in Harlem, and Ebbets. Not coincidentally, Nat Strong had no interest or control over any of them. Ace pitcher Dick Redding was the field manager. High stakes baseball could get rowdy at times in those days. However it was reported that between management's roster choices and Redding's low-key, evenhanded supervision, the Bacharachs "for their deportment alone are the one semi-pro ball club able to get a lease on Ebbetts [*sic*] Field when the Brooklyn Nationals are out of town."[5] Connor was well aware the team had scored a coup by leasing a major league park. He announced that the Giants would be sharply outfitted in new uniforms for the season, because "we have been able to get Ebbets Field and we will look just as good as the Brooklyn Dodgers on that diamond."[6]

Dick Lundy, a star with the Bacharach Giants. One of the top Negro League shortstops, Lundy was the best home team shortstop at Ebbets Field between Bill Dahlen and Pee Wee Reese (National Baseball Hall of Fame Library, Cooperstown, New York).

On May 16, at the Ebbets Field opener, the Giants looked very good indeed. They played a top level New York area semi-pro team with the unlikely name "Treat 'Em Roughs." That had been the motto of the U.S. Army tank corps in World War I and was adopted for the team by its owner, Arthur Guy Empey, famous for his book about his World War I experiences, plus many pulp-fiction adventures. The team of the Spanish-American war veteran, Connor, beat the World War I hero's team, 8–0 and 11–4. Redding, team captain as well as leading pitcher, threw a two-hit shutout in the first contest. Andrew "Stringbean" Williams won the second.

The Giants were an all-around solid team, but after the pitching, the strongest part of the lineup was the left side of the infield. Oliver "Ghost" Marcelle, a slick fielder who hit .286 in the 29 games for which box scores have been unearthed, played third. Dick Lundy, 22, an original Bacharach Giant from Florida who was acknowledged as one of the best Negro shortstops, is described as "a superb fielder with a wide range and an exceptionally strong arm.... A switch-hitter who hit for average and with power."[7] The available 1920 statistics give him a .313 batting average.

Playing several games a week, the Giants shuttled between Atlantic City and New York. Their return to Ebbets Field on July 11 was by any standard their most important set of games of the year. Their rivals for the title of best black team in New York, which really meant best in the entire East, were the Lincoln Giants. The teams were closely matched — the Bacharachs had Redding, Lundy, and Marcelle, the Lincolns ace pitcher Joe Williams and outfielders Spotswood Poles and Clarence "Fats" Jenkins, all household names among black baseball fans. Redding and Williams, "Cannonball Dick" versus "Cyclone Joe," as the papers called them, once teammates on the Lincoln Giants, had a longstanding, unfriendly, personal rivalry.

It was hard to know how closely matched the teams were until now, because they never played each other. There was an underlying enmity between the owners that surpassed the Williams–Redding falling out. The Lincoln Giants' white owner, James Keenan, was a member of the Nat Strong group. In addition to wrestling over control of playing sites, the two teams worked behind the scenes trying to raid each other's rosters in an age where playing contracts were poorly enforced or completely nonexistent.

The *New York Age*, a black weekly newspaper, took credit for bringing the teams together through its blanket coverage of the success of the newcomer Bacharachs: "It was through the pointing out of the growing popularity of the Bacharachs by the *Age* that the Lincoln players were aroused to the point where they demanded of their owners to be allowed to show their superiority."[8] Whatever the intensity of the feud among the owners, Connor, Wilkins, and Keenan (and Strong) could hardly ignore the positive publicity, not to mention paying attendance, which would accrue to both their teams from a matchup. The Lincolns played at Olympic Field in Harlem, which was nothing like a major league ballpark. So Ebbets Field was the obvious choice for the showdown.

Redding and Williams were matched up in the first game of the doubleheader, which the Bacharachs won, 5–0: "It was Dick's day and he pitched airtight ball."[9] The Lincolns won the second game, 7–5. Attendance was announced at 16,000 in the *Age*, more than half the capacity of Ebbets Field at the time. The *Age* sportswriter "Ted" Hooks reported that when its "representative" (presumably him) tried to get Williams and Redding to pose for a photo shaking hands, they refused. The matchup had been a success and Hooks wrote that "The public eagerly awaits a second clash between these two teams."[10]

The eager public was not to be disappointed. The two teams of Giants played again at Ebbets on August 29. Charles Ebbets arranged beforehand for a portion of the gate to go to a fund to buy and distribute coal for the winter among Brooklyn's needy residents.

But what the Lincolns needed that day was more runs and less Redding. Matched up against Williams again, Redding shut out the Lincolns on three hits in the opener, 6–0, then came back with a complete-game 7–3 win in the nightcap. Marcelle had a double and a triple in the opener and leftfielder Elias "Country" Brown also tripled. Lundy, who had two hits in each game, homered in the second one. Attendance was lower due to a rainy day and a streetcar strike on the Brooklyn Rapid Transit system, but still topped 6,000 in the *Brooklyn Daily Eagle's* report.[11] The Bacharachs continued to use Ebbets Field for big games against other top black teams. On August 22, they played a doubleheader with the Chicago American Giants, the champions of the first season of the Negro National League (NNL). The games followed a disastrous Bacharach road trip to the Midwest in which they lost to Chicago, the Indianapolis ABCs, and other members of the prestigious Negro National League.

Negro Leagues aces Dick "Cannonball" Redding (left) and Smokey Joe Williams, flanking two unidentified fans. Redding and Williams hooked up at Ebbets Field in 1920, with Redding prevailing, 5–0 (National Baseball Hall of Fame Library, Cooperstown, New York).

All of that was in the past though, as on the 22nd, the Bacharachs lit up Ebbets Field for 11,000 fans, winning 7–0 and 4–1. Redding and Mervyn "Red" Ryan each pitched complete-game wins. Lundy had two hits in each game, and Marcelle had three in the opener. On September 6, the Giants got their revenge on the ABCs, too, sweeping a rain-soaked Labor Day doubleheader before a reported 12,000 fans that came despite the weather and the continuing transit strike. Regular catcher Julio Rojo, pinch-hitting in the sixth, tripled with the bases loaded for a final 5–4 lead. In the second game, the first ABC hitter Red Ryan faced tripled and scored, but he shut the Hoosiers out the rest of the way as the Bacharachs won, 4–1. Andrew "Rube" Foster brought his Chicago Giants back to Ebbets Field on October 17 while barnstorming the East, and this time scored a double shutout of the Bacharachs, 2–0 and 1–0. Redding and Ryan gave up only four hits the entire 18 innings, but to no avail.

The Bacharach Giants continued to use Ebbets Field to host their most distinguished opponents, the Negro National League teams touring the East, during the 1921 season. The Brooklyn opener on June 5 featured Hilldale, a Philadelphia squad, another of the best black teams in the East. The teams split a twin bill. Hilldale surprisingly racked Redding up in a nine-run fifth inning on the way to a 13–6 win. Eventual Hall of Famer Louis Santop had four hits, including a home run. The Giants got even with a 6–5 darkness-shortened nightcap victory. The teams were at it again at Ebbets Field the following

Sunday. This time the Giants won 14–7 and 5–1. Redding and Stringbean Williams were the winning pitchers. Long before pitchers were more or less automatically expected to be anemic hitters, Redding led the Giants in batting in the first game with three hits, including a homer, and Williams had two in the second. An attendance of 5,000 was reported for the first doubleheader, and 8,000 for the second.

Back at Ebbets Field once again on July 2, the Bacharachs walloped the All Cubans, the Eastern version of two Cuban teams playing black U.S. ball, by a 13–2 score in the opener of a doubleheader, and then hung in for a 4–3 victory in the second game. In the first game, Red Ryan threw a four-hitter, Marcelle had three hits, and the first baseman, Bill Pettus, popped a home run. Lundy was back from an ankle injury, with a hit in each game. Rookie pitcher Henry "Long Tom" Richardson gave up five hits over seven innings for the second win.

The Bacharachs spent August, the high month of the resort season, and early September playing in Atlantic City, including eight games against Negro National League opponents, who had left their Midwestern parks and were swinging through the East. But before they hit the Boardwalk, they hosted the ABCs in Brooklyn on July 31. Indianapolis was run by C.I. Taylor, a black baseball veteran and one of four brothers famous for their Negro League exploits. Brother Ben, who had once been a Bacharach Giant, played first base. The Giants broke a 2–2 tie with four runs in the sixth inning, eventually beating Indianapolis, 11–3, on a rainy day that washed out the second game shortly after it had started. Lundy, nicely recovered, and his infield mate Marcelle each had three hits. Two of Ollie's hits were doubles, and Country Brown tripled.

The *Daily Eagle*, Brooklyn's major paper, sent a reporter to the game who, while perhaps overwhelmed by being in the presence of so many black folk, and all too aware of the differences between him and them, waxed poetic: "Ebbets Field was a riot of color. Every colored lady and gent from the uppermost stretches of Harlem came down to help their Brooklyn brethren cheer on the dusky phenoms. There were plenty of empty seats in the bleachers and grandstand, but the eight or nine thousand of them that were filled provided enough sociable company to keep the players from feeling lonesome. Naturally, when the gallery was so responsive and ready to show its appreciation, the dark boys couldn't help playing completely out of themselves."[12]

After the move back to Atlantic City, the Bacharachs returned to Brooklyn for what turned out to be their final game at Ebbets Field, defeating regional rival Hilldale, 4–3. The Chicago American Giants hit town October 1 for a three-game series which was advertised as "the colored baseball championship of the world."[13] The first two games were played in Harrison, New Jersey, right across the Hudson River from New York, and at Harlem's Dyckman Oval, since the Robins were at home both days. The Bacharachs won the first game and the American Giants the second. The deciding game was played on October 16, long after the white National League season was over, but while the matchup qualified for the marquee display at Ebbets, it was not played in Brooklyn. Instead, it was staged at the Bronx Oval, a field in the South Bronx near the East River in the Hunts Point neighborhood. The papers, neither black nor white, carried any comments on why the Bacharach Giants stopped playing at Ebbets Field, but this mid–October game at another site was no onetime thing. It was announced before the contest (which

Chicago won) that the Giants had signed a lease to play at the Oval in 1922.[14] However, when the new season rolled around the Bacharachs turned out to have a different home field, the New York Oval, located just south of where Yankee Stadium would rise two years later. Actually, the New York Bacharach Giants played there and the Atlantic City Bacharachs played in Atlantic City because the franchise had split in two.

The original owners, Tom Jackson and Henry Tucker, apparently forced the New Yorkers out of Atlantic City and played as the "Original Bacharach Giants." The New York team, still the property of Connor and Wilkins, generally referred to itself in press releases as the "famous Bacharach Giants." But this was the last season for the New York team, famous or not. Wilkins and Connor discontinued the squad, and Jackson and Tucker's team became charter members in the first eastern Negro league, the Eastern Colored League, in 1923. Wilkins and Connor never had another top flight baseball team. In fact, neither had long to live.

Wilkins died in May of 1924 from an occupational hazard. Occupational, that is, if your vocation was providing illegal liquor and other forms of vice to paying customers, and your avocation was helping people in need. He was getting a breath of fresh air outside his Exclusive Club the night of May 24 when one Julius "Yellow Charleston" Miller, a bootlegger who may have been a Wilkins supplier, ran up to him. Miller, a reputed regular drug user, had just fatally shot Joseph Parker, the big winner in a dice game, who had refused to loan Miller money to keep playing. Miller demanded $100 getaway money from Wilkins, who told him no. Miller pulled his trusty pistol and shot Wilkins twice, killing him. Miller was arrested the next day and later was electrocuted at Sing Sing prison for the two murders. Connor, who was one of Wilkins' 16 pallbearers, suffered a stroke and died in July of 1926 from a cerebral hemorrhage. Dick Redding was one of his pallbearers. Between Wilkins' and Connors' deaths, in April of 1925, the two men who helped make their Ebbets Field success possible also passed on. Charles Ebbets died of heart failure and his co-owner, Ed McKeever, who caught a cold that led to pneumonia at Ebbets' funeral, soon followed him.

The next attempt at making Ebbets Field home for a black team was the result of a fan's disapproval of the way the Negro Leagues were run and his determination to do something about it. The Great Depression nearly killed off major league–caliber black baseball. But most of the well-established black teams stayed in business, however marginally, by playing independently, though their leagues folded. By 1932, the Negro Southern League, usually regarded as a quality segregated minor league, was the only sizeable one left. But the desire for the competitive framework that could only be provided by an organized league brought new investors and some existing owners together in 1933 to form the second Negro National League, the successor to the original NNL that had folded in 1931.

The league drew the admiration, tempered with criticism, of Abraham Manley. Manley, a North Carolina native who had originally made money running an illegal, but popular, numbers gambling business (what is now a state lottery, but which then lacked government sanction), liked Negro baseball and wanted in. But Manley also had his reservations. While he valued black baseball highly, he did not care for teams spending most of their time playing substandard opposition on the road, "barnstorming" as it was known, or owners who took advantage of their fellow league colleagues when they deemed it necessary.

As he told his wife, Effa, one day in 1934, "Barnstorming is for the birds.... Negro Baseball is never going to get anyplace until it becomes completely organized, and learns to operate again under real league conditions."[15] Effa, who was a baseball fan herself (she maintained that she met her future husband at Yankee Stadium during the 1932 World Series), debated the subject with Abe, and in the new league's third year, the Manleys had a new franchise, the Brooklyn Eagles. As Effa later recalled, "It seems that Abe had sold his associates on the proposition that a new club could be formed to operate out of Brooklyn, a major baseball metropolis of the first rank."[16] There had not been a Negro League team with a New York City address since 1927, but the 1935 Negro National League was going to feature two: the New York Cubans in Harlem and Manley's Eagles in Brooklyn. Negro teams often played in New York, particularly at Yankee Stadium, but the league was now really trying to put down more permanent roots in the city.

Alejandro Pompez, a longtime baseball promoter whose new team was the New York Cubans, and who, like Manley, had made most of his money in the numbers business, had bought the Dyckman Oval for his home park. But the Eagles were moving into a much nicer baseball neighborhood — Manley forged a deal to lease Ebbets when the Dodgers were not using it. At that time in Negro League history, the Eagles were the only black major league club with a major league home park. They paid a percentage of gate receipts for rent and were responsible for paying the ballpark help, usually the experienced Dodger ushers and ticket takers.[17]

From this distant vantage point, it is not clear who or what prompted Manley to contact the Dodgers. What *is* clear is that, in 1935, the president of the Dodgers, Stephen "Judge" McKeever, Edward's brother, was a fan of the Eagles. The *Brooklyn Daily Eagle* noted that, "when the Eagles are in town, Judge McKeever watches them from his cushioned chair at the back of the grandstand just as he does each Dodger contest."[18] Even after they moved their team from Brooklyn, Manley and his wife had good relations with the Dodgers' front office and rented Ebbets Field on several occasions for individual games and an all-star series they were promoting.

It seemed that everybody liked Abe. He was, in the parlance of the 1930s, a "sportsman," an avid spectator of sporting events who also saw them as social events. As a team owner, Manley excelled in scouting players. He seems to have been good at doing his own "bird dog" scouting, that is, following up on tips from others and making eyeball evaluations of young players. Over the years, the Eagles specialized in finding much of their own talent, rather than depending primarily upon trades or signings from the ever-fluid Negro League free agent market. He was also quick to make friends among other Negro National League owners — he almost immediately became a league officer. His players remember him as an owner who took opportunities to ride the team bus on trips, standing beside the bus door peeling off meal money from a green roll as they exited, and who was also happy to spend hours drinking beer and playing cards with "his boys."

Other than control of the meal money bankroll, Abe apparently had no particular facility, nor love, for the business side of running a team. That is where Effa Manley came in. As an organizer, she was everything that her husband was not. A Philadelphia high school graduate, she thirsted for a place in black society, and her marriage to the well-off Abe gave her the opportunity. She became a fundraiser for charities in Harlem and, in 1934, secretary of the Citizens' League for Fair Play, an organization that pressured white department store owners in the heart of Harlem's business district to hire more black sales clerks.

Effa was highly intelligent and extremely well organized. It was not long before she was not only the business brains behind the Eagles, but was also usually their public face outside of the ballpark. Already a fan of the sport in general, she became a fierce advocate of Negro League ball. In the first month of the 1935 season she attended a Cubans game at Dyckman Oval, where fisticuffs between a sliding runner and an infielder precipitated a general brawl. Lewis Dial, the sports columnist for the *Age* reported: "One Cuban business man was heard to say that he was through with Negro baseball. We were glad to hear Mrs. Manley, wife of the Brooklyn Eagles owner, severely censure him and just about change his mind. If there is such a thing as a lady fan, Mrs. Manley is twins, as far as the Brooklyn Eagles are concerned."[19]

When they made their deal for Ebbets Field, the Manleys had little else in tangible assets. Soon, though, they hired veteran Negro Leaguer Ben Taylor to be their manager, and Abe and Taylor started looking for players. Mostly, Manley and Taylor signed players from organized teams that were not members of the Negro National League, and thus not covered by league anti-tampering rules. The New York Black Yankees, the Kansas City Monarchs, and the Atlantic City Bacharach Giants all made "contributions" that they probably would rather have not made, as did several lesser-known independent black clubs.

The spring training roster included well-established veterans such as outfielder Clarence "Fats" Jenkins (15 years of baseball); shortstop Bill Yancey (eight years); catcher Clarence "Spoony" Palm, a real journeyman joining his ninth team in eight years, and seven-year veteran Ted "Double Duty" Radcliffe, who earned his nickname because he was capable of both pitching and catching, sometimes in the same doubleheader. On the other end of the experience spectrum there was Leon Day, an 18-year-old right-handed pitcher who had spent 1934 with the hometown Baltimore Black Sox, but signed with Brooklyn when the Sox dropped out of the National League. Day, elected to the Baseball Hall of Fame after a 20-year career in the Negro Leagues, Caribbean ball, and the finally-integrated minors, played for the Eagles until 1947. A batterymate, Leon Ruffin, was a rookie in Brooklyn in 1935 and spent the greatest part of his subsequent 15-year career on Manley-owned teams. Ed Stone, a left-handed hitting outfielder, came from the Bacharach Giants in his fourth season, and spent the rest of the decade, and most of the war years, with the Eagles.

After barnstorming their way north from spring training in Jacksonville, real league play began the next Sunday, May 5, in Irvington, New Jersey, when the Eagles swept a doubleheader from the Newark Dodgers. With the Brooklyn Dodgers home until the middle of May, the Eagles stayed on the road. They lost two of three in Philadelphia to the Stars the following Saturday and Sunday, and one more to Philly in Chester, Pennsylvania, the next day, before coming to Ebbets Field for their Brooklyn debut.

Throughout their ownership, the Manleys were firm believers in promoting their home community, particularly the black community and Opening Day was no exception.

The 1935 Brooklyn Eagles called Ebbets Field home before moving to Newark, New Jersey, and greater glory (Lawrence D. Hogan Collection).

New York Mayor Fiorello H. La Guardia was prevailed upon to throw out the first ball. Always on the lookout to promote the successes of high-ranking blacks in the government and business world, the Manleys also made Hubert T. Delaney, a lawyer and, at the time, city tax commissioner, James S. Watson, one of the first African American judges in the city, and the Rev. John H. Johnson, a leading Harlem cleric, their honored guests.

Although Mayor La Guardia, 5 feet, 2 inches tall and rotund, undoubtedly did not have the best fastball on the field, his ceremonial toss may have been the top Eagles pitching performance of the day. Radcliffe and his relievers were raked for 22 hits, and the Homestead Grays won, 20 to 7. Effa Manley could not stand the rout, and although by her own admission "the mayor had to stay for the whole game. I went home in the third inning and had my first drink of whiskey."[20] George Giles, the team's first baseman and captain recalled that "Mrs. Manley loved baseball, but she couldn't stand to lose.... I think she'd take it more seriously than anybody."[21]

The Eagles quickly rebounded against the Grays, splitting a Sunday doubleheader the day after the Opening Day debacle (scoring 18 runs in their win) and then beating Homestead again on Monday for a series split. The team continued an up and down performance, playing .500 baseball through the season's first month. If Effa Manley hated to lose, Abe must not have liked it much better, for by then they had fired Taylor, the veteran manager. According to Giles, who replaced him as playing manager, the 47-year-old Taylor, who had begun a long playing and managing career in the low-offense Deadball Era, could not adjust to the home run conscious 1930's: "He played for one run.... One run wasn't no good with the lively ball."[22] A Midwestern fixture as a Negro Leaguer who had scratched his itch to play in New York, the great metropolis, Giles took over on the field while Abe continued to tinker with the roster.

By early July, Radcliffe had been released, supposedly for insubordination, but a 2–4 won-loss record and an earned run average near six may have had a little to do with the move.[23] The veteran outfielder Rap Dixon had been traded and Dennis Gilchrest, who had been the starting secondbaseman on Opening Day, was also gone. The 38-year-old Christopher Columbus "Crush" Holloway, a Negro League outfielder since 1921, was signed around mid–July, but was released a month later when he proved to have little left but his reputation and interesting name.

The only Latin American player on the team, Javier Perez, proved to be an important pickup at the end of May after being released by the cross-town Cubans following a suspension for punching an umpire. He took over third base, allowing the versatile Harry Williams to move to second for the rest of the season. Williams, Giles, Jenkins, Stone, and Palm were constant regulars, while Manley and Giles interchanged the other pieces of the lineup. The young Leon Day, who stood 5 feet, 9 inches tall and weighed 170 pounds, became the Eagles' number one starting pitcher, while 37-year-old submarine pitcher Will Jackman, a hulking 6-foot, 3-inch righty, was the other regular starter after Radcliffe left. The Negro National League played a split-season schedule in 1935, designed to produce two half-season winners who could square off in a playoff. When the first half ended on July 5 the Eagles were still at .500, 15–15, which left them in fourth place in the eight-team league. They were respectable, but not close to the playoffs.

The Eagles finished strongly in the first half, winning three out of four in Chicago, but stumbled at the beginning of the second half. After losing a doubleheader to the Philadelphia Stars in Philadelphia on July 6, the Brooklyn club split two games with the Stars the next day at Ebbets. The landlord Dodgers were on an extended road trip, so the Eagles had Ebbets Field to themselves for the whole month until the July 27–28 weekend. The potential "home park advantage" did not kick in, though — they won only three of the seven games played there during the period. Toward the end of the home stand a New York black weekly, the *Amsterdam News*, noted the Eagles "are still finding their first season of Negro National League baseball an uphill fight."[24] The uphill road never leveled off, and the Eagles sank in the second half standings, to sixth place with a 13–16 record. The team played league opponents 26 times at Ebbets Field, including some postseason exhibitions, winning exactly half.

Since almost all coverage of Negro League games was in the weekly black newspapers, which did not always carry box scores, team and individual statistics were not rigorously kept. But recent research has captured about 70 percent of the Eagles' games against league opponents, and shows them to have been a good-hitting club with pitching problems. These studies give the Eagles a .274 batting average, averaging nearly five runs per game. Williams (.366), Perez (.353), catcher-infielder Tex Burnett (.309), and Giles (.301) led the club in batting average. On the mound, though, past Day's 7–3 record and 2.66 ERA, things declined. No other pitcher had an ERA under 4.00, and the club ERA was 4.93.[25]

The majority of Negro League games were scheduled on weekends, often as doubleheaders, to attract maximum crowds. The weekdays were devoted to traveling between league cities for games against nonleague opponents to further enhance teams' revenues. These games, against local semiprofessional or amateur teams who usually drew well at the gate when hosting the black clubs and were more or less on the team bus route to the next league city, were the stuff of the "barnstorming" trips so well associated with the Negro Leagues. Barnstorming was not without its hazards. As Lew Zeidler of the *Brooklyn* Daily *Eagle* reported in his "Just Below the Majors" column, after an Olean, New York contest:

> They [the Eagles] finished this game, and without so much as a quick shower piled into the team bus, anxious to drive through to New York during the night so they might get a night's sleep before engaging the N.Y. Cubans on Saturday night. But about 50 miles south of Buffalo one of the pistons in the bus' motor shot its way right out of the cylinder head and the bus rolled to a stop.[26]

The bus was going to be out of action for at least a couple of days, according to the mechanic who was found to take a look at it shortly after sunup. This sent traveling secretary Eric Illidge out on a hunt for cars to carry the team more than 300 miles back home. "He rounded up three and commandeered them for the trip, paying almost as much for their hire as the team received in guarantees that night."[27] That was only a passing setback, though. The chronic problem was not a closely guarded secret — the Eagles were steadily losing money in Brooklyn due to circumstances beyond their control. The biggest cause was simply too much local competition, magnified by the possibility their own league failed to give them the protection they were due as members.

New York City was a hot bed of professional and semipro baseball and Brooklyn was its hottest borough. In 1935, in addition to the Eagles and Cubans in the Negro National League, there were the three teams in the white majors, the Dodger, Yankees, and Giants, plus the New York Black Yankees, an independent squad of Negro League ability. Then, there were the many semipro teams. Three of the most powerful, the Bay Parkways and Bay Ridge in Brooklyn, and the Bushwicks on the Brooklyn-Queens borough boundary, played their home games within six miles of Ebbets Field, often at the same time as the black or white home team there. This did not seem to affect the well-established Dodgers — their average attendance of 6,111 in 1935 was fourth best in their National League and seventh best among all 16 white major league teams.

The competition was, however, murdering the Eagles at the box office. Although the team was slaughtered in its home opener by the Grays, it soon rebounded to be competitive on the field. The enduring problem was highlighted during the opener when the much-ballyhooed game drew fewer than 3,000 fans. Things never got better, as Effa Manley recounted: "It was all downhill for us through the remainder of that season. The Eagles did reasonably well on the road, but our homestand campaign was a dismal flop, from a box office point of view."[28] By late August, Abe Manley was assuring black newspaper readership that the Eagles would be back in 1936: "When I started the Eagles last spring I did so with the idea of building for the future. Some of my contemporaries in the city operated for fifteen years before their clubs won seventy-five percent of their games or even showed a profit. I'm not expecting the world after one full season."[29] However, the fact he had to address the club's future in Brooklyn shows that the subject was on people's minds.

The semipro competition in the Brooklyn area was a very real problem. The clubs played doubleheaders every Sunday on their home fields, which they either owned or had longstanding permission to use. Their baseball was serious stuff— there were a number of former white major and minor leaguers in their ranks, as well as college boys either passing up the per-game money to keep their amateur status intact or playing under assumed names. Since home games were the rule on Sundays, the Brooklyn semipro clubs rarely played each other. Opponents came from Long Island, Pennsylvania, and New Jersey, and the bearded, long-haired House of David teams based in Michigan paid frequent calls as well. But many of their opponents were black clubs, either longtime independents such as the Black Yankees and the Brooklyn Royal Giants or Negro League dropouts like the Bacharach Giants and Baltimore Black Sox. There was no logical reason for them not to play the semipros — the Brooklyn and Queens teams often drew in the thousands of fans on Sundays. The Bushwicks had their own park and sometimes drew more than 10,000.

But the prominent semipro clubs like the Bushwicks also invited in Negro National League teams. Nat Strong had died of a heart attack in April of 1935, but his ghost lingered on in the very real form of the Bushwicks and the lucrative games at their stadium. Strong had been a partner in the team with Max Rosner and had enforced his usual policy at the team's Dexter Park of only giving a flat guarantee, not a percentage of the gate, to visiting clubs. This did not sit well with the Negro League clubs, who, maintaining a fully-salaried operation, wanted a potentially bigger slice of the attendance pie or a percentage of the gate.

Rosner changed that. In early June he and the NNL announced an agreement that invited the league teams to Dexter on better terms. The Pittsburgh Crawfords immediately scheduled a game for June 7, and although they were rained out, they returned for a Sunday doubleheader June 16. The Homestead Grays moved in for two the following Sunday. By the end of the season, only two teams in the NNL had not played the Bushwicks, the Chicago American Giants and the Brooklyn Eagles.

The news story announcing the agreement between Rosner and the league stated that "it is being conceded that Abe Manley will see that the Eagles get their share of the applause out on Long Island."[30] An Eagles–Bushwicks matchup was, in fact, advertised for lucrative July 4, but when the holiday came, Dexter Park was occupied by a Black Yankees–Cubans doubleheader. Manley's and Rosner's teams do not appear to have played each other in 1935. *New York Age* sportswriter Lewis Dial wrote that the arrangement was "tough on the Brooklyn investment which seems to have no territorial rights despite the fact that [it] is duly franchised and protected by the league constitution."[31]

Since at first the games of the other NNL teams in Brooklyn were scheduled when the Eagles were not at home, the additional games may have diluted the demand for Negro League ball, but at least there was no head-to-head competition. This did not last, however, either because with so many teams conflicts were unavoidable, or because the other black teams did not care if they were hurting the Manley's team. On the Eagle's last league home date of the season, September 1, both the Elite Giants and the Cubans played semipro teams in direct competition with a doubleheader at Ebbets Field against Newark. On September 15, when the Eagles were hosting a doubleheader against a team of minor league all-stars, Philadelphia was playing the Bushwicks (before 12,000 fans), Newark was at Bay Ridge, and the Elite Giants were playing the Bay Parkways.

Abe Manley may have told the press in August that the Eagles would be back in 1936, but he did not necessarily say where. According to Effa's memoir, the couple decided to abandon Brooklyn, despite their amicable relations with the Dodgers, long before the 1935 season ended.[32] They found a new home in Newark by buying out Charles Tyler, a restaurateur who owned the Negro League Dodgers, a perennial second-division club, and merged the two squads. They made a deal with the New York Yankees similar to the one they had with Brooklyn: to use Ruppert Stadium, home of the minor league Newark Bears, for a percentage of the gate, with the Manleys also picking up game-day expenses.

The couple remained active in the Negro National League until selling out in 1949, when Negro League ball was on the decline, coming back to Ebbets Field for an occasional game, as did other Negro League teams. In 1945, they sponsored a three-game series there pitting Negro League all-stars against a team of major leaguers getting in shape for a Far East tour. Abe Manley died in 1952, but his younger wife lived until 1981. By that time, the lost Negro Leagues had been rediscovered by baseball historians. As one of the very few black executives still living, she was much in demand for interviews and in turn, she pushed for belated recognition of the black leagues, including the induction of its stars into the Baseball Hall of Fame. Effa herself was elected as an executive in 2006, becoming the only female member of the Hall.

The two Negro Leagues, the National and the American, emerged from World War II financially thriving and with the seeming potential to remain strong. The 1945 preseason, however, brought an announcement of competition from a third major league, the United States League (USL). Although events were soon to prove otherwise, in January 1945 the founders of the USL could not be criticized for believing there was a place for them in black baseball. The birth of the league also brought Negro League ball back to Ebbets Field on a regular, and perhaps conspiratorial, basis.

Abe and Effa Manley, the owners of the Eagles. Effa is the only woman to date who has been elected to the National Baseball Hall of Fame (courtesy NoirTech Research).

Several of the league's founders certainly believed they deserved a place in the Negro Leagues. They had been there previously, but had been forced out by financial setbacks or internal politics, or both. Even the president of the new league, Cleveland attorney John Shackelford, was a former Negro League player, who had previously lost out in a bid to become American League president. But the primary founder of the USL, William A. "Gus" Greenlee of Pittsburgh, had at one time been such an integral part of Negro League ball, and had been working so hard, but unsuccessfully, to get back in, that it was difficult not to think of the enterprise as, at least in part, a weapon of revenge.

Greenlee had led a fascinating life. Emigrating from North Carolina to Pittsburgh on a freight car in 1916, he had, like Barron Wilkins, made his money providing people with what they wanted, not necessarily what the law and society said they ought to have. Greenlee began by running illegal booze in the trunk of his taxicab. Then, like Manley and Pompez, he became a numbers banker. Gus parlayed his business success into a series of nightclubs, some closed by police for late-night goings on. His last, the Crawford Grille on Wylie Avenue, the main street of the city's black community, became the hottest black spot in town, featuring famous musicians and having tables always available for business and political wheeling and dealing. In 1932, Greenlee purchased a locally successful semipro team, the Crawfords. Spending as if he had not heard there was a Depression going on, he took advantage of this extremely weak period in organized black baseball to stock his team with local new talent, i.e., the stars of other teams. Greenlee was the driving force behind the reestablishment of the Negro National League in 1933, and his bulked-up Crawfords were a force to be reckoned with. He even stopped being a tenant of white teams and city parks by building his own ballpark, Greenlee Field, in 1934.

But Gus could not make money appear out of thin air, any more than could the other black owners (or many of the white ones, for that matter), in the troubled '30s. The team was supported by his profits from substantial numbers revenue. The overall take from bettors, before payoffs, was estimated at around $25,000 a day for him and his partner, William "Woogie" Harris.[33] But as competition for bettors' dollars grew, Greenlee suffered other financial setbacks (including being pursued by the IRS for unpaid taxes), and Greenlee Field itself proved to be a money-losing proposition. Greenlee Field shut down and was demolished for a housing project and the Crawfords were sold. Gus lost his team and his position as the power of the NNL. He twice petitioned the league to let him back in, but he was turned down each time. The stated reason was the fear that Greenlee's still festering financial problems would infect the league's economics, but some owners that Gus had manhandled the first time were still around, particularly his longtime Pittsburgh rival, Cumberland Posey.

The USL began play with six franchises in Pittsburgh (Greenlee's Crawfords, of course), Chicago, Detroit, Toledo, Philadelphia, and —*Brooklyn*. Some early juggling of teams and owners (an indication of the precariousness of the whole enterprise) saw prospective teams in St. Louis and Atlanta fail to materialize and Toledo partly fill the resulting gap. Then, the owners of what was supposed to be the Philadelphia franchise (which, due to its inability to find a suitable park in its supposed home city, was to play in the minor league park in Harrisburg), split. One owner, Joseph Hall, took a team to Brooklyn, with a deal for his Brooklyn Brown Dodgers to play in Ebbets Field while his former partner, Irving Mazzer, continued on in Philadelphia/Harrisburg, giving the USL its desired six teams.

Hall and the first version of the Brown Dodgers ran out of money, and lost their franchise in July, as did Mazzer, in Pennsylvania. The Brown Dodgers were revitalized by Webster McDonald, a well-known Negro League pitcher and manager. The Dodgers were one of four teams to finish both the 1945 season and the final campaign in 1946, as the springtime high hopes for the new league again faded. It has to be said to the credit of Greenlee, Shackelford, and the other owners and league officials who strived to keep the USL alive that they left no stone unturned. Most innovative was the mass player acquisition made in June 1946 by Brown Dodger owner George Armstrong, a Pittsburgh businessman Greenlee had brought in to finance the team after Hall's ownership collapsed. Armstrong, with help from Greenlee, bought the entire 14-man roster of the St. Louis Giants, a semi-pro team that included highly-regarded young righthanded pitcher Herbert "Doc" Bracken, and turned them into Brown Dodgers.

Black baseball historian Neil Lanctot accurately summarizes the short life of the USL: "Greenlee's ambitious plans failed to materialize, however, as the actual operation of the USL proved to be anticlimactic. As anticipated, the level of play was mediocre, featuring only a few established players. Moreover, promotions in major league ball parks drew poorly, and league games were soon being scheduled in smaller venues."[34]

Overall, the United States League was doomed to fail. The organizers, if they had been blessed with higher levels of self-realization, might have figured out that their desire to get back into major league ball, and possibly extract some revenge along the way, were driving them past the point of financial prudence. But even so they were going to face a bigger problem, one that no one could see coming as spring arrived in 1945. Professional baseball was on the verge of integrating for the first time since the 1880s, and the slowly growing presence of black players on heretofore white teams, beginning in 1946, would quickly draw the best talent and the hearts of the black fans away from the Negro Leagues. The Negro National League was history by the beginning of the 1949 season. The Negro American League stumbled along, with fewer and fewer top-quality players and less and less attention from the baseball world, until it winked out in 1960.

But the United States League has a place in history, and that place was on Montague Street in Brooklyn where the Dodgers offices were located. There, on May 7, 1945, Branch Rickey the Dodger president, and Shackelford, the USL president, held a press conference to announce Rickey was supporting the USL. The arrangement included renting Ebbets Field to the Brown Dodgers, which Rickey acknowledged would help both sides of the deal by bringing more business to Ebbets. But in addition to that self-interested show of support, Rickey went much farther. He voiced "an interest in Negro baseball on an organized basis. Both Rickey and Shackelford expressed the hope that by the end of the 1946 season the league will be so well organized that it will be recognized by the National Association of Professional Baseball Clubs [white major league baseball, in other words]."[35]

Rickey dwelled repeatedly on the need for good organization, in the process denigrating the two existing Negro Leagues for their uneven schedules, lack of control over players jumping contracts, and their dependence on barnstorming, characterizing them as "no leagues at all."[36] Effa Manley was one of only two executives of the existing leagues to attend (Shackelford said the American and National officers had been invited, but had not responded). She tried mightily to corner Rickey about his attitude toward the existing leagues, but, playing on his field, just served as his foil to extol the virtues of the USL compared to the NNL and ANL.[37]

Rickey had been a light-hitting catcher and manager of some mostly mediocre teams in St. Louis early in the century. His .239 lifetime batting average and .473 managerial winning percentage were anything but Hall of Fame material. But as an executive, he made two enormous contributions to the progress of professional baseball, either of which could have been the basis for his 1967 election to the Hall. As general manager of the St.

Louis Cardinals in the 1920s, he developed the minor league farm system. And as Brooklyn Dodger president in 1946, of course, Rickey engineered the quantum leap of introducing Jackie Robinson to white professional ball, breaking a "color line" that had been firmly in place since before the turn of the century.

Even though the farm system soon became the organizing principle of professional baseball, Rickey had made some strong enemies by introducing it, not least the longtime major league commissioner, Kenesaw Mountain Landis. But in backing the USL, he antagonized even more people. The black sporting press was suspicious, to say the least. At the press conference, Rickey, not at all willing to stick his neck out regarding integration, although he had been thinking about it since at least 1943, was equivocal about the possibility of USL players getting into the white majors. This led Fay Young, sports columnist of the black *Chicago Defender*, to wonder if "Rickey, playing the role of a savior for Negro baseball, is really wearing the black hood of one who seeks to form or sponsor a Negro organization in order to stave off the clamor of the white and Negro fans to have Negroes integrated into the major leagues."[38]

Rickey's fellow major league owner, Clark Griffith of the Washington Senators, whose tenants, the Homestead Grays of the NNL, filled both his Griffith Stadium and the Senators' bank account with big crowds, accused Rickey of trying to become a "dictator" of black baseball, intent on destroying the existing leagues.[39] The owners of the existing leagues, while not as hostile as Mrs. Manley, kept Rickey and the USL at arms' length. About the only well-known ally he had was Gus Greenlee, an odd pairing with Rickey, the tee totaling, rock-solid Methodist.

Rickey kept a low profile throughout this feuding, how low practically no one else knew. He had Dodger scouts fan out quietly to observe Negro League players, ostensibly for berths on the Brown Dodgers. One scout, Clyde Sukeforth, dispatched to Chicago to check out Kansas City Monarch shortstop Jackie Robinson, figured it out, though: "'Now Clyde,' the old man went on, 'if you like this fellow's arm, bring him in. And if his schedule won't permit it, if he can't come in, then make an appointment for me and I'll go out there.' Mr. Rickey go out there? To see if some guy named Robinson was good enough to play shortstop for the Brooklyn Brown Bombers [*sic*]? Well, I'm not the smartest guy in the world, but I said to myself, *this could be the real thing*."[40]

It was for real, more real than Rickey's supposed interest in the United States League, which became the first of the black leagues to go under in the flood tide of support by black fans for the newly integrated majors. Jackie Robinson played for the Dodgers' Montreal Royals farm team in 1946 and started at first base for the Dodgers themselves in 1947, on April 15 at Ebbets Field. His appearance in the field in the top of the first inning immediately consigned all previous black baseball at Ebbets Field to history, but as stepping stones to that day, not to irrelevancy.

Notes

1. Nelson Johnson, *Boardwalk Empire: The Birth, High Times and Corruption of Atlantic City* (Medford, N.J.: Plexus, 2010), 39.
2. *Boyd's Atlantic City Directory, 1917–18* (Philadelphia: C.E. Howe, 1918) 412; *Boyd's Atlantic City Directory 1919–20* (Philadelphia: C.E. Howe, 1920), 463.

3. Robert Peterson, *Only the Ball Was White: A History of Legendary Black Players and All-Black Professional Teams* (Englewood Cliffs, N.J.: Prentice-Hall, 1970; reprint, New York: McGraw-Hill, 1984), 67 (page citation is to the reprint edition).

4. James A. Riley, *The Biographical Encyclopedia of the Negro Baseball Leagues* (New York: Carroll & Graf, 1994), 749.

5. "Redding and Williams Are Idolized by Adoring Fans," *New York Age*, August 7, 1920.

6. "Bacharach Giants on Their Way Home," *New York Age*, April 17, 1920.

7. Riley, 497.

8. "Lincoln Giants to Play Bacharachs Next Sunday," *New York Age*, July 10, 1920.

9. "Redding Trims Williams," *The Chicago Defender*, July 17, 1920.

10. "Redding and Williams Are Idolized by Adoring Fans," *New York Age*, August 7, 1920; Philip Lowry, *Green Cathedrals: The Ultimate Celebration of All Major League and Negro League Ballparks* (New York: Walker, 2006), 39.

11. "Redding Stages 'Iron Man' Stunt," *Brooklyn Daily Eagle*, August 30, 1920.

12. "Bacharachs Revel in Hits and Runs," *Brooklyn Daily Eagle*, August 1, 1921.

13. "Bacharachs and Chicago Giants Play Pennant Deciding Games," *New York Age*, October 1, 1921.

14. "American Giants Take Series Off Bacharachs," *New York Age*, October 22, 1921.

15. Effa Manley and Leon Hebert Hardwick, *Negro Baseball ... Before Integration*, ed. Robert Cvornyek (Haworth, N.J.: St. Johann, 2006), 41.

16. Ibid., 42.

17. Ibid., 47.

18. "Just Below the Majors," *Brooklyn Daily Eagle*, August 25, 1935.

19. "The Sports Dial," *New York Age*, June 1, 1935.

20. John Holway, *Voices from the Great Black Baseball Leagues* (New York: DiCapo, 1992), 320.

21. John Holway, *Black Diamonds: Life in the Negro Leagues from the Men Who Lived It* (Westport, Ct.: Meckler, 1989), 65.

22. Ibid., 66.

23. Negro League Researchers & Authors Group (NLRAG), Larry Lester, Richard Clark, and Lawrence Hogan, directors.

24. "Eagles Seeking to Cop Pennant," *New York Amsterdam News*, July 20, 1935.

25. Negro League Researchers & Authors Group.

26. "Just Below the Majors," *Brooklyn Daily Eagle*, August 28, 1935.

27. Ibid.

28. Manley and Hardwick, 46.

29. "Manley Plans to Continue at Ebbets Field," *New York Amsterdam News*, August 25, 1935.

30. "Rosner Effects Combine with Negro Teams," *New York Amsterdam News*, June 8, 1935.

31. "The Sports Dial," *New York Age*, June 22, 1935.

32. Manley and Hardwick, 47.

33. Rob Ruck, *Sandlot Seasons: Sport in Black Pittsburgh* (Urbana: University of Illinois Press, 1987), 145.

34. Neil Lanctot, *Negro League Baseball: The Rise and Ruin of a Black Institution* (Philadelphia: University of Pennsylvania Press, 2004), 268.

35. "Negro Leagues with Brooklyn Club Is Set Up," *New York Herald-Tribune*, May 8, 1945.

36. "Rickey Reveals Formation of Negro League," *Washington Post*, May 8, 1945.

37. Manley and Hardwick, 69–71; "Rickey's Ultimatum: Join U.S. League or Else," *Pittsburgh Courier*, May 12, 1945.

38. "Through the Years," *Chicago Defender*, May 26, 1945.

39. "Griffin Attacks Rickey," *New York Times*, May 16, 1945.

40. Donald Honig, *Baseball: When the Grass Was Real* (New York: Coward, McCann and Geoghegan, 1975), 185.

Ebbets Field
Sporting Venue and Community Center
Paul G. Zinn

Part of Brooklyn's long-time leadership role in baseball included building ballparks such as Union Grounds (1862) and Capitoline Grounds (1864), which were among the first enclosed playing fields. However, building such facilities cost money, in amounts owners then and since planned to recapture (and then some) from admission charges. It probably did not take long for early ballpark owners to realize no matter how many baseball games were played in their new buildings, the facilities sat empty more often than not. This inevitably led to using facilities built for baseball for other revenue generating events, a trend that has continued to this day.[1]

It was no surprise, therefore, that a baseball executive as astute and financially challenged as Charles Ebbets, used his new ballpark to host a wide range of revenue generating events. This was hardly a new concept for the Dodgers' headman since Washington Park had been a venue for Brooklyn high school football games. Although making Ebbets Field available for additional events was primarily driven by the need for revenue, Charles Ebbets did not ignore his community responsibilities. In fact, it appears the first non–Dodger event at the park was a field day for orphans, sponsored by the Brooklyn Elks. Shortly thereafter, over 20,000 Brooklyn and Queens public school students were guests of the *Brooklyn Daily Eagle* and witnessed championship baseball games and relay races. In reporting on the event, which would take place at least four times in the next five years, the paper noted the ballpark "had been donated for the occasion."[2]

This was quickly followed by the first attempt to generate revenue from something other than a Dodger game. During July and August of 1913, there was a series of athletic meets, which involved "two of the strongest tug-of-war teams in the country" and races between "the fastest runners in the world." Although scheduling a baseball game between the Brooklyn Union Gas Company and their counterparts from Philadelphia boosted attendance at the second meet, by the third and final installment on August 9, "only a handful of spectators" were in attendance. Another significant 1913 event was a baseball game between Harvard and Yale, who had split the first two games of a best of three championship series. Before a crowd of 15,000, the Crimson triumphed, 6–5. As the wide range of early 1913 events suggests, Dodger ownership explored many possible options, a trend that would continue.[3]

Among the options that were tried or at least considered were lacrosse and tennis to name a few, but the three major nonbaseball revenue producing sports at Ebbets Field were boxing, football, and soccer. Boxing was introduced with great success by promoter

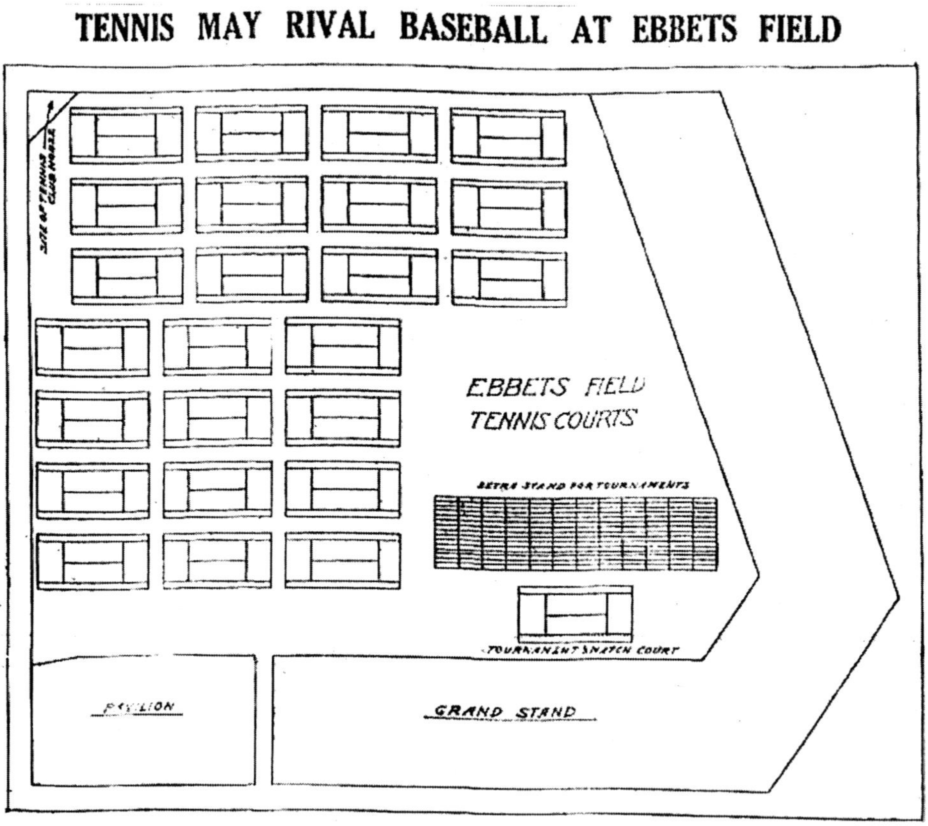

TENNIS MAY RIVAL BASEBALL AT EBBETS FIELD

Many alternative uses were considered for Ebbets Field, but tennis was one that apparently never got off the drawing board (*Brooklyn Daily Eagle*, January 13, 1918).

Johnny Weismantel on Decoration Day in 1915. Coming over from the Broadway Sporting Club, Weismantel hosted an enticing five-bout card that drew 15,000 spectators and produced over $12,000 in ticket sales. The ring was "pitched" near home plate with ringside seats on the field and additional capacity in the grandstand. The crowd featured "many well known Brooklynites," as well as "a score of big politicians from all the boroughs," and well-known labor leader Samuel Gompers. While the initial boxing event was an afternoon affair, night cards quickly became the norm at Ebbets Field, allowing for multiple uses of the park on the same day. Five of the remaining 1915 boxing cards took place following a Dodger afternoon game. Although attendance never reached the opening day mark of 15,000, boxing was clearly popular, but it was not long before legal issues got in the way.[4]

The Frawley Act had legalized boxing in New York in 1911, but in 1917 it was repealed, bringing the sport to a grinding halt in New York. After a three-year hiatus, Senator James J. Walker got a new law through the legislature that again legalized boxing in the state. By forcing nearly everyone associated with boxing to be licensed, the bill centralized the sport and still governs it today. New York was already a hotbed of boxing talent, and Walker's bill allowed local fighters and their fights to stay at home.[5]

As with the 1919 law legalizing Sunday baseball, Charles Ebbets and the McKeevers also took advantage of the new boxing legislation. Working with Jimmy O'Connor, a highly regarded promoter, the first card was scheduled for May 30, 1921, almost exactly six years after the first bouts at Ebbets Field. Unfortunately, the event did not go well, and 7,000 unsatisfied fans booed a card that included "12 long, weary rounds" of stalling in one bout and "a high fancy diving exhibition" in another. To make matters worse, shortly thereafter the boxing license of the Ebbets-McKeever Exhibition Company was suspended for discourteous treatment of a commission representative and irregularities with tickets.[6]

Jim O'Connor was one of a number of boxing impresarios who saw Ebbets Field as an attractive boxing venue (*Brooklyn Daily Eagle*, January 27, 1921).

After these problems, Charles Ebbets and Ed McKeever decided not to mix the management of boxing and baseball. While still willing to see Ebbets Field host fights, the Dodger owners believed it would only be profitable on a championship scale, and did not think they had the expertise to put on these kinds of programs. There was also concern that sponsoring "minor" contests had, in Edward McKeever's words, "lowered the dignity, so to speak, of Ebbets Field, which bears the same relation to Brooklyn as the Academy of Music does to arts and sciences." The trio, therefore, turned things over to the International Sporting Club, which wanted to sponsor championship bouts at the Brooklyn ballpark. The I.S.C. came in with a bang on July 25, 1921, as Peter Herman took back the bantamweight title he had previously lost to Joe Lynch the prior year, looking like "pretty nearly a perfect boxing machine." Twenty thousand spectators showed up, but there were still problems, including rumors of a "wild riot and disorder," exacerbated by the lack of a police presence. Supposedly, the reports were exaggerated, but Ed McKeever said that, at least temporarily, future title bouts would be held during the afternoon, if that were even possible since the I.S.C.'s license had been temporarily suspended, "pending" an investigation. The result was the I.S.C. returned its boxing license to the commission and refused to take part in the review, noting it would hold its fights on private grounds going forward.[7]

In spite of reservations about mixing boxing and baseball management, the Ebbets-McKeever Exhibition Company was back at it in 1922 with David Driscoll as its "matchmaker." There were some major bouts at Ebbets Field that year. On May 13, 1922, on the way to his historic 1923 heavyweight championship fight with Jack Dempsey, Luis Firpo knocked out Jack Herman in the fifth round. Then in August, before what was reportedly the largest boxing crowd yet at Ebbets Field to date, Frankie Genaro won a decision over Pancho Villa, an excellent Asian fighter, after "10 furious rounds of boxing." A week later, Harry Wills, knocked out "Tut" Jackson in the third round. Wills was a veteran heavyweight also looking for a shot at Dempsey for the title, but a scheduled bout for the crown was cancelled by the Governor of New York because of fear of race riots. Although the Willis–Jackson match was not very competitive, Dave Driscoll was praised by Thomas Rice because he "has done a lot to put Brooklyn in the limelight of boxing and to bring it to the fore for the most important matches by having had almost uniform success in producing plenty of action in his shows."[8]

Boxing was absent at Ebbets Field for the next few years but came back with a vengeance in 1926, with perhaps the biggest bout the park ever hosted, Jack Delaney vs. Paul Berlenbach. On the night of July 16, an estimated 42,000 spectators crammed into the park, the largest crowd to attend any event at Ebbets Field to date. Supposedly, another 25,000 were turned away. The record attendance may have been facilitated by a change in the layout. Photos in the *Brooklyn Daily Eagle* indicate the ring was now located in short center field, allowing for temporary seats to be placed throughout the rest of the infield and outfield. The expanded on-field accommodations led to sightline issues for those in the more expensive box seats, who could not see when those on the field stood up. The crowd was full of celebrities, including New York City Mayor Jimmy Walker, the governors of New Jersey and Maryland, not to mention Morgans, Rockefellers and Astors, as well as Babe Ruth. The huge crowd saw Delaney easily win the light heavyweight title from Berlenbach. The *Eagle* proclaimed it was "a gala night for this boro. Many who had imagined that Brooklyn was a village or a town and not the biggest boro of the five in Greater New York were astounded at its magnitude." Those seeking a bleacher seat, the least expensive ticket at $3, began arriving at 6:45 A.M., even though the gates did not open until 4:10 P.M. A ringside or box seat was priced at $27.50 and was being scalped for $100. It was an impressive performance on any scale, the *Eagle* reporting the attendance was the seventh largest in boxing history, and the gross receipts of almost $462,000 trailed only two of Jack Dempsey's heavyweight fights for the largest purse in history.[9]

The Delaney–Berlenbach bout was arranged by Humbert Fugazy, who along with David Driscoll, formed the Brooklyn Exhibition Company, which was organizing a two-pronged effort to bring football and boxing to Ebbets Field. In addition, an owner of the Brooklyn Horsemen Football Team, which also played at Ebbets Field, Fugazy put on bouts throughout the 1920s and early 30s. Fugazy was a visionary for the attendance potential of outdoor fights, and he was correct as boxing at Ebbets Field continued to draw large crowds. 1926 was a breakout year with the record-setting July crowd of 42,000 followed by another 35,000 in October that saw Jack Sharkey defeat Harry Wills.[10]

Fugazy also brought some unique characters to Ebbets Field, including Monte Munn, a Nebraska legislator who fought George Godfrey in 1927. Described as a "slow, clumsy" fighter that "'telegraphs' his blows like an expert Western Union operator," Munn had an impressive record against unimpressive competition. Tired of criticism of his accomplishments, Munn was stepping up in class against Godfrey, who finished his career with a 97–20–3 record. The referee called off the bout in the fourth round, as Munn was "hopelessly outclassed." Fugazy was also an advocate of Roberto Roberti, an Italian heavyweight,

Nebraska legislator Monte Munn's attempt to establish his boxing credentials fell flat in a 1927 Ebbets Field bout against George Godfrey (*Brooklyn Daily Eagle*, September 15, 1927. Copyright unknown).

who fought numerous times at Ebbets Field and had visions of becoming a champion. Alas, it was not to be.[11]

Boxing continued to be popular at the Dodgers' home through the end of the decade. Another intriguing Ebbets Field fighter was featherweight Kid Chocolate, who made his debut at the Brooklyn ballpark on July 10, 1929, with an easy decision over Ignacio Fernandez in front of 15,000 spectators. Chocolate began boxing as a newspaper boy in his native Havana "to defend his sales turf" and did not suffer his first defeat until 1930, losing to Jackie "Kid" Berg in front of 40,000 at the Polo Grounds. Chocolate held both world featherweight and junior lightweight titles during his career. One of Kid Chocolate's major competitors was Brooklyn product Tony Canzoneri, who defeated the Cuban pugilist at least twice. In the early 1930s, Canzoneri was "considered the best fighter, pound-for-pound, in the world." His first bout at Ebbets Field was on August 17, 1927, when he knocked out Pete Samiento before 25,000. Canzoneri is one of only three boxers to hold three different divisional championships: featherweight, lightweight, and junior welterweight. The Canzoneri fight in 1927 was held on a Wednesday, which was becoming a pattern at Ebbets Field. Most likely because of the large number of venues in the New York metropolitan area, the State Athletic Commission began assigning one day of the week to each facility, with Wednesday being the day or night for boxing at Ebbets Field (Thursday was the rain date).[12]

Although fights continued at Ebbets Field in the 1930s, they became less frequent and by 1936 had tapered off altogether, which had to be at some level an effect of the

Great Depression. Finally in 1941, Chick Meehan, Brooklyn Boxing Association President, brought the sport back. Tami Mauriello, a middleweight, defeated Steve Mamakos in a technical knockout, despite dislocating two fingers on his right hand. Meehan's satisfaction with the attendance of 8,000 and a gate of $12,000 showed how far expectations had fallen. Fights continued in 1941 but then did not resume again until after World War II. In 1946, promoter Bill Johnston of the Zenith Sporting Club tried to bring the sport back to Ebbets Field in a big way, hoping it would "emerge as a powerful rival" to Madison Square Garden. Although Johnston was hoping for a gate in the $50,000 range at the first fight in June, he had to settle for $18,000 from 8,500 fans, who filled about one-third of the available 26,000 seats.[13]

Johnston's efforts lasted only one year and, in 1947, Andy Niederreiter of Brooklyn Fights, Inc., was promoting bouts at Ebbets Field. Mauriello, who had fought so heroically in 1941, was featured on what turned out to be the last two cards at Ebbets Field. He first fought and defeated Jimmy Carollo in May before 11,000, and then took on Gus Lesnevich in late July as part of a charity event, with the proceeds going to the Runyon Memorial Cancer Fund. The latter was billed as "Brooklyn's greatest boxing carnival in many years," and Lesnevich won in a "grueling 10-round victory." There were 21,955 in attendance, generating a gate of $102,955, and afterward, Ben Gould of the *Brooklyn Eagle* confirmed "this was Brooklyn's greatest boxing carnival since July 22, 1931, when Jack Sharkey and Mickey Walker attracted 33,156 fans and a gate of $238,831." Getting caught up in the moment, Gould went on to claim "the guy who kept chirping that 'Brooklyn can't draw big fight crowds' held his peace." Unfortunately, the "guy" would be proven correct as this was the last big bout ever held at Ebbets Field.[14]

The success of boxing at Ebbets Field in the 1920s was a reflection of the popularity of sports and entertainment throughout the decade known as the "Roaring Twenties." This period reflected the new energy of the post-war era, and the end of the more conservative norms of the late 19th and early 20th centuries. The popularity of new pastimes, combined with the availability of new and larger venues, led to entertainment innovations such as opera at Ebbets Field. Early in July of 1925, it was announced there would be free performances of three operas at the Brooklyn ballpark, beginning with *Aida* on August 1. Sponsored by the Mayor's Committee on Music, the initial performance would be followed by *Cavalleria Rusticana* and *Pagliacci* on August 5, with *Faust* as the closing event on the 8th. Since admission was free, applicants were limited to two tickets to one performance.[15]

Significant preparations went into the event as Director Josiah Zuro held nine auditions (both indoor and outdoor) for over 100 singers before casting the parts. While the Dodgers would be on the road during the performances, rehearsals at the ballpark began during the end of a home stand, so that "the sharp crack of the Robins bats" was mingled with "the sad measures of *Aida's* hymn of farewell." In order to make the experience more accessible to the general public, it was announced *Faust* would be performed in English. After the Dodgers' last game of that home stand on July 26, a massive stage was erected behind second base with a "tented city" behind it for dressing rooms and other support areas.[16]

With everything in place, the only remaining challenge was the weather, which cooperated each night, particularly for the opening when *Aida* was performed under a "clear sky and soaring moon." Over 25,000 witnessed the spectacle, which featured a cast of 400-plus elephants, horses, and camels. The crowds grew on each of the next two evenings with 40,000 on hand for the finale of *Faust*. According to police estimates, another 30,000 were turned away.[17]

Even more out of the ordinary was an event the following spring — the wedding of a couple picked as "Mr. & Mrs. Brooklyn." Sponsored as a fundraiser by the Young Folks' League of United Israel Zion Hospital, John Iverson and Ella Codner (both orphans) were chosen from 350 couples vying for the honor. Ticket sales for the ceremony benefited the hospital, and the event got some unexpected publicity when the Rev. Horace Leavitt of Union Church of Bay Ridge refused to officiate, calling it a "Roman holiday." Fortunately the Rev. Thomas Lawler of Grace Reformed Episcopal Church stepped in, and the wedding or show could go on. Although 17,000 tickets were sold, only 3,000 "braved the cold" to attend the ceremony on Saturday, June 5, 1926, which did not start until 10:15 P.M. Keeping with the spirit of the night, Mr. and Mrs. Steve McKeever served as best man and matron of honor, heading an *Aida*-like cast of 100 bridesmaids and an equal number of ushers. Along with 25 flower girls and pages and one ring bearer, the "cast" processed from dugouts usually inhabited by ballplayers to a $1,500 altar placed over second base.[18]

While boxing certainly had its moments at Ebbets Field, it was football — at three different levels — that was far and away the most popular sport after Dodger baseball. The Brooklyn ballpark hosted longtime and well-attended high school football rivalries and St. John's and Manhattan collegiate contests, as well as a few "big-time" matchups. In addition, the pro football Brooklyn Dodgers played there for 19 years, many of them at the National Football League level. Football was a different sport in the early 20th century, and the amateur game was extremely well liked. "New York City once was the place to play college football," wrote David Maraniss in *When Pride Still Mattered*, noting that

In 1917, 30 years before Jackie Robinson, Rutgers All-American Paul Robeson led his school to a 14–0 upset win over the undefeated and unscored upon Newport Naval Reserve (courtesy Rutgers University Special Collections and Archives).

Fordham, Columbia, and New York University all played the best competition at the Polo Grounds and Yankee Stadium. Although Ebbets Field never obtained that stature, it certainly was not left out of the equation, even hosting an Army–Notre Dame contest in 1923, considered at the time to be a major rivalry.[19]

Unlike high school football, it took a while for Ebbets Field to schedule its first college contest. In the end, however, it was a matchup worth waiting for—a game between the undefeated and unscored upon Newport Naval Reserve and once-beaten Rutgers College, one of the game's founding institutions. Although the contest may not have seemed especially noteworthy at first glance, the Naval Reserve team was made up of former college stars, including a number of All-Americans. Rutgers, on the other hand, had its own All-American in Paul Robeson and had shut out five opponents on its way to a 6–1–1 record.[20]

Credit for bringing the game to Brooklyn belonged to the son of the ballpark's builder and namesake, Charles H. Ebbets, Jr. While his father was attending the minor league meetings, the younger Ebbets reached out to the managers of both teams after learning plans to hold the game at the Polo Grounds had fallen through. By November 20, the matchup was set for the following Saturday, and tickets were on sale "around town." As the game approached, padded goalposts were erected in front of the left field scoreboard and near where Jake Daubert played first base for the Dodgers.[21]

Although George Foster Sanford's Rutgers squad had enjoyed an excellent season, gamblers were not impressed since "it was generally believed that the team [Naval Reserve] was practically invincible." The former college stars were installed as 3:1 favorites. However, they and the rest of a chilled crowd, estimated between 12,000 and 15,000, were in for a big surprise. The Naval Reserve lines may have outweighed their Rutgers' counterparts by almost 20 pounds per man, but "never for a moment during the play was it anybody's game, but Rutgers." After a long Rutgers' drive stalled at the Naval Reserve 20-yard line, the New Jersey school forced the former college stars to punt. Then starting another long drive that extended into the second quarter, Rutgers hit pay dirt for a 7–0 lead. Eschewing standard practice, the New Brunswickers followed their score up with an onside kick, which they recovered inside Naval Reserve territory. Unable to move the ball, Rutgers punted, but a Naval Reserve fumble gave the collegians possession at the five-yard line. From there, a John Whitehill to Paul Robeson pass provided Rutgers with a 14–0 lead they would hold for the rest of the game.[22]

So dominant was the New Jersey school "it was a wonder that Rutgers scored only twice." In a game where the longest run from scrimmage was only ten yards, the New Brunswickers made 12 first downs to only two for the opposition and dominated by running the football, outgaining the servicemen by 187 yards to 58 in spite of the latter's size advantage. Playing both ways without a single substitution, Rutgers was equally dominant on defense. The New Jersey school was led by Robeson, "a grim, silent and compelling figure," who was "a veritable Othello of battle." At game's end, Robeson and Whitehill were carried off the field by "a wild serpentining mob of rooters," while "'On the Banks of the Old Raritan' echoed through Flatbush." As one of the country's first prominent African American college football players, Robeson's performance would anticipate by 30 years Jackie Robinson's historic achievements on the very same field. Perhaps buoyed by its 1917 success, the Rutgers football team returned to Ebbets Field almost 12 months later to take on another service team, the Great Lakes Naval Station, but they were routed, 54–14. A crowd of 10,000 witnessed the contest, so the two games established that Ebbets Field was a viable venue for major college football and positioned the Ebbets and McKeevers to take advantage of an even greater opportunity five years later.[23]

By 1923, St. John's University was playing its home games at Ebbets Field, but the big news that year was the opportunity for the ballpark to host one of college football's most historic matchups. Army and Notre Dame were supposed to renew their rivalry on October 13 at either Yankee Stadium or the Polo Grounds, but with both the Yankees and Giants in the World Series, neither venue was available. As a result, the game was moved to Ebbets Field. Given the magnitude of the event, the field, which typically ran parallel to the left field stands, would run from home plate to the flagpole in center field, in order to provide a better perspective for fans on both sides. Army was an Eastern power, while Notre Dame, under Knute Rockne and his inventive forward-passing scheme, was considered to be the premier team in the Midwest. Army had always struggled against the Fighting Irish, but this was viewed as one of its best opportunities for a victory. The Cadets' primary weapons were bruising running back Tiny Hewitt and a great offensive line. Army's squad also took experience to a new level since Hewitt had already enjoyed a full varsity football career at Pittsburgh before coming to West Point. However, he was a relative rookie compared to Army's center and future College Football Hall of Famer, Edgar Garbisch, who was playing his seventh season of college football. The Notre Dame squad was much younger and had Rockne looking for the right combination of talent, although he did have a promising backfield of Harry Stuhldreher, Don Miller, Jim Crowley, and Elmer Layden.[24]

The game was scheduled to begin at 3:15 P.M., and Army was a slight favorite, with the *Brooklyn Eagle* warning "don't let anything short of murder keep you away from Ebbets Field on Saturday." Fans answered the call with over 35,000 cramming in, and 10,000 more left looking for tickets. Missing from the crowd would be the Notre Dame student body since the faculty decided it was "too long a trip." Although their trip was much shorter, the Corps of Cadets (including the football team) had a challenging day, beginning with 4:50 A.M. reveille and a morning of classes. The 1,200 Cadets then took trains to Weehawken, New Jersey, ferries to Manhattan, and marched to Times Square to board subways for Brooklyn's Franklin Avenue station. Finally from there, they marched in formation to the ballpark. Their gray uniforms, along with Notre Dame's "midnight blue jerseys" and Army's gold ones (the first time they had ever worn them), created a colorful scene.[25]

Unfortunately, the game was not as colorful, with the Fighting Irish riding their team speed to a surprising 13–0 victory. According to George Trevor of the *Eagle*, it was a case of one team "playing 'October football' of the common garden variety against an outfit that had already attained November form." Interceptions set up both touchdowns, with Elmer Layden catching a scoring pass in the second quarter and Don Miller running for six in the final stanza. With the loss, Army still had not beaten Notre Dame since the end of the First World War. The game foreshadowed the following year's matchup when Grantland Rice gave immortality to the same Notre Dame backfield, calling them "The Four Horsemen."[26]

In the most high profile college football game ever played in Brooklyn, Notre Dame defeated Army, 13–0, on October 12, 1923. The Fighting Irish were led by a backfield that a year later at the Polo Grounds would be dubbed "The Four Horsemen" by Grantland Rice (courtesy Notre Dame Archives).

Three other colleges — Manhattan, St. John's, and Brooklyn College — also saw significant action at Ebbets Field. Of the trio, it was the Jaspers who seemed to have the most success, playing a national schedule including the likes of Michigan State, LSU, and North Carolina State at the Brooklyn ballpark. Although Manhattan had other home fields, Ebbets Field was the primary one for the Jaspers from 1932 to 1937, when they played at least six games there each season.[27]

After defeating St. John's at Ebbets Field in 1928, Manhattan began playing regularly in Brooklyn in 1932. Quarterback Bill Pendergast led the Jaspers to 6–3–2 and 5–3–1 marks in 1932 and 1933, respectively. While playing at Ebbets Field, the team was drawing as many as 20,000 spectators on multiple occasions. And Pendergast, along with nine other teammates, closed out their collegiate careers at Ebbets Field with a 7–0 victory in 1933 over a Catholic University team amidst mud and snow, which Harold C. Burr wrote, "changed a season of disaster into a season of sunset success." It was the Jaspers' first win over Catholic in three tries. And with coach John F. "Chick" Meehan having a strong sophomore class for 1934, things looked promising. The team struggled that season, however, finishing 3–5–1, but played a more national level of competition, including a 13–13 tie with Kansas State and a 39–0 loss to Michigan State, both at Ebbets Field. In the latter defeat, one wonders how the Jaspers must have felt as the Spartans showed no mercy, scoring three times in the fourth quarter. Manhattan also opened the season at home, defeating St. Bonaventure, 6–0, at night, under light provided by portable electric equipment.[28]

Manhattan continued to play both local and intersectional foes in 1935, finishing 5–3–1 despite a brutal three-week stretch at Ebbets Field that included losses to LSU and North Carolina State and a tie with Holy Cross. The latter contest, played in front of a "heavy drinking crowd" that was fighting in the stands, ended 13–13 against an undefeated Crusaders' squad that had not been scored on all year until Manhattan broke through in the fourth quarter. The Jaspers' late rally included an 82-yard punt return for a score by Jim Whalen. Holy Cross would finish that season 9–0–1. Manhattan improved against national foes in 1936, earning a 6–4 mark while knocking off North Carolina State and Kentucky at Ebbets Field. It set up 1937 for what was supposedly Chick Meehan's "dream team," and the best of his six years at Manhattan. The squad finished 6–3–1 but seemed to live up to the billing, particularly at Ebbets Field, where they defeated Michigan State, 3–0, Detroit, 7–0, and North Carolina State, 15–0. It was definitely a schedule of national prominence, as the losses came to Texas A&M (Polo Grounds), at Kentucky, and to a Villanova team that Manhattan never found a way to beat during the 1930s. The defeat to the Wildcats was the lone loss at Ebbets Field that season.[29]

Meehan's tenure ended after 1937 and effectively marked the end of big-time college football at the ballpark. St. John's run at Ebbets Field, which went from 1923 through 1928, against a lower level of competition, was much less eventful. After an impressive 5–0–1 mark in 1923 (with four of the games at the Brooklyn ballpark), St. John's had an overall 10–24–4 record over the next five seasons. One of the highlights at Ebbets Field was a 13–0 victory over Villanova in 1924 that future Dodger football player Rex Thomas keyed with two field goals and a touchdown reception.[30]

College football did make a brief resurgence at the park in the late 1940s, hosting four Brooklyn College–City College rivalry games. Brooklyn College would win three of the meetings, and the teams tied in the other. Most significantly, the Kingsmen's first two wins were their seventh and eighth straight against City College, allowing them to take a series lead, 11–9. Equally impressive was the attendance, with three of the games drawing 15,000+, including the largest mark ever for either school when 16,904 showed up in 1948. Ebbets Field seemed to truly bring out big crowds for games with local flavor.[31]

While college football played a major role at the ballpark, the high school game was more popular and important to the park's relationship with Brooklyn. More than any other activity or sport, high school football was how Brooklynites got to actually play at Ebbets Field. From 1913 to 1953, the park hosted over 200 high school football games, involving at least a dozen Brooklyn high schools, both public and private, including many important rivalry contests. Schools such as James Madison, Brooklyn Tech, and Boys High played at the Brooklyn ballpark at least 25 times, while Poly Prep, New Utrecht, Brooklyn Prep, and St. John's Prep took the field on at least a dozen occasions. A number of other Brooklyn Schools played there at least once. The countless experiences of players, cheerleaders, and bands at the home of Brooklyn's baseball heroes further strengthened the connection between the community and Ebbets Field. Although the 25-plus games played there by James Madison, Brooklyn Tech, and Boys High is impressive, it pales in comparison with the totals of Erasmus and Manual Training School. During the same period, the two institutions played each other 41 times at Ebbets Field, and each had another 40 or so contests against other opposition.

Since Charles Ebbets had hosted high school football at Washington Park, it was no surprise he would do the same in his new ballpark. Not long after the end of the Dodgers' first season at Ebbets field, it was announced an Election Day high school doubleheader would take place at the borough's new venue. For the inaugural matchup, Boys High would square off against Poly Prep, while Erasmus would meet Manual. In an interesting twist, the first two schools would play the first half followed by the opening two quarters of the second matchup. Then, the games would be played to their conclusion. This practice would continue at Ebbets Field twin bills until 1917, when it was abandoned to spare the players the downtime between halves. The event was a big hit as 10,000 spectators watched Poly shut out Boys, 13–0, and Manual blank Erasmus, 12–0, in "perfect weather." Reflecting on the day's success, the *Eagle* noted Brooklyn was a "great town for scholastic sports" and only lacked a "good setting." With that in place, the paper was confident high school football would be as popular in Brooklyn as the "big college football games."[32]

Of the Election Day matchups, Boys and Poly had the longer history, dating back to 1892. Erasmus and Manual were relative newcomers, having met for the first time in 1909 — a 5–5 tie symbolic of how close the series would become. Perhaps the start of the rivalry and the opening of Ebbets Field were mutually reinforcing, helping each other grow. By 1922, the *Eagle* pronounced the annual contest to be "as important in school boy ranks as the Yale–Harvard clash is in collegiate circles." The events between the two schools were big, colorful spectacles and drew large crowds, such as the 35,000 that showed up in 1927. That afternoon, "there was a brilliant scenic effect where the spectators were housed in the home of the Brooklyn Robins," wrote James J. Murphy, noting the contrasting colors of the two schools. Murphy went on to say "The picture was completed by the Erasmus band behind first base attired in blue sweaters, bearing the inscription 'Erasmus Hall,' white duck trousers, with brown berets as head coverings. The cheer leaders were spic and span in blue and white togs. The Manual band on the third base side was without uniforms, but the cheer leaders made up for this in blue sweaters and white trousers with blue berets and gold tassels dangling from the uppermost parts of the French chapeaux." The Manual–Erasmus contests typically also included halftime skits. For example, during that 1927 game, fans witnessed the "Good Ship Manual" sail in at halftime on a motorcar, accompanied by two boats, one reading "Life Boat" and the other "No Hope," insinuating the Manual ship was sinking. Typically each school would hold a "mimic funeral" at halftime, hanging or burning an effigy of the other side.[33]

The rivalry saw no greater player than Erasmus' quarterback Sid Luckman, who went on to Columbia University, and then a Hall of Fame career with the Chicago Bears. In the process, he "became the first successful 'T' quarterback." Luckman entered Erasmus in 1931, with his school not having defeated Manual in six years, losing five times and tying once. Erasmus would win the 1931 and 1932 meetings, however, with Luckman playing a particularly key role in the latter victory. However, even he was not immune to the hazards of rivalry football, as Luckman's 1933 fourth quarter fumble at the Manual two-yard line ended Erasmus' last chance to break a scoreless tie. Led by the quarterback, some of the great Erasmus teams went on a 17-game winning streak from late 1930 through the very end of the 1932 season, when the Buff and Blue were upset by Madison.[34]

All told, Erasmus and Manual played 41 times at Ebbets Field, the last meeting at the Dodgers' ballpark occurring in 1952. Attendance had fallen to about 4,000 by the early 1950s, and the Dodgers notified both schools that 1953 would be the last contest at Ebbets Field, because it typically cost close to $10,000 to repair the damage to the field caused by the game. Since the schools were also losing money on the game, they decided to forgo one last meeting at Ebbets Field. After the 1952 contest, which Erasmus won 48–7, they led the series 20–17–8. At that time, Ebbets Field had hosted 41 of the 45 total meetings, with Erasmus holding the edge, 19–15–7.[35]

Interestingly, the best football players who ever played at Ebbets Field probably generated the least interest. Although professional football there periodically produced excitement, it never matched the levels of college and high school football. The first National Football League game at the ballpark was played on October 10, 1926, when the Brooklyn Lions defeated the Hartford Blues, 6–0, on a fourth quarter touchdown from St. John's product Rex Thomas. Thomas himself may have identified the problem when he said pro football "had everything but color, you do miss the old rah-rah spirit."[36]

Brooklyn owner Edmund Butler had been granted an NFL franchise earlier in 1926, but there was local competition from the rival American Football League, which also had a Brooklyn franchise named the Horsemen. They were owned by the aforementioned boxing promoter Humbert J. Fugazy and played at Commercial Field. Fugazy's AFL team quickly failed, however, and merged with the Lions in November of 1926, becoming the Brooklion Horsemen. There were few highlights in an inaugural season that saw the team go 3–8, starting as the Lions and ending as the Brooklion Horsemen. The largest crowd of the campaign, some 7,000 fans, attended the first interborough professional football game on Thanksgiving Day and watched the New York Giants defeat Brooklion, 17–0. Brooklyn's inability to defeat their rivals would be a pattern for the franchise. Although supposedly in the league's future plans following the initial season, the Brooklyn team was one of 10 dropped after the opening campaign. NFL football would not return to Ebbets Field until 1930 when William V. Dwyer and John Depler purchased the Dayton Triangles and moved them to Brooklyn.[37]

Brooklyn Dodger star and Pro Football Hall of Famer, Clarence "Ace" Parker (Brooklyn Public Library — Brooklyn Collection).

Now called the Brooklyn Dodgers, with Ebbets Field as their home, the team would struggle in the 1930s, much like their baseball namesakes, finishing over .500 only twice under five different coaches. After going 7–4–1 in 1930, the Dodgers went a "whopping" 33–63–8 from 1931 to 1939. Their first 1930 and first ever franchise win came on the road against the Staten Island Stapeltons, followed by a 32–0 Ebbets Field victory over the Newark Bears, keyed by Thomas, who was still on the squad. The campaign ended with games against the Giants, the Dodgers actually winning the first at the Polo Grounds, before losing the return visit in front of 30,000 fans. Perhaps caught up in the moment, Harold Parrott of the *Eagle* felt the large crowd was "noisy evidence that pro football had made the grade." Depler, who had been a standout player at Illinois, served as the coach that first year, but after a 2–12 mark in 1931, former New York Giant Benny Friedman took over as a player/coach. However, the team's 3–9 record in 1932 was scant improvement.[38]

In 1933, Friedman moved into a playing-only role, as the NFL made numerous changes that shaped the game we know today, including allowing quarterbacks to pass from anywhere behind the line of scrimmage, rather than more than five yards behind. The league also split into two divisions (Brooklyn was part of the five team East), and the Dodgers would again find themselves under new ownership as Dwyer, who had lost $30,000 to $50,000, sold the team to former college greats, Chris Cagle and John "Shipwreck" Kelly. The two men would be player-owners. Coach John "Cap" McEwan led the squad to a 5–4–1 finish and second place in the Eastern Division, but a 4–7 mark in 1934 brought things back to normal. That team also supposedly had issues with late-night partying amongst the players and insubordination. Before the 1934 season, future New York Yankees baseball owner, Dan Topping, had taken over Cagle's interest in the team and would work as the treasurer, while Kelly remained as president.[39]

Over the next five years, the Dodgers would show signs of competitiveness. A 10–6 home win over the Boston Redskins in 1934 demonstrated "a lot of promise," but a 21–0 loss to the Chicago Cardinals buried "the championship hopes of the Brooklyn Dodgers." That game was played in "ankle-deep mud," due in some degree to the Erasmus–Manual contest earlier that day, something unthinkable today. In 1935, the Dodgers came closer to respectability, finishing 5–6–1 under new coach, Paul Schissler. Things seemed even more promising in 1936 when the Brooklyn football squad beat a highly-regarded Detroit Lions team, 12–10, but things went downhill thereafter and they finished with a 3–8–1 mark. As a result Schissler was replaced by George "Potsy" Clark for the 1937 campaign. Although the best Clark could do in three seasons at the helm was a 4–4–3 record in 1938, he would play a significant role in the Dodgers' best seasons by helping to select Clarence "Ace" Parker when a college draft was instituted in 1936. Parker would go on to a Hall of Fame career as a "triple-threat, two-way back" for Brooklyn. While scouting the Dodgers, Redskins coach Ray Flaherty said, "Parker can do everything. He can pass, run, block, and is a good defensive man." Flaherty warned that no one should be "surprised if Parker stands head and shoulders above any player in the league." The pieces seemed to be falling into place in the late 1930s, to the point the rallying cry more frequently associated with the baseball Dodgers, "Wait Till Next Year," was heard after a 13–13 tie in 1937 with the archrival Giants.[40]

After the 4–4–3 season in 1938, Brooklyn Dodger football fans could have been excused for thinking and hoping 1939 would be that "next year." After winning their first two games that season, however, things went downhill, and the club went 2–6–1 over the remainder of the campaign, causing Potsy Clark to resign. One of the defeats was a 7–6 near miss against the Giants, with the largest pro football crowd ever at Ebbets Field (just over 34,000) looking on. A week earlier, history of another kind was made as the Dodgers–Eagles game at the Brooklyn ballpark became the first NFL contest ever televised, giving Ebbets Field the distinction of hosting the first baseball and football games shown in that new medium. The telecast reached some 1,000 receivers in the New York area on NBC.[41]

An October 19, 1941, pro football game between the Brooklyn Dodgers and the Chicago Cardinals. Note the Abe Stark sign in the background (Roger A. Godin Collection).

The beneficiary of the groundwork laid by Clark was the new headman for the 1940 season, Jock Sutherland, who had been very successful in his previous coaching position at the University of Pittsburgh. In another quick start, Brooklyn was 3–1 in 1940 before dropping to 4–3 after another loss to the Giants. The Dodgers were not dead, however, and responded on November 10 with a 16–14 victory in front of a big crowd of 33,846 over Sammy Baugh and the Redskins, who were previously undefeated. *Brooklyn Eagle* reporter Lou Niss called the contest "the most thrill-packed game of the season." After another home victory over the Cleveland Rams the following weekend, the Dodgers defeated the Chicago Cardinals, 14–9, on "Ace Parker Day," to improve to 7–3 and keep their slight divisional title hopes alive. Included in Parker's gifts was a suit from Abe Stark, which he apparently got without having to hit the sign in right field. Brooklyn ultimately finished 8–3, including a victory over the Giants, to come in second behind the Redskins. For their exploits, Ace Parker received the Joe F. Carr trophy for NFL MVP and, along with Bruiser Kinard and Perry Schwartz, made the All–NFL team.[42]

Although hopes had to be high for the 1941 season, the Dodgers (now called "Topping Tech" by the *Eagle*) got off to a rocky start. They won their opener, but a tough road trip brought them back to Ebbets Field 2–2, where they lost to the Chicago Cardinals, 20–6, putting the team in third place with little chance of their first-ever divisional title. To make matters worse, Parker, although he would return the following week, suffered a concussion. With their season hanging in the balance, the Dodgers rebounded, upsetting the undefeated Giants, 16–13, at Ebbets Field before 28,675, who the *Eagle* described as "mostly incredulous." Parker, though banged up with both head and leg problems, keyed the win. Tommy Holmes wrote, "It was a great victory for the Dodgers — a ball game that rescued Sutherland's club from a desperate situation and placed it in a spot from which it might soar to a prosperous season." Home victories against the Eagles and Redskins got the team to 5–3 and back into the divisional race, which was "tangled up like a basket of eels." The Dodgers win over Washington knocked the Redskins into second, while Brooklyn was third at 5–3 with supposedly the easiest schedule. But the Pittsburgh Steelers, supposedly a weak team, would get their only victory of the season, 14–7, to drop the Dodgers to 5–4 and ultimately seal their second-place fate at 7–4.[43]

Perhaps the future of Brooklyn Dodger football might have been different if the war had not intervened, but the reality is the remaining Dodger teams would be extremely unsuccessful. In their final six seasons, playing in two different leagues, the franchise went through six-plus coaches, never finished better than 3–8 and, overall, went a putrid 13–58–2 with a .178 winning percentage. Sutherland went into the service in 1942, line coach Mike Getto took over, and things simply fell apart. Historian Roger A. Godin wrote, "There is no question that Jock Sutherland, whatever his human relations deficiencies, was a tough act to follow." The Dodgers also lost their star, Ace Parker, to the military. There was one big crowd in 1942 when 31,643 came to see the Chicago Bears and local product Sid Luckman dismantle the Dodgers, 35–0. It was just one of eight losses in a disappointing 3–8 season, almost a direct reversal of the prior year. Things continued to

Demonstrating his running ability, triple-threat Ace Parker of the football Dodgers runs for 15 yards against the Washington Redskins on November 9, 1941 (Roger A. Godin Collection).

spiral downward as the 1943 team went only 2–8. Midway through that campaign, with Pete Cawthon at the helm, the team had lost 12 straight, spanning the last two seasons, and eight of the first 10 were shutouts. Amazingly, 1944 produced a worst-ever record at 0–10, albeit with a different team name: the Brooklyn Tigers. New General Manager Tom Gallery changed the name, claiming the Dodger nickname caused confusion with the baseball franchise. It made little difference, and NFL football ended at Ebbets Field after the 1944 season as Topping merged the Tigers with the Boston Yanks and moved the merged club out of Brooklyn.[44]

After one season with his new team, Topping shifted the club to the All-America Football Conference, a rival league to the NFL. The AAFC was founded in 1944, and Brooklyn would actually obtain a new franchise for the 1946 season. After two unsuccessful campaigns, Branch Rickey took over the team for the 1948 season, bringing the baseball Dodgers and football Dodgers under the same ownership. Despite repeated claims by Rickey that the team would be successful, they folded after just one season. On the field, futility reached a high, or low, point on November 21, 1948, when San Francisco outscored Brooklyn, 63–40. The game "featured" 16 touchdowns and 12 balls lost in the stands on extra points. The cost of the lost footballs was symbolic of the "red ink bath" Rickey was taking with his new venture. Incredibly after that game, coach Carl Voyles, "with true Dodger optimism," claimed "by 1950 we'll give Brooklyn the best football team in the world." Unfortunately for Voyles and the few remaining fans, the team had only two games left, not two years. The 1948 season ended with a 31–21 loss to the Cleveland Browns in the final professional football game played at Ebbets Field. In their last three contests, the Dodgers surrendered 132 points, which was not that surprising considering the opposing quarterbacks were Frankie Albert, Y.A. Tittle, and Otto Graham. Prior to the 1949 season, the Dodgers would merge with the New York Yankees, and professional football left Brooklyn forever. Pro football never drew especially well at Ebbets Field. Over 15 seasons, the NFL franchise broke 20,000 in average attendance only twice. Not surprisingly, the highest average attendance of 24,400 came during the successful 1940 campaign. Things got even worse during the AAFC years, as the average attendance fell gradually from just over 14,000 to just above 10,000. Considering there was no television revenue, it was no surprise the team could not survive financially.[45]

As the biggest public facility in the borough, Ebbets Field was occasionally used for large, nonsporting events, such as the opera in 1925. As world tensions escalated in the late 1930s and early 1940s, Ebbets Field was seen as a possible venue for more political purposes. With war raging in Europe in 1941, the Brooklyn chapter of the America First Committee tried to rent the ballpark for a peace rally. Not surprisingly, outspoken team president Larry MacPhail refused and reportedly used "offensive and insulting language" to convey the decision to William Leonard, committee chair. MacPhail's attitude raised the ire of local lawyer and peace activist George Friou, who made thinly-veiled threats of legal action regarding the noise caused by night baseball at Ebbets Field. MacPhail stood his ground, however, claiming the home of the Dodgers was not available for "propaganda" rallies.[46]

Whether MacPhail would have differentiated between politics and propaganda during the 1944 presidential campaign was a moot point as the Dodger leader was in the military.

Recognizing Brooklyn and the surrounding county had on three previous occasions given him "thumping pluralities," Franklin D. Roosevelt made an October 21 campaign visit to the boro, including addressing a rally at Ebbets Field. A crowd estimated at 10,000 to 15,000, some of whom arrived as early as 5 A.M., braved the rain for the President's 11:00 A.M. arrival. As Roosevelt's car entered through the center field gates, the crowd gave him a standing ovation. Then, in the course of a speech urging the reelection of Democratic senator, Robert Wagner, FDR said he was a Dodger fan and wanted to come back to see the team play. Sadly Roosevelt had only about six months to live and was unable to make good on the wish.[47]

While Ebbets Field hosted boxing and football in its early days, both sports had faded out by the late 1940s and early 1950s. Soccer, however, which got a later start at the Brooklyn ballpark, not only survived the other two sports, but the Dodgers themselves. In November of 1925, Ebbets Field hosted its first significant soccer event when 5,000 spectators watched the U.S. National Team defeat Canada, 6–1, led by four goals from Archie Stark (presumably no relative of Abe), the American Soccer League's leading scorer. Considering the game was played in bad weather, it was a good crowd, which prompted

President Franklin D. Roosevelt visits the home of the Dodgers as part of his 1944 presidential campaign (Brooklyn Public Library—Brooklyn Collection).

the Eagle to predict "it follows that one of the semi-finals or finals for the U.S.F.A. and American League cups might well be brought to Brooklyn in the not far distant future."[48]

Unless the paper was trading on inside information, it was certainly prophetic, as on April 11, 1926, Ebbets Field was the site of the National Challenge Trophy Championship game of the U.S. Football Association. The crowd of 18,000 (a United States soccer record) represented a coming-out party for the role the Brooklyn park would play in the sport's future. Once again, Archie Stark was active, leading Bethlehem to an easy 7–2 victory over the Ben Millers of the St. Louis Soccer League. No doubt pleased, the *Eagle* wrote, despite the lopsided score, "yesterday's game put this boro more solidly than ever on the soccer map." The large crowd did not witness much drama since Bethlehem led 3–0 at halftime and cruised to their sixth and final National Cup Title. Ironically, the Pennsylvania team was only fourth best during the 1925–26 American Soccer League season.[49]

It was the Brooklyn Wanderers, playing in the American Soccer League, who saw the most action at Ebbets Field, primarily between 1926–1928. The ASL was formed for the 1921–22 season with eight teams from the Northeast, and the Wanderers would join for the league's second campaign after the Todd Shipyards, another Brooklyn squad, folded. The person most responsible for bringing quality soccer to Brooklyn was Nathan Agar. Agar had founded the club and was now the owner-manager of the Wanderers and even played occasionally. Developing an interest in soccer in his native England, he had been active in the sport in the New York City area since at least 1905. In addition to league games, the Wanderers played a significant number of matches against international teams, something Agar believed strongly in. For example, he brought the Hakoah All-Stars, an All-Jewish team from Vienna, to the U.S. on an international tour in 1926, and a number of them remained in the United States to play for Agar and the Wanderers.[50]

The Hakoah's visit to Ebbets Field was the ninth match of their 12-game American tour. The visitors built a 6–1 halftime lead and hung on for a 6–4 victory in front of 22,000, which again broke the Ebbets Field attendance record for a soccer match. In addition, the Wanderers competed in the inaugural International Soccer League, which paired three teams from the ASL with four Canadian teams. Brooklyn played more contests than the other participants and made the finals, called the Nathan Strauss Cup, where they lost to Ulster United of Toronto at Ebbets Field on November 20, 1926. However, despite struggling in 1926 against international competition, the Wanderers did well enough for the *Eagle* to write that the sport's "devotees will be knocking for admission into the charmed circles of the major sports."[51]

The Wanderers also struggled in the ASL during the 1927–28 campaign, even though they had Johnny Nelson, one of the stronger goal scorers in the league. In 1927, the Uruguay National team continued to add international excitement, playing three of their 13-game schedule at Ebbets Field against the Wanderers. The best the Brooklyn club could manage was a tie despite playing their opponents tough. During 1928, the most significant international match was against the Glasgow Rangers on June 2. Another large crowd of 20,000 saw the Scottish team defeat the Wanderers, 4–0. But on August 19, Brooklyn provided a glimpse of what was to come next season, defeating a favored Italian team, 3–2, behind two goals from former Hakoah player, Joseph Eisenhoffer. The *Eagle* even wrote that "the championship pennant of the American Soccer League may flutter from the flagstaff at Hawthorne Field."[52]

The hypothetical pennant would have flown at Hawthorne Field because while the Wanderers played important weekend matches at Ebbets Field, their home pitch was the prior facility, also located in Brooklyn. The newspaper was nearly prophetic as the Wanderers sported their best ASL record during the first half of the 1928–29 campaign. The league had split its schedule into a first and second half, and in the first part, the Wanderers spent most of the season in second place, patiently waiting to make a move on first place Fall River. Janos Nehadoma provided much of the excitement and ultimately finished tied for the scoring title, with 43 goals for the entire season. Nehadoma played a key role on December 16 when the Wanderers knocked off the New York Nationals, 4–3, to finally take over first place. In some curious scheduling, however, a match between the two front runners the following Sunday would take place at Hawthorne Field, despite the *Eagle's* warning that the facility's capacity "will be taxed to its utmost." That contest with Fall River ended in a tie, and Brooklyn maintained first place into January. However, the close race ended in disappointment when Fall River knocked off the Wanderers, 2–1, amidst a snowstorm and questionable officiating to finish one point ahead.[53]

The Wanderer's near miss seemed to auger well for the future of professional soccer at Ebbets Field, but amidst the exciting play, the ASL was falling apart. The league was at war with the United States Football Association and was already considered to be an outlaw league. Control and timing of the National Challenge Cup were major issues, and three teams had already left the ASL. For the most part, this ended a local pro soccer team calling Ebbets Field home, at least part of the time. Although the club continued to play in a reconstituted ASL, the Wanderers folded prior to the 1931–32 campaign.[54]

From that point on, most soccer matches at Ebbets Field were local stops on international tours. Amazingly, on at least two occasions, a night soccer game followed an afternoon Dodger game. Unthinkable today, the scheduling shows once again how much baseball club owners, in the days before television revenue, needed to generate more income from their ballpark. The numbers did not lie either as a June 18, 1948, Liverpool–Djurgarden (Sweden) match drew 20,000 fans, compared to only 9,703 (including 2,500 knot holers at reduced prices) who saw the Dodgers play that afternoon. A year earlier, an even larger crowd of 25,000 saw Hapoel of Palestine play an American all-star team. Although such international matches were sporadic, leading European clubs like Real Madrid and Liverpool visited the home of the Dodgers. The last of these contests took place in 1959, two years after the final Dodger game in Brooklyn.[55]

As with all enclosed ballparks, Ebbets Field was used throughout its existence to generate additional revenue for its owners. However, non–Dodger events there became something more than alternative sources of revenue. Although its lasting image is as a small, intimate place, Ebbets Field was a big project at the time of its construction, and Brooklyn took great pride in its new state-of-the-art facility. It was fitting that it hosted major events, including the Yale–Harvard baseball game and the Army–Notre Dame football game. At the same time, Brooklynites did not just spectate at Ebbets Field, a number of them actually competed on it through programs like the field days hosted by the *Eagle* and many other high school events. This was a further reason Ebbets Field was more than just a ballpark, particularly to the people of Brooklyn. Instead of just furnishing an additional revenue stream, these events provided yet another thread that bound Brooklyn to Ebbets Field.

Notes

1. Neil W. MacDonald, *The League That Lasted: 1876 and the Founding of the National League of Professional Baseball Clubs* (Jefferson, N.C.: McFarland, 2004), 7–8; Harold Seymour, *Baseball: The Early Years* (New York: Oxford University Press, 1960), 48; *New York Times*, December 22, 2010.
2. *Brooklyn Daily Eagle*, June 18, 1913, June 28, 1913, June 23, 1914, June 25, 1914, June 26, 1915, June 24, 1917.
3. *Brooklyn Daily Eagle*, June 20, 1913, June 22, 1913, July 10, 1913, July 21, 1913, July 27, 1913, August 3, 1913, August 10, 1913.
4. *Brooklyn Daily Eagle*, May 31, 1915, June 1, 1915, July 2, 1915, July 21, 1915, July 24, 1915, August 20, 1915, September 10, 1915, January 13, 1918, May 6, 1923, www.retrosheet.org.
5. Jack Cavanaugh, *Tunney: Boxing's Brainiest Champion and His Upset of the Great Jack Dempsey* (New York: Ballantine Books, 2007), 73–74, 77.
6. *Brooklyn Daily Eagle*, May 20, 1921, May 31, 1921, June 27, 1921, June 29, 1921.
7. *Brooklyn Daily Eagle*, July 11, 1921, July 26, 1921, July 27, 1921, July 28, 1921.
8. *Brooklyn Daily Eagle*, May 14, 1922, July 5, 1922, August 23, 1922, August 30, 1922, October 4, 1922; http://www.ibhof.com/pages/about/inductees/oldtimer/wills.html.
9. *Brooklyn Daily Eagle*, July 16, 1926, July 17, 1926.
10. Bob McGee, *The Greatest Ballpark Ever: Ebbets Field and the Story of the Brooklyn Dodgers* (New Brunswick: Rutgers University Press, 2005), 94, 108; *New York Times*, November 13, 1925; *Brooklyn Daily Eagle*, October 13, 1926.
11. *Brooklyn Daily Eagle*, August 10, 1927, September 14, 1927, September 15, 1927, August 16, 1928, September 6, 1928; http://www.ibhof.com/pages/about/inductees/oldtimer/godfrey.html.
12. *Brooklyn Daily Eagle*, July 11, 1929, August 18, 1927; *New York Times*, May 7, 1930; http://www.ibhof.com/pages/about/inductees/oldtimer/chocolate.html; http://www.ibhof.com/pages/about/inductees/oldtimer/canzoneri.html.
13. *Brooklyn Daily Eagle*, July 10, 1941, June 12, 1946, June 13, 1946.
14. *Brooklyn Daily Eagle*, May 29, 1947, July 30, 1947, July 31, 1947.
15. *New York Times*, July 7, 1925.
16. www.retrosheet.org; *New York Times*, July 12, 1925, July 18, 1925, July 19, 1925.
17. *New York Times*, August 2, 1925, August 6, 1925, August 9, 1925.
18. *Brooklyn Daily Eagle*, June 3, 1926, June 26, 1926.
19. David Maraniss, *When Pride Still Mattered: A Life of Vince Lombardi* (New York: Simon & Schuster, 2000), 31.
20. *Brooklyn Daily Eagle*, November 23, 1917; *Newark Evening News*, November 27, 1917; *New York Times*, November 25, 1917; *New York Herald*, November 24, 1917; *Rutgers 2010 Football Media Guide*.
21. *Brooklyn Daily Eagle*, November 11, 1917, November 20, 1917, November 22, 1917.
22. *Brooklyn Daily Eagle*, November 25, 1917; *New York Herald*, November 25, 1917; *New Brunswick Sunday Times*, November 25, 1917.
23. *Brooklyn Daily Eagle*, November 25, 1917, November 17, 1918; *New York Times*, November 25, 1917; *New Brunswick Sunday Times*, November 25, 1917; *New York Tribune*, November 25, 1917; *Rutgers 2010 Football Media Guide*.
24. *Brooklyn Daily Eagle*, August 23, 1923, September 29, 1923, October 7, 1923, October 9, 1923.
25. *Brooklyn Daily Eagle*, October 9, 1923, October 12, 1923, October 14, 1923.
26. *Brooklyn Daily Eagle*, October 14, 1923.
27. http://www.luckyshow.org/football/manhattan.htm.
28. http://www.luckyshow.org/football/manhattan.htm; *Brooklyn Daily Eagle*, November 19, 1933, September 23, 1934, October 21, 1934.
29. *Brooklyn Daily Eagle*, October 20, 1935; http://goholycross.com/sports/m-footbl/archive_results.pdf.
30. http:/www.luckyshow.org/football/redmen.htm; *Brooklyn Daily Eagle*, October 26, 1924.
31. *Brooklyn Daily Eagle*, November 2, 1947; November 7, 1948, November 6, 1949, November 5, 1950.
32. *Brooklyn Daily Eagle*, October 19, 1913, November 5, 1913, November 5, 1917.

33. *Brooklyn Daily Eagle*, November 1, 1914, November 6, 1922, November 9, 1927, November 8, 1933.
34. *Brooklyn Daily Eagle*, November 8, 1933; *New York Times*, November 4, 1931, November 9, 1932, December 4, 1932; http://www.profootballhof.com/hof/member.aspx?PlayerId=135.
35. *New York Times*, November 4, 1953; *Brooklyn Daily Eagle*, November 7, 1934, December 2, 1934, October 4, 1950, October 13, 1950, November 2, 1950, October 22, 1952, November 5, 1952, October 13, 1953, October 20, 1953.
36. *Brooklyn Daily Eagle*, October 12, 1926, October 13, 1930.
37. *Brooklyn Daily Eagle*, November 26, 1926; Roger A. Godin, *The Brooklyn Football Dodgers: The Other "Bums"* (Haworth, NJ: St. Johann Press, 2003), 2–3, 5–8.
38. Godin, pp. 8, 11, 15–16, 24–25, 408; *Brooklyn Daily Eagle*, December 8, 1930.
39. Godin, pp. 33–35, 42–43, 52, 408.
40. *Brooklyn Daily Eagle*, October 1, 1934, November 7, 1934, November 26, 1937, November 25, 1938; Godin, pp. 53, 55, 63–64, 77–78, 408; http://www.profootballhof.com/hof/member.aspx?PlayerId=172.
41. *Brooklyn Daily Eagle*, October 30, 1939; Godin, pp., 115, 120–122, 131.
42. Godin, pp. 136–137, 155, 177; *Brooklyn Daily Eagle*, November 11, November 18, November 15, 1940.
43. *Brooklyn Daily Eagle*, September 22, October 20, October 27, November 10, 1941; Godin, pp. 204, 215, 223–225, 408.
44. Godin, pp. 232–233, 277–278, 282, 290–291, 317–318, 408; *Brooklyn Daily Eagle*, November 9, 1942; http://www.profootballhof.com/hof/member.aspx?PlayerId=172.
45. Godin, pp. 318–319, 321, 371, 396; *Brooklyn Daily Eagle*, October 31, 1948, November 22, 1948, November 29, 1948, December 6, 1948.
46. *New York Times*, June 14, 1941, June 15, 1941, June 18, 1941.
47. *Brooklyn Daily Eagle*, October 22, 1944; *New York Times*, October 22, 1944.
48. *Brooklyn Daily Eagle*, November 9, 1925.
49. *Brooklyn Daily Eagle*, April 12, 1926; http://homepages.sover.net/~spectrum/year/1926.html.
50. http://homepages.sover.net/~spectrum/year/1922.html; http://homepages.sover.net/~spectrum/year/1923.html; http://homepages.sover.net/~spectrum/year/1926.html; *Brooklyn Daily Eagle*, October 4, 1926; *New York Times*, June 26, 1978.
51. http://homepage.sover.net/~spectrum/year/1926.html; *Brooklyn Daily Eagle*, November 21, 1926; December 26, 1926; *New York Times*, May 23, 1926.
52. http://homepages.sover.net/~spectrum/year/1927.html; *Brooklyn Daily Eagle*, December 27, 1927, June 3, 1928, June 24, 1928, August 20, 1928.
53. http://homepages.sover.net/~spectrum/year/1929.html; *Brooklyn Daily Eagle*, December 17,1928, December 24, 1928, December 28, 1928, January 14, 1929.
54. http://homepages.sover.net/~spectrum/year/1929.html; http://homepages.sover.net/~spectrum/year/1930.html; http://homepages.sover.net/~spectrum/year/1932.html.
55. *Brooklyn Daily Eagle*, June 18, 1947, June 19, 1948, July 9, 1948; *New York Times*, July 16, 1959, August 17, 1959.

Ebbets Field by the Numbers

Ronald M. Selter

Although the popular memory has a fixed image of the layout and configuration of Ebbets Field, in reality the park evolved throughout its 45-year history. Built more or less in the standard Deadball Era (1901–1919) model, the original facility had vast space in left field and center field, with all of the stands in foul territory. In the course of two large ballpark modifications, additional seating absorbed some of the space in left field and in center field, creating the more intimate park remembered today.

The Brooklyn club had used Washington Park for 15 seasons before moving to Ebbets Field for the 1913 season. The site of Ebbets Field had previously been used as the community garbage dump. The ballpark was located, on what was at the time, the outskirts of Brooklyn in an area known as Flatbush. In 1913, the ballpark site was bounded by Montgomery Street on the north, by Franklin Avenue (later Cedar Place) on the west, Sullivan Place on the south and Bedford Avenue behind the right field wall on the east.[1] Note that Sullivan Street did not run east-west, but had a slightly southwest-northeast orientation, and thus did not form 90-degree angles with either Cedar Place or Bedford Avenue. The dimensions of the park site were 478 feet along Sullivan Place, 638 feet along Cedar Avenue, and 474 feet along Bedford Avenue. The east-west dimension along Montgomery Street on the north, that limited the right field dimensions for the life of the ballpark, was 450 feet. The shape of the park site was thus not a rectangle, but a trapezoid. Because of the trapezoidal shape, the first base portion of the grandstand was parallel to Sullivan Place, and that made the right field line intersect the right field wall at more than 90 degrees. On the west side, the third base portion of the grandstand was parallel to Cedar Place, and the left field line converged with the third base bleachers. The total area of the park site was 6.0 acres — less than average for the classic ballparks. The trapezoidal shape and limited size of the park site were dictated by the surrounding streets. As a result there was a deep left field (the north-south direction) and a shallow right field (the east-west dimension). Home plate, the center of the grandstand, and the main entrance — a neo-classical rotunda — were all located in the southwest corner of the park site at the intersection of Cedar Place and Sullivan Street.[2]

Ebbets Field, one of the best-known and best-loved of the classic ballparks, was built largely of steel and concrete and had an initial seating capacity of about 19,000. The ballpark's stands, in the Deadball Era, consisted of (1) a double-deck steel and concrete grandstand, which ran from the right field corner around the infield and beyond third base, and (2) a large set of concrete bleachers that ran from the third base end of the grandstand down the left field line to the left field wall. There was no seating in the outfield. The left field line was canted a few degrees to the west of a north-south orientation, and as a result, the left field foul line intersected the left field wall at 80 degrees. As the left field and right field walls intersected in the center field corner at 90 degrees, the right field foul line intersected the right field wall at 100 degrees. For the last 20–25 feet of the left field foul line, nearest to the left field wall, there was zero foul territory. The foul line near the left field corner in 1913 was in fact the front of the bleachers.

No sooner was the park opened (an exhibition game vs. the Yankees on April 5, 1913), than a serious design flaw was discovered.[3] The ballpark had only two entrances — the one on Cedar Place for the left field bleachers, and the main entrance to the park and only entrance to the grandstand, which was the ornate and circular rotunda. The problem was the ticket windows were inside the rotunda, and fans with tickets had to push through the lines of other fans in line to buy tickets. In addition, at the end of the game, the thousands of fans in the grandstand all tried to exit through the rotunda. Charlie Ebbets was quick to act. By April 29, 1913, four new entrances were added to the ballpark: two on Cedar Place and two on Sullivan Place.[4] In addition, to help with the outflow of fans at the conclusion of the game, an exit gate was cut into the wall in right-center field. This exit gate limited the extent of the center field double-deck stands during the 1931 expansion.

The configuration of Ebbets Field was substantially modified late in the 1920 season.

This photograph gives a good sense of the size of the playing field prior to the 1931 expansion.

The Dodgers that season were in a hard-fought, and as it turned out, successful pennant race. In order to accommodate the increased demand for seats — particularly on Sundays — (Sunday baseball in New York state had just become legal early in the 1919 season after a long campaign by Charles Ebbets, other owners, and fans) the Dodgers in early September installed temporary bleachers in left field. These bleachers extended from the front of the permanent left field line bleachers nearly to the center field corner. At the center field end of these new bleachers, a low fence extended to the right field–center field wall, thus putting the flagpole out of play. The new bleachers that provided additional seating were referred to as "circus seats" in the press. However, the club's official designation for them was "emergency grandstand," which allowed the Dodgers to charge the higher grandstand price for the seats, instead of the lower bleacher price. The front of these bleachers consisted of a low fence, which was all of two-and-a-half feet high. The left field dimension at the foul line was now 384 feet, and the straightaway left field distance 374 feet. Dead center field was now 450 feet, and the center field corner was 470 feet. The right field dimensions were unchanged. The center field interior fence lasted only as long as the 1920 World Series. A 20-foot wide running track was added before the 1929 season.

In late August of 1930, the Dodgers erected a 19-foot screen on top of the right field wall. This screen ran all the way from the right field corner to almost the center field corner. The purpose of this screen, that made the right field barrier 38 feet high in all, was not to curb home runs. The Dodgers built the screen with a half-inch offset behind the right field wall. This arrangement, and the park's ground rules, made the screen out of play, and thus balls hitting the screen were home runs. If not to cut down on home runs, then what was the purpose of the screen? The concern of the Dodgers was the potential liability for balls hit over the right field wall (typically during batting practice) and striking pedestrians on Bedford Avenue — the thoroughfare that was immediately behind right field. The right field wall/screen situation became even more complicated in the 1931 season when a large scoreboard (34 feet high, five feet in depth and about 85 feet wide) was built in front of the right field wall and blocked a portion of the new right field screen. The scoreboard protruded from the right field wall and reduced the outfield distances for about one-third of right field by five feet. For the 1931–1935 seasons, balls hitting the right field wall and scoreboard were in play. Balls hit to the left or right side of the upper part of the scoreboard, and thus hitting the screen, were out of play and home runs. Starting with the 1936 season, the Ebbets Field ground rules were changed, and the right field–center field screen was now in play. Thus for the 1936 and later seasons, over-the-fence home runs to right field had to clear the wall and the screen.

After the 1930 season, the Dodgers decided to expand Ebbets Field. The original expansion plan was to double-deck the stands down the left field line and add a deep set of double-decked stands in left field. To accomplish this, the Dodgers planned to have the city relocate Montgomery Street (the street behind the left field wall) onto the property (owned by the Dodgers) on the north side of Montgomery Street. The Dodgers would then build a deep set of double-decked stands in left field and extending into center field. This plan fell through as the city would not agree to reroute Montgomery Street.[5] Instead, the Dodgers were limited to double-decking the left field foul line bleachers and building the double-decked outfield stands within the limits of the existing park site. Construction started on February 17, 1931, and rapid progress was made. By May 1, 1931, all but the last section of the stands in center field were opened and in use. The new sections of seating had greater width than the seats in the old grandstand sections, thus the increase in capacity (21,600 to 32,000) was not as great as early press reports estimated and as might have been expected. In addition, a dark green canvas screen was erected in front of the seating section in dead center field to serve as a batter's eye. However, for games which experienced a heavy demand for tickets, the screen was removed. This was hard on the batters, but good for the Dodgers' gate receipts.

The next big change to Ebbets Field was the installation of lights during the 1938 season. Ebbets was the second major league ballpark to host night games. The first night game at the ballpark was on June 15, 1938. For the huge crowd (38,748 in a park with a listed capacity of some 32,000), it was a memorable game as Cincinnati Reds' pitcher Johnny Vander Meer threw his second consecutive no-hitter. The not-so-good lighting

The more intimate park with which most fans are familiar (Brooklyn Public Library — Brooklyn Collection).

in 1938 did nothing to make Vander Meer's second no-hitter any more difficult to accomplish. The number of night games was at first limited to seven games per season — one night game against each of the other seven teams in the National League (NL). By 1950, the Dodgers were scheduling 21 night games out of the season total of 77. In 1955, 30 night games were so scheduled.

Before the 1947 season, a small increase in the ballpark's seating capacity occurred. Three rows of box seats were added to the outfield sections of the grandstand (about 800 additional seats), and the outfield walls were now 12 feet closer to home plate.[6] The capacity of Ebbets Field had now reached its historical maximum: 33,700. The expansion of the seating in the left field and center field stands, by reducing the left field and center field dimensions, made the park very attractive for right-handed power hitters. For right-handed batters, left field was now an average distance of 345 feet, with an eight-foot fence, while right field had an average distance of 326 feet, with a 38-foot barrier to home runs. Before the 1948 season, in a move to prevent or reduce injuries, the outfield walls were padded — this change came too late for Brooklyn outfielder Pete Reiser, who had made a habit of running into the outfield walls while making spectacular catches in the early 1940s.[7]

In the Dodgers last two seasons in Brooklyn, seven home games in 1956 and eight home games in 1957 were moved to Roosevelt Stadium, across the Hudson River in Jersey City, New Jersey. Attendance was not all that great at Roosevelt Stadium, so the Dodgers decided to try another location farther west for the 1958 season — Los Angeles, California.

Ebbets Field was demolished in 1960. An interesting piece of trivia: The wrecking ball used to demolish Ebbets Field in 1960 was also used to demolish the Polo Grounds a few years later after the New York Mets used that ballpark for the 1962 and 1963 seasons. The former Ebbets Field site was used for the Ebbets Field Apartments housing development in 1963 — renamed Jackie Robinson Apartments at Ebbets Field in 1973.

The Basis of Ebbets Field's Configurations and Dimensions

The basis for the initial 1913 configuration of Ebbets Field was the original Ebbets Field plans.[8] These plans included several ballpark diagrams that showed the park's boundaries, the location of the stands, and the perimeter fences. In addition, the location of home plate and the foul lines were included. Home plate was in the southwest portion of the park. The right field and left field dimensions, derived from the park diagram in the original plans, match exactly the left field and right field dimensions for Ebbets Field in 1913, taken from *Green Cathedrals*: LF was 419 feet and RF was 301 feet.[9] Dead center field in the original plans was at the center field corner — a tremendous distance of 507 feet from home plate.

There were generous amounts of foul area in the infield. From home plate to the backstop, the distance was 76 feet and nearly as much (72 feet) from home plate to the grandstand, along extensions of each foul line. The foul area narrowed down to 55 feet at both first and third base. In addition, the plans show the location of home plate and the foul lines. Home plate was in the southwest portion of the park. The unique 19-foot high right field wall featured a slanted lower section and a vertical upper section. The capacity of Ebbets Field, when it opened, was about 19,000. Despite extensive research, no firm figures on seating capacity were uncovered.

For the 1914 season, a small change was made in the ballpark's configuration. Home plate was moved nine feet towards the left field corner and about two feet towards the right field corner. A revised park diagram for 1914–1919 was developed, and the new dimensions calculated. This move of home plate made the backstop distance 85 feet. The infield foul areas were now no longer symmetrical. The left field dimension became 410 feet and the right field dimension 300. Dead center field, now just to the left of the center field corner, was 496 feet. The deepest point in the park was still the center field corner, which was now a distant 500 feet. It appears the reason for this configuration change (at least the portion of the move of home plate toward right field) was to eliminate the zero amount of foul territory in the left field corner that had existed with the original configuration. Such a move would have eliminated disputes about balls hit into the left field corner being in or out of play.

The next major change in the configuration of Ebbets Field was the installation in early September 1920 of what was, at first, temporary bleachers (made permanent in the 1921 season) in left field and in a part of center field. These bleachers were installed for the late-season pennant race and retained for the 1920 World Series. They extended into the left side of center field but not to the center field corner. Instead, a low interior fence extended from the front left corner of the bleachers to the junction with the right field– center field perimeter wall. This configuration is evidenced by an aerial photo of Ebbets Field that appeared in the *Philadelphia Public-Ledger* during the 1920 World Series. The dimensions for this configuration were based on the listed left field dimension in *Green Cathedrals* (384) and verified with a photo of the temporary bleachers from *Diamonds.* In this photo of the 1920 World Series, there are 13 rows in the left field bleachers. The bleachers reduced the left field dimension by 26 feet or from 410 to 384. The straightaway left field (374), left center (391), and center field (450) dimensions were obtained by adding the bleachers and center field interior fence to the 1914–1920 diagram of Ebbets Field and measuring the above dimensions. An interesting effect of the center field interior fence was it put the center field flagpole out of play, behind the interior center field fence. This configuration did not last long. Photos in the 1920s showed the center field interior fence had been removed. In addition, game accounts in the 1920s referred to extra base hits being driven to the center field flagpole, which proved the flagpole was again in the field of play, and the center field interior fence had been removed. It has been assumed that the interior center field fence was removed at the start of the 1921 season.

The largest change to Ebbets Field was the double-decking of the left field line bleachers, and the building of the new double-deck stands in left field and center field. This expansion cost $450,000 and increased capacity to 32,000. After the major expansion that was effective with the start of the 1931 season, the Ebbets Field average left field distance was reduced to 358 feet. Ebbets Field now had the second smallest left field in the NL — only Baker Bowl in Philadelphia was slightly smaller, with an average left field dis-

Thirteen rows of bleachers were added in time for the 1920 World Series (Library of Congress, Prints & Photographs Division, Bain Collection [LC-DIG-ggbain-31275]).

tance of 357 feet. In terms of overall size, Ebbets Field, with a composite average outfield distance of 359 feet, was the second smallest ballpark in the NL — again only Baker Bowl was smaller. This major expansion increased both the seating capacity and visual appeal of the ballpark. However, the timing of the expansion, at the beginning of the Great Depression, was terrible. Ebbets Field attendance dropped substantially in both the 1931 and 1932 seasons.[10]

The following tables show the configuration data for the life of the ballpark: dimensions, fence heights, and average outfield distances.

Table 1: Dimensions (Calculated from Park Diagrams)

Years	*LF*	*SLF*	*LC*	*CF*	*RC*	*SRF*	*RF*
1913	419	417	441	507	388	326	301
1914–1920*	410	408	431	496	378	321	300
September 1920	384	374	391	450	378	323	296
1921–1930	384	374	391	496	378	323	296
1931–1946	353	353	378	399	378	318	296
1947–1952	343	340	363	384	378	318	297
1953–1957	348	345	378	384	378	318	297

*1914–August 1920

Table 2: Average Outfield Distances

Years	*LF*	*CF*	*RF*
1913	422	455	333
1914–1920*	414	449	330
September 1920	379	425	328
1921–1930	379	433	328
1931–1946	358	397	326
1947–1952	345	383	326
1953–1957	350	384	326

*1914–August 1920

Table 3: Fences Height (From Green Cathedrals)

Years	*LF*	*CF*	*RF*
1913–1920*	20	20	19
September 1920	2.5	2.5–20	19
1921–1930	2.5	2.5–20	19
1931–1935	8	8–19	19–34**
1936–1957	8	8–38	38

*1913–August 1920. **Only the Scoreboard was 34 feet in height

Table 4: Additional Information

Architect:	Clarence R. Van Buskirk
Capacity:	19,000
September 1920	21,600
1931	32,000
1940	32,970
1947	33,700
Park Size Composite Average Outfield Distance:	
1913	400
1914–August 1920	394
September 1920	377
1921–1930	380
1931–1946	359
1947–1952	351
1953–1957	353
Park Site Area:	6.0 acres

The Impact of the Park's Configurations and Dimensions on Batting

The best measure of a ballpark's effect on hitting is park factors. Park factors are computed by taking the batting data for a team and their opponents (e.g., the Brooklyn Dodgers and opponents) at the team's home park (Ebbets Field), relative to the batting data of the team and their opponents in road games at the other NL ballparks. A batting park factor is defined as the ratio of the home park batting statistic to the batting statistic in road games by a given team and opponents (e.g., a home park batting average of .300

and a road batting average of .280 equals a ratio of 1.07). Batting park factors are multiplied by 100 (1.07 × 100 = 107) and adjusted by the other park correction factor. The other park correction factor is used to normalize the home/road ratio to the league average, since the league average park factor for each batting category is by definition of 100. Thus, batting park factors of more than 100 indicate a hitter's ballpark, while batting park factors of less than 100 indicate a pitcher's park.

Ebbets Field in its seven Deadball Era seasons (1913–1919) was very close to an average offensive park. The ballpark's run park factor was 102, or two percent above the NL average, while the home run park factors were in a range of 88 to 125 (See Batting Park Factors in the eighth table below). While the home run park factor was definitely average, it was held down by the low number of over-the-fence (OTF) home runs. However, the generous dimensions in left field and center field led to many inside-the-park home runs. In the history of the ballpark (1913–1930, when the left field and center field walls were in place), no home runs were ever hit over the distant perimeter left field or center field walls. Unlike at most other major league ballparks in the second decade of the Deadball Era, the proportion of inside-the-park home runs (IPHR) was large and remained large — amounting to 68 percent of the total home runs hit in Ebbets Field's seven Deadball Era seasons.

In the Deadball Era, Ebbets Field had a park factor for runs of 102. Consistent with this park factor for runs, the batting average and on-base park factors were both 100, and the slugging park factor was 101. All in all, as far as batting statistics went, Ebbets Field was a typical NL Deadball Era ballpark. Ebbets Field, in 1915, had the second-largest left field (only Robison Field in St Louis was larger) and the largest center field. Despite the ballpark's generous dimensions in left field, left-center and center field, Ebbets Field posted only slightly above average park factors for triples — an average of 117 for the 1913–1919 seasons. The home run park factor was a very ordinary 102. Unlike many other Deadball Era parks with modest park factors for triples and home runs, Ebbets Field had a park factor for doubles of a sub-par 89 for the same 1913–1919 seasons.

Ebbets Field became much less asymmetrical and a more typical sized NL ballpark with the installation of the (originally temporary, then permanent) left field — center field bleachers in early September of 1920. In the 1921–1930 decade, Ebbets Field was roughly average in size for an NL ballpark. The average outfield distance for the NL ballparks in that decade was 381 feet, while Ebbets Field was 377 — a one percent difference. The batting park factors for the same decade were not much changed from the Deadball Era. The park factor for batting average dropped from 100 to 97, on-base percentage from 100 to 98, and slugging percentage from 101 to 97. From these park factors, one can conclude that Ebbets Field was a slightly below average park for batting. In the category of extra base hits, the batting park factor for triples decreased (117 to 107) with smaller dimensions in left field and left-center, while doubles also decreased, from 89 to 85. The home run park factor stayed virtually the same (103 to 102), as the number of OTF home runs increased, while the number of IPHR decreased. (See Tables 5–8 below.)

Ebbets Field, in the Deadball Era, was a very asymmetrical ballpark with an average left field distance of 414 feet and an average right field distance of 330 in 1914–1919. The question comes to mind — to what extent did Ebbets Field in the Deadball Era favor left-handed batters over right-handed batters? Home/road batting data were compiled for all

Brooklyn left-handed and switch-hitting batters in the Ebbets Field Deadball Era seasons of 1913–1919. The batting data for Brooklyn right-handed batters was obtained by subtracting left-handed and switch-hitting batters from the total team home and road batting data. In their home games played at Ebbets Field, the Dodger left-handed batters had marks (batting average, on-base, and slugging) of .302, .360, and .411 vs. marks of .252, .295, and .329 for the right-handed batters. A first impression of this data is Ebbets Field favored left-handed batters. One obvious possible alternative explanation is the Dodgers had better left-handed batters than right-handed batters. Since the Dodger's left-handed hitters in these years included two-time batting champion Jake Daubert and Hall of Fame outfielder Zack Wheat, there may well be obvious merit to this argument. If the left-handed batters were better hitters than the right-handed batters, then the left-handed batters should have hit better at home and on the road. In fact, that is exactly what happened. The road batting marks for the Dodger left-handed batters were .282, .340, and .373 vs. .239, .277, and .306 for the right-handed batters. This established that the Dodger left-handed batters were, in fact, better hitters than the Dodger right-handed batters. A relative comparison was made of the home/road batting marks for both left- and right-handed batters. The Dodger left-handed batters had home/road batting ratios (batting average, on-base, and slugging) of 1.083, 1.074, and 1.104. The equivalent marks for the Dodger right-handed batters were 1.054, 1.060, and 1.078. Bear in mind the above home/road batting ratios reflect the general home park advantage, as well as the particular park effects unique to Ebbets Field. For comparison, the average NL home/road batting ratios, in this decade (1910–1919), for batting average, on-base, and slugging were: 1.044, 1.044, and 1.061. From this data, one can see the Dodger left-handed batters had home/road batting ratios only two to four percent better than those of the Dodger right-handed batters. Not a very large difference for a strikingly asymmetrical ballpark such as Ebbets Field.

There is one inherent problem with using ratios of home/road batting data in the Deadball Era. In the second decade of the Deadball Era, the average NL ballpark is believed to have favored left-handed batters. As evidence as to why this might have been true, consider that in 1915 the average left field distance for all NL ballparks was 383 feet, while the average right field distance for all NL ballparks was 351. Thus, for the Dodger left-handed batters to have had home/road batting ratios better than the Dodger right-handed batters, Ebbets Field would have favored left-handed batters more than the average NL park did so. It is the author's conclusion that accurately measuring the impact of ballparks on left vs. right-handed batters would only be possible if all of the other parks in the league were roughly symmetrical. The complete 1913–1919 home/road batting data for Dodger left and right-handed batters is shown in Table 9 below.

After the 1920 season, Ebbets Field was less asymmetrical with a 1921–1930 average left field distance of 379 feet and an average right field distance of 328. In the NL, the average left field distance was 370 feet vs. a right field average distance of 349 in 1921–1930. But Ebbets Field, in this decade, was still more asymmetrical than the average NL ballpark and still appeared to favor left-handed batters. Thus, the question arises: How did Dodger left-handed and right-handed batters hit in this new configuration of the ballpark? Surprisingly, left-handed batters hit no better (relative to the other NL ballparks) in Ebbets Field than right-handed batters. The home/road batting ratios for left-handed batters of 100, 101, and 103 (batting average, on-base percentage and slugging) were close to the home/road batting ratios for right-handed batters (97, 102, and 98). Only in the category of home runs did left-handed batters post noticeably higher marks (117) than right-handed batters (82). See Tables 11–12 for the 1921–1930 data of Dodger left-handed and right-handed batters.

In the seven Deadball Era seasons, the number of home runs at Ebbets Field amounted to the modest total of 26.4 per year. After the installation of the left field bleachers late in the 1920 season reduced the left field and center field dimensions, home runs increased dramatically to an average of 68.2 per season in 1921–1930. Ebbets Field had not become a bandbox or homer haven, the ballpark had merely caught up (roughly speaking) with the rest of the NL in regard to home runs — the entire league averaged 73.0 home runs per park per season in 1921–1930. One area in which Ebbets Field exceeded any other ballpark, AL or NL, was in bounce home runs.

Before the 1931 season, any fair-batted ball leaving the field of play on a bounce and doing so at a point at least 250 feet from home plate was a home run (except as limited by the ground rules at individual ballparks). The 250-foot minimum distance was added to the official rules starting with the 1926 season. Before the 1926 season, there was no minimum distance at all for a bounce home run. During the Deadball Era, there were a number of instances at various major league ballparks of roughly 100-foot bounce home runs, where fair-batted balls were deflected by an infielder into the stands in foul territory.

There were 18 seasons of baseball at Ebbets Field (1913–1930) when bounce home runs were possible under the then current rules. During these 18 seasons, there were two principal configurations of Ebbets Field. In Ebbets Field's original large configurations (the two configurations before the addition of the left field bleachers in September 1920), inside-the-park home runs were common (some 65 percent), and bounce home runs were rare. In fact, in the nearly eight seasons of the park's large configurations, there were only seven bounce home runs — all seven of which were, in the author's judgment, flukes. The first bounce home run at Ebbets Field happened in a game on May 6, 1916. A ball hit to right field by the Dodgers' George Cutshaw rolled up the slanted lower portion of the right field wall and skipped over the top. To make this bounce home run even more memorable, it was a walk-off home run that occurred in the 11th inning. There were two other bounce home runs hit to right field: one struck the kinked right field wall and bounded into Bedford Avenue, and the other went through an open gate into the field level stands down the right field foul line. In addition, there were two bounce home runs hit to center field; both went through the exit gate in center field. The final two bounce home runs in this time period were hit to left field. Both were the result of left fielders kicking the ball into the third base stands.

Starting in September 1920, after the installation of the temporary bleachers in left field, the now much closer left field home run barrier had only a 2.5 foot height at the front of the bleachers. In fact, it was now possible to hit a bounce home run into the LF bleachers on the second or even third bounce! The new bleachers had a tremendous effect on the number of bounce home runs at Ebbets Field! In the original configurations, bounce home runs were less than one per season. With the left field bleachers in place (10 plus seasons), a total of 92 bounce home runs were hit at Ebbets Field, of which 88 went into the bleachers. Of these, 80 went into the left field sections of the bleachers, six into the left-center field portion of the bleachers and two into the center field section. There were two bounce home runs hit into the foul area stands — one down the left field line and one down the right field line. Two other bounce home runs were hit to right field. Both of these were ones that struck the canted lower portion of the right field wall and climbed over.

By comparison, there were a total of 353 bounce home runs hit in the major leagues for the 11 seasons of 1920–1930. Ebbets Field, the leading major league ballpark for bounce home runs, with 92 alone, accounted for 26 percent of the total. At Ebbets Field for these 11 seasons, bounce home runs outnumbered inside-the-park home runs (92 to 66).

The home run data and batting park factors for Ebbets Field 1913–1930 are shown below in Tables 5–12:

Table 5: Home Runs by Type at Ebbets Field

Years	***Total***	***OTF***	***Bounce***	***IPHR***
1913–1919	185	60	7	125
1920–1930	720	653	93	67

Table 6: OTF Home Runs by Field at Ebbets Field (Excluding Bounce)

Years	***Total***	***LF***	***CF***	***RF***	***Unknown***
1913–1919	53	1*	0	49	3
1920–1930	560	114	10	426	10

*Into temporary bleachers in front of the LF wall

Table 7: Inside-the-Park Home Runs by Field at Ebbets Field

Years	***Total***	***LF***	***LC***	***CF***	***RC***	***RF***	***Unknown***
1913–1919	125	44	14	56	5	5	1
1920–1930	67	7	3	43	9	0	5

Table 8: Batting Park Factors at Ebbets Field, 1913–1930

Years	***BA***	***OBP***	***SLG***	***2B****	***3B****	***HR****	***BB*****
1913–1919	100	100	101	89	117	102	102
1920–1930	97	98	97	85	107	103	100

*Per AB. **Per Total Plate Appearance (AB+BB+HP)

Table 9: Home/Road Batting Data Brooklyn Dodgers, 1913–1919

Left-Handed Batters (LHB)

Park	*AB*	*H*	*2B*	*3B*	*HR*	*BB*	*HP*	*BA*	*OBP*	*SLG*
Home	5025	1517	196	94	54	427	30	.302	.360	.411
Road	5398	1521	202	92	35	431	46	.282	.340	.373

Right-Handed Batters (RHB)

Park	*AB*	*H*	*2B*	*3B*	*HR*	*BB*	*HP*	*BA*	*OBP*	*SLG*
Home	11644	2939	362	202	41	627	83	.252	.295	.329
Road	12190	1521	396	144	41	567	62	.239	.277	.306

Table 10: Home/Road Batting Ratios Brooklyn Team, 1913–1919

Group	*BA*	*OBP*	*SLG*	*2B**	*3B**	*HR**
LHB	107	106	110	104	110	166
RHB	105	107	108	96	147	105

*Per At Bat

Table 11: Home/Road Batting Data Brooklyn Dodgers, 1921–1930

Left-Handed Batters (LHB)

Park	*AB*	*H*	*2B*	*3B*	*HR*	*BB*	*HP*	*BA*	*OBP*	*SLG*
Home	8807	2746	452	155	227	797	48	.312	.372	.476
Road	9549	2968	523	155	210	824	52	.311	.369	.464

Right-Handed Batters (RHB)

Park	*AB*	*H*	*2B*	*3B*	*HR*	*BB*	*HP*	*BA*	*OBP*	*SLG*
Home	15328	4062	583	213	100	1253	91	.265	.324	.350
Road	16198	4343	708	168	129	1115	63	.268	.318	.356

Table 12: Home/Road Batting Ratios Brooklyn Team, 1921–1930

Group	*BA*	*OBP*	*SLG*	*2B**	*3B**	*HR**
LHB	100	101	103	94	108	117
RHB	99	102	98	87	134	82

*Per At Bat

Once again, this major reconfiguration of Ebbets Field had little effect on the ballpark's batting park factors. For batting average, on-base percentage, and slugging percentage, the park factors increased from 97–98–97 for 1921–1930 to 99–100–101 for the 11 seasons of 1931–1941. Only for doubles was that a significant change — the park factor for doubles went from 85 in 1921–1930 to 108 in 1931–1941. Given that Ebbets Field, in the 1931–1941 time period, was the second smallest ballpark in the NL, why were the batting park factors so average? One theory is the construction of stands (in 1931) in dead center field led to the white-shirted fans in center field creating a poor batter's background.

Before the 1947 season, the seating capacity of Ebbets Field was increased, while the left field and center field dimensions were decreased. The average outfield distance at Ebbets Field was now 351 feet, compared to the NL average of 370. For the 1953–1957 seasons, a relocation of home plate before the 1953 season increased the average outfield distance slightly to 353 feet. A natural question is what effect this change in 1947, reducing the left field and center field dimensions, had on the Ebbets Field batting statistics. In the 11 seasons with the smallest configuration in the ballpark's history (1947–1957), the Ebbets Field batting park factors were above average in every batting category except triples. For home runs, there was a dramatic effect — a 92 percent increase in the park factor (as shown in Table 13 below) from 1946 to 1947–1957. It is interesting to note that only with the 1947 season did Ebbets Field become a slightly better-than-average hitter's park. A notable exception is the home/road ratios for home runs for left-handed batters in 1913–1941. In summary, Ebbets Field was a good hitter's park only for left-handed power hitters until 1947, when it became a better hitter's park for right-handed power hitters.

Table 13: Batting Park Factors at Ebbets Field, 1931–1957

Years	*BA*	*OBP*	*SLG*	*2B**	*3B**	*HR**	*BB***
1931–1941	99	100	101	108	109	105	105
1946	97	100	96	115	110	61	107
1947–1957	101	102	105	108	95	117	105

*Per AB. **Per Total Plate Appearance (AB+BB+HP). Note: Excludes 15 games at Roosevelt Stadium Jersey City in 1956 and 1957.

Table 14: Home/Road Batting Data Brooklyn Dodgers, 1931–1941

Left-Handed Batters (LHB)

Park	*AB*	*H*	*2B*	*3B*	*HR*	*BB*	*HP*	*BA*	*OBP*	*SLG*
Home	11854	3301	613	170	233	1222	54	.281	.351	.421
Road	12075	3474	572	157	184	1068	66	.288	.349	.407

Right-Handed Batters (RHB)

Park	*AB*	*H*	*2B*	*3B*	*HR*	*BB*	*HP*	*BA*	*OBP*	*SLG*
Home	16245	4313	816	186	172	1491	65	.265	.330	.370
Road	17230	4413	723	135	170	1303	54	.256	.310	.343

Table 15: Home/Road Batting Ratios Brooklyn Team, 1931–1941

Group	*BA*	*OBP*	*SLG*	*2B**	*3B**	*HR**
LHB	98	101	104	110	111	129
RHB	105	106	106	120	146	107

*Per At Bat

Table 16: Home/Road Batting Data Brooklyn Dodgers, 1946–1957

Left-Handed Batters (LHB)

Park	*AB*	*H*	*2B*	*3B*	*HR*	*BB*	*HP*	*BA*	*OBP*	*SLG*
Home	8237	2334	450	93	278	1124	42	.283	.372	.462
Road	8671	2303	380	80	279	1037	28	.266	.346	.424

Right-Handed Batters (RHB)

Park	*AB*	*H*	*2B*	*3B*	*HR*	*BB*	*HP*	*BA*	*OBP*	*SLG*
Home	21190	5693	925	169	691	2647	141	.269	.354	.426
Road	22169	5764	897	178	561	2462	123	.260	.337	.392

Table 17: Home/Road Batting Ratios Brooklyn Team, 1946–1957

Group	*BA*	*OBP*	*SLG*	*2B**	*3B**	*HR**
LHB	107	108	109	125	122	105
RHB	103	105	109	108	99	129

*Per At Bat

A portion of this chapter appeared previously in *Ballparks of the Deadball Era* and is used with the author's permission.

Notes

1. *Ebbets Field: The Original Plans,* ed. Rod Kennedy Jr. (New York: Brooklyn Dodgers Hall of Fame, 1992), 10.
2. Ibid.
3. *New York Times* April 9, 1913.
4. *New York Times* April 29, 1913.
5. Bob McGee, *The Greatest Ballpark Ever* (New Brunswick, N.J.: Rutgers University Press, 2005), 116.
6. Ibid., 198.
7. *New York Times* April 16, 1948.
8. *Ebbets Field: The Original Plans,* 10.
9. Philip J. Lowry, *Green Cathedrals: The Ultimate Celebration of All Major League Ballparks* (New York: Walker, 2006), 38.
10. McGee, 120.

II — Memories of Ebbets Field

A Few More Wrinkles That May Be Introduced at Our New Ball Park

Even before it was built, there was anticipation that Ebbets Field would produce new and different kinds of memories (*Brooklyn Daily Eagle*, January 25, 1912).

Visiting Players Reminisce About the Brooklyn Ballpark

I remember how small it seemed to be, but that was only an illusion. Right field was very short with a very high wall. The top of the wall in left seemed like it was even with the batter's head.—**Jim Bolger played the outfield for the Reds, Cubs, Indians, and Phillies over seven seasons from 1950 to 1959.**

The ballpark was very small, particularly in right field where you had the high scoreboard. The dugouts were very, very low, so much so you could bang your head if you got up too quickly. I only played there twice, but one of the ballgames I played in, Emmett Kelly was there. He was a real clown, probably the number one clown in the United States in the '50s and '60s. Kelly would go up to someone in the bleachers, in the front row, and he would eat a head of lettuce right in front of them. He would look at them while he did it, and he would just keep looking. They would look away, but when they looked back, he would still be looking at them.—**Eddie Bressoud was a member of the Giants, Red Sox, Mets, and Cardinals between 1956 and 1967. Although he played every infield position, he was primarily a shortstop. He hit a personal-best 20 home runs in 1963 for Boston and had a .963 career fielding percentage at shortstop.**

I came up as a rookie at the end of June in 1954 and replaced the first African American ever to play with the Cardinals, Tom Alston. I'm from New Jersey, and I used to be a Yankees fan growing up. I remember going to play my first game in Ebbets Field. They had a great ballpark and all of these great players, like Campanella, Hodges, Snider, and Pee Wee Reese. And here I am playing against the Dodgers. It was quite a thrill. The Dodger fans were great. We had Stan Musial, and he used to hit so well at Ebbets Field, they called him "Stan the Man."

Of course, in '54, we were struggling. We didn't have great pitching, and we didn't win many games. I did set a Cardinal record for two pinch hits in one game in the same inning against the Dodgers. In St. Louis on my birthday, I hit a three-run homer against Carl Erskine. Of course, he struck me out three times in Ebbets Field, and some of my family members were there. Once after Stan Musial hit a home run off of Preacher Roe, Roe drop kicked his glove into the stands.

They [the fans] could be rude every now and then. We would wear white shirts and ties to the ballpark, and going to the Dodgers' stadium, you had to be careful because if they lost, they would squirt a water pistol with red or black ink. It was a small ballpark.

There was lots of signage. The stadiums were built closer to the field then. The fans had a better perspective of the game.

Sometimes when I was in a slump, I used to bunt. And once when we were playing the Dodgers, I was in a slump, and I bunted at Billy Cox, the Dodger third baseman. I ended up getting a base hit and scored a run. The next time I was up there was a runner on second, and I got a hit, and I drove in a run. I was out of the slump. Well, after the game we go into the shower room, and Eddie Stanky chewed me out like I have never been chewed out in my life. Stanky said you don't bunt against a team like the Dodgers in a small stadium. I tried to explain, but I don't think he ever understood.—**Joe Cunningham played for the Cardinals, White Sox, and Washington Senators in a 12-year major league career. A first baseman and right fielder, he made the All-Star team in 1959 en route to a .345 batting average.**

The first memory I have is that when I first went out onto the field, I was really surprised it was that small all the way around, and that it was so short to right field. Carl Furillo was the right fielder then, and I remember hitting a ball to right field, and as I was going down to first base, I was jogging. I thought I had it, and the next thing I knew he almost threw me out at first base. That's how short it was. The playing surface, if I remember, it was pretty good. It had all grass. They kept the field in pretty good condition. It was nice playing there, and they had a really good team at the time. If you won there, you were really lucky. The atmosphere for them was phenomenal every time we went in there, and you really had to play extra well to beat them. They drew really well no matter who the opposition. I remember one game where we were winning, 3–1, and Duke Snider came up and hit two home runs in two times at bat, and they beat us.—**Bob Del Greco played for the Pirates, Cardinals, Cubs, Yankees, Phillies, and Kansas City Athletics. Spending most of his career patrolling the middle outfield spot, Del Greco recorded a .981 fielding percentage during his tenure in the big leagues.**

The ballpark itself was very small. I think down the left field line it was a little bit over 300 feet, and right field was only 240 or 250 feet. It was built on a block of streets in Brooklyn itself, and the streets were very narrow, and the right field line was built right on the street. The wall was also right up by the street. It was a very good field for a left-hander to get base hits, and even the right-handers because it was so short to go to right field and try to just hit the wall.

The right field wall consisted of a concrete base, and this was the craziest thing about the ballpark. The field was a weird shape because it was built on a city block. As for the concrete base, it was slanted, like Cincinnati [Crosley Field]. You had to be very cautious because it was very difficult to defend in the outfield. The concrete base extended up a few feet, and then they added the fence, and the fence at that time was corrugated metal, and it went way up. And then on top of that fence was another fence, so it extended I guess two stories high, and I guess they had to do that because it was short. A pop fly could be a home run.

That fence extended down to center field along that city block. When they cut the field over [toward left field], the block was still going on. There wasn't another street going that way [with the fence], so the stands were built [in between the city block and the fence that went toward left field]. The wall there wasn't too high, maybe 5–10 feet high. Those stands went to the left field line. It was the same type of setup as Sportsman's Park in St. Louis. So it was a very small ballpark. I will always remember that park because Stan Musial used to hit them over the right field fence, and they would hit the building across the street two stories high.

The pitchers had a tough time there because you'd get base hits that were cheap, but playing defense, you had to learn how to play the ball when it would hit the wall. And let's say it went to right-center, it could take a bounce over your head back to the infield. If it hit on top of the concrete part, the ball could either go left or right from the grooves in the corrugated steel. Then in center field, there was also a little corner where you had to catch flies sometimes. It was a very trying field to defend from center field and right field.

The Brooklyn fans were tremendous. They were very loyal, and they didn't like the opposing club. They would get all over you in that respect. You'd get used to them hollering because they were so close to you that you could hear everything. They were very noisy and loud.

I never cared to play in New York because you had a hard time getting to the ballpark. You had to take the underground subway. You had to get there on your own, and you couldn't afford a taxicab. They [the fans] knew where the door to your hotel was, and they would meet you at the door and walk with you until you signed an autograph. You got to the subway, and you had to put a dime in. They would jump over the turnstile and keep hounding you and would get on the train with you. The thing went in reverse when the game was over. They would meet with you coming out and follow you to the subway. So they were tough, but they were tremendous baseball fans. It was a decent ballpark, but it wasn't the best in the world. The outfield grass was so-so. It wasn't the manicured fields that you like. It was just a playing field. There was a grass infield with dirt all the way around the bases. There was no foul territory. You'd pop up a ball, and it was in the stands because it was built on the small block. But the playing field wasn't great at all. The locker room was small. They had little cubby-hole, wooden lockers, and you could barely hang up your clothes. There were little wooden showers, not real sanitary.

Also in a game in 1947 we were tied with them going into the 10th inning, and they had men on first and second base. Eddie Dyer put me in right field in the ninth. And Eddie Stanky was on second base, and there were two outs, and Dyer put me in right field for defense, and they got a base hit in the hole, and I threw Stanky out at home. It was still tied, and in the 12th inning, Whitey Kurowski hit a home run, and we won. All the sportswriters were around Whitey Kurowski because of the home run that he hit, and this lone reporter came up to me, and said, "Chuck, you look lonely. If you hadn't thrown that guy out at the plate, you wouldn't have won the ballgame." — **Chuck Diering played for the Cardinals, Giants, and Orioles from 1947 to 1956. Primarily an outfielder, he had a .987 fielding percentage in over 700 Major League games.**

My first memory of Ebbets Field is when I worked out with the Dodgers in 1947. I was in high school getting ready to graduate and Branch Rickey wanted to sign me. I spent a week with them. If you remember '47, that was when Jackie Robinson first came into the major leagues. I met the guys, was in the locker room, and worked out with them everyday and sat up in the stands and watched the games. I decided it was a zoo. In my opinion, nobody has ever really seen a baseball game unless they've seen one in Ebbets Field. It was a place all its own.

My first game in the majors, I was with Cincinnati, and we played the Dodgers at Ebbets Field. That was in 1953. The things that happened, the people they had. They had the Sym-Phony Band, they had Hilda Chester with the cowbell. It was a tight little park. You could almost throw the ball against the right field fence from home plate, but it had a high screen. It was a hitters' ballpark. They had a loyal following. Brooklyn fans were like no other fans I've ever seen. In my opinion, you find the best baseball fans and the most studious ones in the New York City area. They've been exposed to baseball for a long time. They know the game of baseball and how it should be played. Of course, a lot of that's changed now. That's a little better than 50 years ago. It was baseball. You had camaraderie with the guys you worked with. They were there. There were no computers. No one was making any money, and everybody was happy.

There was one time though, a Sunday, we were going over to play a doubleheader, and four or five of us were riding the subway, and Dale Long was wearing a white linen suit, and one of the Brooklyn fans squirted a blue ink pen all over it when Dale did not give him an autograph. The people there expressed opinions, but they were good fans. They were knowledgeable and most were courteous.

The surface of the field wasn't like today. Not many ballparks were in the condition that they are in today. You had Happy Felton who had the Knothole Gang down the line in right field. So it was an adequate ballpark, but by today's standards, it would be called a cow pasture. I don't care who you were or where you played, your ground crew doctored the field according to the home team. If you had some fast runners on the opposing team, the ground crew would dig up between first and second and fill it up with sand.

The Dodgers had Carl Furillo playing right field, and he had a cannon for an arm, and if a ball was hit to him, you didn't take an extra base. Center field was the hardest field to cover. It was the deepest part of the ballpark, and they had Pete Reiser, who would bounce off that wall. Most of their players were students of the game. They would try to steal signs from the pitcher or whatever. All is fair in love and war. It was a real friendly ballpark, like Fenway park. What they did was a different world to me. I was a little country boy from Virginia coming to the big city. It was just a pleasure to put a uniform on and go out and play. — **Hank Foiles caught in the major leagues for 11 seasons with seven different teams and made the National League All-Star team in 1957.**

I played the last game ever played there, and I also played the last game at the Polo Grounds a week before in 1957. There were only 6,000 people in the stands because they were so mad that the Dodgers were going to move, and I think that there were only 11,000 at the Polo Grounds.

I think it was about 330 down the line, 375–380 to the power alley in left-center, and to center field it was not even 400. Right field was really short because they had the screen up high and all that jazz. I didn't hit that way anyway, so I didn't pay attention. And if you hit one that way, Carl Furillo would grab it.

The first time up in 1955, it was like 36 degrees, and I didn't start the game. My brother George and I were on the bench because Curt Roberts was playing second, and Sid Gordon was playing third. We were just sitting on the bench and we're getting beat, and our manager Fred Haney, said "Freese, go hit." I told my brother George to hit, but I ended up going up there. [Public address announcer] Tex Rickard sat right behind the Dodger dugout. In the lineup card, they didn't have our names, just our first initials. And Tex wanted to know who I was, and Don Zimmer told the guy leaning into the dugout that it was Augie, and that's how I got my nickname, which stuck. I was hitting against Carl Erskine and got a base hit over Pee Wee Reese.

Then I got on first base and people are throwing stuff at me from the stands. They were kind of crazy. Gil Hodges had me stand in front of him, and said they wouldn't throw stuff at him. Of course, he said that if I got a big lead, they would throw stuff again.

One time I was playing third base and Jackie [Robinson] was on third, and it was 1956, his last year. And someone hit a fly ball to left field, and he tagged up too soon I thought. So I went to the umpire Al Barlick, and I had already been thrown out four or five times that year. I get the ball, and I stand on third, and he said, Safe." I said, "You're a homer." He said, "I'm going throw you out of here, and from now on, a lot of guys are going to throw you out until you correct yourself." — **Gene Freese was a member of the Pirates, Cardinals, Phillies, White Sox, Reds, and Astros between 1955 and 1966. An infielder, who spent most of his time at third base, Freese hit a personal-best 26 home runs and 87 RBI in helping lead the Reds to the 1961 National League pennant.**

They called it the bandbox. It was small. You knew you had to have your "A" game when you went in there. There was a lot of excitement at Ebbets Field. They had the band playing, so there were many things going on. They packed the stadium just about every time we were there.

It was a great place. The short fence in right field, where it was 297 down the line. Then it was 390 to center field and 335 to left, where you had the double deck. It was a great ballpark. It was one of the all-time greats. It was a pretty ballpark. It had a lot of charisma. That's what baseball was. The fences weren't symmetrical. There was a lot of history. It was like Yankee Stadium.

It was an exciting place to play, in and out of the ballpark. They used to drop cherry bombs into the bullpen from the left field seats. They had a lot of action. Leaving the ballpark, if you beat them, you always got harassed. A lot of times we had to have the policemen usher us out. They got on you when you walked on out from the ballpark to your bus.

It was a good playing surface. The infield looked like red clay. It was a shade of red. The clubhouse was typical of the old clubhouses, not very big. I really learned how to pitch in Ebbets Field. I pitched a lot of baseball games in Ebbets Field and had some pretty good ones against the Dodgers, and that was one of the great teams at that time.

I had a game there on May 31, 1955. I wasn't pitching too well at the time, and Roy Campanella had just hit a line-drive home run over my head into the seats in center field where it was 390. It probably carried 410. Fred Haney came out, and was going to take me out. I kind of begged him to stay in, and he let me. We ended up getting them out and went on, and we scored a few runs. I pitched a complete game and struck out nine. That was a turning point for me, and I ended up winning the ERA championship [2.83].

That was a big game for me. I hit a home run off Mad Monk Meyer there into the left field seats on September 25, 1954, and he kept cussin' me as I did my home run trot around the bases.—**Bob Friend played with the Pirates from 1951 to 1965, before splitting his last season (1966) with the Yankees and Mets. A part of three All-Star teams and the 1960 World Series champion Pirates, the right-handed pitcher led the National League in innings pitched twice, wins once, and ERA once.**

When I think about playing at Ebbets Field against the Dodgers, the word that comes to mind is claustrophobic, and not just because of the size of the ballpark. That lineup was just overwhelming—Reese, Snider, Hodges, Robinson, Campanella, Furillo, Pafko—it never stopped. No matter how well we played, we just couldn't beat them. And if their offense wasn't enough, they played great defense. Carl Furillo was magnificent in right field. My rookie year in 1952, they beat us 19 out of 22.

I played my first game that year against the Giants at the Polo Grounds. Then in my second game I faced Billy Loes at Ebbets Field. Like all those Dodger pitchers, he tried to knock the bat out of your hands. It was a tough way to break in. The infield at Ebbets Field was one of the best I ever played on. The ball always bounced true. I don't remember any bad hops.

The fans at Ebbets Field were very enthusiastic, but they always treated me well. They supported their team, but I never found them to be abusive. Day games were tough, however, because there were no team buses in those days, so we took the subway or a cab from our hotel in Manhattan. We usually wore sports jackets, and a lot of mine got torn by kids chasing me for an autograph.

After my rookie year in 1952, I spent the next two years in the military. My first year back [1955] the Dodgers ran away with the pennant, but in 1956, the pennant race came down to the last weekend when we played three games at Ebbets Field. The Pirates had just played at the Polo Grounds, and we had a few days off before the series in Brooklyn. Two sportswriters, Milt and Arthur Richman, took Bill Virdon and me to Grossingers to play golf. It was my introduction to a game I have loved ever since. During the round I got hit on the knee with a ball, and it really swelled up. I was worried because the series in Brooklyn would help decide the pennant, and I had to play. After using a lot of ice, I was able to play all three games and even went 4 for 8. It was no where near enough, however, as the Dodgers won all three games and their last pennant in Brooklyn. Just being part of it was something special.

Of course, the next year was the Dodgers last year in Brooklyn, and I played in the last game at Ebbets Field. In fact, I also played in the last game at the Polo Grounds, and I assisted on the last out there. I don't think we were really conscious of being part of the last game at Ebbets Field. It felt just like a typical end of the season game. The next year when we realized that we weren't going back to New York and Brooklyn to play was when it really hit us. While we never had any real success against the Dodgers at Ebbets Field, I have a lot of fond memories of the place and hated never being able to play there again. To me, the Frank Sinatra song, "There Used to Be a Ballpark Here," says it all about Ebbets Field.—**Dick Groat played for the Pirates, Cardinals, Phillies, and Giants during a 14-year major league career. He was the starting shortstop for two World Series champion teams—the 1960 Pirates and the 1964 Cardinals—and was the National League MVP in 1960.**

I did have one hair-raising experience there with the Reds. I was sitting in the bullpen one real cold day, and the starting pitcher got in trouble right from the get-go. I was sitting in the bullpen, and I hadn't thrown a pitch. Rogers Hornsby comes out of the dugout, and we were all hiding and hoping it wouldn't be us. He waved his right hand, and I ended up coming in. I had eight warm-up pitches, and the bases were drunk. Andy Pafko was up, and he hit a ball on a 3–2 pitch so damn high in the infield, I thought it would never come down. Finally, we got out of the inning. They had some tremendous ballplayers on their club at that time, and a couple of interesting managers with Durocher and Dressen.

The atmosphere was unbelievable. It was very tight and very, very noisy. They had little jazz bands all over the seats and the bleachers constantly playing. Red Barber was always coming through and doing interviews before the game. It was a great ballpark for me to pitch in. You were almost on top of the catcher because the backstop was right behind the plate. Ebbets Field was so close and tight that I always felt real comfortable with my control. I was a breaking ball pitcher, and the Dodgers were a fastball hitting club. So in 1951 and 1952 I got to pitch against them quite a bit. All the National League clubs stayed at the Commodore Hotel in Manhattan, so when you factored in the Giants with the Dodgers, you would have two clubs checking in and two clubs checking out. Consequently, you would have four clubs in the same hotel.

I remember once Duke Snider hit a pitch off of me, and I've never seen a ball hit so hard. The right field fence went straight across the outfield and joined the left field fence in deep center field. The right field fence was extremely high, and Snider hit a ball that was still going when it hit the corner where the two fences joined. I couldn't believe it went so far. The right field fence down the line was pretty short, but it was very, very high. There were a lot of base hits off of that fence that would have gone out in most ballparks. They came back probably for a double.

When I got traded in 1953 to the Reds, I was in Brooklyn at that time, and they called me in after warm-ups and announced that I had been traded to Cincinnati. They said to pack up my bags and head for Philadelphia where the Reds were playing the Phillies. As I was leaving, I went right past the Dodger clubhouse, and Jackie [Robinson] came out of the door. We had a great relationship. I probably faced him 13 or 14 times, and he got his hits, and I also got him out. I always respected him and never knocked him down or anything like that. He saw me leaving and backed me up against the wall.

He said, "What are you doing?" I explained to him that I had been traded, and I was demoralized. That was the time when a lot of white guys were giving him a lot of grief. It was embarrassing the way they yelled at him. He took the time to build me up and said, "You are going to do great there." That was amazing.

It was very noisy, and there were all kinds of people in there all the time. You would go to get in a cab to leave after the game, and if you had the window down, the kids on the sidewalk would be zipping baseball cards or anything else they had through the window to get signed. The patronage and excitement were exciting. It was terrible for the community when they left.—**Bob Kelly pitched for the Cubs, Reds, and Indians between 1951 and 1958.**

It was a great place to play, mainly because the fans were so entertaining, and you also had characters, like the members of the Brooklyn Sym-Phony band, and everything else that went on there. The fans were really the main thing about playing in Ebbets Field. They had great teams and great fans, and it was always packed, so it was something you always looked forward to.

The dimensions were small, but that was really offset because they had such outstanding pitching. But the ballpark itself was really small compared to other parks, in regards to the dimensions. And they had the unusual fence in right field. There was cement way up high and a screen on top of that, so you got a different bounce.

They had the Abe Stark sign on the fence, and if you hit the sign, you got a new suit of clothes. That was almost impossible to hit because it was so low to the ground. It probably went from the ground to about three or four feet high. And Carl Furillo would stand in front of it and make it nearly impossible to hit, and we would always joke that Furillo should get a suit because of that.

The dugouts were really small, in terms of height. A manager would get enthusiastic and hit his head on the top and literally knock himself out. It was that low. It was fine for sitting but not for standing. The tunnel or the runway to both clubhouses was the same for both teams, and they were adjacent to each other and you could hear what was going on. You would always try to pick up information that way. When we went to the clubhouse, it was screened off. The fans couldn't get to the players, but you would be able to communicate with them. This was on a dirt runway that both teams used to get to the clubhouse under the stands on the first base side.

It was the time when the bubble gum cards started, probably in the 1950s. Kids would take postcards, and they would throw them into our cab, or whatever, as we were leaving the park. It would have their address, and when we got back to the hotel, we would be able to sign an autograph and send it to the kids. That was the start of the bubble gum cards and the autograph frenzy. That was the first time I think I saw that in major league baseball.

They had a double deck in left field, and I almost hit one on top of the roof. I don't know if anyone ever did that. The wind was blowing out most of the time, so that made it a good park for hitters. I hit for the cycle there, which was the only one of my career. A triple is really unusual there because the fences are short, and of course, the triple is the toughest of the four to get.

We had a pitcher named Sullivan, and he had a tough night the night before, and he came the next day for a day game. And he crawled inside the drum that held the tarp, and he probably would have been okay sleeping off a tough night there. But it started to rain, and when they put the tarp on the field, they rolled him on to the field.—**Ralph Kiner played for the Pirates, Cubs and Indians over a 10-year major league career. Best known as a power-hitting leftfielder, Kiner went to five All-Star games and held at least a share of the National League home run crown for seven straight seasons, including a career-best 54 in 1949. Kiner was elected to the Hall of Fame in 1975.**

We rode the subway out to get there, and then you had to walk two blocks. Usually when you got to the ballpark, you had to walk by a lot of kids who wanted your autograph, and you had better sign for them, or they would throw ink on you. But we signed, so it was no big deal.

Ebbets Field was an interesting park. You could hit home runs there. I even hit one or two. Their guys, Duke Snider, Carl Furillo, Roy Campanella, and Gil Hodges, all those guys — even Pee Wee Reese — when you got through half the season, they usually had just about 20 home runs. It was an easy park for hitters. It wasn't too friendly for pitchers.

The fences weren't that far away. It seemed like they were only 315–325 feet. They had the scoreboard and the screen going up in right field. It was easy to hit home runs, and with their particular lineup, they had the guys that could do that. Carl Furillo played the right field wall better than I've ever seen. He could play a ball off the scoreboard into a single.

There was a game when Jackie Robinson told our coach, Clyde Sukeforth, "I'm going to beat you." Clyde had been a coach with the Dodgers, but he came to Pittsburgh after Branch Rickey. Jackie said that to him, and then he backed it up, stealing second, third, and home to win the game in the ninth inning. It was an interesting park to play in, and the fans were very rabid of course. And when they pulled out [to Los Angeles], it was a sad day. They loved their Dodgers.—**Vern Law was a pitcher, playing his entire 16-year career with the Pittsburgh Pirates. He won 162 games and went 2–0 with a 3.44 ERA during the 1960 World Series victory over the Yankees.**

I played there in 1956 and 1957. And of course, that was when they still had Roy Campanella and Jackie Robinson. We always stayed in New York City and would go across the Brooklyn Bridge to the ballgames. And it was a small ballpark. I think my brother Von won his first game there [June 16, 1957] in Brooklyn, in relief, when he came up at age 18.

I didn't have very good luck there. I lost a game, 2–1, when Junior Gilliam stole home plate in the 10th inning [June 14, 1957]. And then I lost a game there, 4–2 [May 4, 1957]. I would have lost it 2–1 except I hit a home run off of Roger Craig that tied the game at two. Then Charlie Neal came up and hit a home run, and we lost, 4–2. Charlie

Neal hit the home run to straightaway center field. He wasn't that big a guy, so it was not too hard to hit a home run there. The air was heavy because it was at sea level, so your good stuff would work well, and they always had good [pitcher's] mounds. It was a tight mound, so there wasn't loose dirt. I think I was very successful there considering the ballpark. I just wasn't very lucky. They were low-scoring games.

I always thought the Dodgers had a neat organization. They had a lot of stability in the organization. It was kind of the Dodger way of playing. Of course, they had Walter Alston, who was the manager for 18 years with one-year contracts all of those years. They stressed pitching and defense, doing the little things to win, such as moving runners over, stealing bases. They played the game the way I thought it ought to be played. That distinguished them from the Giants, who were all power, rather than doing the little things. My impression is a lot of the Dodger players were real gentlemen — Campanella, Hodges, Jackie Robinson, and Pee Wee Reese.

It was a small ballpark, and it had some funny angles. And of course, the fans were right on the field, and they were pretty vocal. Like a lot of ballparks in those days, the clubhouse wasn't very much. I think our showers were next to the street. And people could throw soda pop through a screen into the shower from the street. The shower had a screen at the top that faced the street. Most of those clubhouses in those days were pretty dismal things. — **Lindy McDaniel enjoyed a lengthy major league career, playing for the Cardinals, Cubs, Giants, Yankees, and Royals. Primarily a reliever, he participated in one All-Star Game (1960) and went 141–119 while pitching over 2,000-plus innings.**

My experience was that I had a good year in the minor leagues and was brought up to the Cardinals at the end of the 1950 season. I reported to Ebbets Field for my first game on Saturday, September 16, and I went to the gate, and I had my little bag with me and shoes and sweatshirt and stuff like that. I said to the gatekeeper, "I'm Ed Mickelson, I'm supposed to be in here with the Cardinals." He replied, "You're not on the list." I said, "I don't care, I need to get into the clubhouse." I got a little bit riled, and the clubhouse was just a little bit away from where we were. I asked him to go into the clubhouse, and authenticate me. He did, and I got in. I went into the clubhouse, and there were all my heroes. I'm wondering what I'm doing here.

Then I put on my uniform with the birds on the bat, and go into the Cardinal dugout, and I see Hodges at first, Robinson at second, Pee Wee Reese at shortstop, Billy Cox at third, then Carl Furillo in right field, Snider in center field, and Gene Hermanski in left. Then Campanella was behind the plate. I thought maybe that gatekeeper was right, maybe I don't belong here. I think this was on a Saturday. I didn't play. I was just there for one game, and the next day was a Sunday, and we went to play the Giants at the Polo Grounds, and I pinch hit.

It was just a big thrill for me to be there at Ebbets Field with all those great players. And Brooklyn, that was a tremendous team, golly. That was just a tremendous bunch of ballplayers out there on the field. My observation as I looked at the field was the fans were right on top of you, and it was really not that big a ballpark. Even though I didn't

Music was always part of the atmosphere at Ebbets Field (Library of Congress, Prints & Photographs Division, Bain Collection [LC-DIG-ggbain-17204]).

play, I still remember it.— **Ed Mickelson was a first baseman, who played for the Cardinals, Browns, and Cubs between 1950 and 1957.**

The crowd was absolutely fantastically noisy. They got on you pretty good in Brooklyn. I remember the Brooklyn Sym-Phony Band. It was beautiful. I remember Gladys Goodding at the organ. I remember the public address announcer, and one time when he said, "Pitcher Ralph Branca has left the game. He has a blister that has busted." I never forgot that. It was so fantastic.

I remember taking the subway there and walking through that fantastic area to the ballpark. There were all kinds of occupations, stores, and then the mounted police on horseback around the ballpark all the time. I really liked it. It was great playing there and wonderful because they had such a great team. They had the best teams in the league, so it was always a challenge to play there.

It had a short fence in right field, and it had that ledge on the fence in right field, where the ball could get up there, hit, and get stuck there instead of bouncing down. As a pitcher, I didn't like that short fence in right field. But it added to the character of the ballpark. It was a wonderful, wonderful ballpark, with all the great players they had there. The tunnel where the two teams came in from their locker rooms, there was just a slight partition separating both tunnels. I loved that. Everything was unique and wonderful.

I thought they had a nice mound there, and I thought the playing surface was excellent. I thought it was a beautiful little ballpark. There was a lot of tradition and all the advertising on the walls. Watching the Dodgers run on the field with those white uniforms and blue trim, what a thrill. When you beat them, you couldn't wait to get out of there because they had police on horsebacks trying to keep the fans away, and they had to because the fans would throw stones at you.— **Bob Miller pitched for the Philadelphia**

Phillies from 1949 to 1958. A starter and reliever, Miller appeared in the 1950 World Series.

My rookie year was in 1955 with the Cincinnati Reds, and I pitched in relief a few times at Ebbets Field. Like most players, what I remember the most is how small the park was. Of all the parks in both leagues that I visited as a player, it was the smallest. As a rookie when I took the mound, I felt like everything was closing in on me, but after a few minutes I was able to settle down and relax. The Dodger fans were something special. Dodgers who were just average ball players were treated like they were kings. At the same time, they were always fair to visiting players like me. Of all the Dodger hitters, Carl Furillo was the most difficult for me — he was the hardest to get out.— **Rudy Minarcin played for the Cincinnati Reds and Boston Red Sox from 1955 to 1957.**

The most important thing to me was when I was a rookie and it was the first time I had ever been to Ebbets Field [1954]. I was in the clubhouse and all I had was pants and a T-shirt and my uniform. I was looking out a window that was about 10–15 feet up from the concrete sidewalk. There was a little kid there and he said to me, "You must be Dick Murphy." I was a rookie, I had never been to Brooklyn, and I had just joined the club, so I don't think he had ever seen my picture. It just speaks to how much they knew about the game. It had a real short porch in right field. The wire fence was probably 30 feet high, and Duke Snider used to hit them over that fence like pop flies.— **Dick Murphy played for the Reds in 1954.**

It was an extremely close park. The dugouts were so close to each other you could needle the other team. There was so little foul territory that if you fouled out, they said you were in a slump. It was the most intimate ballpark around. The close proximity and the fans were right there. They were great fans. All of the parks had character back then. I thought that Ebbets Field was a great park to play in. It wasn't a short porch as they used to say. You had to hit the ball. The bullpens were adjacent to the foul lines and almost on the field, kind of like Wrigley Field today, except closer.

Every park was different, and I liked that about our time. For the old-time player, I think what was great is it was straight baseball. Now there's little boats running around, the grounds crew coming out every three innings and dancing, and this pitch is sponsored by so and so.

The Dodgers had Happy Felton, who was an interviewer down in the right field bullpen, and he would interview the player of the game. That was the only major league park that we played in that had advertisements. They had an Abe Stark sign beneath the scoreboard and Happy Felton advertisements in right field. So it was colorful. The other parks were just baseball and no advertisements.

I thought that was the best infield surface that I ever played on. It had the best consistency. Pittsburgh was hard between short and third, and sandy up the middle. The

Cincinnati infield sloped back. The Polo Grounds' infield had a sandy, white tinge. In Milwaukee, the stands were so low, the fans used to sit there on Sunday, and they'd wear white, and you could lose the ball in their shirts or the background. St. Louis, because of the weather, was hard as a rock. You adjusted to the infields that had a different setup, but that was the one thing I really liked about it. The infield was perfect. You didn't even see a rock out there.

When we came out of Seattle University, we played in the NCAA basketball Tournament in 1953 in Corvalis, and we finished on a Saturday night. On Sunday afternoon, we [Eddie and twin brother Johnny] signed with Pittsburgh. On Monday we went home and spent a night with my father, and then on Tuesday, we flew to Havana to meet the Pirates for spring training. We worked our way back up and opened the season at Ebbets Field. It was a great thrill for us because we were 30 miles from home [born in South Amboy, New Jersey], playing at Ebbets Field to open the season. We didn't get in, but I just remember looking around, and it was a great thrill to start my major league years there.

We played them once the last game of the season [1956], and they were a game ahead of Milwaukee. We played them in Ebbets Field, and Vern Law started for us and Don Newcombe for them. If they beat us, they won the National League championship. And of course in those days, whoever won the championship, went to the World Series. At the time I was playing center field, and in the first inning, Duke Snider hit one over my head into the center field bleachers.

The Dodgers went on to win, and they had a champagne celebration after the game in the clubhouse. Gil Hodges came over from their locker room and gave us some bottles of champagne. He said, "We beat you 13 times during the year, so you helped us win the pennant, so I figured we should give you a few bottles of champagne." He was one of the nicer guys that ever played the game.—**Eddie O'Brien was a member of the Pirates in 1953 and again from 1955 to 1958. He was a true utility man, appearing in games as a pitcher, shortstop, second baseman, third baseman, and all three outfield positions.**

As I recall there wasn't a lot of excitement at the last game in 1957. Both pitchers pitched good games. We just got beat, 2–0, Danny McDevitt pitched that day for Brooklyn and was opposed by the Pirates' Benny Daniels, who was making the first start of his career. Daniels' chore was not an easy one.

We had a young team, and the Dodgers were loaded [with a lot of sluggers].

It was a small park. It held about 35,000, but there was a very lively atmosphere for the most part. They had a heck of a ball club, and you go in there with a young pitcher pitching against those guys in a small park, it was a challenge for a young pitcher to pitch a good game in a park like that.

It was a sober type atmosphere because there wasn't a lot of hollering from the stands. The players didn't seem to be overly excited about playing in the last game. Usually in Ebbets Field, they had the five-piece band always playing, walking through the stands and the fans — it was a very lively type atmosphere. That didn't happen in this game. I don't remember that. It was kind of a lackadaisical kind of game, not a lot of action, not a lot of excitement in the stands or from the players in the field.

At the last game at the Polo Grounds, people were coming out of the stands, tearing up the sod, the bases, and even home plate. At Ebbets Field it didn't happen that way, maybe because the clubhouses were not in center field. At the Polo Grounds, you had to walk clear across the field, and it was deep — maybe 460 ft. At Ebbets Field, the clubhouses were behind the dugouts, so we made outs in the top of the ninth, and we just went behind the dugout to the clubhouse. The clubhouse itself was very small, kind of a cramped, a small type of clubhouse. It was an old ballpark, and a good one to play in. The fans were always hollering, and they had the band going. It was a fun place to play. It wasn't like that at the Polo Grounds.

I hit one of my three home runs in Ebbets Field. And on that day, I also had a single and two walks. Happy Felton had a program after the game, and I thought — oh boy, I hit a home run and got two walks. I thought I had a chance to be the star of the game, but he picked Frank Thomas instead. — **Harding "Pete" Peterson was a catcher for the Pirates in 1955 and 1957–1959.**

I think the first thing that I remember was the ball club that was playing there was awfully good. When I came into baseball, the Dodgers were one of the top teams. The ballpark itself had very small dimensions, but it wasn't any different than Wrigley Field in Chicago.

When we won the pennant in 1950 that was my best memory, besides getting married and being inducted into the Hall of Fame. That was the third highlight. [Richie] Ashburn threw a runner out at home plate in the bottom of the ninth or else we would have been playing the next day. We would have been tied. That was the big play, and then the three-run home run by Dick Sisler in the 10th. That was a great moment for the Phillies. We had been down for so many years as an organization. We finished third in 1949, which showed improvement. And then we won in 1950, so at least we have that good memory. After clinching the 1950 pennant at Ebbets Field, we went back to Brooklyn on Opening Day in 1951. And we won that game as well. I pitched and beat Carl Erskine.

In that ballgame when we won the pennant, right field was close, and there was a high fence with a concrete wall halfway up and then screen wire the other half. For the Dodgers' run, Pee Wee [Reese] hit a ball to right field. The ball hit the screen and stuck on top of the concrete part. He circled the bases, and they gave him a home run. Of course, there was no ground rule that covered that. But there was a ground rule from then on.

The Phillies' fans weren't much different [than the Dodgers' ones]. Brooklyn fans had a certain accent that you recognized. The fans were so close to the field. That was different. The Brooklyn situation in baseball was one of a kind. You knew that when you went there. We used to take the subway to the game, walk from where you got off to the ballpark, and the fans would holler, "The bums are going to get you." If we won, we went right past them on the way out. If we lost, we found another way. — **Robin Roberts,**

World Series games produced long lines outside the ballpark in both 1920 (top) and 1947 (bottom). Notice the diversity in the 1947 crowd, surely due to Jackie Robinson (Library of Congress, Prints & Photographs Division, Bain Collection [LC-DIG-ggbain-31442; Brooklyn Public Library — Brooklyn Collection).

who became a member of the Hall of Fame in 1976, played most of his career with the Phillies (1948–1961), before finishing it with the Orioles (1962–1965), Astros (1965–1966), and Cubs (1966). His list of accomplishments includes five All-Star teams, one World Series appearance, and 286 career wins with a 3.41 ERA. In addition, Roberts finished with 20 or more wins each season from 1950 to 1955 and led the National League in victories the final four years during that period.

It was cozy and small. There was no foul territory. The stands came right down to the foul lines, and the people were right on top of you. They were very, very boisterous. I can remember my first game there in 1956. I played against Carl Erskine. I can remember them hollering, "Com' on Ersk."

It was always kind of a special place to me because I was born in Brooklyn. My family moved when I was nine or 10 years old up to White Plains. But my allegiance was to the Dodgers when I was a kid, and it stayed that way until I had to bump heads with them. As for the dimensions of the park, I just wished to hell I was a left-handed hitter. You could stand at the plate, and you were almost at the right field wall. It was tall, but it was close.

What always fascinated me about the difference between the two leagues was the National League had smaller ballparks. So the pitchers were mainly breaking ball or sinkerball pitchers because they wanted you to hit the ball on the ground. In the American

Unable to get in or unwilling to pay the admission charge, fans sometimes used alternative means to see their beloved Dodgers (Library of Congress, Prints & Photographs Division, Bain Collection [LC-DIG-ggbain-31443]).

League, they would throw you the high, hard ones and let you hit it nine miles because you couldn't hit it out of center field.—**A Brooklyn native, Art Schult played for the Yankees, Reds, Senators, and Cubs at first base and the corner outfield spots.**

Back in those days, we would be at one hotel in Manhattan and play at Ebbets Field and the Polo Grounds for a few days. We would ride the train to the game.

As we got off the train, we had our sports coats on, and if you missed one of the kids [for an autograph], they would squirt ink on you. The dimensions were fairly close, and it was a great hitters' park. Being on the Pirates, we were young and just in awe of the Dodgers' success. I really enjoyed playing there because I hit, and it was a hitters' park. It was fun playing there, but the results usually weren't good. Because of Carl Furillo in right field, it was almost impossible to advance too many bases because it wasn't that far, and he had a great arm. The playing surface was fine, and the gaps — there was quite a bit of room in there.

I had a grand slam home run there one time off of Monk Meyer. And he stared at me all around the bases and threw his glove in the air. In those days, we were a young team, and we were capable of playing with the Dodgers for 6–7 innings. We had good, young pitchers, and it took them 6–7 innings to catch up to our pitchers, but once they did, they would just knock us out of the box.—**Primarily a leftfielder, Bob Skinner played for the Pirates, Reds, and Cardinals, hit .277 for his career, and appeared in two All-Star games and two World Series. Along with Dick Groat, he was a member of both the 1960 Pirates and the 1964 Cardinals World Series championship teams.**

It was a bandbox. It was a really small ballpark and a great hitter's ballpark. Yankee Stadium was 461 to deep center and 457 to left center. Ebbets Field was nothing. It was a small ballpark. It was a great ballpark to hit in. I would have had a lot more home runs if I had played there more. Ebbets Field was beautiful, and the people were great. They drew a lot of fans. They really loved the Dodgers.

In the 1956 World Series, I went 0-for-4 against Sal Maglie in Game 1, and Casey [Stengel] benched me for the next five games including the fifth game when [Don] Larsen threw the perfect game. I was upset because I had 23 home runs and 90 RBIs, and I got benched after the 0-for-4 game and didn't think I would get back in.

Then in game six, Jackie Robinson hit a line drive to left field, and Enos Slaughter misplayed it. And after the game I'm standing between Mickey [Mantle] and Billy Martin, and Mickey's crying. Casey asked what's wrong, and he said, "Why don't we put Elston Howard in left instead of Enos Slaughter and put 'Moose' at first base?" The next day we were in the lineup, and Yogi [Berra] hit two home runs, Elston one, and I hit a grand slam.

Before the grand slam, Roger Craig was coming in to start the seventh, and I thought Casey was going to take me out, but Roy Campanella said he wouldn't. Casey called me back to the dugout and said he wanted me to take two shots at right field. I went back out there and Campanella said, "See I told you he wasn't going to take you out." The

A packed house at Ebbets Field during the glory days (National Baseball Hall of Fame Library, Cooperstown, New York).

first pitch was low and away, and I hit it over the left field wall. I got back to the dugout and Casey said, "Way to pull it," and everyone laughed.— **Bill "Moose" Skowron was a member of the Yankees, Dodgers, Senators, White Sox, and Angels. The first baseman appeared in four All-Star games and eight World Series, hitting eight home runs, having 29 RBIs, and batting .293 during his World Series career.**

My first memory of Ebbets Field is Opening Day in 1953, and the pitcher for Brooklyn was Carl Erskine. I was the first hitter of the year and led off the game. I hit a line drive to left center, and it looked like a sure double, but Duke Snider ran it down. In that game, I did have two hits. I had a single and a double. But it wasn't off Erskine, it was the relief pitcher — Joe Black. I was an outfielder, but when I got to spring training in 1953 [my rookie year], Branch Rickey told me I was going to play first base. So Opening Day of that season was the first time I had played first base.

In a doubleheader on August 16th, 1953, I had four hits [a triple and three singles]. I was chosen by Happy Felton, who had a sports program after the game, as the player of the game. I was asked to represent the Pirates with Duke Snider of the Dodgers. He had three home runs in the doubleheader. Also, in the first game of the doubleheader on the 16th, I hit against Preacher Roe in the first inning to lead off the game. I could run pretty well, so I bunted down the third base line and the ball stayed fair and stopped on the line. He walked all the way over to first base, me not knowing what was going on, and said, "That was the damndest bunt I've ever seen in my entire life." And then he walked back to the mound.

Another memorable moment for me was the first game of a doubleheader on April 21, 1957. Don Newcombe was the pitcher for Brooklyn. It was the third inning, and we hit three home runs, back-to-back-to-back. The first was hit by Frank Thomas, then I hit one, and then Dick Groat, all on five pitches.—**Paul Smith played for the Pirates and Cubs as a first baseman and corner outfielder. He hit .270 for his career.**

They talk about rivalries. Nothing compared to the Dodgers and Giants back in New York. Every game you would have two or three knockdowns. The players just got up, dusted themselves off, and went about their business. It was just part of the game. It was almost unbelievable. When we went to Ebbets Field, their fans were really into it, and it was the same thing when they came to the Polo Grounds. You can't imagine it unless you were there.

Ebbets Field was a hitters' ballpark. Duke Snider was the luckiest hitter because he never had to face a left-handed pitcher in his own park. It was a hitters' paradise. Everybody hit home runs in Ebbets Field. Of course, they had some good pitchers and other good players. They took advantage of that little ballpark. I don't know what Duke Snider and Roy Campanella would have done in another park, but they sure did well in Ebbets Field.

I sometimes wonder how many more home runs Willie Mays would have hit if he had played his six years in Ebbets Field instead of the Polo Grounds. He hit an awful lot of 400-foot drives in the Polo Grounds that would have been home runs in Brooklyn.

It was just a great atmosphere. It was just a great ballpark to play in. It wasn't quite the same when we went to San Francisco and Los Angeles. We still had the rivalry, but it was nothing like Brooklyn.—**Daryl Spencer played for the Giants, both in New York and San Francisco, as well as the Cardinals, Dodgers, and Reds over a ten-year major league career.**

Ebbets Field, one of the greatest memories I have is playing in that park. I think any ballplayer that ever played there has very special memories. A ballplayer that never had the opportunity to play there has no idea what baseball is all about. It was the epitome of my career, and I feel very fortunate to have played there. It was quite an experience. I feel sorry for any ballplayer that never played there. Of course, I was with the Giants, and there was the intercity fight thing. Everybody disliked everybody else.

There was a parking place across the street from the ballpark for the players. You had to be ready when you got there though. There were lots of kids with fountain pens filled with ink, and they would shoot that stuff. If you didn't have time to stop and sign autographs, you were vulnerable. You would have a white shirt with a nice streak of ink. And you hadn't even gotten in yet.

It was some ballpark. The ballpark itself was small. The fans were practically on top of you. It was different than any other park I played in. The rivalry was so great you didn't know what was going to happen. I played there in the 1951–1952 timeframe, and they had one heck of a team with Snider, Robinson, and the rest of their stars.

One of the greatest pitching feats I ever saw happened there. In 1952 [April 20 and May 27], Sal Maglie had two consecutive starts there and shut them out for 18 innings. One game was a two-hitter and the other a four-hitter. He had their number for some reason. It was a tough ballpark with the club they had at that time. I was a sinker ball pitcher, and was aware of that short porch in right field.

The best play I ever saw Willie Mays make was in that park. It was a line drive to left-center field. Mays was playing center straightaway, and Monte Irvin was playing left field. Mays starts after it, makes the catch, and then slides on the dirt, knocking himself out on the wall. Monte Irvin had to come over and pry the ball out.

The clubhouses were right together, and there was a door between the clubhouses. One time, they had whipped us pretty dog darn good, and we heard Mr. Robinson saying that the rivalry was dead. We were badly bruised, but we weren't dead yet.—**George Spencer was a member of the Giants and Tigers between 1950 and 1960. A relief pitcher for the most part, Spencer was part of the Giant team that defeated the Dodgers in the 1951 playoff.**

I enjoyed playing there. It was a good ballpark, and we were playing against the Dodgers, who at that time were the elite team of the National League. They had good ballplayers, and we played against Jackie Robinson, Gil Hodges, Pee Wee Reese, and Duke Snider. The atmosphere was great. You had Vin Scully, who was the greatest announcer, and then Gladys Goodding, who did the cheers from the stands. It was a great atmosphere almost every time you went there. We didn't fare well against the club, but we had a good time, and I've got a lot of good friends in Brooklyn.

Ebbets Field was the ideal ballpark for anybody. It was 330 down the line in left, 375 in left center, 400 to dead center. And then right was short, so that was good for Duke Snider. It was ideal for left-handed hitters because there was a short right field fence. And if you hit a high fly ball, it was a home run, and it went out onto Bedford Avenue.

It was the ideal ballpark for any major leaguer who wanted to play baseball. It was a very, very well maintained park, the infield and the outfield. It was a joy for me to play there, and when you play against a great team, it brings out the best in you. It was a ballpark that drew a lot of fans because it was a great ballpark, and they had a great ball team. When you have a great ball team, you don't need any of the stuff that you have today with the mascots.

The fans were great. They were good to me. I don't know why they were good to me. I never had any problems with any of the fans in Brooklyn at all. When I used to come out of the clubhouse, there were five or six girls that I would always talk to. They were young girls, probably 13 or 14 years old, and they became very good friends with my family when I went to the Mets in 1962. They would take my wife and my kids to Coney Island and to the World's Fair while I was at the ballpark. What's really sad is four of the six have died from cancer. One girl lived on Hawthorne Street, and they would invite me over for an Italian dinner, and every time I went, the next day I hit a home run.

I remember when Sal Maglie was pitching for Brooklyn, and I hit a home run to win the game. The next day I was on "The Big Payoff" with Bess Meyerson. Another game that I remember is the last game that we played there in 1954 when Sandy Amoros was playing left field, and he made a shoestring catch. Because he was a left-handed thrower, he reached out with his right hand. That catch kept me from hitting .300 that year.— **Frank Thomas played for the Pirates, Reds, Cubs, Braves, Mets, Phillies, and Astros over a 16-year major league career. A three-time All-Star, he played all three outfield positions, as well as first, second, and third base and hit 286 career home runs.**

I played there [Ebbets Field] about eight different years. I played in the Milk Benefit Game against the Dodgers, which was a charity game. I also played in the World Series there in 1955 and 1956. Probably the best game I ever pitched in my whole major league career was pitched in Ebbets Field. That was the game after Don Larsen pitched the perfect game, and I pitched a four-hitter. It should have been a no-hitter. I set a Yankees' World Series strikeout record with 11. Clem Labine was the opposing pitcher who beat me in 10 innings.

Enos Slaughter was in left field for us, and he had just come over and gotten on the team for the World Series and was at the end of his career. With two outs in the 10th, Jackie Robinson was the hitter. He hit a line drive right at Enos, and all Enos had to do was stand still. But he came charging in, and it went over his head, and I lost the game, 1–0. They got only one run in the last three games of that '56 World Series, and that's why we came back to beat them. It wasn't so much the hitting but the pitching.

It was a very small ballpark, so I can see why the Dodgers hit so many home runs against other pitchers. But for me, being a hard thrower, guys would swing hard and hit a lot of popups. I pitched pretty good ball in Ebbets Field. There was nothing like the fans. We took a bus to the park for the '55 World Series, and when we got off, there were a bunch of teenagers there, and they squirted ink all over us as we were going into the ballpark. The fans were very rabid. It was a fun ballpark. For me it was, anyways, although I didn't win any games there.

It was an old ballpark. It was in the middle of Brooklyn, and there were signs up, and the whole city came out for the World Series and exhibition games. It was an exciting time. In a way, I hated to see them move to California, but I understand why. O'Malley was limited to how much money he could make in that ballpark.

The playing surface was good. There wasn't a lot of foul territory so it was good for hitters, which is partially why the Dodgers had so many good hitters. The ball would go into the stands instead of being caught by the first or third baseman. It was a baseball fans' ballpark, and the fans were right on top of the field.—**A pitcher, Bob Turley was a member of the Browns, Orioles, Yankees, Angels, and Red Sox. Turley won the Cy Young Award in 1958 when he led the league with 21 wins and 19 complete games, while posting an ERA of 2.97. He pitched in one All-Star Game and five World Series, including 1958 when he was named World Series MVP, going 2–1 with a 2.76 ERA.**

Ebbets Field—it was just a special place. As with most ballparks, you had the alleys in left and right field. But Ebbets was like playing in a great big shoebox. There were no alleys. When you hit a ball on the button, it was in the seats. You hit a ball in the alley, you were either out or it was a home run. Even center field—it was something like 409 feet—that's a pop fly to center field.

It was all together different from the other parks. The stands were so close to the infield, especially at home plate. The box seats you could almost spit into it. Any pop fly foul ball that had an arc on it would end up in the seats. They talk about a hitters' ballpark—that was it. It was just a crazy place to play. But it was fun. The atmosphere is what it was. I played in both leagues, but there was only one Ebbets Field. Duke Snider and I were both from California, and once in a while we'd get together before the game. And I would say Duke, "you should give half of your salary back getting to play in this place."

I hit my first grand slam there, and I hit about six or seven. I hit it off Hugh Casey. He got a fastball up in my eyes, and I hit it out of the park with the bases loaded. It was 1947—my first year with the Pirates. I was from the country, and we were going East for the first time—to Boston, New York, and Philadelphia. We were in New York City for a three-game series with the Dodgers and a two-game series with the Giants. We got rained out all five days and never left the hotel. So the third trip in July, in Brooklyn, the first day, they had us play a doubleheader to make up one of the games from the first trip. In my first at bat of the first game, the bases were loaded and I cleared them with a double. Then, in the seventh inning, they were loaded again, and I hit a grand slam. That was the only time of my career I had seven RBIs in one game. Of course, the next time up I was knocked down. That was commonplace then.

The next night Ralph Branca, the dean of the staff, was starting. I had decided I was going to look over a pitch and get a look at it under the lights. He didn't wait long, and the first pitch was going down my mouth. I got out of the way. I don't know how. It just dusted my check. From that day on, Mr. Branca and I had no love for each other.—**A member of the Pirates, Cardinals, Reds, Indians, Orioles, and Phillies between 1947 and 1956, Wally Westlake played all three outfield positions and third base. A career .272 hitter, he appeared in the 1951 All-Star Game and 1954 World Series.**

I was on the other side, a Giant coming into Ebbets Field, so they were the enemy. When I first walked in there in 1953, I could hardly believe it was a baseball park. When you walked in from the field, and then you went from the dugout to the clubhouse, it was all dirt in that area underneath, which was unusual.

It was a nice place to play but not anything like what they moved to in L.A. It was just an experience going there. The fans were close to the field, and when they'd announce Alvin Dark, 29,000 people would holler, "Boo!" That was a little tough right there. That's what they did to each of them. Left field was not long, and right field was a short field. It was a real experience.

I remember the second game [July 11, 1953] I ever pitched in the big leagues was there. I shut them out, 6–0, and you remember the ones you win. I was a little scared going there. I drove over with Jim Hearn and Sal Maglie, and I didn't know much about the big leagues. I hardly knew anything about the Dodgers, and here I was going to pitch against them. I had heard how good they were, and they won the pennant that year. That was the only time they got shut out that year, so that was good for me. I also pitched against them when Carl Erskine pitched a no-hitter against us, 3–0 [May 12, 1956].— **Al Worthington played for the Giants — both in New York and San Francisco — and the Red Sox, White Sox, Reds, and Twins between 1953 and 1969, and was a member of Minnesota's 1965 pennant winner.**

The Home Team
Recollections of the Brooklyn Dodgers

Most of the games I played at Ebbets Field were as a visiting player with the Reds and Cubs. Then in 1955, Duke Snider got hurt, and the Dodgers picked me up from the Reds as a defensive replacement, but I didn't play very much. The two things I remember the most are the right field wall and the fans. The wall was so big, and there were so many different angles that the right fielder had to learn how to play. Of course Carl Furillo was great at it — holding batters to singles when they should have had doubles. There weren't any other parks that had a wall like it.

The other thing is the fans. They were strictly for Brooklyn, and they treated the Dodgers well. As a visiting player, they didn't like you very much. They didn't boo us, but they liked to get on us. Of course, the fans were always so close to the action. Only Wrigley Field was similar. In the other parks, the fans weren't that close.

The one game that I especially remember at Ebbets Field was May 21, 1952, when I was with the Reds. The Dodgers scored 15 runs in a first inning that lasted almost an hour. In the outfield, I was chasing a lot of line drives, wishing I was wearing armor. They really hit the heck out of the ball. The final score was 19–1 and the Dodgers set a number of records. — **Bob Borkowski played in the major leagues from 1950 to 1955, primarily with the Reds and the Cubs, though he played briefly for the 1955 Dodgers.**

The two things that I remember the most about Ebbets Field both happened during the 1955 season. On July 17, I pitched and won my first major league game, a 6–2 complete-game victory over the Cincinnati Reds. I gave up a run in each of the first two innings [one was unearned] on a total of three hits, but then for the last seven innings, I didn't allow a run or a hit. The clubhouse at Ebbets Field was very small, and I remember my first locker was a nail. But after my win, John Griffin, clubhouse man, gave me a real locker the next day. He said, "Looks like you might be around awhile."

Your first major league win is important for any pitcher, but the game I remember from 1955 was important for the Dodgers and all of Brooklyn because it was the fifth game of the World Series. As probably everyone knows, we lost the first two games, and then won the next two. I had been warming up in the bullpen for all of the games. After the fourth game, Walter Alston came to my locker and asked me how I felt. I said, "I feel great, I want to pitch." He said, "You're pitching tomorrow, kid." In the game, I pitched six innings, and we won, 5–3. Clem Labine pitched the last three innings in relief. Before the game, Alston was criticized by the press for starting me, but it worked out great!

Those were my two best memories of Ebbets Field. I guess my worst memory is

Parking was never easy at Ebbets Field (Library of Congress, Prints & Photographs Division, Bain Collection [LC-DIG-ggbain-22423]).

giving up a grand slam to Moose Skowron in the seventh game of the 1956 World Series. It was the seventh inning, and we were already behind 5–0, but that didn't make it hurt any less.

Ebbets Field was a rough park to pitch in, but I was pretty lucky. My lifetime record there was 16–5. The playing field was always immaculate. Both starting pitchers warmed up in front of the stands on each side of home plate. The difference between Ebbets Field and other major league parks I played in was that Ebbets was so small, and the fences were short. It was only about 349 feet to right center and about 383 to center field. The fans were [it seemed] so close to the playing field they could almost reach out and touch you as you walked by.—**Roger Craig pitched in the National League for five major league teams between 1955 and 1966. He also managed the Padres (1978–79) and Giants (1985–1992), winning two division titles and one National League Pennant.**

I was just a skinny kid from Indiana who was lucky to play for that team, at that time, in that place. The whole experience meant so much to me that I want to do what I can to preserve the history of that time. It is probably no surprise that my best and worst memories of Ebbets Field have to do with games that I pitched there. However, for someone who pitched two no-hitters at Ebbets Field, it probably is a surprise that those games rank only as my second and third best memories. My top memory at Ebbets Field was the third game of the 1953 World Series against the New York Yankees. It was a matchup between Vic Raschi and me — Casey Stengel used to say that if he needed a pitcher to win one game, his choice was Raschi. Not only did I win a close pitcher's duel, 3–2, I struck out 14 Yankees, a World Series record at that time.

The other fascinating thing about that game was that Roy Campanella was scheduled to be on the first Edward R. Murrow "Person to Person" show the next night. Since it was a live show, they rehearsed on Friday at Campy's home. The rehearsal went well, and at the end Murrow said to Campy, "Now all you need to do is hit a home run to win the game tomorrow." And sure enough that's exactly what happened.

My worst memory of Ebbets Field was in a relief appearance. When I came up to the majors, there were no pitching coaches who were former pitchers, they were almost all catchers. So to be successful, you really needed to rely on other pitchers as mentors. My mentor was Preacher Roe; he was a great teacher and I idolized him. Preacher started a game against the Braves at Ebbets Field and led 2–0 after eight innings, but he got sick and couldn't finish the game. I came on in relief; promptly walked the first two batters, and then Sid Gordon hit a three-run homer to cost us the game. I felt so bad that I couldn't face having to go into the locker room and apologize to Preacher. I literally wanted to dig a hole in the field and hide.

What I remember the most about Ebbets Field was the intimacy, no foul territory and very short fences. With those disadvantages, you would think that as a pitcher I would have disliked the park, but I actually liked pitching there. To me the fact that I might give up more runs there was more than offset by the fact that the Dodgers always scored a lot of runs. I don't remember the records, but I don't think the Dodgers of those days were shut out very often. Even with the negative factors, I enjoyed some real success at Ebbets Field, including two no-hitters. I got an award a few years ago called the Casey Stengel "You Can Look It Up" award for something that was both obscure and noteworthy — in my case it was the fact that I was the only pitcher to throw two no-hitters at Ebbets Field. There were something like nine all told, but I was the only one to pitch two there.

One of the people that everyone remembers from Ebbets Field is Gladys Goodding, the longtime organist. Not surprisingly, the song she played more than any other was the "Star Spangled Banner." But people might not know that the song she played the most after that was "Back Home in Indiana." During my time in Brooklyn, there were three of us from Indiana on the Dodgers: me, Gil Hodges, and Billy Herman, our third base coach. Anytime I came in to pitch, Billy Herman went out to third base, or Gil Hodges hit a home run, she would play that song. I am very proud of my home state, and it always made me feel good to hear that song. I also really appreciated it when the sportswriter, Roscoe McGowen, referred to me as the "gentleman from Indiana."

In some ways that kind of thing reflects the way things were in Brooklyn. People treated us like we were part of the family. It was never because we were famous. We just knitted together into one community. I think a lot of it had to do with Brooklyn sort of being an orphan borough, no glitz, a residential area with a lot of different ethnic groups. The intimacy of Ebbets Field may have contributed to that; the fans were so close it was easy not only to talk to them, but to hear everything they said. I often wondered whether the sense of community in Brooklyn had something to do with Branch Rickey's decision to bring in Jackie Robinson — the culture was right for that kind of change. While the

Dodgers had some periodic success before Jackie got there, after that we were either in the World Series or contended every year. I think that gave the people of Brooklyn something to be proud of that they didn't have before.

One of the fans I remember is Captain Joe Dodd, the dispatcher for the Moran Towing Company, a tugboat company. He went back to the days of Zack Wheat and Dazzy Vance and became friends with Gil Hodges, me, and other Dodgers. He used to take my sons and me out on a tugboat on an off day and sail all around New York harbor, sometimes going on an ocean liner. Captain Joe also used to take Gil Hodges, me, and others out fishing in Sheepshead Bay. I remember Ernie Harwell going the one year he was in Brooklyn. Captain Joe was almost suicidal when the Dodgers left Brooklyn. We stayed in touch after the Dodgers went to Los Angeles and I retired. One year he was my guest at an Old-Timers Day in New York, and I took him to a dinner afterwards at Toots Shor's. All the old Dodgers and Yankees were there, and he had to call his wife to tell her where he was. I heard him say, "Martha, I have died and gone to heaven." He was the Godfather of the Dodgers.

There's a famous picture of Jackie Robinson in a rundown with five Phillies in the picture. It happened at Ebbets Field on May 31, 1951. In a major league rundown play, you are not supposed to throw the ball, you are supposed to run at the runner and tag him. Jackie Robinson was so quick he would cause a major league team to forget the fundamentals. In the picture, Andy Seminick, the Phillie catcher, has the ball, and he made a bad throw into left field. Jackie broke for home and beat Russ Meyer's tag with his slide, accidentally spiking Meyer at the same time. Although you can't see it in the picture, I think the Phillies left fielder was backing up third, so there are actually six Phillies in the play. I didn't realize I was the pitcher in that game or that I got three hits. I am glad to hear that.—**Carl Erskine won 122 games in a 12-year Dodger career from 1948 to 1959, including two no-hitters. He also won two World Series games.**

It was a nice field. It was in good condition. We all liked it. It helped defensively because the field was in such good shape. When we played well, the crowd was with you. When we played badly and made errors, they booed. I would imagine it was the same as the Giants' park. I liked him [Jackie Robinson] as a person. He was a hell of a ballplayer. He did all the things you had to do to get into the Hall of Fame and win a pennant. In his first game, he played first base, and we played the Boston Braves. He scored the winning run, and we won the game. They [the crowd] were cheering him. You had the first black player in baseball, and he's playing well. The reaction was much worse on the road. But he was the right person for the right job.—**Gene Hermanski was a member of the Dodgers, Cubs, and Pirates between 1943 and 1953. A corner outfielder, Hermanski was a career .272 hitter and played in the 1947 and 1949 World Series for the Dodgers. Prior to his death in August of 2010, he was the last surviving member of the Dodger starting lineup on April 15, 1947, the day Jackie Robinson broke the color barrier.**

Before I was traded to the Dodgers, I played for five years for the Chicago Cubs, so my first experience of Ebbets Field was as a visiting player. We always felt like we came through the front gate two runs behind because the Dodgers had so many great players — Robinson, Hodges, Reese, Snider, and the rest. Other teams in the National League didn't have that kind of talent.

I remember the infield as being good in terms of true bounces, compared to other National League parks. It was an old park. I played third base, and if I took two steps, I was next to the stands and able to talk to the fans. It was dangerous during batting practice. Fans had to pay attention for line drives. If you came early to sit along the base lines, you really needed to watch batting practice. The only other park that was similar in this respect was Wrigley Field. In the others, you weren't that close to the fans. At the Polo Grounds, it was an overnight hike to talk to the fans.

Another thing at Ebbets Field was how loud the fans were. You really had to concentrate. I remember playing a few games in Boston before the Braves moved to Milwaukee, when there would be only about 2,000 fans present, and you could hear the conversations of people in the stands during the game. Brooklyn was very different, and there was also the Sym-Phony band. Other parks had people playing the trumpet or ringing bells, but Ebbets was the only field that had its own band.

From the standpoint of a hitter, Ebbets Field had a pretty good hitting background. That kind of thing wasn't important to owners in those days, so in a lot of parks, including Ebbets Field, you had fans sitting behind the pitcher wearing white shirts, which made it difficult to see. Ebbets Field was a park where I always played well, both as a visitor and as a Dodger. There are just some parks where you feel comfortable as a player, and Brooklyn was one for me. Milwaukee was a place where I never played well.

After the 1955 season I spent the winter in Chicago, which was a big mistake because of the weather. A sportswriter called me and said you have been traded. I immediately started worrying about what team it could be, and then he told me I had been traded to Brooklyn. I asked him if he was teasing me, but fortunately he wasn't. I think every major league baseball player wants to do two things: play in an All-Star game and play in a World Series. I had already played in two All-Star games, so this was my chance to make it to the World Series, which happened that year.

I was disappointed no one from the Cubs ever called me to say I was traded. That kind of thing would never happen with the Dodgers, who were always a first-class organization. When I got to spring training, the theory was that I was going to take Jackie Robinson's place. I always admired Jackie because he could beat you in so many ways. The night before the season opened, Walter Alston called me into his office and said that Jackie and I both had similar results in spring training, but given Robinson's history with the Dodgers, he would start. That was fine with me and I said, "Great!" Jackie got off to a slow start that year, and after about a month, I took over and batted cleanup. It was quite a thrill for me to have batted cleanup for the Dodgers for a few months. Unfortunately during the All-Star break, I cut my left thumb very badly on a porcelain shower knob, opening it up all the way to the bone. Jackie came back into the lineup and played great from that point on.

My favorite memory of a game at Ebbets Field was during that 1956 season. We were losing to Philadelphia, 5–2, going to the bottom of the ninth. Gilliam walked, and Duke Snider hit a home run to make it 5–4, and then I hit a home run to tie it up. Gil Hodges was up next. He also hit a home run, and we all went home. I have seen numerous other times when a team had three consecutive home runs, but I don't remember seeing any where the last one won the game. Since we won the pennant by one game, every win was important. I also hit the last home run in Brooklyn Dodger history, but it was in Philadelphia the last weekend of the season.

I don't remember anything in particular about the last game at Ebbets Field. I don't think we were told that the team was going to Los Angeles until after the season was over. At that point it was just a typical end of the season game, and if your team wasn't going to the World Series, everyone was just thinking about going home for the winter. There are only nine of us left who played with Brooklyn in 1957 and went on to Los Angeles.

When I was a Dodger, most of us came to the ballpark by car and subway. We would go through the main entrance, walk through the rotunda and down the hallway to the locker room. The locker room was small, but not that different from the rest of the stadiums. The fans would recognize you when you came through the gate, and they would pat you on the back and encourage you. I always liked the fans, and I made an effort to talk with them and sign autographs. The fans loved the players, and there was always plenty of enthusiasm. It was part of being with a habitual winner, and that's great for a player.

I also remember Happy Felton and the Knothole Gang. Happy would pick three kids who would field and throw for a player who evaluated their performance. The player then picked one kid who would come back another time. One time I got a letter from Florida from a man who I had picked one day at Ebbets Field. He told me about how much that meant to him, which was a very nice thing for him to do.— **Ransom (Randy) Jackson played for the Cubs, Dodgers, and Indians over a ten-year career. He made the National League All-Star team in 1954 and 1955.**

My memories of Ebbets Field are as follows:

1. The great fans! Hilda Chester, Shorty, and the Sym-Phony Band!

2. It was in Ebbets Field that I won both ends of a doubleheader in relief versus the St. Louis Cardinals [August 22, 1951].

3. Playing with Jackie Robinson on Opening Day in 1947! At Ebbets Field! Exciting!

4. Playing the New York Giants and the great crowds. Almost always there was a fight then.

5. Gladys Goodding playing the organ when we came on the field: For instance, with Pee Wee Reese, she played "My Old Kentucky Home!" For me, she played "Carolina in the Morning!"— **Clyde King played for the Dodgers and Reds between 1944 and 1953. A relief pitcher for the most part, King enjoyed his best season in 1951 when he finished 14–7. Following his playing career, King also managed the Giants, Braves, and Yankees, finishing with a better than .500 career record.**

I was with the Dodgers for part of two seasons. Unfortunately I never got to pitch at Ebbets Field. I first came up to Brooklyn in September of 1956 after winning 20 games with Montreal. What stood out about Ebbets Field was the scoreboard and the right field wall with all the nooks and crannies that a ball could bounce off. I think I saw two inside-the-park home runs that fell where the ball hit the wall and then shot on a line past third base. Of course, they were hit by Dodgers, not the other team. That didn't happen when Duke Snider and Carl Furillo were in the outfield — one would play the carom, and the other would back him up. Carl had an arm that wouldn't quit. I remember one sportswriter asked him how he learned to play the wall. He said, "I worked at it!" Actually he used an earthy adverb, but that couldn't be printed.

The other thing that I remember about the park is that the left field wall came straight across at an angle so that the left field line was almost as short as right field. That's why left-handed pitchers got killed there. I remember Rube Walker telling me that pitchers would get ahead of Roy Campanella 0–2 and try to waste one, and he would just overpower the pitch and hit it into the left field seats. Another thing I remember is Saturday afternoons when they would let in the Knothole Gang — all the kids in the left field seats raising hell.

During the 1956 pennant race, we were fighting the Braves, and at the end of the season, the Braves kept losing. Jackie Robinson came into the clubhouse at Ebbets Field and yelled "they are just waiting for us to beat them," and that's what happened. We clinched the pennant on the last day of the season. I was in the bullpen, and as the game ended, someone said grab your hat and glove because the fans will be over the place as indeed they were. That was an old Dodger team, but they didn't miss games, no matter how much they were hurting.

I was also with the club at the beginning of the 1957 season and again at the end, including the last game at Ebbets Field. I don't remember anything special about that game. It was a typical end-of-the-season game. The team wasn't going anywhere and everyone just wanted to end the season and go home. Danny McDevitt pitched and won for Brooklyn and Joe Pignatano caught part of the game. Joe was born in Brooklyn and Danny in New York, so it was an all–New York battery at the end of the game. — **Fred Kipp played for the Dodgers for part of their last season in Brooklyn and moved to Los Angeles with the team for the 1958 and 1959 seasons.**

The thing that stands out the most about Ebbets Field for me is the short right field fence. Next were the wonderful, avid fans. Happy Felton used to have his Knothole Gang down in right field before the game. The kid who won the contest got to choose the player he wanted to talk to. Even though I was new and only there for part of 1954, I was chosen once. If you were chosen, you got $50 from the sponsor. It was very nice. Something else is that Lucky Strike put a pack of cigarettes in every player's locker. That way they could say the Dodgers smoked Lucky Strikes even if each of them didn't.

The Dodgers had a hell of a ball club in those days, and I think Walter Alston acquired me because of how well I hit against his Montreal teams when I was with Rochester. He thought I would be a good pinch hitter, but I was the world's worst pinch hitter. I had to play every day to be effective. I played first base, and I wasn't about to replace Gil Hodges. Same thing with the Reds, I was competing with Ted Kluszewski, and you know who won that competition. A lot of the Dodgers were really nice guys and friendly to a newcomer like me, especially Gil Hodges, Junior Gilliam, Carl Furillo, Roy Campanella, Johnny Podres, Preacher Roe, and Carl Erskine.

The Dodgers acquired me from Detroit during 1954. Walter Alston asked me to meet him in St. Louis. When I got there, he said, "I want to use you in today's game, but there's a problem, you have to sign a contract, and I don't know how much they're willing to pay you." I said, "Write down a dollar." He asked if I would sign a blank contract and trust him. I said, "Yes." I signed and got into the game as a pinch runner.

When we got back to Brooklyn, Buzzie Bavasi called me in and said, "We need to sign you to a new contract." I told him that I had been making $7,500 in Detroit, and the general manager had promised me a raise if I was with the team after June. This was past June, but the Detroit general manager hadn't given me the raise. Buzzie picked up the phone to call the Detroit general manager, but then put the phone down and said, "I don't have to check, how about $9,000?" It was a lot of money to me in those days. Buzzie was a good guy. The Brooklyn Dodgers were always a first-class organization. The Los Angeles Dodgers still send me publications and material on a regular basis.—**Chuck Kress played for the Dodgers in 1954 and for the Reds, White Sox, and Tigers between 1947 and 1957.**

I only had a very short "cup of coffee" at Ebbets Field in 1953, but my memories of that time will never be forgotten. I spent two years in the Medical Corps (during the Korean War) and having saved my leave time, I was invited by the Dodgers to spring training at Vero Beach in 1953. I pitched 15 exhibition innings against other big league clubs, giving up no runs and having a great spring. I was with the Dodgers when they headed north as Dressen wanted to keep me. But regretfully, I still had 40 days to serve at Fort Sam Houston, so I went back to the Army until May 15.

When I got out, the Dodgers had a set lineup, so they sent me to Fort Worth. In two months there, I was 8–5 with a 1.78 ERA (made the All-Star team), and the Dodgers needed help again, so Dressen called me up. Not having been in baseball for one full season and getting called to the big leagues was obviously a dream at 22 years of age. I was in awe when I walked into Ebbets Field, and just to be on the same field with the "Boys of Summer" was something I will never forget. I really didn't think that much about the field itself but later knew that it wasn't exactly the best pitcher's park—the ball did carry!

I knew that Jackie Robinson went to UCLA and had a good time talking to him about Bruinville. He was only one of two ballplayers I ever played with or saw that could start to steal second base, know he was going to be thrown out and go back to first. He had great lateral movement and an explosive start. That's what made him such a great athlete at UCLA in track, baseball, football, and basketball (I believe he was the only person to letter in four sports there). He was truly an amazing athlete and a person that will forever be etched in baseball history.

Don Zimmer and I used to see who could be the fastest off the field, into the shower, and out of the park. Pee Wee would say, "First out of the club house, first out of baseball" as he watched us. He along with Hodges, Campy, Jackie, Billy Cox (probably the most underrated player on that club), Dick Williams, Duke, Don Thompson, and Carl Furillo, along with all those great pitchers, were legends, and I loved being with them.

When I look back at Ebbets Field and compare it to Dodger Stadium or Anaheim Stadium, it was truly a park that you had to go to. But the nostalgia and ambiance of that park will never be duplicated, and those fans were something to behold, especially for a young kid like me!!

As we got out of a cab to go into the park one day, a large group of fans circled around us for autographs. Jim Hughes (who was with me in the cab) said don't stop and to keep going, but being a rookie, I thought it was a privilege to sign my name. Wow, was I wrong!! I had pen marks all over my shirt and pants and had to fight my way into the park!

Manager Wilbert Robinson led the Dodgers to two National League championships. For many years during his tenure (1914–1931), the team was known as the "Robins." The name stuck to such a degree that newspaper coverage in 1957 still referred to the club as the "flock" (Library of Congress, Prints & Photographs Division, Bain Collection [LC-DIG-ggbain-31065]).

The only sign in the clubhouse I remember was in the bathroom. It said, "We aim to please, you aim too, please," and "Players with short bats please step up to home plate!" This was all put up by John "Senator" Griffin, our clubhouse guru.

I have never figured this out, but Dressen brought me out of the bullpen to face Ted Kluszewski as the first person I pitched to in the bigs. This guy had arms bigger than my legs, and his shirt cut off so that those arms would fit the uniform! I got two strikes on him and just hoped that he didn't hit up the middle and kill me, so I pitched him away—where I thought that Campy wanted it. The pitch was away, and Klu hit it into the left field stands and probably knocked five seats loose! When I got the side out and came back to the dugout, Johnny Podres was laughing and said, "Don't feel bad, Mick, I throw from the left side and he has hit several off me!"—**Glenn Mickens pitched briefly for the Brooklyn Dodgers in 1953 before playing in Japan, followed by a 25-year coaching career at UCLA.**

I just remember the fans. They were like Philadelphia fans. They were really rabid and very loyal. A better comparison would be Chicago fans. The ballpark was an old-time ballpark. There were signs on the wall, and if you hit it the suit sign, you would get a suit. I remember the locker rooms would be the equivalent of a Class D locker room today.

I remember the first time I put on the uniform, standing next to Pee Wee Reese and Duke Snider. I'm 17 and with all of those big-time players, and they treated me like an equal. That was a great experience. I remember stepping out onto the field. I got fined for not signing an autograph because I was too embarrassed. Walter Alston came by and said that would cost me $1,000. I asked him why, and he said it was part of my contract to be signing autographs at that time. He was just being stern. Of course, we got the money back after the season. I remember the hot dog salesmen, and they were getting paid a percentage of what they sold, so they went about their job in earnest.—**Rod Miller played briefly for the Brooklyn Dodgers in 1957.**

My best memory of Ebbets Field is that my boyhood dream of playing in the major leagues had come true. I played for the Dodgers for three seasons and never had a bad moment there. What I remember the most is the small ballpark with the fans sitting so close to the field. It was loud with many of the same fans at every game. It was a great place to play.—**Bobby Morgan was an infielder with the Brooklyn Dodgers and three other National League teams over eight seasons.**

In 1945, I pitched in 15 games, starting 10 and relieving in five. My record was 3–2. First when you came to the park, it was a magnificent looking ballpark from the outside, where it was rather ornate. But when you got inside, it was different. It was much smaller. And the tunnels, as well as the areas where the concessions and washrooms were located, were very small.

The dimensions were small, and it stayed that way until they moved to Los Angeles. The right field fence was over 300 feet down the line when it was built. But when I played there, it was 295. So I have a little bit of a different memory of the park. It was small, and as a youth, I had been to Wrigley Field and Comiskey Park, which were more expansive.

The left field wall was longer than right field. Left field is where Hilda Chester spent some of her time — her commotion getting the crowd going. She was all over, but I think that was her spot to sit and cheer. There was an Abe Stark sign at the base of the wall in right field. And if you hit that sign, you got a free suit. There were a lot of different signs. Wrigley Field didn't have any of those advertisements, and neither did Comiskey Park. I stayed at a hotel in Brooklyn with Clyde King, until my wife joined me.

My first start was on a Monday. I came to the ballpark for extra-men batting practice. I was in the outfield and Charlie Dressen, the pitching coach, said he wanted to talk to me. He asked if I had thrown at all. I said no — just the ball back into the infield. And he said Leo [Durocher] would like to talk to you. He asked me the same question. I said no. He said I was the starting pitcher. I had relieved in two games before that. The start was against Pittsburgh's Preacher Roe. In the seventh, we scored three to take a 4–1 lead. In the eighth, I walked two men on eight pitches. So I see Leo staring out from the dugout and motioning the bullpen to get up. I did not want to come out, as I was used to pitching nine innings. So I kicked some dirt around the mound, and Mickey Owen came out and settled me down and said, "we'll get the next guy," who was a pinch hitter. Then Leo came out and asked if Mickey told me how to pitch this guy. I said, "Yes." He said, "I don't know what I came out here for then" and went back to the dugout. We got the guy out and then got the side out in the ninth for the win.

My contract said I couldn't pitch on Sunday because of my faith, and Leo wanted to get me some work, so he pitched me on Saturday before we went West. I gave up four runs in the first inning, and we got four runs in the second half. So he sent me back out, and I loaded the bases. I still hold the record for one of the longest home runs given up at Ebbets Field. Andy Pafko hit it off of me. I got out of the second, but they still pinch hit for me.

There was another time — I was going to pitch on a Monday. We had a doubleheader on Saturday and used a lot of pitchers. It was 1–1 in the eighth, and Don Lund pinch hit for me. Don Lund pinch-hitting for Lee Pfund. Then Clyde King pitched five shutout innings, and a Howard Schultz single in the 13th won it. Leo gave each of them a $100 bill in the clubhouse. Ebbets Field was an unusual place to play, and I got to pitch in all the old ballparks. My career was short-lived as I suffered a season-ending knee injury in a Red Cross benefit game in Washington, D.C., on July 17, 1945.—**Lee Pfund pitched for the Brooklyn Dodgers in 1945.**

❖ ❖ ❖

The playing field was excellent. It was very beautiful. It was good — a lot better than what I played on in the minors — a lot, lot better. As for the fans, they loved us like children. They were in the ballgame as much as we were. And boy if you made a mistake, they let you know about it. The stands were not far from the playing field. It was only maybe 20 feet if it was that much.

It was a small ballpark. It wasn't a very big one. It was about 340 down the left field line and 355 in left-center. And it was 401 in center field, and I think 258 down the right field line, but it had a 40-foot fence and a scoreboard on it. If someone hit a line drive on one hop to Carl Furillo in right field, he'd throw them out at first base. Every game was great. Every game we tried to win. We had a good ball club.

Fans would try almost anything to get to a game at Ebbets Field — even telling the truth (*Brooklyn Citizen*, April 8, 1913).

It was kind of sad the last game of the 1957 season. I caught the last game in Ebbets Field. We all didn't know what was happening. We kind of figured we were going to Los Angeles, but we were never told that we were. We were hoping we would stay in Brooklyn. I was a Brooklyn boy, and I wanted to stay. I went because, hey, I was in the big leagues. There weren't many people in there, and Gladys Goodding played at the end of the game. I was the last player off the field and the skipper was right behind me. He was the last one of the club to go down those steps and go to the clubhouse. I was next to last. They [the fans] were mad. They knew we were going. They just said, "Bye," and "We'll see you somewhere along the line" because they were still diehard Dodger fans. And most of them became Met fans.—**Joe Pignatano played for the Dodgers in both Brooklyn and Los Angeles, as well as for the Kansas City Athletics, Giants, and Mets. A catcher, Pignatano was part of the Dodgers' 1959 World Series championship team.**

One of the things that I remember the most about Ebbets Field is the nearness of the fans to the field and the players. Also, it was a hard place to pitch. Not only was the left field fence close, but it was actually lower than home plate — a tough place for pitchers. Some of the words I would use to describe it are impressive, old, and traditional. In my opinion, it should have remained standing as a tribute to baseball.— **Ed Roebuck pitched for the Dodgers both in Brooklyn and Los Angeles from 1955 to 1963, before finishing his career with Washington and Philadelphia. All but one of his 460 major league appearances were in relief.**

What I remember the most about Ebbets Field is coming out of the dugout and seeing the field and all the things I had seen pictures of and read about. To top it off, I had Pee Wee Reese's uniform on, as he was in the service. I gave the uniform back the following year. Above all, I liked the fans at Ebbets Field, they were so close to you that you could shake hands with all of them. It was a great park and there wasn't anything I didn't like about it. One game that stands out is a close contest against the Cardinals with Enos Slaughter on third with one out. The ball was hit to right field, and Carl Furillo with his great arm threw the ball to me on one hop as Slaughter was tagging up. The ball got there maybe a step ahead and he hit me and drove me almost to the wall. I lost all of my tools, but the ball was in my right hand, and he was out. What a shot! I felt it for a few days. I saw Slaughter at a B.A.T. [Baseball Assistance Team] dinner and told him about it. His answer — "Can't play the game, get the 'H' out." I said, "You're still mean."— **Mike Sandlock was a catcher and utility infielder for the Braves, Dodgers, and Pirates between 1942 and 1953.**

When I first came up to Brooklyn from Mobile, Alabama, in 1948, I went to pinch hit. A fan started yelling encouragement — "You can do it." "He's afraid of you," things like that. Then I struck out and he yelled, "Send the bum back to Mobile."— **George Shuba played for seven years with the Brooklyn Dodgers, including on the 1955**

World Series championship club. Oral History Interview, 2008, Brooklyn Historical Society.

I got out of the service in 1946, and Bill Killefer, an old Dodger scout, came to see me play. He asked what position I played and my coach said I played all over, so in that game I caught for three innings, pitched for three innings, and played shortstop for three innings. He then invited me to come to Ebbets Field for a tryout on the day of the second National League playoff game between the Dodgers and the Cardinals. I worked out at 8:00 A.M. and then caught batting practice for the Dodgers.

After that I asked the Cardinals if they would mind if I caught batting practice for them. They said they would appreciate it, so I did. My dad and I then watched the game from the stands. It was the first major league game I ever saw. The next day they signed me to a contract, and I started playing in the minors in 1947. The only bad thing about the experience was that my dad had his pocket picked while he was walking up the ramp.

I spent a lot of time over the next seven seasons going up and down from the minors, to and from Brooklyn, usually when Roy Campanella was hurt. In most years, I spent spring training with the Dodgers, but it wasn't until 1954, that I made the team and played in 10 games. The one I remember the most is when I caught Preacher Roe against the Pirates on May 23, 1954, at Ebbets Field. The Dodgers had a policy that the starting catcher would catch the last ten minutes of the pitcher's warm up throws to get ready for the game. Preacher told me that everybody says he threw a spitter, but that I shouldn't worry about it because what he really threw was a screwball. It was actually sort of a changeup. We won the game, 5–4, and I didn't have any trouble with his pitches.

The Dodger players were a great bunch of guys, like brothers. That was due to Branch Rickey. He made it like a close family. I learned a lot of baseball in that organization. I especially remember the right field wall and that Carl Furillo was the only one who could really play it. When I took batting practice at Ebbets Field, I hit a couple on the top of the wall, and I thought this was pretty good, but then I realized it was because the wall wasn't that far away.—**Tim Thompson played for the Brooklyn Dodgers in 1954, before spending three years in the American League with the Athletics and Tigers.**

Vox Populi

The People Remember Ebbets Field

My first Dodgers game at Ebbets Field was in 1942 when, at the age of six or seven, I saw a loss to the St. Louis Cardinals, who were World Series champions that year. After that I was hooked. While I could have walked to Ebbets Field from where I lived, most of the time we took the Brighton Beach Line of the BMT. As you came out of the subway, there was a Bond Bread factory across the street, and you were immediately hit with the aroma of fresh baked bread. Walking the two blocks to Ebbets Field, the aroma of the bread mixed with the smell of beer and cigars — the combination of the three was the odor of Ebbets Field. It will stay with me until I die. Like everyone else, what impressed me the most the first time I went to Ebbets Field was the green grass. We lived in an apartment and never saw grass like that. I actually had a brief career as a peanut vendor at Ebbets Field, but it was a short tenure because I was fired for sitting down and watching the game instead of selling peanuts.

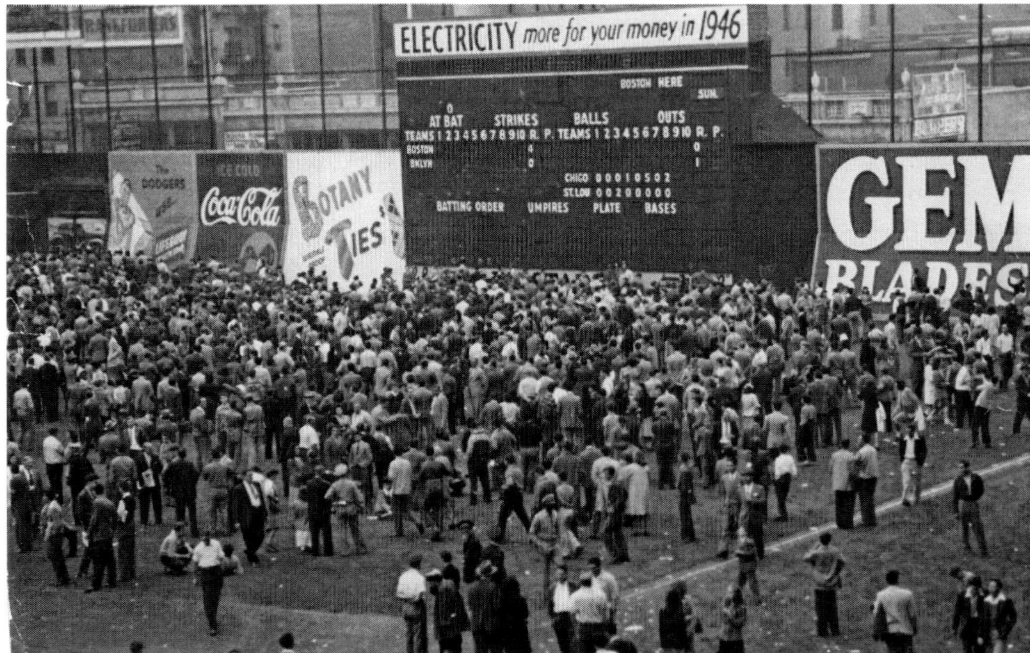

Exiting through the center field gate after a game allowed fans the opportunity to walk on the hallowed ground of their beloved ballpark (National Baseball Hall of Fame Library, Cooperstown, New York).

After the Dodgers left Brooklyn, I founded the Brooklyn Dodger Baseball Hall of Fame. It came out of a project at the Jackie Robinson Intermediate School in Crown Heights, which is located directly across the street from the site of Ebbets Field. The school opened in 1967 and was named after Jackie when he died in 1972. In 1977, which was the 10th anniversary of the school's founding and the 30th anniversary of when Jackie broke color barrier, our school did multiple projects on Jackie and the Dodgers, which led to the creation of the Brooklyn Dodger Baseball Hall of Fame. I think the Brooklyn Dodgers were the first "America's Team" because after 1947 they represented all of America. Brooklyn was probably the only place where the color barrier could have been broken because of the diversity in what was a borough of immigrants where so many different races and ethnic groups lived together.—**Marty Adler—oral history interview, 2010, Brooklyn Historical Society**

I was born in Troy, New York, but my parents moved to Brooklyn and we lived in Bay Ridge near where the Verrazano Bridge is today. My first game at Ebbets Field was in 1938, the year that Babe Ruth was a coach with the Dodgers. We had just moved to Brooklyn and my mother said you have to see Babe Ruth. We went to a late-season game against the New York Giants and I think Carl Hubbell pitched for them. That was before the Dodgers' resurgence under Larry MacPhail. We sat in the upper deck to the left of home plate.

As a kid in the 1940s, I used to love to go to Sunday doubleheaders at Ebbets Field. My mother would give me a bag of bologna sandwiches, a nickel for a Coke, and a nickel for the subway. I would sit in the center field bleachers, which I believe cost 55 cents. To me, it was the best seat in the house, just like the camera angle that television uses for most games today. Pete Reiser was the center fielder. He would have made the Hall of Fame had it not been for the injuries he suffered.,

If St. Louis was in town, you might see pitching matchups between Mort Cooper and Howard Pollet of the Cards and Kirby Higbe and Whitlow Wyatt of the Dodgers. Often in the second game, the people in the box seats had left, so you could move down into those seats. I was a baseball fan, not a Dodger fan, so I loved seeing teams like the Cardinals and the panorama of baseball at Ebbets Field. Something else that stands out is the satin uniforms that the Dodgers wore for night games during World War II. They were white satin with a blue stripe down the shoulder.

Then, when I was in high school, I was a copy boy for the old *New York Sun* and my girlfriend, Maureen, who has been my wife for 56 years, and I used to go to Friday night games at Ebbets Field and sit in the lower left field stands. I don't especially remember any specific games, but the one thing that stands out is Jackie Robinson running the bases—the way he would jitterbug back and forth off a base.

The physical feature that stood out the most was the scoreboard and the wall in right field—the ads on the wall and the scoreboard like Schaefer beer. Stan Musial used to hit line drives off that wall and sometimes over the wall—Ebbets Field is where he got his nickname of "the man." Another physical feature that I remember was the center field exit gate where the wall joined the center field stands. After the game was over you could go down on the field, walk around the infield, and go through left field and center field out the gate onto Bedford Avenue. You didn't have to go out that way, but it was an option.

I was the only kid in my neighborhood that went to see the old NFL Brooklyn Dodgers play at Ebbets Field during World War II — nobody else I knew liked pro football. For example, I saw Sammy Baugh play for the Washington Redskins. The games weren't well attended and the team ultimately went out of existence. Then there was another Brooklyn Dodger football team in the postwar era that played in the All-America Football Conference. Although the NFL Dodgers weren't that good, they had some great players — such as Hall of Famers Ace Parker and Bruiser Kinard.

The Dodger baseball team I remember the most was the 1953 Dodgers, which was the best Brooklyn team of the era — that's my opinion and it was the players' opinion as well. They won the NL by 13 games and led both leagues with 208 home runs. Duke Snider hit 42 and Roy Campanella hit 41.

I covered the last Dodgers' game at Ebbets Field for the *Journal American*. I wasn't the beat writer; he was off covering the American League pennant race, so I went to that game. After the game was over, Bill Roeder (*New York World-Telegram and Sun*) and I were the last two to finish. We were always the last. It was about 1:00 A.M., and we took the elevator to what was called the "night watchman's gate." There were still cleaning people in the building. We got to the gate and I let Bill go first, and as I went out, I realized I was the last baseball writer to leave Ebbets Field after the last Dodger game. I didn't plan it that way and I never wrote about it until the Brooklyn Cyclones started and the *Times* asked me to write about baseball in Brooklyn.

The only notice that was taken of it being the last Dodger game at Ebbets Field was by Gladys Goodding through the songs she played on the organ — for example, "California, Here I Come." The move wasn't official yet, but everybody knew it was coming. O'Malley had Los Angeles in the back of his mind for three or four years before that. You read now that Robert Moses was the villain, well O'Malley was the villain. The last game wasn't made into a big deal because it hadn't been officially voted on by the National League owners. O'Malley handled it so there was no emphasis on it being the last game at Ebbets Field.

I remember all the characters among the fans like the Sym-Phony band, the guy who yelled "Cookie," and Hilda Chester. When I was a kid in the center field bleachers, I would be about 10 rows behind Hilda with her cowbell. There was always something going on — it was like a country fair. And they were real fans. They didn't need a color commentator.

I got started as a sportswriter at the age of 22 in 1951 as a $40-a-week clerk at the *Eagle,* no other sports departments were hiring. I did things like answer the phone to take down high school scores plus a little writing. Then in 1952, Lou Niss the sports editor told me he wanted me to cover some Yankee and Giant home games which I did. The Dodger beat writer was Harold Burr, but early in the 1953 season, he fell in Cincinnati and broke his hip. The other reporters didn't want the job because it meant being away half of the season. I realize now that Lou Niss was grooming me in case he needed a beat writer, which it turns out he did.

So in May of 1953, I suddenly was the Dodgers' beat writer. I was in awe of the other writers. I learned how to do it in self-defense by keeping my mouth shut and listening. The other writers were people like Dick Young of the *Daily News*, Bill Roeder of the *World-Telegram and Sun*, Roscoe McGowen of the *Times*, Roger Kahn and Harold Rosenthal of the *Herald Tribune*, Gus Steiger of the *Daily Mirror*, Mike Gavin of the *Journal American*, Jack Lang of the *Long Island Press*, Sid Friedlander of the *New York Post*, and sometimes Bill Dougherty of the *Newark Evening News*.

In those days, you covered spring training plus all of the home and away games, so you almost never got a day off. All the road trips were by train except at the end of a trip to the west like St. Louis or Chicago when the team would fly home. Fortunately for me, Tommy Holmes liked to cover Sunday doubleheaders at Ebbets Field both to write an article and his notes column, so I got Sundays off. It was the best beat in the city; the Yankees won all the time, but there were more stories and action with the Dodgers. I think I may have been only the sixth or seventh beat writer for the *Eagle* with the Dodgers. Before me there was Harold Burr, then Harold Parrott, who became a Dodger executive, Tommy Holmes, Tom Rice, Abe Yager, and maybe even Henry Chadwick himself.—**Dave Anderson**

I was born in 1937 and lived on Clarkson Avenue, just off of Bedford Avenue, until 1949 when we moved to Long Island. We were only 10 to 12 blocks away from Ebbets Field, so I got there fairly frequently between 1945 and 1949. Almost all the games I saw were from the bleachers in center field, which cost 50 cents a seat.

In the 1940s, the teams used to break spring training and work their way up the coast, playing mostly minor league teams. When the Dodgers reached New York, they played a three game series with the Yanks. My father took me to my first game in the spring of 1945, and I saw Joe DiMaggio play for the first and only time in person. I can still envision the #5 on his back, as we sat directly behind him in the bleachers. If you sat in the bleachers, you could not see parts of the outfield below you, including the big iron gate at the 399 mark in center field. Only if you sat in the first row of the bleachers, which was first come, first serve, could you view all of the field. During July, if you were sitting in the bleachers, you could see the fireworks at Coney Island.

In April, of 1946, my brother Tom and I saw Ed Head's no-hitter. We went alone. I was eight and a half, and I took my four-year-old brother. We walked the ten blocks or so, crossed Empire Boulevard, and bought our own tickets. I think it was Ferrel Anderson who hit a home run in the 5–0 game. It was only when we got home that we were told we had just seen a no-hitter. One time my father and I were at a game against the Cardinals watching batting practice and saw Stan Musial pound the ball off the right field fence. "He's playing handball off the wall," my father said.

Another game that stands out was against the Braves when Carvel "Bama" Rowell hit a ball into the Longines clock atop the scoreboard, shattering the glass. I heard that Bernard Malamud may have been at that game and used the scene as part of "The Natural." On another occasion, I saw Eddie Stanky tag Lennie Merullo of the Cubs (or perhaps it was the other way around), and both stood atop second base hitting each other like Rock-

'Em Sock'Em Robots. The dugout emptied out, and the next day cops were sitting in the dugout to prevent another outbreak.

In 1955, I went to a game with our family doctor, Dan Bradley. He had written letters of recommendation for me and another guy for his alma mater, Notre Dame. We both got in, and he invited us to a game and we ate in the Stadium Club or whatever it was called. We sat in the upper deck over third base. It was Pee Wee Reese Night. About a half dozen cars came on the field through the big gate in centerfield and Pee Wee got to pick a set of keys from a fishbowl. He picked a two-tone car, the predominant color being pink, which Pee Wee later characterized as "a little gay." This was at a time when gay had other connotations. Then they turned out the lights, and everyone struck a match or a cigarette lighter (everyone carried them) and sang "Happy Birthday" to Pee Wee.

As I look on it now, interesting memories from just a few games in a short period ... all seen in person.—**Jack Barthel**

The last conversation I had with my father a few days before he died was about baseball. His health had begun to deteriorate following an accidental fall, and I think he knew that he was facing, at age 97, his last few days with us. Baseball kept us talking, and I will miss the weekly conversations we had about the game and the players.

Over the course of his last few months, we had been talking about the Brooklyn Dodgers. As a 12-year-old, my father's older brother had escorted him to his first Ebbets Field game in 1924. I asked my father if he had any distinct memories of that first trip to Ebbets. "I think my brother paid 50 cents for a ticket, but I really remember that he bought me a soda and a hot dog for a nickel each."

My father lived just a few blocks from Ebbets Field, at 675 Empire Boulevard, and he was able to attend many games over the years, especially after his mother let him go with his friends and without adult supervision. Born in Brooklyn, he lived with his parents, two sisters, and three brothers until he married in 1948.

My father's memory of Ebbets really centered on the postwar years. "The smartest man was that Abe Stark," he recalled, "because of that sign. 'Hit Sign, Win Suit.' Very few hit that sign. It was under the scoreboard, and it was hard to hit. I think you could hit it on a bounce, too, but I never saw that happen either." Abe Stark owned a men's clothing store in Brooklyn. "I never shopped there because he was too expensive," my father remembered.

There was no recall of the great Dodger players before Pee Wee Reese, Carl Furillo, Cal Abrams, Duke Snider, Jackie Robinson, and the "Boys of Summer." My father lived and breathed the "Wait 'Til Next Year" slogan until his Bums triumphed in 1955. By then he had moved his family to the Long Island suburbs.

I'll never forget one of the best days in my life with my father. In 1957, the Dodgers had announced that they would be leaving Brooklyn and heading west. My father was philosophical about this. After all, he had abandoned Brooklyn as well. But he wanted me to experience the charm of Ebbets Field before it was demolished. He drove me to Ebbets near the end of the season, but the game was sold out. We walked over to nearby Prospect Park, and to an eight-year-old, this was paradise. Years later I regretted not having seen a game in Ebbets, but I have never regretted the time spent with my father, Harold Bernstein. Over the years, we disagreed on many things, but it was always baseball that kept us connected and interested in each other's lives.—**Sam Bernstein**

My story of Ebbets Field actually begins some nine months before I ever saw or heard of Ebbets Field. Somehow, my father, who was a big baseball fan, got a ticket to one of the World Series games of 1952, played between the Dodgers and Yankees. This was a big deal to me (I was five years old at the time) because I was Yankee fan. And I was a Yankee fan because they were the only team I had ever heard of. I don't know which game he saw, but I do remember that my mother put on the TV so that I could try to see my father sitting in the stands. This was obviously a ploy, so she didn't have to keep an eye on what I was doing. Needless to say, I never saw my father in the stands.

That evening when my father came home I asked him about the game, and he said he wasn't happy because the team he was rooting for had lost. I asked him who that was, and he said the Dodgers. Now being a highly intelligent five-year-old, I couldn't understand why everyone wasn't rooting for the Yankees. He explained that the Dodgers were in the same league as his team, and that's why he was rooting for them. I asked him who his team was, and he said the Giants. I said that if he was a Giant fan then I was also a Giant fan, and from that day forward I have been a Giant fan.

Flash ahead nine months to July 11, 1953. It was a bright, sunny day, and it's my first live baseball game. The Giants are playing the Dodgers at Ebbets Field. We're sitting in the upper deck along the third base line. There is a large man sitting to my left, and he keeps writing something in the program. Not knowing any better, I asked him what he was doing, and he explained that he was keeping score of the game. I asked him why he needed to do that because the score was on the scoreboard. He laughed and explained that he was keeping a record of what each batter did during the game. I asked him why. This man obviously had a lot of patience. He told me he was a Dodger fan and went to a lot of their games and liked to have a record of the games.

A Dodger fan? There is such a thing? I don't understand. My father is a Giant fan, I'm a Giant fan, isn't everyone a Giant fan? Interesting that nine months earlier I was a Yankee fan and couldn't understand why everyone wasn't one, and now I couldn't understand why everyone wasn't a Giant fan.—**Bill Bess**

I grew up in the Crown Heights section of Brooklyn, and the highlight of every summer was when my Uncle Tom took me to a doubleheader at Ebbets Field. This began when I was about nine and continued until I went off to college. We would get two seats in the bleachers (I think they cost 55 cents) and watch the Dodgers for six or seven hours—it was fantastic! I went to high school at Brooklyn Prep, and sometimes the Dodgers would run out of ushers so they would call over to the school and ask for a couple of seniors. If your grades were good enough you might get picked, and I was fortunate enough to do it a couple of times. It was great, and sometimes someone would give you a nickel or a dime as a tip. During World War II if you donated metal, you could get into a game for free. My friends and I would scour the neighborhood for pieces of metal. I think sometimes we even stole a few garbage can tops. Ebbets Field and the Dodgers were a very important part of life in Brooklyn and they held the borough together. When the Dodgers left, it marked the beginning of a decline that took decades to recover from.— **Joseph A. Califano, Jr., oral history interview, 2010, Brooklyn Historical Society**

I went to Dodger games at Ebbets Field on a regular basis when I was a student at Horace Mann, a private school in New York City. At that time, the Dodgers played mostly day games and since our school got out earlier than most schools, my friends and I would take the subway to Ebbets Field. It was a long trip between 1½ and 1¾ hours and then a long trip back to where I lived on Central Park West at 94th Street. On the ride over we would be figuring out batting averages. I am not good at math, but I could always figure out batting averages.

We always got to Ebbets Field early enough for batting practice when there was hardly anyone there. Of course, we wanted to get a ball and we would move around from left to right depending on the hitter. One time the Cincinnati Reds were taking batting practice, and there was a right-handed batter up so we were in left field. A left-handed batter, Ted Kluszewski was up next, he always pulled the ball in batting practice. Since the outfield stands were not connected, I had to run all the way down the left field line to the home plate area and then up the first base line to the right field stands in foul territory where I got a foul ball off of Kluszewski's bat that ricocheted off the seats. It was a long way to go, but since it was a small intimate park it wasn't as difficult as it might sound.

As I remember it, the grandstand seats were $1.50, which is where we sat. The box seats were probably owned by corporations and usually no one came to the day games, so the ushers let us go down and sit in the box seats. I always wanted to play third base, so I would go on the third base side, where I felt like I was part of the infield, playing next to Billy Cox with Pee Wee Reese just on the other side. Jackie Robinson was a little further away at second and Gil Hodges was the furthest over at first base. In addition to being small and intimate, there wasn't any extraneous noise like today — the only sounds were the sounds of baseball, the bat hitting the ball. After the game, we had a long subway ride home for dinner. I always took a lot of notes on my scorecard on things such as how the runners advanced from one base to another. On the way home, I would be doing more batting averages — all in my head since there were no calculators — as well as analyzing RBIs and things like that.

I was at Princeton in 1957 when the Dodgers left Brooklyn. I never took seriously the idea they would leave; I guess I probably just couldn't believe it. I had this terrible feeling of injustice and I hated Walter O'Malley. It was only when I wrote *The Power Broker* that I understood that Robert Moses had a lot of responsibility for what happened. When the Dodgers left Brooklyn, it was a pivotal event in my world view — something I thought was permanent was gone for no valid reason. To this day, I can't enjoy baseball, even though I like other sports.

A lot of it was the ritual of going to the game: the long subway ride, the walk to the ballpark, the ticket windows and then such a perfect setting — the field, this wonderful green space. The building itself may have been deteriorating, but we didn't care about that. All we cared about was that beautiful field and being so close to the players. There were also the landmarks like the Abe Stark sign in right field and being allowed to roam unfettered through the park by the ushers who were gruff, but gave us plenty of freedom. Plus, of course, the sense of familiarity with the players especially since other than the left fielder, the lineup was the same from year to year. What it came down to was that Ebbets Field was a home and all of the people were the family who lived there. That began with the players, but also the people who worked there, the fans who were there every day sitting in the same seats in the grandstand and, of course, the Sym-Phony band.

And then there was Jackie Robinson. In *Master of the Senate* when discussing the rising tide of civil rights consciousness, I wrote the following about Jackie Robinson: "when you saw the dignity with which Jack Roosevelt Robinson held himself in the face of the curses and the scorn and the runners coming into second base with their spike high, you had to think at least a little of America's shattered promises." Those lines were for me what civil rights was all about and for me and many Jewish kids in New York City, Jackie Robinson was civil rights.

When Robinson started playing for Montreal in 1946 there were no box scores in the papers, but periodically there would be a few paragraphs that would let you know he was doing well. Then he came to Brooklyn and he was so noble — a great hero right in front of me. My fondest thrill at Ebbets Field was leaning over the rail on the third base side, watching him dance off the base. You could see the fear in the pitcher's eye. Would he or wouldn't he go? And then every so often, he would go and steal home.

Such a wonderful age, such a magical time. Ebbets Field was a shrine for me, so special a place, one of the foremost things of my youth. — **Robert Caro**

John Griffin, the Brooklyn Dodgers' last equipment manager. was my uncle — I was in the wedding party when he married my Aunt Peggy. Uncle John was called the Senator, and he retired when the Dodgers went to California since he didn't want to leave Brooklyn. Although I was only 10 when the Dodgers left, I had a lot of opportunities to go to Ebbets Field and even went into the locker room a few times. As I look back on that, I am surprised I was able to go in there. We lived fairly close to Ebbets Field, and my father and I would walk. To a little girl, the park seemed large, and the seats were too big for me. What I remember most is the food, especially the hot dogs because we seldom had that kind of food at home. Since this was post–1947 there was diversity in the crowds, which were very loud and supportive of the Dodgers. — **Ann Brown Chapin, oral history interview, 2010, Brooklyn Historical Society**

My father and my uncles used to take me to Ebbets Field. Sometimes we would use the subway, but we would also walk from Brooklyn Heights, which had to be more than a two-mile walk. The feature of the park that stands out the most was the rotunda with all that marble. When my wife and I went to Citi Field for the first time and walked through the rotunda, I had tears in my eyes. The other two things that I remember the most are the Schaefer beer sign and the Abe Stark sign. From the rotunda, the entranceway branched out to the seats. We usually had box seats at field level, so we were close to the action. My father and uncles always tried to get tickets for games against the Giants.

I was born in 1949, and my first game was in 1955. I tried to follow the action, but at five, I didn't understand the game that clearly. However, at that age, a year makes a big difference, and the next season I had a much better idea of what was going on. We went for the first time that year shortly after Easter. Jackie Robinson was playing second base, which wasn't his primary position then, and I especially remember how he yelled encouragement to his teammates. My best day at Ebbets Field came later, when we were there when the Dodgers clinched their last National League pennant on the last day of the 1956 season against the Pittsburgh Pirates. I believe that Duke Snider and Sandy Amoros hit home runs, and Don Newcombe was the starting and winning pitcher, but Don Bessent finished the game in relief. I will never forget the cheering and the excitement. I am pretty sure it was a full house — a lot was written about attendance falling off, but it always seemed packed when I was there.

We also went to games in 1957 and were there for the only game ever called on account of fog. I was very annoyed. When the Dodgers lost, my father told me that it would help teach me about life. One of my uncles didn't look at it that way — to him it was a personal insult when the Dodgers lost. When my father told me that the Dodgers were leaving, I said I guess we will root for the Giants, and he said they were leaving, too. So I said I guess we will root for the Yankees, and he replied that we would never root for the Yankees. When Ebbets Field was being torn down, I was going to go there with my friends to try to get some bricks, but I made the mistake of telling my mother and she stopped me.— **Gil Cividanes, oral history interview, 2010, Brooklyn Historical Society**

We used to sneak in. We never paid. That was the best for doubleheaders. We used to go there in the afternoon and stay there all night long. It was an iconic kind of a team and an iconic kind of ballpark. There were so many great players on the Dodgers. We took it for granted because we lived in Brooklyn. I remember Carl Furillo, Leo Durocher, Duke Snider, Pee Wee Reese, and Roy Campanella. They were our heroes. And you know they were called Bums. Today they would be called dynamite. And they would be making a lot more money today. This was home to the people in Brooklyn. They remember Brooklyn and Ebbets Field. It was just wonderful.

It was in a neighborhood. They would never do that today. You could walk out of your house and walk right into Ebbets Field. People would watch the game on a rooftop, and you didn't have to pay a dime. When Leo Durocher went to the Giants, you never saw such anger and hate for a guy. It was a neighborhood baseball field. It was just a magical era. There was more respect and dignity. That was our home — Ebbets Field. That was ours. It was such a wonderful thing.— **Pat Cooper**

During the late 1940s, we lived near Asbury Park, New Jersey. I was starting my teen years, and my father took me to a few ball games at each of New York's ballparks. My first game at Ebbets Field was the day game of a day-night doubleheader. We arrived by subway from Penn Station (another skill my father taught me — how to get around New York City's subway system). The Dodgers were playing the Braves, and we sat in the upper deck, above the first base dugout. I remember the Dodgers won, and that my father noted the Braves did not get a hit after the first inning. — **Jerome Crosson**

I have many Ebbets Field stories. Let me first state that my father had box seats along the third base line for many years until the end. My uncle worked for Western Union and sat in the press box teletyping Dodger games to the rest of the sports world. I have fond memories of being in there with the great sportswriters of that era. When the Dodgers were on the road, I used to delight in my uncle's deciphering the Morse Code clicks on the Dodger broadcasts and giving us the play-by-play before Red Barber announced it.

I will never forget the sight on one cool afternoon in the spring of 1947 when a magnificent athlete wearing number 42 stepped up to the plate for the first time at Ebbets Field — Jack Roosevelt Robinson. I witnessed the many hardships he went through that first year. I remember Eddie Miksis rolling hysterically in the dirt with the winning run after Cookie Lavagetto's two-base hit that broke up the Yankees' Bill Bevens' no-hitter in that famous World Series. I remember Pete Reiser colliding against the center field wall and being carried off the field, while the announcement was made that a #4, Duke Snider, a newcomer, was replacing him.

I remember countless great throws by Carl Furillo cutting runners down from right field. I remember greeting the players outside the park after the game. I will never forget the wink and big smile from the great Stan Musial when he cruised into third base one time. I remember a young wild pitcher starting his first game with many walks and strikeouts. He did not impress me at the time. His name was Sandy Koufax. Another lefty impressed me more who came through in 1955: Johnny Podres.

The fond off-key rendition of the Brooklyn Sym-Phony's "Three Blind Mice" when the umpires came out at the start of the game still plays in my mind, along with Gladys Goodding's organ music. I remember Don Newcombe pitching shutouts with his blazing fastball, and Roy Campanella screaming at him in his high-pitched voice to stop throwing the local and show him the express. He and Jackie were always pushing him. The Dodgers were part of our family, as with the rest of Brooklyn, we lived and died with them. One could walk a street on a spring day and not miss a word of Red Barber's description of a game through open windows. Ebbets Field was a shrine decimated by Robert Moses and Walter O'Malley. So many memories. So little space. — **Les Davidson**

Although born in Brooklyn, we moved to New Jersey when I was five, so I was a Dodger fan by birth but not geography. Around May 1952, at age 16, a friend and I decided to see our first major league game. Without drivers' licenses, our transportation was the bus to the Port Authority and a subway ride to the stadium. Purchasing general admission tickets, we visited the hot dog concession and settled down to watch a real game. I don't remember who the Dodgers played or even if they won, but there was a rain delay which made the game even more interesting. We watched the tarp being unrolled, and luckily for us, rolled up again when the sun came out. The subway and bus ride home seemed longer than the trip there, but the experience was worth the effort. Although I never got to Ebbets Field again, I still felt cheated when the Dodgers moved west.— **Richard Denby**

I lived in Flatbush many years ago. As a youngster, I delivered the newspaper, the *Brooklyn Eagle*, to a designated route in my Flatbush neighborhood. One of my customers was the Gil Hodges' family. When collection day came, Joan would always answer the door, pay me for the paper subscription but I never received a tip. I didn't complain — it was an honor none of my friends ever shared (I was often offered "bribes" just to switch routes). Well, one day, Gil answered the door. I was shocked. He said, "Well, how are you young man and what is your name?" "Fine, Sir — my name is Bobby." He said, "Tell me now, how much does Mrs. Hodges give you as a tip?" Panic set in. How would I answer this? I lied and said that I couldn't remember. He gave me a dollar tip. That was unheard of in those days.

But the story doesn't end there. Several years later, my father and I were walking on Glenwood Road in Flatbush headed for the bus stop (Avenue J bus) on the corner of Glenwood Road and Nostrand Avenue. As we approached the bus line, I saw him. The first thing I saw was his neck. I didn't say anything to my father. Why not? My father was a diehard Giant fan. He hated the Dodgers with a passion. I thought he might do or say something regrettable. We stood right behind Gil, who eventually turned around and saw me. I could see he was trying to place the face, but I was keeping quiet. Finally he said, "Well how are you, Bobby?" I almost died. First, because I couldn't believe that he would remember my name, and then I thought that my father would definitely cause a scene now. My father knew who he was, as did, I would guess, everyone else in Brooklyn.

So Gil asked, aren't you going to introduce me to your father who, by now, had his head down staring at the cement refusing to acknowledge Gil's presence. So I had to do the talking. I explained to Gil that my father was a Giant fan and while he really detested the entire Brooklyn team, he had no particular dislike for Gil, personally. I said this at the risk of hearing about it later from my father. Gil stuck out his hand for my father who reluctantly shook it (still with the head down). Ever the gentleman that he was, he said to my father, "I wish your team the best of luck."

If my father ever discussed this chance meeting with anyone else, I don't know. I do know that he and I never discussed it again.— **Bob Donnelly**

My first major league baseball game was on June 23, 1956, the Cincinnati Reds against the Dodgers at Ebbets Field. I was seven years old. I went with my Dad and sister on Ladies Day, a Saturday afternoon. I'll never forget (a common memory I've heard from others) the sight of the field as I walked up the ramp from the darkness. The field was the greenest of green. The bluest of blue on the uniforms, and I even recall the blackest of black as I noted number 42. (Yes, I recall that he stood out by his color. Sure, there were Campy and others, but Jackie was beautiful in his sheer contrast.)

But this game was noteworthy in a sad way because young reserve infielder, Don Zimmer, was struck by a Hal Jeffcoat fastball, fell unconscious as his teammates surrounded him, and was carried off on a stretcher. I never forgot the image and shared my recollection with Zim at a book signing a while back. He was impressed that I remembered the game so vividly and signed a microfiche copy of a *New York Times* article that I had gotten at the library.

By the way, a young Koufax started the game and fell behind, but the Dodgers rallied for a walk-off victory in the ninth. I remember two less well-known Dodgers, Rocky Nelson (1B) and Ransom Jackson (3B; three hits), were keys to the victory. The dramatic win left me happy, though I worried about Zimmer and was pleased that he recovered (and went on to spend a few more years with the game). As I got older, I dreamed that Ebbets Field would return to Brooklyn. Sigh.—**Robert Dorin**

My uncle, Joseph B. Stevens, was the head of the concession firm, Harry M. Stevens (HMS); HMS sold scorecards, hot dogs, and other items at Ebbets Field. When I was a young boy growing up in New Rochelle, New York, my brother and I would take the subway to Ebbets Field to sell peanuts at the ballpark. Because my hair was red, I usually got a lot of business.

I remember many things about baseball at Ebbets Field including less well-known players like Erv Palica, Tom Lasorda, Eddie Miksis, Andy Pafko, and others, who came alive through my baseball card collection. Like many other people, I loved watching Jackie Robinson take leads off first base. I have never seen anyone bother a pitcher more. Pee Wee Reese was my hero; when I wished on my birthday cake, I hoped to be the shortstop for the Dodgers. I loved watching Happy Felton's Knothole Gang and dreamed of being on the show and meeting my favorite players. My other favorites were Duke Snider and Don Newcombe.—**Mort Dukehart**

I became an avid Brooklyn Dodger fan during 1947, Jackie Robinson's first year. Going to Ebbets Field was a great experience. If you went there once, you were hooked. It was like being part of a family—you always felt that you belonged. Even between the innings, there was always something going on, like the Sym-Phony band, Gladys Goodding on the organ, or Hilda Chester ringing her bell. Since the park was so small, we were always close to the players, even in the bleachers, which I believe cost only 50 cents.

The game that stands out the most in my mind was Opening Day of the 1953 season. It was the only time that I ever played hooky from school. It was an exciting day because in addition to being Opening Day, the Dodgers raised the 1952 National League pennant. I don't remember exactly how we got the tickets, but we sat behind home plate, which was my first time out of the bleachers. It was very cold, and I think we basically drank the place out of hot chocolate. I also remember a man sitting near us, who every time that Roy Campanella came to bat, he would say "chop wood, Campy, chop wood." That was typical Brooklynese, with the natives using their own pet expressions. It was also the first time I waited outside the players' entrance to get autographs — it was a very exciting day. — **Irwin Fenichel, oral history interview, 2010, Brooklyn Historical Society**

I went to Ebbets Field about 300–400 times. I was born on Staten Island, New York, in 1930, and then moved to Omaha in 1968. I went to high school in Brooklyn. There was a lot of skipping school because it was approximately 20 minutes away from Ebbets Field by subway on the BMT line. From Staten Island itself, you would get on the Staten Island train or the New York Ferry, and then the BMT line — this would take the better part of three hours. At first, I would go with relatives, but I finally had the spending money in the mid–1940s and started going on my own then. As I remember it, bleacher seats were 75 cents, unreserved seats down the first and third base lines were $1.25, reserved seats were $1.75, and box seats were $2.25. When the game was over, you'd go across the street and get a hot dog and cream soda for 25 cents on Bedford Avenue, which was adjacent to the stadium.

I remember once seeing a young lady standing on the subway platform after the game. She was holding a scorecard, and I tried to impress her with numbers, and she knew everything. I didn't end up getting home until 4 A.M. that night. The Dodger Sym-Phony, if you were a Giant fan or Cardinal fan, they'd stand in front of you and blow away with their music sheets. There was one player — Pete Reiser, an outfielder — who kept running into the wall as a rookie in the same spot, and as a result, Dodger management put padding in that one spot.

I was at the game when Leo Durocher came back (July 26, 1948), and the crowd was booing. He came out to talk to his pitcher and complained to the umpire that because of the crowd, he couldn't hear his pitcher. The umpire made an announcement to the crowd, and the place got even crazier. You can imagine what happened then. The World Series games were tough to get tickets to. I never went to one. I did go to a game against the Phillies in the heat of a pennant race, in the final days of the season, when the Dodgers lost to the Phillies on an extra-inning home run. Here again, one of the greatest memories was a loss, but here again, fans would clap and recognize players on other teams, except the hotheads. Most of the games I remember are losses. In fact, some of the *most* memorable games were games we lost.

There was a guy that would stand outside the stadium with a cup and ask people as they came in, "Do you know what the score is before the game begins?" Everyone fell for it, and of course, the score before the game begins is 0–0. Additionally, I remember trying to buy tickets and being told none were left and seeing that you had to pay the ticket sales person 25 cents to get him to sell you a seat. They sold peanuts, and the guy would stand four to five rows below and throw you the peanuts, and you would throw the money back, and he never missed.

I was at the last game at Ebbets Field. Oh boy. The fans were quiet. They really disliked the city's political people for not providing reasons for the Dodgers to stay there. They didn't want a new stadium; they just wanted parking, and the city cried poverty. There will never be another field like Ebbets Field.—**Jim Gardner**

I became a Dodger fan in 1955 when I was eight, but I didn't go to a game at Ebbets Field until 1957, the Dodgers' last year in Brooklyn. We lived in the Bronx, not far from Yankee Stadium, so on a Friday night in May, my father and I took what seemed to be a really long subway ride to Brooklyn. I especially remember the brick exterior, which was almost like a brownstone and very Brooklyn, plus walking through the rotunda. Since all my knowledge of Ebbets Field to that point was through black and white television, all the different colors, including the big green space, made a big impression on me. There was also the smell of the place, a combination of Cuban cigars, beer, and peanuts, which is something that has stayed with me.

I went to four games that season, the final one was in September, the next to the last game the Dodgers played at Ebbets Field, which was a Sunday afternoon against Philadelphia. The things that impressed me about the ballpark were the smaller size, which I liked, and all of the ads on the outfield walls. The crowds were mostly men my father's age, many smoking cigars, who were frequently also a little loud. I remember one man sarcastically singing "California, Here I Come," which bothered me because I was trying to pretend that it wasn't going to happen. The physical features that stand out the most are the front entrance and the right field wall. Something else that is interesting is that the buildings outside the walls of Ebbets are still standing. They used to put ads up on those buildings as well. About 12 years ago, I went past the site, and you could still see some of the faded ads. In many ways, my experience with the Dodgers and Ebbets Field was like a short love affair—one season and it was over.—**Edwin Gerstein, oral history interview, 2010, Brooklyn Historical Society**

My first visit to Ebbets Field took place in 1946 when I was nine years old. My brother was going, and I decided I wanted to go as well. We bought bleacher seats, which seemed like they were four miles away. I wasn't satisfied and was determined to get down to the field. The next year my parents bought season tickets, reserved grandstand, which I think cost $1.25 per seat, per game, which still wasn't close enough for me. I would wear a little Brooklyn Dodger uniform and move close to the dugout and hang round there whenever I could. I got to know a number of the ballpark personnel, including Joe McDonald, who was an usher and went on to be the general manager of the Mets. Charlie DiGiovanni, who was the batboy, saw me and asked if I wanted to be his assistant. It didn't take me long to say yes, so before and after the games, I would help him set up and put away the bats. I got to meet all of the players and their wives, so I was basically a 10-year-old boy living out his fantasy. Ebbets Field was a special place for me. I particularly remember the rotunda, with the lights made in the shape of baseballs. It was very much like going back to old New York City. I don't have such fond memories of the food, which was not too delectable — the hot dogs in particular were nasty. — **Hal Glicksman, oral history interview, 2010, Brooklyn Historical Society**

My first game at Ebbets Field was during the summer of 1949. Before that, I listened to games on the radio and imagined what a game at Ebbets Field was like. So it was very exciting to compare the reality with what I had imagined. Like so many other people, the first thing that impressed me was the rotunda with all the baseball designs in the floor. It seemed huge to me. Then, after walking up the ramp, there was that moment of seeing the diamond and the park for the first time. I get a very similar feeling when I go to Fenway Park for the first time each season.

The sight of that huge expanse of green was unforgettable. I didn't live in the city itself, but it was the largest green space I had ever seen. I had never seen so many people in one place before, and there was a tremendous energy in the park. Although in reality Ebbets Field was one of the smallest parks, it was so much bigger than I had imagined. It seemed huge to a six-year-old.

We would almost always take the train from Long Island and then the subway to Flatbush Avenue and walk to Ebbets Field. The walk to the park was also a memorable experience — this large group of people all so fervent, talking happily. It was a real feeling of comradeship. Again, I have the same feeling when we get close to Fenway Park for a Red Sox game.

What stood out about Dodger games is that the park was so crowded that you felt like you were part of what was happening on the field. The opposite of the experience you get in a domed stadium today. I think the greatest aspect of Ebbets Field was how close we were to the field. I went to both Yankee Stadium and the Polo Grounds as a child, and neither of them had that same home-like feeling of Ebbets Field. Of course, part of that was due to the fact that Yankees and Giants weren't my team, but the difference in size had something to do with the experience.

The two games I remember the most are "Rockville Centre Night" in 1951 and Pee Wee Reese's birthday celebration in 1955, the two games I wrote about in *Wait Till Next Year*. I don't remember a bad game or a bad time there. The players still stand out in my mind after all those years — Jackie Robinson running the bases and intimidating the pitcher; Duke Snider, who was so handsome (I had a crush on him at one time); and Gil Hodges, who was so decent and classy. If he had been a character in *The Wizard of Oz*, he would have been the one with the heart, something that we saw when he was a manager.

Like most people, the physical features of Ebbets Field that I remember are associated with the right field wall and scoreboard. Especially the Abe Stark sign and the Schaefer beer sign that would light up to signal a hit or an error. Hilda Chester always stood out because of her loud voice, but also because she was big physically. I believe she always wore a print dress. At the time I thought she was great because we were for the same team, but I realize now how irritating she must have been to the other team. She was what might be called an obnoxious pleasure. The Brooklyn Sym-Phony also stands out with their songs like "Three Blind Mice," "The Worms Crawl in — the Worms Crawl Out," and "Somebody Else Is Taking My Place," when the opposing pitcher was taken out. Their choice of songs was very creative. — **Doris Kearns Goodwin**

My memory is mostly of the physical layout. In a way, I can still visualize it. If you stood in front of the rotunda, there was a street that went down the left-hand side. If you walked about a half block, that's where the press entrance was, and as soon as you went through the gate, if you took a hard right, there was an elevator that took you up to the press room. It was more like a bar. To the left of it, there was a little studio I believe, and then you'd walk out, straight to the upper level of Ebbets Field. And to get to the actual press box, you walked over a catwalk, and then into the press box. It was just so intimate. And I can still almost visualize the elevator operator. Whoever he was, he was there forever at the press elevator. Everybody was like family. Everybody was on a first-name basis, and the people who were working there, covering the team, spent more time with that family than their actual family.

My Dad was a sportswriter covering the team for a number of years. I knew some of the players — Jackie Robinson, Gil Hodges, Pee Wee Reese — so it was like a second home. When I say a second home, I was probably 10 years old or younger when I started going. It was a special place. And it went beyond Ebbets Field. A lot of the players lived in Brooklyn during the offseason. One was Gil Hodges, who even owned a bowling alley in Brooklyn.

Happy Felton's Knothole Gang was very much part of the Ebbets Field scene, and they would do the show live. The Dodger bullpen was down the right field line, and when you went under the stand, that's where the clubhouse was. The bullpen area was where the show was done. There were two or three cameras, and it was a very simple show. There were three Little League players, and on every show a Dodger player would take time out to give three Little Leaguers a work out, and then would select a winner. Every kid got a bat and a glove, and the winner got an autographed baseball from the player. The winner also got to come back for the next show, and at the end of the show, he would interview his favorite player just outside the Dodger dugout.

I was fortunate enough to be on the show once. Pee Wee Reese gave us the workouts, and I won, so I got to come back to interview my favorite Dodger — Gil Hodges. So the next game, I'm in the Dodger clubhouse with my Dad, and he sees Hodges, and he says, "Gil get ready, you are going to have a tough interview before the game even starts." At that time, Hodges' wife was 9½ months pregnant, and all of Brooklyn wanted to know when she was going to have the baby. My Dad told me I had to ask him about that. I said, "Dad, I'm 11 or 12 years old, and I'm not going to ask Hodges about his wife and their baby." He said, "Then you should ask him for advice on how to hit a low, outside curveball." Hodges had a spread eagle stance, and was vulnerable to that pitch. We're on live, and I popped the question. He stares at me, and says, "Do you have that problem in the Little League?" I said "Yeah, and it's been bothering me lately." He said, "Well, I've been trying to figure out how to hit that pitch my entire career, and I've finally figured that if a pitcher hits the outside corner, with his breaking pitch, then he deserves a strike."

As we're walking into the dugout, he [Hodges] said, laughing, "Where's your Dad? I need to talk to him."— **Ed Goren**

My favorite memory of Ebbets Field is the excitement of Opening Day. I was a majorette for the bugle, fife, and drum corps for my school at St. Louis parish. On Opening Day, we would march to the ballpark. There would be so many people out on the streets, and it was so exciting that I have always remembered it.— **Adele Irene Grande, oral history interview, 2010, Brooklyn Historical Society**

The rotunda was the means of access to the inside of Ebbets Field for most fans. This was the place where they frequently saw players going to the locker room (courtesy Los Angeles Dodgers).

I grew up in Brooklyn, on Parkside Avenue near the corner of Flatbush Avenue, just about midway between Ebbets Field and Erasmus Hall High School, where my (1956–1959) classmates included Neil Diamond, Barbra Streisand, Billy Cunningham, and Bobby Fischer.

After school most days, when the Dodgers were playing at Ebbets in a day game, I walked home the approximate half mile along Flatbush Avenue, where I quickly disposed of my school books. Then I continued rapidly forward, mostly along Flatbush Avenue an additional half mile or so to the Sullivan Place and Bedford Avenue, home of my beloved Brooklyn Dodgers, the "Boys of Summer."

At about the seventh inning, when at least some fans were beginning to exit the ballpark, the security guards gave generally wide berth to the group of kids (myself among them) who were hanging around outside, essentially allowing them to "sneak" into the stands (for me in the upper deck along the first base line). It was in that way that I got to watch the later innings of countless games, often hoping for extra-inning affairs.

If I got there too early, I would hang out on Bedford Avenue, hoping to retrieve a home run ball hit over the right field wall.

After the game, I would, among others, wait outside the player exit gates to get players to autograph their Topps baseball cards, especially *en masse* as visiting players prepared to board the team bus. Players readily and freely provided autographs — no baseball card shows, no long lines, no charge. Those autographed cards were traded among friends, flipped to the sidewalk to the heads or tails winner, or flipped to a wall with the closest to the wall or "leaner" being the winner. My mom, along with most moms, and with very little foresight, eventually tossed those very same autographed cards in the trash, including those signed by some of my adolescent heroes, such as Jackie Robinson, Roy Campanella, Pee Wee Reese, Gil Hodges, and especially Duke Snider.—**Stuart Grant**

My friend Pam was the one who introduced me to baseball, the Dodgers, and Ebbets Field. One day she told me that from her kitchen window we could see the top of Ebbets Field, and sure enough, we could. We used to go over to Ebbets Field around the eighth inning, when they would start opening the gates to let the crowd out, and go in and watch the end of the game. When the game ended, we would wait outside the locker room for autographs. It was usually a small group, and the players were so friendly and accessible. Sometimes we would self-address a postcard and give it to them, and they would send us their autograph when it was more convenient for them.—**Jane Grodenchik, oral history interview, 2010, Brooklyn Historical Society**

My school was very close to Ebbets Field, so when school got out about 3:00 or 3:30 P.M., we would walk the two blocks to Ebbets Field when they were opening the gates for people to exit. The ushers were very tolerant of kids sneaking in, and we would go sit in box seats behind the dugout and talk to the players. I would also stand outside the player's clubhouse exit and wait for autographs. I accumulated quite a collection, which I still have. A number of the players would walk up Franklin Avenue to the IRT, and we would walk with them and talk with them. The things I remember the most about the features of Ebbets Field are the Abe Stark sign, Hilda Chester, and the Brooklyn Sym-Phony band. On the days that I didn't sneak in, other kids and I would stand on Bedford Avenue with our gloves and hope to catch a home run. There was a big gate there, through which they used to admit motorcades, and there was a gap in the gate so you could see part of left and center field.

I remember during the 1944 presidential election campaign, Franklin Delano Roosevelt gave a speech at Ebbets Field, and his motorcade came down Eastern Parkway and

I watched him pass by. Sometimes I would go with my father, and we would walk to the ballpark—it was less than a mile down Franklin Avenue, which was a nice commercial street. When I went on my own, I would usually buy a bleacher seat. The crowds in the bleachers were verbal and boisterous, but there were never any major problems. I always felt safe.—**Ed Gruber, oral history interview, 2010, Brooklyn Historical Society**

I am an 85-year-old Giant fan who lived in Brooklyn and loved Ebbets Field because it was small and you were close to the action. The best ballgames were between the Giants and Dodgers at Ebbets Field. I remember seeing Pete Reiser bouncing off the outfield wall trying to catch a ball. I remember going to a diner (Toomey's) across from Ebbets Field on Empire Boulevard, about an hour and a half to two hours after a game. You could have a hamburger and sit across from Medwick, Camilli, Stanky, and other ballplayers. When the fans yelled, I could hear them at my home at Parkside Avenue and Bedford Avenue. I remember O'Malley, the president, wanted the street next to Ebbets Field to make the ballpark bigger, but the mayor said no. So O'Malley moved the team to California. I also loved the band that played in the stands with a cowbell. God bless the fans and Ebbets Field—and this comes from a Giant fan.—**Walter Hafner**

One of my fondest memories was the day I chased Jackie Robinson across the street outside of Ebbets Field in pursuit of his autograph. He (Jackie) sees a car coming, grabs my hand, crosses me to the sidewalk, and after chiding me about running in the street, he so kindly signed my Dodger book on his photo. He smiled, I said thanks and he reminded me again about running in the street. I went home that day and told my mother, with a beam on my face, "Jackie Robinson held my hand crossing the street." My memory of him is of a sweet, kind, gentleman and the honor it was just to have met him, if only for that brief period in 1950.

Another time I was at Ebbets Field early while they were taping the Knothole Gang. I told the guard I worked for my high school (Erasmus) newspaper (a lie) and asked if I could please sit closer to the show. He let me in, and I was two rows from the field. Carl Furillo was at bat practicing—he hit a ball down right field, and I jumped up, bent over the fence and grabbed the ball as it passed. I sat back down so proud of that opportunity, thinking it can't get any better than that. Well, it did. Carl Furillo was interviewed that day by Happy Felton and signed the ball I got during practice.

Pee Wee Reese's autograph was hard to get, and one day I read in the newspaper that he and his wife Dottie lived in an apartment building within walking distance. So off I went, thinking and hoping he wouldn't mind if I rang his bell. I got there and was really nervous. I rang his bell, he answered, and I saw his wife sitting on a couch. She smiled at me, and Pee Wee said, "Hi, can I help you?" I politely asked for his autograph, while I was apologizing for ringing his bell. He said, "Sure," smiled and signed my book, then told me to "have a nice day." I said thanks and practically ran from the building. I can't imagine doing anything like that today. What probably helped was I was around

16, but looked about 11 years old. I am now 75 years of age and consider my love for the Dodgers unmatched.—**Mary Walsh Heagney**

I was born and grew up in Brooklyn, New York, where I learned to worship the residents of Ebbets Field. At 19 years old, my grandfather, Herman (Jake) Hehl, pitched for the Dodgers during the 1919 season.

Two years after "Them Bums" won the World Series, beating the much-hated Yankees, I was seven years old. My father came home one day and announced that someone gave him *box seat* tickets for Ebbets Field. These were far too expensive for my Dad's meager income, and I never would have been able to sit in this section if it were not for this gift. The seats were a few rows behind the end of the third base dugout. Finally, I was actually going to see my team in action—live and in person. I barely slept the night before.

The day finally came. We traveled there by EL and then subway. I remember my first view of Ebbets Field. To me it was the biggest structure that I have ever seen to that point, much bigger than I had imagined. During the game I found myself marveling at the inside of this magnificent ballpark and at the huge crowd, as much as watching the game. It was indeed a dream come true.

One thing that stuck in mind was the good fortune of one fan who was sitting ahead of me in the first row. He was right at the outfield end of the dugout, on the fence that separated the stands from the field. During the game he caught and went home with three foul balls and a bat. The bat slipped out of the hands of a player and landed at the fence. He just bent over and picked it up. A discussion ensued, and the fan gave the bat back to the player. He was then given another bat to take home. At the end of the game, I remember him walking past me with the biggest smile ever, holding his four prized possessions.

Shortly thereafter, I suffered my first heartbreak with the departure of my team and have not recovered since. I am an avid baseball fan and till this day am unable to truly root for another professional baseball team. These emotional scars run deep! I have been lucky enough to see baseball games at 20 different stadiums in the USA and also at stadiums in Puerto Rico, the Dominican Republic, Mexico, Canada, the Philippines, and Taiwan. My presence at all of these venues put together does not even come close to that one day at Ebbets Field. Thank you, Charles Ebbets, for your magnificent ball park and my memories!—**Mark Hehl**

In the early 1950s, I guess around 1952 or 1953, I went to Ebbets Field with a church group or the Boy Scouts, as part of a group of 10- to 13-year-old kids. We were guests of Happy Felton's Knothole Gang. Our seats, as I remember, were far up in the upper deck and even farther from home plate. I don't remember a thing about the game, except that my friend and I snuck back into the corridor and bought a beer from a passing vendor—my first illegal beer! I don't remember the price, but it was probably "outrageous," at around 25 cents, and we were "only" five or six years away from being "legal" (the drinking age was 18 then in New York as *all* New Jersey teens knew). While not remembering the game at all, I will never forget the thrill of *buying* my first illegal beer in Ebbets Field. Ain't baseball great! — **George Hirai**

My father came to the United States in 1939 with my mom and my three-year-old brother. I was born in 1947. Settling in Brooklyn, my father tried to become Americanized, but he had certain old-world passions, the greatest being soccer. As a child, I, like my big brother, detested soccer. We loved basketball, football, and best of all, baseball, played anywhere, but especially at Ebbets Field.

Dad would come home in the evening and tell me to finish my homework (or put down that stickball bat) because he was dragging me off to another interminable, boring soccer match. My brother would save the day by saying, "Sorry dad, but I'm taking the little guy to a Dodger game tonight." He even did this when the Bums were on the road!

One afternoon in 1953, my father decided to join us and learn firsthand about baseball and its hold on Americans. It was the bottom of the 8th, with Milwaukee ahead by one run and the Dodgers had two men on base and our favorite, Duke Snider, was stepping to the plate. "Oh boy," said dad, "it's the Dookis of Schneider. He's got two blintzes on this plate (or two ducks on the pond to the native-born). The Dookis will hit a home run and give us the lead." But Del Crandall signaled the pitcher (Bob Buhl, I recollect) to put the batter on base.

"*What is this*?" my father exclaimed.

"They are giving him four balls, I said.

"*But they can't do that*," he shouted. "*It's the Dookis' turn to hit*."

"It's called an intentional walk," my brother explained, "They won't pitch to him."

"*And you call this America's pastime*?" Dad retorted.

"Yes," we replied.

"*Then all of you Americans are a bunch of cowards*," he screamed. Dad slammed his beer cup on the ground, and rising to leave, declared: "*How could America beat the Axis when it doesn't have the guts to pitch to the Dookis of Schneider*?" — **Alan J. Hiss**

It was a hot, sticky September day in 1959, one of those last summer days before school starts. The Dodgers had left Brooklyn, and we knew that Ebbets Field was going to be torn down. My twin brother Steve, along with friends, Ricky, Norman, Gerry, and I, decided it was time for action. We got on our bikes and rode to Ebbets Field, carrying hammers and screwdrivers and a box to put the cornerstone in and take it home with us. To our surprise, when we arrived at Ebbets, we discovered that the cornerstone was almost as high as our 10-year-old bodies. We started to hammer away, banging and chipping at it until pieces of the stone fell off. I was working on chipping off the date. I wanted to keep those numbers, but they were ingrained in the granite, not to be removed. I continued banging at those numbers. Soon the damage was done, and you could no longer see the date clearly. So I started to chip and bang in the upper right hand corner. A big chunk of stone fell off, and I put it in the box. Now, I thought, my family was going to be rich; there would be pictures in the newspapers and maybe the Ocean Avenue kids would be on TV. Holy Mackerel! I put the pieces in the box and rode my bicycle back home. We were all excited since we knew in our 10-year-old minds that we had a piece of history, something that was never to be again. I raced back home and showed it to my Mom, who didn't appear to be impressed. She told me I should go back and bring home the whole stone! She put the pieces of the stone in the closet. Like us, my mom had no idea how big the cornerstone really was.

Many years after that hot, historic (for me) day in Brooklyn, I was the mother of an eight-year-old boy. As all parents of little boys know, especially ones that are fanatic baseball fans, a trip to the Baseball Hall of Fame at Cooperstown is a rite of passage. Never did I imagine how emotional it would be for this 40-something mom on my first trip there. As a young girl, I was known as a "tomboy," a girl who played baseball up until my early teens with the boys, since back in the 1950s and 1960s, girl teams did not exist. Living less than half a mile from Ebbets Field, baseball was in my blood. A trip to Cooperstown sounded very enticing, even though I had lost the baseball part of me and had switched to the more respectable sport of tennis.

Upon arriving at Cooperstown with my family in mid-winter, we bought a three-day pass to the Hall of Fame. The Hall of Fame was three stories high and much bigger than I expected. One could spend several days looking at all the exhibits and the history of baseball. We lingered at each exhibit as long as we could with my then eight-year-old son, Ross, who scurried from exhibit to exhibit. When we finished the exhibits on the first two floors, I climbed the stairs to the third floor. As I opened the door and came

Susan Horowitz and her son, Ross, with the Ebbets Field cornerstone at the National Baseball Hall of Fame (courtesy Susan Horowitz).

upon the first exhibit in the middle of the floor, I literally froze! There it was, right in front of me; the very same cornerstone of Ebbets Field. I always wondered what had happened to it, and there was the original, red, granite Ebbets Field cornerstone right in front of my eyes! Yes, there it was in big bold letters — EBBETS FIELD — and underneath that, 1912. It was hard to read part of the date because as I well knew, it had been chiseled away. Right here my own piece of history came to life.

The upper right hand corner of the cornerstone was missing. There were chisel and hammer marks all over the cornerstone. The last number of the date was chipped away and impossible to read, just as we had left it all those years ago. I could not believe my eyes. The memories would not stop coming back to me, of my parents, of my glorious childhood, of all the kids who moved away and got on with their lives. The memories of my first boyfriend Ricky came back to me. Ricky, the boy who gave me my first kiss and died years later, way too young, a victim of the drugs of the 1960s. I thought we would all grow old together, but it wasn't meant to be. The emptiness in my heart was still there, and the tears came and did not stop.

All these emotions and memories came flooding back to me. I felt both happy and sad at the same time. I felt as if I were 10 years old again, back in Brooklyn, chipping away at the stone, secure and safe and also knowing it will never, ever be that way again. I touched the stone. It was cold. I hugged the stone. I wanted to take it in my arms and hold it like a baby, with all the memories in place. I placed my hands on the numbers, the letters, and the place where the big chunk in the right hand corner was missing. I could not stop touching the stone. It felt the same as it did on that September day, 40 years ago. I wanted to take the whole stone home to remind me of what I had. Over the next three days, I went up to the third floor, to the cornerstone, over and over again, to touch it and to remember. I did not want to leave. I explained to my son what this cornerstone meant to me and told him about my childhood and how we rode our bikes with no fear and about growing up in Brooklyn in the 1950s.

Everyone has their memories, but for me that day in September, 40 years ago, will forever be special. I will always know that a little piece of my childhood history will live on in that cornerstone forever. People who visit that cornerstone will see the marks on the face of it and the missing chunks and date. I will tell my son about that day in Cooperstown on the third floor and what it meant to me. And I will tell him to pass the story on down to his children and show them the cornerstone. Show them, tell them, and teach them about a glorious time in the past that once was and will never be again. And tell them that his mom left a small mark forever on a huge part of history, the history of the Brooklyn Dodgers and Ebbets Field.— **Susan Horowitz**

When I was a little boy, my father would take me on the elevated subway train to Brooklyn. I remember the slowly whirring ceiling fan, the straw rattan seats, and the windows you could open. Then we would arrive at Ebbets Field! There was no feeling quite like the first visit to the ballpark every spring; suddenly there was the bright green of the grass, and the bright blue of the number 39 on the broad back of Roy Campanella. Our seats were right behind home plate!

Many, many years passed, and the old park was gone. I had a grown-up job conducting surveys for a public opinion pollster, and one day I found myself doing interviews in a housing project that bordered on Flatbush Avenue. I had an inkling of something, and I asked on old-timer, "Was Ebbets Field around here?" He replied, "Follow me," and led me down to the laundry room. "This," he said, "was home plate." And in that moment, I remembered my father.—**John Jiler**

My father owned Claridge Bar and Grill about 25 blocks from Ebbets Field, and he had season tickets to the Dodgers games at Ebbets Field. When he didn't take one of his customers, I would get to go. My first game was when I was about eight years old, probably 1947. At one of my first games, I was wearing a Dodger hat, and when they played the National Anthem some man behind us said, "Sonny, take the cap off." I was so embarrassed, but when I took the cap off and my hair fell out, nothing more was said. My father and I used to take the trolley, but later when I went with my girlfriends, we walked the 25 blocks or so in order to save money. My father's season tickets were originally behind home plate, but he wanted to be able to see into the Dodger dugout, so we moved to seats between third and home. My girlfriends and I would typically sit in the bleachers.

Arriving at Ebbets Field was so exciting, with the beautiful green grass and the white uniforms. After a night game, they would sometimes let you walk on the field and exit through a gate in the outfield. I used to pick up some dirt and take it home. Once the game was over, we would often walk across the street to where the Dodgers parked their cars and get autographs. I remember getting autographs from Duke Snider, Gil Hodges, Jackie Robinson, Pee Wee Reese, and Carl Furillo, among others. The players were all such gentlemen. The area around the park was like a little community. There was a bowling alley and a diner where we would go for ice cream after the game. I never had to cut school to go to Dodger games. I went to a Catholic school that let us out early on Wednesdays so the kids from public schools could get religious instruction, and those were the days I would go to Ebbets Field.—**Marjorie Burns King, oral history interview, 2010, Brooklyn Historical Society**

I became a Dodger fan in 1947 because of Jackie Robinson. Before that I liked baseball but didn't root for a particular team. I grew up in Verona, New Jersey, and everyone in my family, as well as all of my friends, with one exception, were Yankee fans. My first game at Ebbets Field was against the Cardinals because in addition to being a Dodger fan, I wanted to see Stan Musial. My father took my cousin and me, and we drove into Brooklyn from Verona, which was difficult, parked on a street, and walked to the ballpark. We went through the rotunda, which was very small, and then walked up a ramp where we got a first view of the field. I couldn't believe how big and green it was. I was certainly used to seeing green space, but this really impressed me—it may have been going from the dark into the light.

After that first time, my dad took me other times, and the recreation department in Verona used to sponsor bus trips. Almost every time I went, I would go down the right field line before the game to watch the telecast of Happy Felton's Knothole Gang. We always went to day games. I never saw a night game there. As I remember the crowds, they were mostly men, very few women and children. There was not a lot of drinking going on, people went to see the game. Watching Jackie Robinson was always a thrill, and I also remember seeing Duke Snider hit a home run over the scoreboard. Like most people, the feature I remember the most about Ebbets Field was the right field wall and scoreboard. Everything that has been said about how Carl Furillo played the wall is true — I remember seeing him throw out a runner at first base. The last time I was there was in 1955 or 1956 to watch the Cubs and Ernie Banks. I was in the Marines in 1957, so I missed the last season at Ebbets Field and all of the controversy of the Dodgers leaving Brooklyn. — **Ken Kistner**

My father, Arthur Leible, was the circulation manager for the *Brooklyn Daily Eagle.* He worked first for the *Brooklyn Daily Times*, until they were acquired by the *Eagle.* The paper would also give him assignments, sort of like a stringer, covering games and special stories at Ebbets Field because he was a good writer. Through him I was able to meet all the Dodgers. I only got into the locker room once, and what I remember is the camaraderie, especially the laughter of Campanella, who was one of the leaders with the jokes, as was Pee Wee Reese and Robinson. Leo Durocher was also very nice to me. He picked me out of a crowd of autograph seekers outside of Ebbets Field in order to get everyone in an orderly line so that he could sign autographs. From then on, I guess I became one of his favorites.

I used to get coffee for Red Barber — he always wanted it black and would pay me a nickel for getting it for him. My father would never use the *Eagle's* passes because there was always someone more deserving than us. I used to save up 50 cents to get into the bleachers, and then when I was older, I had a G.O. (government organization) pass so I got in for 30 cents. I also used to collect the Borden's milk cartons, which got you in at a reduced price.

My first game was in 1941, but I don't remember that much about it. The first game I remember was in 1946 — Carl Furillo played center field, and I remember him throwing a runner out at second. I was also there for Jackie Robinson's first game, and that was always my biggest thrill at Ebbets Field. I remember going out there with my dad. It was a bright day. I knew why I was going. I knew why he let me miss school. And I looked and I saw white uniforms glistening, and I saw this black face. He [Jackie Robinson] was the greatest ballplayer I've ever seen, and I've been around a long, long time. If he had come up at the age of 21, he would have broken so many more records.

Nowhere but Brooklyn could he have been embraced like that. They were all for him. There were no dissenters. Everyone was immediately in love with him. I think it's because Brooklyn itself was a so-called melting pot. Either parents or grandparents knew what it was to come here, earn a living, and be accepted. And that's why they accepted Jackie so readily. When he came up to bat or was in the field, or when he was on the back end of a double play, it seemed like all eyes were focused on him. Even watching him in the dugout and on the Dodger bench, it didn't seem like there was any prejudice toward him.

My favorite place to sit was in section 27, just above the Tydol Gas sign because you could see the whole park. Once at a Dodger–Giant game, Whitey Lockman was playing left field, and Eddie Miksis hit a ball that I thought was going to come into the stands. I reached for it and my fingers hit the top of Lockman's glove. He caught the ball anyway and did he swear at me as he ran off the field! I was afraid he was going to come after me when the game was over.

I was fortunate enough to be on the Happy Felton show once — the Little League coaches picked the players, and I was picked and competed against two other third basemen. Billy Cox was the player who judged the three of us and he wanted to pick me since he knew me, but I muffed two balls so I didn't give him enough reason to do so. You got a ball, a bat, and a glove for being on the show, which was great.

I was at the last game in 1957. I took a girl I was dating and trying to impress her — she had hardly ever been to Ebbets Field. We sat there behind third base, and I just cried the entire time — she wasn't impressed. I was just about to be drafted into the army, so the two things were equally depressing. When I was in the army at Fort Leonard Wood, I called my dad and asked him to go to Ebbets Field and see if he could get some kind of souvenir, but he said he wouldn't go near the place.

I went to Erasmus High School and remember the Election Day football games against Manual. Erasmus was more of an upper-class school — you had to pass an admissions test to get in. Manual was more of a trade school, but their players were much bigger than ours and you always wondered how Erasmus could ever win a game.

I don't have any bad memories of a game there — I was just happy to be there, and I used to go at least 30 times a year. It had a tremendous ambience — it was a warm and friendly place, not like some of the places you see today. — **Mike Leible**

I was a rabid Dodger fan at an early age, like only young kids in Brooklyn could be. My father worked long hours at his business, so my Uncle Morris used to take me to Ebbets Field. My first game was when I was seven or eight, either 1945 or 1946. I have especially vivid memories of 1947, the year that Jackie Robinson broke in. I was actually there for what was really the first game that Robinson played at Ebbets Field, not the April 15 game that everyone talks about, but an exhibition game a few days earlier. In those days, the Dodgers and Yankees used to play a couple of exhibition games right before the season began. I saw him play first base at Ebbets Field in an exhibition game before opening day, and he made one of those iconic Robinson catches. Another famous Dodger player was Pete Reiser, but my memory of him is after he played for the Dodgers. Reiser was traded to the Braves, and I saw him play against Brooklyn at Ebbets Field, another time that I went with my uncle. Reiser was at bat with the bases loaded, and I told my uncle that I had never seen a grand slam home run and Reiser promptly hit one. — **Ron Lightstone, oral history interview, 2010, Brooklyn Historical Society**

I am a third generation Dodger fan. My grandmother, who was born in New York City in 1879, was a Dodger fan. I remember just when I began to root for the Dodgers, as I recall listening to Red Barber announcing the game on the radio while returning from the 1939 World's Fair at Flushing Meadow. The pitcher was Al Hollingworth and the catcher was Al Todd. They only played together for one year.

A neighbor, Al Weiss, who was a furrier, had a client named Jocko Conlon, the umpire. Jocko said if Al's kids wanted to go to Ebbets field, all they had to do was show up at the Press Gate and ask for two tickets for Lew Carson. The tickets were free, all you had to pay was the tax. Luckily for me, Al's kids were Giant fans, so they never went to see the Dodgers play. I went so often as Lew Carson that my rain check collection is in the Hall of Fame Baseball Museum in Cooperstown.

Among the games that I remember attending are Ed Head's no-hitter in April of 1946, opening day in 1951 when it was freezing, and a game that was called off because a swarms of green gnats that showed up at game time. Other memories include Dixie Walker getting a hit to tie a game and a fan jumped out of his seat, ran up to Walker, and kissed him on the cheek. I also remember 16-year-old shortstop, Tommy Brown, throwing the ball over first baseman Howie Schultz's head, even though Schultz was six foot six. When *The Encyclopedia of New York City* first came out, it listed the right field fence at 310 feet and the left field fence at 297 feet. I had to straighten them out on that. — **Bud Livingston**

I went to my first game at Ebbets Field with my father when I was no more than 10, so it would have been in the early 1950s. I was a Giant fan, so after the top of the seventh, I stood up for my team and some fans told my father that it wasn't a good idea, but I don't remember any incidents. I especially remember the Sym-Phony band, which was like Spike Jones with a lot of crazy sounds. Their specialty was "The worms crawl in, the worms crawl out," which they played when an opposing player struck out. They would play that song loud and out of tune until he sat down and then made an unflattering noise. Some players would play along and refuse to sit down.

Another memory I have is the first time a member of my family got a foul ball. I think it was 1955, and Dick Williams hit one that landed on top of my sister's arm — she didn't have to do anything, it just landed there. There was, of course, a lot of scuffling for the ball, but then a voice behind us said, "The girl has it," and that was the end of that. The features that stand out in my mind are the right field fence, the Abe Stark sign, and what seemed to be this vast expanse of green to an urban kid. They also used to do the Knothole Gang show down the right field line. There is apparently one surviving recording of an episode, and I found the winner and wrote a story about him.

The crowd was rowdy, but not as vehement and scary as it is today, with nothing like the "Boston s...." chants. In fact, Stan Musial got his nickname, "Stan the Man," from the fans at Ebbets Field — think of a player today getting a "printable" nickname from the opposing team. The best part of Ebbets Field was the closeness to the action; there were some posts and obstructed views, but you were so close that you could hear the chatter from the field. It's a shame Ebbets Field wasn't saved; it would be like Wrigley

No player or fan who heard them ever forgot the Brooklyn Sym-Phony Band (National Baseball Hall of Fame Library, Cooperstown, New York).

Field and Fenway Park today.—**Lee Lowenfish, oral history interview, 2010, Brooklyn Historical Society**

My first visit to Ebbets Field was with my father and two of his friends. I have vivid memories of this large green space. The player who made the biggest impression on me is Jackie Robinson. The other visit that I especially remember was during the 1953 World Series. There was a big iron stanchion in front of us, which partially blocked the view, but it was part of the charm of the place. Leo Durocher and his wife were sitting three rows in front of us, and I remember he was shouting at people and they were shouting back at him. We lived on Long Island at the time, so we would drive to the games, park, and then walk and there would be people hanging out of their apartment windows. Ebbets Field was a very intimate park, and every game was like a big celebration—it was so much fun.—**Malcom MacKay, oral history interview, 2010, Brooklyn Historical Society**

In 1955, my high school (W.C. Bryant in Woodside, Queens) baseball team played at Ebbets Field for the Public School Athletic League championship. The entire student body was in attendance. One of Bryant's top players was Freddie Van Dusen, a tall, blond left-handed hitter with a classic stance. Freddie crushed one out over the right field fence onto Bedford Avenue. I remember the baseball scouts at the game scribbling furiously on their note pads. Bryant won the game and the championship.

I often wondered whatever happened to Freddie. I assumed that he never made it to the major leagues, but I was wrong. I learned only in recent years that he was signed as a bonus baby by the Philadelphia Phillies and made an appearance late in the 1955 season. He, however, played in only one major league game and batted only once and was hit by a pitch.

I also attended a 1954 game when the Giants clinched the pennant behind the pitching of Sal Maglie. As we were leaving the ballpark, below us on the ground level I observed Walter Alston and Leo Durocher shaking hands to acknowledge the end of the pennant race. I often have thought what a terrific photo this would have made. But, alas, I didn't have a camera with me. It was also a memorable evening because for some reason or another my father didn't take the expressway in driving from Astoria, Queens, to Flatbush. So it seemed like we drove through every neighborhood in Brooklyn to reach Ebbets Field and that it took forever to get there.—**Anthony Marcantonio**

My father used to take me to Ebbets Field with him, and I think the first time was when I was seven or eight, which would have been in the late 1930s. My father took me, but never took my sister so it was part of a private experience for the two of us. He taught me how to keep score, about the game itself, and how to be a baseball fan, which has continued ever since. We mostly went to day games when he was off from work, and it would be at least once a month. My father would say to my mother, "I'm taking your daughter to the Dodger game so she won't be able to help you around the house." My mother would pack a big brown bag of food, but my father didn't get to eat much of it since he was always so excited, yelling, and even standing on his seat. I'm embarrassed to say it, but he was really a Yankee fan. We went to Ebbets Field because it was more convenient, and he did root for the Dodgers unless they were playing the Yankees.

My fondest memories are of the façade and the rotunda. There was always so much energy in the rotunda, people were excited and it would get others excited. I remember my father pointing out the different players to me as we walked through the rotunda. I went to an all-girls Catholic high school and also used to go to games with my friends. My best memory of a game at Ebbets Field is one where Brooklyn was behind 12–0, and people were leaving, but the Dodgers came back and won the game in the last few innings. I remember saying to people that you can't leave early, you have to stay to the end. I don't have any memories of a specific bad game, but any time the Dodgers lost, it was a bad game.—**Josephine Marchesano, oral history interview, 2010, Brooklyn Historical Society**

My Dad took me to Ebbets Field on a Sunday in July of 1957. My aunt lived in Brooklyn, and her brother-in-law worked as a member of the grounds crew. He got us the tickets for a doubleheader with the Phils. The teams split the games. On the way out we were allowed onto the field, and my Dad told me to scoop up some dirt from around second base. I still have the dirt, which is saved in an instant Maxwell House coffee jar. I also have the ticket stub.—**William Markert**

In the summer of 1956, my friend Vinny and I went to Ebbets Field on tickets we got by collecting a number of Borden's ice cream cup lids. Needless to say, the seats we got were in the upper deck and quite a distance from the field. We decided to try to sneak down into some better seats closer to the field. After some slick maneuvering, we managed to arrive at two empty seats right on the third base line about ten rows from the field. You could imagine how happy these two 14-year-old boys were after their successful attempt to get away with such a stunt. We were just settling down in our seats to enjoy the game from our new vantage point when the announcer said that the Dodgers were honored to have as their special guests members of a VFW chapter, who also were all World War I veterans. The announcer requested that all the veterans stand and that the crowd give them an ovation. All these much older men around us stood up to thunderous applause, and it was then that Vinny and I discovered that we had managed to sneak into the one section of the ballpark where we could not blend into the crowd. A few moments later, one of the ushers came to us and asked to see our tickets. When we produced our tickets, he politely escorted us to our original seats. Thus ended my one chance to see a Dodger game from the vantage point of a box seat.—**Gene Martincz**

A common trip to Ebbets Field when I was young meant standing in line at the bleacher gate with a Knothole Gang cardboard tag hanging from a buttonhole. It meant free admission. I would be clutching a paper bag with a meatball sandwich my mother made while the famous fan, Hilda Chester, waved a cowbell around until the gates opened. Always early enough for batting practice, I recall coach Cookie Lavagetto tossing baseballs up to us kids in the bleachers during batting practice. It was home to us 20 to 30 times a year, every year. It was small, intimate, and lovable. Everyone around you talked baseball with each other.—**Andy Mele**

It was August 11, 1956, a Saturday. My father asked me if I would like to go to the ballgame for my birthday. I was seven, going on eight, the following week. The Dodgers would have been on the road on my birthday, so this was the best time to go (it was Saturday and my father was off from work). The Dodgers played the Phillies. We had seats directly behind home plate, first row above the net. Great seats, and the only game I ever went to at Ebbets Field. The Dodgers won the game, 5–2. The one thing I will always remember about the game was third baseman Randy Jackson hit an inside-the-park homerun, which was unheard of in a small bandbox like Ebbets Field. I also remember walking hand in hand with my father through Prospect Park. We lived on the west side of the park (Park Slope). A few years ago, I located the box score of that game on the Internet.

I made a copy and had it enlarged and framed. Every time I look at it, it brings back the memories of that Saturday, the walk through the park, and the game.

On an unusually warm Saturday afternoon at the end of February or beginning of March of 1960—less than three years after the Dodgers had left Brooklyn — my friend and I were riding our new bicycles. We rode through Prospect Park and found ourselves at Ebbets Field. There was a construction fence around it, and it was in the process of being demolished. We were just kids, and we found a hole in the fence and we entered. It was Saturday, so no one was working. Half the stands were demolished, and there were big piles of dirt in what used to be the field. However, the Dodger dugout was still there. I found a box in the corner of the dugout containing a pile of old expired Dodger contracts. It was about 10 inches thick. I remember seeing ones for the Duke, Gil Hodges, and many more signed contracts, apparently discarded by management when they left to go to Los Angeles. I took the box, but left it behind when the watchman saw us. We made a beeline back to the hole in the fence.—**James N. Minally**

We were huge Yankee fans from Lincoln Park, New Jersey. I was 12, and while my dad usually had tickets for games at Yankee Stadium, in the summer of 1955, he ended up with two tickets for a Dodger game at Ebbets Field. In our neighborhood, you were either a Yankee fan or a Dodger loser. I had never been to a Dodger game and usually only watched Yankee games on TV, but I was playing Little League ball that summer and wanted to see Gil Hodges bat. He had such an unusual batting stance, and a bunch of us playing ball that summer were trying to imitate his stance. It was the only time I ever went to Ebbets Field and Dad drove, but we ended up walking quite a few blocks and got there just as they were playing the National Anthem. Great game. I saw Hodges get a hit (a single) and came home and used his stance for the rest of summer. Thank goodness the pitching wasn't fast in Little League back then.— **Peter Mitchko**

I lived on Union Street and New York Avenue, which was about three blocks to Brooklyn Prep, where I went to high school. From there, it was another three blocks to Ebbets Field. On game days, you could see the flags at Ebbets Field from the top floor of the school. My first game was when I was about five or six. It was opening day, the mayor was there, they raised the flag, and it was also very cold — so cold that I think it was the first time I had a cup of coffee. The neighbor who took me was embarrassed buying a young boy coffee, but I needed it to keep out the chill.

I think it was about 1937, my sister was nine, and I was seven, and we found that if you waited for the players, you could get their autographs. So I got a copybook, cut out pictures of the players, pasted them in my book, and then asked the players to sign. One of the players I went after was Pepper Martin of the Cardinals, who was called the "Wild Hoss of the Osage." He told me I was very persistent and signed my book. I didn't know what persistent meant, so I had to go ask my mother. Another player I remember from autograph seeking was Dixie Walker — "The People's Cherce." He would sit in his car and sign autographs for every kid who wanted one. I felt bad when he wanted to leave the Dodgers after Jackie Robinson joined the team because Dixie was always nice to the kids.

When I was 10 in 1940, my uncles used to tease me that the Bushwicks could beat the Dodgers. At the time I didn't know who the Bushwicks were, but they were a semi-pro team from Brooklyn. One day, I saw that they were playing at Ebbets Field, so I went and bought a bleacher seat for 25 cents, which is one half of what the Dodgers charged. I got to sit in the first row of the bleachers, which was a good seat in such a small intimate park. I remember looking down at the opposing centerfielder and seeing he was, in the language of that time, colored — it was the first time I had ever seen a colored ball player. My instinctive reaction was I guess they want their own team; I had no idea that they weren't allowed to play in Organized Baseball. The crowds changed a lot after 1947. Before that, there were very few black fans at the games, but after Jackie Robinson broke in, a lot more blacks came to games.

However, my best memory of Ebbets Field is from the summer of 1944 when I was a "stile" boy. I was 14 years old, and so I was too young to get a job at most places, but too old just to hang around. The one place where boys my age could get hired was at Ebbets Field as turnstile or stile boys. It was a good job because you were paid 50 cents plus, and after a couple of innings, you could go watch the game. As the ticket taker tore the ticket in half, the stile boy would press a pedal that would register the admission. The way it used to work was that the main gate would open before the ballgame and the hiring boss would come out and hire the kids, and usually those with experience got picked first. Once he was done hiring, the gate came down and that was it. One day the gate came down, we started to walk away, and then we heard the gate come back up. The hiring boss came out and said I need one more kid for the bleachers. There was a big redheaded man with him, and he said I want an Irish kid. Although I have an Italian last name, my mother's side of the family is Irish and my features look Irish. Like everyone else, I was calling out pick me and they called me inside the gates. Once I was inside, the redheaded man asked me what my last name was. I was sure if I said Natiello, he wouldn't hire me, so I thought of some spinster sisters who lived in our building named Brennan, and I said my name is Brennan, so I got hired. As a result, I had to then put up with my friends calling me Brennan all summer long.

I probably worked one-third of the games that year, and early on, I was told that there was a management spotter who checked to make sure that there would be one turn of the turnstile for one ticket. One day I noticed that two people were getting in for one turn and that every so often the ticket taker would give tickets to the spotter, who took them back to the ticket booth. At the end of the game, the ticket taker told me to meet him under the stands on the third base side near the hot dog stand. When I got there, he gave me $3 as my share, and I celebrated with a second hot dog. This happened a couple of other times, and I didn't know what to do. I certainly didn't want to tell my mother.

Decades later in 2008 I decided I better make good on the roughly $6 that I made on this deal, so I sent the president of the Dodgers a check for $100. He wrote me a thank-you letter and said that the money would go to the Dodgers Dream Foundation. Later I wrote up the story and sent it to Dave Anderson of the *New York Times*, who put an article about it in the paper.

Stile boys were pretty much the youngest employees at Ebbets Field. A number of the ticket takers themselves were postal employees, who worked at Ebbets as a second job. They had flexibility in their postal schedule so they could fit in a day or night game. Most of the hot dog and other concession vendors tended to be older than stile boys, but younger than the ticket takers. All the employees were male, I don't remember any female employees.

During this time I became friends with the Dodger batboy, Lenny Septoff, who ranked just behind the mayor and the parish priest for us kids. He allowed me to help him with the bats, and sometimes I got onto the field before the game and could play catch with the players. He lived only a block away from me, and sometimes I would arrange it to walk to the park with him and occasionally he would help me get in. He also gave me a broken bat once, but it was from Johnny Dantonio, one of Brooklyn's worst catchers.—**Robert Natiello, oral history interview, 2010, Brooklyn Historical Society**

I was born in Brooklyn. I was a fan of the Brooklyn team since I was a little kid. I went to Ebbets Field many times with my father, who loved the Dodgers. There was a little gate on the first base side by the fence, and there was a security guard there. That's where we used to sneak in. And the Dodger bullpen was right there. It was wide open, so you could lean against the railing, and you were right there. The other bullpen was in left field. They [the pitchers] were right there. They weren't behind any wall, and they'd throw their pitches, and they were maybe 10 to 15 feet in front of you. It was all wide open. When you were in front, you were level with the field.

When I was a kid, if you didn't get in, someone would have a radio, and you'd hear, "it's a long fly ball to right field." And we'd run out onto Bedford Avenue to catch it, and traffic would have to stop and the people from the cars would be hollering. We would give the ball to the security guard, and he would give it to the bullpen. That was the ball they used over and over again. It wasn't like today, where you would hold onto it.

There were guys like Duke Snider, Leo Durocher, and Pee Wee Reese. They were all there — Carl Furillo as well. They were very friendly, and they would talk to you. After the game, you would wait outside the dressing room and try to say hello. Of course, someone would pull up with a car, and they'd jump in. I started going in the very early 1930s, and I went right up until they closed it. I remember one game. There was a triple play. That was something. That made the papers.

The fans were very, very Brooklyn. They were different back then. They were diehard Brooklyn fans. Everything was Brooklyn, Brooklyn, Brooklyn. They always had a nice crowd at Ebbets Field. They used to pack the house. They'd be in there good. The Sym-Phony, they were good. They were there all the time, playing around third base. And the crowd loved them. Hilda Chester would get up there, ringing them bells, and everybody would go crazy when she was doing that. She was quite a person.— **Tom Nolan**

My parents took me to Ebbets Field many times when I was an infant, but the first time I remember being there was in 1951 against the Cubs. I saw Clem Labine pitch, Gil

Hodges, who was already my favorite player, got a hit, and Jackie Robinson stole a base. My family didn't have a lot of money, so we almost always sat in the left field bleachers. It was always special there because of the almost juicy diversity — different pockets throughout the bleachers including Orthodox Jews and Hasidim, plus people of color. It was there that I heard my first word of Yiddish — "Yankel" — over and over again in a loud voice — it means Jackie. I have always thought that older African American men were the most knowledgeable baseball people, and with them in that section, there was a lot of informed baseball talk going on. As whites, we were the minority sitting among different people with one thing in common — our love for the Dodgers.

Hilda Chester also used to sit in the bleachers sometimes. My father was an eclectic kind of person who could talk to anyone. He would talk to Hilda as a person, not as some kind of freak, asking her how she was and what she did the night before, things like that. Sometimes when she came through the stands, if there was a vacant seat next to us she would sit down and talk with my father and me. I was always "kid," never Tom. I can see her talking to my father about everyday things in a normal voice when something would happen on the field. Then she would react in a voice like a Fulton Street fish market salesman, using language that would make a sailor blush. But then she would switch roles back and resume the conversation with my father.

The Dodgers loudest, and perhaps most loyal, fan, Hilda Chester, could reportedly switch at a moment's notice from everyday conversation to language that would make a sailor blush (National Baseball Hall of Fame Library, Cooperstown, New York).

In talking about memories of the features of the building, you have to understand the difference between a boy's memories and a man's memories. We lived on the east side of New York in very cramped conditions, so when I came out into the bleachers and saw that vast expanse of green, it was the size of the place that struck me. The only similar areas of big green space that I had experienced were Prospect Park and Central Park. I knew it was an intimate space and that the Polo Grounds and Yankee Stadium were much bigger, but I never thought of Ebbets Field as being small. Part of that was due to the size of the right field wall.

The atmosphere at Ebbets Field was like a carnival, not a circus, but rather a carnival. It started when you got off the subway, even before getting to the ballpark. I especially remember a blind black man selling pencils, offering to bet anyone that he knew the score before the game even started — 0–0 — the oldest con line in the world.

My best memory of a game at Ebbets Field was in 1952 or 1953 when my father had written an article about the Paul brothers, the new owners of the Cincinnati Reds. For the rest of that season, we were given box seats just to the right of the visitor's dugout every time the Reds were in Brooklyn. Two plays in that game always stayed with me, both of which had to do with Jackie Robinson. On one, he scored from first on a double, but as he turned third and headed home it seemed like he was running right at me — I could even hear him breathe. It was a little startling. The other had to do with the Reds catcher, Ed Bailey. Since Robinson took such a large lead off first, catchers would sometimes throw behind him to try to pick him off. Bailey made a snap throw like that to Ted Kluszewski, and the next thing I knew there was a big cloud of dust at second where Robinson had stolen the base. Both of those plays symbolized how Robinson could just take over a game — I never saw another player like him until Willie Mays.

Of course my other favorite memory of Ebbets Field was the fifth game of the 1955 World Series, the one World Series game I was fortunate enough to see there. The two things I remember so vividly are the World Series bunting and the way we hung on every pitch. My first sight of the bunting just told me that this was the World Series — this was something special.

My biggest negative memory of Ebbets Field is how it stunk to high heaven — it was bus terminal cubed. My mother always brought toilet paper with her. That said, I never had an unhappy day at Ebbets Field even though I saw the Dodgers lose many times. It was family-friendly baseball. Although I never experienced it, I heard of some problems with teenage behavior toward the end, but to me it was a family atmosphere — almost bordering on hokey.

As I got older I used to hang out by the players' entrance. I remember a group of the Dodger players arriving in one car — they did actually car pool. Also I remember Duke Snider walking down Montague Street as if he was on his way to work. While there was a distance between the fans and the players, they were accessible. They weren't movie stars, which contributed to the carnival like atmosphere. Also, they had the best organist in the country, Gladys Goodding, who was an important part of the show.

When I interviewed Johnny Podres about the 1955 World Series, he made a very profound point that winning the seventh game was so special because it could never happen again. I think the same thing is true of Ebbets Field since it no longer exists. It is not a relic, but something that lives in memory — it has a certain aura. By the way, around the cherry trees in Prospect Park is the dirt from Ebbets Field, so you can go there and still see Ebbets Field. I am very confident in saying that Ebbets Field will live forever. — **Tom Oliphant**

I remember Ebbets Field as being small, noisy and old, but also charming and friendly. The fans were so close that there was always good communication between the fans and the players. On day games, it was a beautiful scene. I have vivid memories of Ebbets Field as a place people looked forward to going to. It was a place where people would sit next to strangers and become friends.

Over the years, my sister and I got to know a lot of the employees — ushers, grounds crew, among others. There was a lot of continuity, many of them worked for the Dodgers for a long time. They took great pride in their work and were proud to say that they worked at Ebbets Field for the Dodgers. The players were always very nice to me. I was especially friendly with Pete Reiser and also with Bill Sharman, who played only briefly with the Dodgers before becoming a famous basketball player with the Boston Celtics.

A lot of times we went to Ebbets Field by public transportation, and there was a great deal of anticipation about getting there. One story that sticks out in my mind is one that I have heard several times from Danny and Sylvia Kaye. Danny took Sylvia to Ebbets Field for their first date. There was a big crowd in the rotunda, and they got separated. Danny went to the game and Sylvia went home. Afterwards Danny went to Sylvia's house and asked what happened and learned that she didn't know what to do, so she just went home. That was their first date, and they still got married!—**Peter O'Malley, oral history interview, 2010, Brooklyn Historical Society**

I was born in 1921 in Harlem. My father died when I was young, and my mother moved to Brooklyn where her two brothers, who were a doctor and a dentist, lived. My one uncle (the doctor) was a bachelor, and he offered to be in loco parentis for me as a father. He was an enormous Dodger fan, so when I was seven, every weekend that the Dodgers were at home, he would take me to a game at Ebbets Field. We would ride the subway to Empire Boulevard, and then walk to streets with strange names like Sullivan Place and McKeever Place. First we would buy peanuts outside the park since they were only five cents, while they were 10 cents inside, then he would buy a newspaper for two or three cents since it had a scorecard, while inside that cost 10 cents. Finally, we would pay 55 cents for a bleacher seat and go inside. My uncle knew the value of a penny, but he also knew the worth of a dollar because once we were inside, he would generally slip the usher a dollar, and we would end up sitting near third base, not in the bleachers. We would watch the game, while dropping peanut shells on the floor, and I thought if my mother could see this, I would hear about it.

My first games were in the 1920s and early 1930s before the outfield seats were built, so the seats were basically all in foul territory, running from right field to just past third base. That was also before the big scoreboard with the Abe Stark sign was added. The player's names in those days were like they were part of a troupe of clowns—think of it—Van Lingo Mungo, Dazzy Vance, and Babe Herman. I saw two of Babe Herman's high or low points: getting hit on the head with a fly ball and hitting a double which turned into a double play. But on the latter play, the runner on third did score the winning run. I also saw Babe Ruth at the end of his career. I had relatives from South Africa, and one time a cousin, a young girl a few years older than I, was here on a visit. My uncle took us to a game, and the first two times Hack Wilson of the Cubs was up, he hit a home run. The third time he struck out, and my cousin said, very politely, "How inconsistent!"

My greatest thrill at Ebbets Field was a doubleheader against the Cardinals. In the first game, Dizzy Dean pitched a three-hit shutout, and his brother Paul was scheduled to pitch the second game. My uncle said wait until you see him, and he pitched a no-hitter. After seeing Babe Herman get hit on the head with a fly ball, my worst moment was when a foul ball came into my hands, I dropped it, and a man drinking beer picked it up and wouldn't give it to me.

The ballpark was never full unless the Giants were in. Initially, they were almost all white males, very loud, raucous, and beer drinking, but cheerful. Then, after Jackie Robinson started, there was a lot more diversity, which was a good thing.— **Charles Plotz, oral history interview, 2010, Brooklyn Historical Society**

I lived a short hop from the stadium, and it was like a part of me! When the Dodgers left Brooklyn, I was 14, and it felt like losing a limb. I remember sitting behind home plate with my father during a World Series game. To this day, I can easily rattle off the names of many of our beloved Brooklyn Dodgers! They're forever in our hearts and fondest memories, as is Ebbets Field.— **Carol Pozner**

My first game at Ebbets Field was in June of 1954 when I was almost 10 years old. It was against the Reds, and the Dodgers won, 6–3 after Duke Snider tripled with the bases loaded. There was sort of a small cut in the left-center or center field wall, and that's where Snider's ball went, otherwise it would have been a home run. When we got to the game, we walked up ramps until we could see the field for the first time. It was a night game, and the lights were on, so it was this brilliant shade of green. I said something to my father, who was a Scotch immigrant, and he said, "Well, lad, what color did you think it would be," and I said, "Gray," just like on television.

I probably went to about 20 games between 1954 and 1957. It was always like going to a gathering of family and friends, it seemed like everyone knew one another. One of the ways that I got in was through the Sheffield Milk Company. If you saved 10 or so coupons from the side of a milk carton, that and 10 cents or 20 cents would get you into the bleachers, which was a fine place to sit. The crowds were always very interesting — a lot of shouting and riding players, but never any cursing. I never had a bad experience at Ebbets Field.— **John Reilly, oral history interview, 2010, Brooklyn Historical Society**

I lived in Bedford-Stuyvesant, and we used to walk to Ebbets Field — it was a long walk. We used to sit in the grandstand because it was all we could afford. I remember the last Dodger game at Ebbets Field because my sister and brother-in-law went, but I couldn't go because I had to go to a wake. Well, they went to more of a wake than I did. They said it was so sad they all cried.— **Edith Resker, oral history interview, 2010, Brooklyn Historical Society**

My first game at Ebbets Field was supposed to be on June 6, 1944, but my father called me from his work and said we couldn't go because all major league games that day had been cancelled because of the Allied invasion of Normandy. Less than a week later, I did get to go to my first game—a doubleheader against the Boston Braves. It was a bright, sunny day and I was in awe until the game began. The first batter I saw was Tommy Holmes, who was from Brooklyn. He was the leadoff batter for the Braves.

Up to that point I had only been able to listen to games on the radio, so I didn't know what a game actually looked like. That was part of the genius of Larry MacPhail. When he wanted to put Dodger games on the radio, the reaction was that people would listen instead of going to the games. However, what really happened was that it made people more curious, and they wanted to go and see a game for themselves. It certainly was true for me.

After that, I went to a lot of games, especially when we got box seats for the 1955 season. My father knew someone who had eight seats, and he sold two to us. They were great seats, just 11 rows behind the Dodger dugout, and we kept them for the 1956 and 1957 seasons. We wanted to keep them forever, but you know what happened in 1958. Since Ebbets Field was such an intimate ballpark, we were really close to the field.

Before we had the box seats, I became an expert on seats with obstructed views. In the upper deck, the obstructed views started after row eight, so you knew if you got seats in the first eight rows, you didn't have to worry about a pole blocking your view. In the lower deck, the poles started behind the box seats, so any place behind the box seats, you were at risk of not being able to see some part of the field. There were about 7,000 seats at Ebbets Field with obstructed views, and I got to know where they all were.

My best game at Ebbets Field was May 12, 1956: Carl Erskine's no-hitter against the New York Giants. I was well aware of what was going on, and by the 7th inning, I was very nervous. Whitey Lockman almost broke it up in the seventh—he hit a long fly ball that went just foul over the right field fence.

My saddest experience has to be the last game of the 1950 season when the Dodgers lost to the Phillies in extra innings, just missing forcing a playoff. Pee Wee Reese hit a ball that struck the top of the right field fence and fell behind the scoreboard for a home run. To me, Cal Abrams being thrown out at home with the potential winning run in the bottom of the ninth was just a good play by Richie Ashburn.

Everyone always talks about how the short right field fence helped Duke Snider, but I remember a game where it really hurt him. It was a game on June 1, 1955. Duke had already hit three home runs when he came up for the last time in the bottom of the eighth. Duke hit one that was rising from the moment it left the bat. It hit the top of the right field fence and bounced back for a double. If the fence had been a few feet further back, it would have cleared it easily, so this was at least one time when the short fence didn't help a left-handed batter.

The daffiness of the Dodgers was one of the things we loved about them, and even the best of them weren't immune from it. I remember in 1947 Dixie Walker was at the plate with Pee Wee Reese on first. Dixie swung and missed, the bat slipped out of his hands and went down towards first. Pee Wee came off the bag and gave him back the bat. Reese returned to first base only to be called out by the first base umpire. It turned out that he hadn't called time, so the Cubs' pitcher threw the ball to the first baseman, Eddie Waitkus, who applied the tag. I reminded Pee Wee of it many years later, and he said,

"Of all the things I did, why did you have to remember that?" I said it was who the Dodgers were and we loved them for it, and he said I was right.

The night of the last game in 1957, I wanted to go, but my father wanted to take my uncle. I was begging to go, but he told me, "You've been to a lot of games this year. Let us go — there will be other games." Of course, there were no other games in Brooklyn, but there were in Los Angeles, something I reminded my father of on many occasions.

It's amazing when you think about it. In addition to winning six pennants between 1946 and 1957, three times the Dodgers lost out on the last day of the season —1946, 1950 and 1951, the worst one of all. If they had won those times, they would have been a dynasty in the National League, the same way the Yankees are a dynasty in the American League.— **Bob Rosen**

1. Sitting at a hot dog stand between the subway and the ballpark in 1950, eating a hot dog, was the new, young redheaded announcer, Vince Scully.

2. I remember the blind beggar who held out his cup and said (in the best Brooklynese), "*The Dodgas is gonna win! The Dodgas is gonna win!*"

I also remember Campy's Buick: license number KG-39. Once, Jackie Robinson's dark blue Cadillac was parked outside the ballpark in the little players' lot, and I looked in to see a kiddy car seat and an open, half-eaten candy bar. It made him seem very human.— **Oliver Saffir**

I was 11 years old, and because he wanted me to see Ebbets Field before it was history, my Dad took me to my first major league baseball game. Growing up in northern New Jersey, trips into New York were memorable, but infrequent, events.

I was always in awe of the big city, especially the transit system. I remember rattling along in the dark, when suddenly we rushed into the sunlight. "I didn't know the subways could run above ground," I thought. Off his usual commuting path to lower Manhattan, Dad had missed our stop. We had to get off and catch a train back. We were going to be late.

Since my family members were longtime Yankee fans, it was strange that my first, in-person exposure to the big leagues was in the Dodgers' home. The men in blue and white were the mortal enemies of the pinstripers. Logically then, I immediately adopted the Dodgers' opponents that day — whomever they were — and that July day it was the Milwaukee Braves.

We were late. Rushing to our seats in the upper deck, first base side, we scrambled down the aisle. I remember looking up and being struck by the sight of *green grass*. The contrast with the gray and grit of urban New York was dramatic. I can still see it. As we sat down, the first pitch of the game was hit out of the park by some guy named Schoendienst.

Dad bought me a Braves felt pennant — the colorful Indian in full headdress had appeal to an 11-year-old. It was a souvenir that would hang on my bedroom wall for the next seven years, until I shipped off to college.

That first inning, too, my Dad pointed out that their star, Hank Aaron, was batting cleanup. I figured he would hit a homer too, but he didn't. To be honest, the rest of the game was a blur. The Dodgers tied the game in the first, and then there was no scoring until the ninth inning when the Braves went ahead, 2–1. Wanting to beat the crowd, Dad headed for the exit early — missing Gil Hodge's two-run homer that won the game for the Dodgers. It was fairly typical of my family's sense of timing.

That was it — my only visit to Ebbets Field. It made me a Braves fan for the rest of the season, which turned out to be pretty good because they went to the World Series and ... beat my Yankees!

As a postscript, on the 50th anniversary of my visit, my son had the ticket stub I had saved framed along with a portrait of Ebbets Field, and today it hangs in my office — a continual reminder of my introduction to major league baseball. — **George Saltsman**

My first Dodger game at Ebbets Field was in 1952 when I was seven years old, before I had really become a serious baseball fan. I remember walking with my father up the ramp and getting my first view of the field, which was this very intense green. I was so shocked that I just stopped in my tracks. My father asked me what was wrong, and I said, "The grass is the wrong color." He said what do you mean, and I replied that the field was supposed to be black and white, just like it was on television. As I say, I wasn't fully indoctrinated as a Dodgers' fan yet, and I wanted to leave before the game was over, which didn't please my father, but I am pretty sure we did stay until the end.

We lived in the Gravesend section of Brooklyn then, and as I got older I used to go to Dodger games with my older brother and his friends. We would walk to the Kingshighway station and take the Brighton Beach Line. I remember my mother instructing us that if we got a local it would be nine stops, while an express would be only three. Once we would get off of the subway, we would just follow the crowds up to the street where there would be this mass of humanity headed to Ebbets Field. As soon as we crossed Flatbush Avenue, we would see the ballpark. Right near the subway station was a Bond Bread factory, and I remember the smell of the bread was very evident. Interestingly, I don't remember entering the ballpark through the rotunda. We would usually enter through the first base or third base gates. My brother and his friends had a tradition that they would take a Spaldeen to the game, and one of them would throw it on the field. I will never forget the time that it was the turn of a friend, who had had polio to make the throw. When he did, he missed hitting the left fielder by only a foot or so!

At that first game, we had box seats about seven to nine rows behind home plate. I remember there was a beer vendor about 10 to 12 rows to the left who would open the beer can and pour the beer into the cup, giving it a nice big head. I am not sure why, but the beer shot out of the can like a geyser and hit a bald guy on the head. It was a typical Ebbets Field moment.

The first night game I ever went to was in 1954 or 1955, and I was there with my older brother. About the sixth or seventh inning, I started to get this awful earache, which was unusual for me. I didn't want to go home, but it got so bad that my brother called my mother from a pay phone, and she said that he better bring me home by cab. We got in the cab, and the driver was listening to the game on the radio. It was tied in the ninth and went into extra innings, and Don Zimmer won the game with a home run in the bottom of the 10th. The cab driver was overjoyed, but my brother was very annoyed with me that we had to leave the game.

Beyond the features of the ballpark that most people remember like the short right field fence, I especially remember the smell of the hot dogs and beer. Once you got into the park and the seats, it was very distinctive. It wasn't the same in the other ballparks I have been in.

Between 1952 and 1957, I probably went to Ebbets Field about 20 to 25 times. Among the games that I recall is one against Pittsburgh where both Ralph Kiner and Jackie Robinson, who was my favorite player, hit two home runs each. There was another time where a cousin and I were sitting in the second row of the left field stands, and Rip Repulski of the Cardinals hit a home run that went right off my cousin's finger tips and someone else got it. My brother and I were there for one historic moment in Ebbets Field history. We were sitting on the third base side for a game against the Milwaukee Braves, and Joe Adcock hit a home run over the left field roof and out of the park. It was the first and only time that a batter hit a ball in fair territory out of the park in left field. We both knew that it was a record, looked at each other and said, "Nobody ever did that before."

My worst moment at Ebbets Field was also against the Braves. We were sitting in box seats four rows behind first base, and the Dodgers were losing by one or two runs but had runners on base. Rube Walker, a left-handed batter, was up and he hit a screaming line drive towards right field, and we leaped to our feet expecting the Dodgers to tie it up, when Frank Torre (Joe Torre's older brother) snared it out of the air for the last out of the game.

As I said, Jackie Robinson was my favorite player, and I remember one time watching him dancing off third base so dramatically that the pitcher finally balked and Robinson scored. Near the ballpark was a Mobil gas station where the players parked their cars and where fans would gather to ask for autographs. The thing I remember about Jackie Robinson is that he wouldn't leave until every child who wanted an autograph or to shake his hand had the opportunity to do so. In 1997, Joe Dorinson, a professor at LIU, had a symposium about the 50th anniversary of Jackie's breaking the color line. Before one of the sessions, I had a chance to speak with Rachel Robinson, and I told her about that. She said, "Jackie never wanted to disappoint a child."

There used to be a television series called *Brooklyn Bridge* about a family in Brooklyn with two boys. In one episode, the older boy is going to Ebbets Field because he has a chance to be on Happy Felton's Knothole Gang. Before he left, his younger brother reminded him to touch the scoreboard. The boy doesn't win the contest, but then asks the producer if he can touch the scoreboard and the man tells him to go ahead. He stands there and puts both hands on the wall. When I saw that, my eyes teared up because I had done just that after one game. They used to let you exit the park by walking on the warning track to a gate in center field. It was in the show because it was a shared experience of so many boys from that time.

There were a number of times that the beginning of the baseball season coincided with Passover. My mother would make my brother and me chopped liver sandwiches on matzohs that we would take to the ballpark. It was a way to practice two religions simultaneously!

In addition to all the Dodger games, I also went to the circus at Ebbets Field with my father. I especially remember a man being shot out of a cannon from the right field corner and landing near second base. By the way, the last baseball game played at Ebbets Field was not played by the Dodgers. It was a game between LIU and Queens College in 1959.—**Ron Schweiger**

I grew up only five blocks from Ebbets Field, so the Dodgers were a very important part of our community. I went to Catholic school, and I remember that the Dodgers were very important to the priests and nuns of the parish. You could always tell the importance of the game by the number of people and cars that were in the neighborhood. Some people would let fans park their cars in their driveways for some money. My father was a groundskeeper at Ebbets Field, and he was one of about 10 or so who worked for the Dodgers year round. In the offseason, they would work on different maintenance projects around the park, but during the season they worked on maintaining the field itself. Since we lived so close, my father would usually come home for lunch on the day of a day game, and he would ask me if I wanted to go. I would say yes and he would then ask, who are you taking, and I would usually take two or three others, most of the time cousins and friends. My father would leave a pass for us at the press gate—the ticket agent was named Babe Hamburger. We didn't have assigned seats, but the ushers knew me so we would sit in vacant seats and probably had to move 10 times during a game. Sometimes after the game, I would get a chance to go into the clubhouse and see the players.

The groundskeepers also had to share night watchman duty from 4 P.M. to 12 A.M. Every so often my mother and I would take him something to eat and sit with him in a little office off of the rotunda. Part of the job was going on rounds through the ballpark punching time clocks in different parts of the facility. I would go with him—it was fairly eerie with no one in the park, but what I liked was I would get a chance to go down on the field and into the locker room. It was great to go into the locker room and see the uniforms, touch the bats, and even try on Duke Snider's glove.

A lot of the men in our neighborhood worked at Ebbets Field, mostly part-time during the season. Most of the ushers were men in their late 20s and 30s and it seemed to me that most of them did it not so much for the money, but to see the game. Harry M. Stevens had the concessions, but we usually ate at home or brought our lunch. I don't remember there being much beyond hot dogs, peanuts, popcorn, and things like that. One of the nonalcoholic drinks was orangeade and I think also lemonade. I don't remember soda being sold there. The vendor carried around a big aluminum container on his back that had the orange syrup, water, and ice, and he would pour it through a spigot into a cup.—**Joe Setaro, oral history interview, 2010, Brooklyn Historical Society**

Most of my memories of Ebbets Field are tied in with my father. I remember in the early 1950s we had what was then a partial season plan, which included all Saturday, Sunday, holiday, and night games. Today that would have covered almost every game, but they didn't play as many night games then. The seats were behind third base about 20 rows up. I remember the location because when I bought tickets at Yankee Stadium many years later, I chose the same location in honor of my dad, who died in 1960 when I was 16.

One game that really stands out in my mind was in either 1952 or 1953 when I was 10 or 11. I don't remember the opponent or a lot of the specifics, but I do remember that Roy Campanella hit a walk-off home run to win the game. There was a picture the next day on the back page of the *Daily News* or *Daily Mirror*. Although I don't remember any special significance of the game, it is especially vivid in my mind. When "Campy" came up, everyone was standing, and I was standing on my chair praying for him to hit a home run. As soon as it happened, I was hugging my father — I think part of the reason I remember it so well is that it was one of the greatest vindications of prayer that I can recall. I teach a religion course at NYU today, and I tell the students that prayer changes people, not things, but this was one time it worked out the other way.

The three features that I remember the most about Ebbets Field are the rotunda, the scoreboard, and the Abe Stark sign. I especially recall my father telling me it was geometrically impossible for someone to hit the Abe Stark sign and win a suit because the batter would have to hit a frozen rope and the outfielder would have to ignore it. While it wasn't really that large, to a young boy, the rotunda seemed immense with this mass of people going through it to their seats and the field. The rotunda connected the profane and ordinary with the sacred and transcendent. It is what in religious terms is known as a critical threshold.

Ebbets Field is a place that I will always connect with my father. By 1956, he became ill and we didn't go to Ebbets Field anymore, but the memories remain.—**John Sexton**

As a child some of my happiest moments were spent sitting next to my dad at Ebbets Field. He often worked six days a week, but whenever he could he'd take me to a game, where we would always try to sit between first base and right field to be as close as possible to both Carl Furillo and Gil Hodges. One year, the first opportunity he had to take me to a game was during the Passover holiday. Eating at the game, therefore, was going to be a problem since we observed the holiday quite strictly and did not eat non–Kosher food for Passover food. My mother tried to solve the problem by making us chopped liver sandwiches on matzoh and wrapping pieces of gefilte fish in wax paper. I was about seven or eight years old at the time and was quite embarrassed by our now soggy brown paper bag, but when we opened them, other hungry Jewish fans sitting near us leaned over to ask if we could share our repast with them. I recall an older African American man telling my dad that he loved matzoh and asked if he could have some, too. We happily shared with all. I always had a sense that people who went to games at Ebbets Field were all somehow related, and in many ways we *were* a family. Those who never had the chance to sit in those narrow wooden seats, listen to Gladys Goodding on the organ, watch the Sym-Phony band make "music," and sing "Follow the Dodgers" will never understand what it *really* means to bleed Dodger blue. I consider myself blessed to have those memories.— **Burt Siegel**

When I was about five in 1951, my mother died and my father broke up our home and returned to his mother's house in Bay Ridge, Brooklyn. I eventually moved in with and became a permanent part of my mother's sister's family. My dad visited me at least twice a week in the early days after Mom died, and often he and I would to go out or travel together on weekends. Among our many adventures were a series of night baseball games at Ebbets Field, after which I got to stay at the "big house" in Bay Ridge and got to play with my cousins and their friends.

My father had seven brothers, all rabid Brooklyn Dodger fans, but his only sister had the temerity to marry a Giant fan, my very dear late Uncle Pasquale (Pat) Capitti. He was also a Bay Ridge resident, but the fact that he was a Giant fan, almost made it seem like a mixed marriage. During this time my father also resumed his friendship with Joe Palmento, who was "Uncle Joe Pal" to me. Frequently on those weekend trips to Ebbets Field, my Dad and I were accompanied by both my "Uncle Joe Pal" and that unapologetic Giant fan, Uncle Pat Capitti, often for a very much argued over Dodger–Giant game. Even as a small boy, I thought Ebbets Field seemed very small and very crowded for those weekend night games. The big places I saw on TV (a very new thing then) like Yankee Stadium or Fenway Park, all seemed much grander and statelier by comparison. I remember the Dodger fans disputed almost every other call the umpires made and cheered wildly for the Dodgers, but I will never forget my Uncle Pat, who even though he was short and stocky, made more noise than anyone near us rooting for his beloved Giants.— **Dan Sollecito**

All the girls and wives would go over and park in the lot by the stadium. We'd sit in the car until it was close to the time for the game to start. The guys would go into the clubhouse. I saw two little boys flip pens, and ink ran down the back of the shirts. The guys turned around like they were going to chase the kids, and they ran away.

We would usually be seated in the reserve section. And I was there with Kay Maglie, and a couple other girls. Sal Maglie was having a long day on the mound, and the Brooklyn fans were really hot to trot. Something good happened for the Giants, and the four of us clapped. A man behind us stood up, and asked who we were. Kay said she was Kay Maglie, and he hit her across the head with his wallet. After that, Mr. Stoneham wouldn't allow us to go there anymore.— **Billie Spencer — wife of George Spencer, a member of the Giants and Tigers between 1950 and 1960.**

I remember seeing a tank roll onto the field, and there were a couple of Dodgers on the field, as well as Fat Freddie Fitzsimmons. It was a war bond drive in 1944 that the players were participating in. I can remember driving down Bedford Avenue that day, and as a five-year-old, it was a big deal to be there. You didn't know how it (the war) was going to turn out.

The first baseball game I went to was at Ebbets Field in 1946. I kind of remember my father taking me out of school. The Dodgers beat the Reds, 5–3, on September 20, and Dixie Walker hit a home run. That was huge the way it would be for a seven-year-old, and he was a hero in our house, at least for that year. The whole experience was so overwhelming. The players left their gloves on the grass in between innings, and it was the first game I had ever been to, and that struck me. That right field fence is famous, and I've tried to fix it in my head, but I can't say I remember it that day.

My dad was still writing for the *Daily News* during the war. I believe he was still writing part-time in 1946 or had moved to the Associated Press. He had access to the press box, as it was a much more informal time. He took me in, and I can remember a bartender sliding a Coke across the bar for me. With the Mets in 1964, Louis Napolitano was a bartender at Shea Stadium. I asked if he had been at the Polo Grounds before that, but he said he was at Ebbets Field every day. I was able to say to him you gave me a Coke when I was six or seven. He was a mainstay of the early Mets.

I was a student-intern for the athletic department at Hofstra, and I traveled with the baseball team, and we played at Ebbets Field after the Dodgers left. No one had been in a dugout before, and one of our players hit a pop-up. One of the reserves jumped up and skulled himself on the low roof of the dugout, knocking himself out.

Once I went to a doubleheader against the Pirates. I was with my father and some family friends, and I was allowed to go to the hot dog stand, and standing in line was Jackie Robinson. This was '53 or '54. He was in uniform as I recall, and he was heavy and gray. He wasn't playing that day because he was hurt. He was as nice as can be in that setting.

Cartoonist Gene Mack captures the essence of Ebbets Field (courtesy Joseph E. Duggan).

We went to the last game of the 1954 season against the Pirates, and Karl Spooner pitched a shutout. That was his second straight shutout. The last day of the season was always kind of sad because the Dodgers were out of it. The Giants had won the pennant.

I think my first World Series game was at Ebbets Field. It was Game Five of the 1953 World Series. Johnny Podres was pitching, and Russ Meyer came in and gave up a grand slam to Mickey Mantle. I was in the center field bleachers — just to see that ball delivered and coming at you from 300 or 400 feet away was a thrill. It was probably only the second time I've seen Ebbets Field filled. And people wonder why O'Malley left. The 1949 All-Star Game was the first time I saw it filled. My dad got tickets, and they were really good seats. They were behind home plate. Don Newcombe gave up a couple of runs in a couple of innings, and after changing into an elegant suit, shirt, and tie, he was going into the stands to see his wife. He had a souvenir bat with him that all of the All-Stars probably got. I did what any kid would do and scuttled up to him for an autograph, and he was grouchy with me. Over the years, I have become friendly with Don Newcombe. He has had a great life, and I probably annoyed him right after he had a rough outing in the game. I wouldn't mention it now if I did not have such strong admiration for him.

It was a rainy day that game, and they stopped it for about 12 minutes just before Stan Musial batted for the fourth time. He popped the ball up in front of the plate, and Yogi Berra threw him out. He had two base hits and a home run in his first three at bats. Later in the game, Andy Pafko got to second with the National League down by four runs, and there was the energy of a rally, but it never happened. — **George Vecsey**

Appendices

A: Play-by-Play and Box Scores for Ebbets Field's Two 1913 Openers

New York Americans	*AB*	*R*	*1B*	*TB*	*SH*	*SB*	*SO*	*BB*	*PO*	*A*	*E*
Daniels, r.f.	4	0	1	1	0	0	0	0	3	0	0
Wolter, cf.	3	0	1	1	0	0	0	1	1	0	0
Hartzell, 3b	3	0	1	1	0	0	0	1	2	2	0
Cree, lf,	4	0	0	0	0	0	1	0	1	0	0
Chase, 2b	2	0	1	1	0	0	0	1	1	0	0
Stump, 2b	0	0	0	0	0	0	0	0	0	0	0
Chance, 1b	4	1	2	2	0	0	0	0	7	0	0
Sweeney, C	4	0	1	1	1	0	0	0	6	4	1
Derrick, ss	4	0	0	0	0	0	0	0	4	1	0
Caldwell, p	2	0	1	1	0	0	1	0	0	2	0
Fisher, p	2	0	0	0	0	0	2	0	0	1	0
*Midkiff	0	1	0	0	0	0	0	0	0	0	0
Total	32	2	8	8	1	0	4	3	25	10	1

Brooklyn	*AB*	*R*	*1B*	*TB*	*SH*	*SB*	*SO*	*BB*	*PO*	*A*	*E*
Stengel, cf	3	1	1	4	0	0	1	1	4	0	0
Cutshaw, 2b	4	0	1	1	0	0	0	0	1	3	2
Meyer, rf	3	0	1	1	0	0	1	1	0	0	0
Wheat, lf	3	1	2	2	0	0	0	1	1	0	0
Daubert, 1b	3	1	1	4	1	0	1	0	11	0	0
Smith, 3b	4	0	2	3	0	0	0	0	1	2	0
Fisher, ss	3	0	0	0	0	0	0	0	5	1	0
Miller, c	3	0	0	0	0	0	1	0	4	5	0
Rucker, p	1	0	0	0	0	0	0	0	0	3	0
Allen, p	1	0	0	0	0	0	1	0	0	1	1
**Moran	0	0	0	0	0	0	0	1	0	0	0
Total	28	3	8	15	1	0	5	4	27	15	3

*Ran for Chase in ninth inning. **Batter for Rucker in fifth inning. ***One out when winning run scored.

Score by Innings

	1	*2*	*3*	*4*	*5*	*6*	*7*	*8*	*9*
New York	0	0	0	0	0	0	0	0	2–2
Brooklyn	0	0	0	0	1	1	0	0	1–3

Base Hits by Innings

	1	2	3	4	5	6	7	8	9
New York	0	2	0	1	1	0	0	2	2–8
Brooklyn	2	1	0	1	1	1	0	0	3–8

Two-base hits — Smith. Home Runs — Stengel, Daubert. Balk — Allen. First base on errors — New York, 2. Left on bases — New York, 7; Brooklyn, 5. Time of Game — 2 hours and 1 minute. Umpire — Emslie and Hurst.

Pitcher Summary

Name	*Innings*	*AB*	*R*	*H*	*BB*	*SO*	*HP*	*WP*
Rucker	5	18	0	4	1	1	0	0
Allen	4	15	2	4	2	2	0	0
Caldwell	6	21	2	6	3	3	0	0
Fisher	2⅓	7	1	2	1	2	0	0

Brooklyn Daily Eagle— April 6, 1913

FIRST INNING — Daniels led off for New York, and Rucker slipped over a strike as the crowd roared. Then he died, Rucker to Daubert. Wolter followed with a short fly to center which Stengel dragged down. Hartzell waited and walked, being first man to reach first. Hartzell was caught by an eyelash stealing second, Miller to Fisher. NO RUNS.

Stengel opened the first round for Brooklyn. Caldwell slipped over a strike on the first ball pitched. Stengel rapped one sharply to Derrick, who pegged low to first, but a great stop by Chance saved the play. Cutshaw tore off the first hit on the new grounds, a clean-cut wallop over second. Meyer whipped a single into right, which dropped fair by six inches, Cutshaw stopping at second. Hartzell fell over the base drum and cornet trying to get one of Wheat's fouls. Wheat then lifted a short fly to Cree. Cutshaw was caught stealing third, Sweeney to Hartzell, retiring the side. Hartzell was spiked making the play. NO RUNS.

SECOND INNING — Cree died, Cutshaw to Daubert. Chase sliced a clean hit to center. This brought Chance up and the crowd roared another welcome. Chance responded by whaling the first ball pitched for a clean hit to right, driving Chase to third. The drive was low and hard, and tore through Meyer's fingers. Sweeney tapped to Rucker, and in the run down, Chance was out, Rucker to Miller, who made the play at third, Chase sticking at third, and Sweeney went to second. Derrick punched a line drive to center which Stengel gathered in. A close call for Rucker. NO RUNS.

Daubert struck out. Smith doubled over second, Chase dived headlong after the ball, but could not catch it. Caldwell threw out Fisher. Smith raced to third on the play. Caldwell settled down and struck out Miller. NO RUNS.

THIRD INNING — Caldwell struck out, Miller dropped the third strike, and threw him out at first. Daniels flied out to Stengel. Wolter punched one through Cutshaw for an error. Wolter was caught napping, Rucker to Daubert. NO RUNS.

Rucker flied out to Daniels. Stengel struck out. Cutshaw lined to Daniels for a nice catch. NO RUNS.

FOURTH INNING — Hartzell opened with a hard smash to center for a single. Cree rolled to Daubert, Hartzell going to second. Fisher threw out Chase, and Hartzell went on to third. This brought Chance up with a chance to drive the first run, but the sphere dropped to Stengel in center. NO RUNS.

Meyer walked. On a hit and run Wheat singled to right, and Meyer went to third, Wheat pulling up on second with the throw in. Daubert fouled out to Hartzell. Derrick went into short left, making a pretty catch of Smith's pop fly. Fisher fouled to Chance and the New York contingent cheered Caldwell's game stand to a finish. NO RUNS.

FIFTH INNING — Sweeney slashed a line drive to right, but a wonderful leaping catch by Daubert snagged it with his gloved hand and shut off a two-base hit. Cutshaw threw out Derrick. Caldwell chopped off a single over second. Daniels forced Caldwell, Cutshaw to Fisher, making a very nice play. NO RUNS.

Chase ran into center for Miller's short fly. Moran batted for Rucker, and got a base on balls, but was caught napping at first, Caldwell to Chance. Stengel drove a hard slash to center, and caromed off Wolter's knee for a home run. Tough luck for Caldwell, as it should have been an easy two-base hit and no more. Cutshaw flied to Daniels. ONE RUN.

SIXTH INNING — Allen went in the box for Brooklyn. Wolter walked. Hartzell bunted to third, and Smith by clever work, forced Wolter at second, Fisher covering the base. Cree struck out. Allen balked and Hartzell went to second. Allen tossed out Chase at first. NO RUNS.

Hartzell threw out Meyer. Wheat walked, but was nailed stealing, Sweeney to Derrick. Daubert whaled a home run by Wolter who lost track of the ball in the shade of the stand. It was a hard wallop, but Wolter didn't see the ball until it was past him. It really should have been a single. A fine stop and throw by Hartzell nailed Smith. ONE RUN.

SEVENTH INNING — Cutshaw fumbled Chance's infield tap. Sweeney popped to Fisher. Chance was nailed stealing, Miller to Fisher. Derrick line viciously to Cutshaw. NO RUNS.

Fisher now pitching for New York. Fisher fouled out to Sweeney. Miller flied to Cree. Allen struck out. NO RUNS.

EIGHTH INNING — Fisher struck out. Daniels singled to center. Wolter by fast work beat out a short liner to short. Daniels stopping at second. Hartzell flied to Wheat. Daubert made a fine catch of Cree's foul near the stand. NO RUNS.

Stengel walked. Cutshaw bunted in front of the plate and Sweeney pegged to Derrick, forcing Stengel. Brooklyn roared over the decision which looked to be bad. Cutshaw was out stealing, Sweeney to Derrick. Meyer struck out. NO RUNS.

NINTH INNING — Chase walked. Midkiff running for Chase. Chance singled to center, Midkiff stopping at second. Derrick bunted in front of the plate and Sweeney was run down, Miller to Smith to Cutshaw. Sweeney laid down a perfect bunt down the third base line, which Allen grabbed and hurled into right field for a bad error, on which Midkiff and Chance raced home tying the score. Sweeney, who reached first on the hit went to second on the error. Derrick bunted in front of the plate and Sweeney was run down, Miller to Smith to Cutshaw. Fisher struck out, Derrick was nipped stealing, Miller to Fisher. TWO RUNS.

Stump now playing second base in place of Chase. Wheat outran a slow bunt in front of the plate and took second on Sweeney's wild peg to first. Daubert sacrificed, Fisher to Chance, Wheat moving up to third. Smith singled to center, scoring Wheat and winning the game (*Evening Mail*— April 5, 1913).

Philadelphia

Name	***AB***	***R***	***1B***	***TB***	***SH***	***SB***	***SO***	***BB***	***PO***	***A***	***E***
Paskert, cf.	4	0	1	1	0	0	1	0	1	0	0
Knabe, 2b.	3	1	2	3	0	0	0	1	2	0	0
Lobert, 3b.	3	0	1	1	1	0	0	0	2	1	0
Magee, rf.	3	0	0	0	1	0	0	0	2	0	0
Dolan, lf	4	0	1	1	0	0	0	0	0	0	0
Luderus, 1b.	4	0	0	0	0	0	1	0	12	0	0
Doolan, ss.	3	0	0	0	0	0	1	0	1	5	0
Dooin, c.	3	0	2	2	0	0	0	0	6	5	0
Seaton, p.	3	0	1	1	0	0	1	0	1	2	0
Total	30	1	8	9	2	0	4	1	27	13	0

Brooklyn

Name	*AB*	*R*	*1B*	*TB*	*SH*	*SB*	*SO*	*BB*	*PO*	*A*	*E*
Stengel, cf.	4	0	0	0	0	0	1	0	1	1	0
Cutshaw, 2b.	4	0	1	1	0	0	0	0	2	4	0
Meyer, rf.	2	0	0	0	0	0	1	1	0	0	2
*Erwin	1	0	0	0	0	0	1	0	0	0	0
Wheat, lf	4	0	0	0	0	0	1	0	2	1	1
Daubert, 1b	3	0	1	1	0	1	0	0	12	1	0
Smith, 3b	3	0	0	0	0	0	3	0	1	2	0
Fisher, ss	3	0	1	1	0	0	0	0	3	1	0
Miller, c	3	0	2	2	0	0	0	0	6	4	0
Rucker, p	2	0	1	1	0	0	0	0	0	2	0
**Callahan	1	0	0	0	0	0	0	0	0	0	0
Ragan, p	0	0	0	0	0	0	0	0	0	0	0
Total	30	0	6	6	0	1	7	1	27	16	3

*Batted for Meyer in ninth inning. **Batted for Rucker in eighth inning.

Score by Innings

	1	*2*	*3*	*4*	*5*	*6*	*7*	*8*	*9*
Philadelphia	1	0	0	0	0	0	0	0	0–1
Brooklyn	0	0	0	0	0	0	0	0	0–0

Base Hits by Innings

	1	*2*	*3*	*4*	*5*	*6*	*7*	*8*	*9*
Philadelphia	3	0	0	1	1	1	1	1	0–8
Brooklyn	1	0	1	0	1	1	0	2	0–6

Two-base hit — Knabe. Passed ball — Dooin. First base on errors — Philadelphia, 1. Left on bases — Philadelphia, 4; Brooklyn 4. Time of game —1 hour and 33 minutes. Umpires — Klem and Orth

Pitchers Summary

Name	*Innings*	*AB*	*R*	*1B*	*BB*	*SO*	*HP*	*WP*
Seaton	9	30	0	6	1	7	0	1
Rucker	8	27	1	8	1	3	0	0
Ragan	1	3	0	0	0	1	0	0

Brooklyn Daily Eagle, April 10, 1913

FIRST INNING — Paskert hit the second ball pitched through short for a single, but died stretching it. Wheat to Cutshaw. Knabe doubled to right field. Stengel made a good catch of Lobert's fly. Knabe took third on the catch. Myers dropped Magee's fly and Knabe scored, Magee taking second on the error. Dolan singled to center, Magee tried to score, but was out, Stengel to Miller. ONE RUN.

Stengel grounded out, Lobert to Luderus. Cutshaw beat out a roller over second. Myers struck out. Cutshaw was out stealing. Dooin to Knabe. NO RUNS.

SECOND INNING — Luderus out, Cutshaw to Daubert. Miller held on to Doolan's high foul fly. Dooin line flied to Wheat. NO RUNS.

Wheat flied to Luderus. Doolan and Luderus took care of Daubert. Smith struck out. NO RUNS.

THIRD INNING — Seaton fanned. Paskert went out, Smith to Daubert. Cutshaw and Daubert sat down Knabe. NO RUNS.

Fisher popped to Seaton. Miller drove a single over first, but died stealing. Dooin to Doolan. Rucker grounded out to Luderus unassisted. NO RUNS.

FOURTH INNING — Lobert singled to center field. Magee sacrificed, Rucker to Daubert. Dolan hit to Fisher and Lobert was out at third, Fisher to Smith. Wheat made a sensational catch of Luderus's line drive. NO RUNS.

Stengel struck out. Cutshaw tapped in front of the plate and was out, Dooin to Luderus. Myers lined to Knabe. NO RUNS.

FIFTH INNING — Doolan flied to Cutshaw. Dooin singled to left, and kept on to second when Wheat booted the ball. Seaton went out, Cutshaw to Daubert. Paskert was out the same way. NO RUNS.

Wheat went out, Doolan to Luderus. Daubert singled to left field and lost no time stealing second. Smith again fanned. Daubert was out stealing third. Dooin to Lobert. NO RUNS.

SIXTH INNING — Knabe singled to center. Lobert sacrificed, Miller to Daubert. Magee hit in front of the plate and was out, Miller to Daubert. Knabe took third on the play. Dolan foul-flied to Daubert. NO RUNS.

Fisher flied to Magee. Miller out, Seaton to Luderus. Rucker singled to right. Stengel flied to Paskert. NO RUNS.

SEVENTH INNING — Fisher ran to the grand stand for Luderus' foul fly. Doolan struck out. Dooin singled to left field, but was caught stealing. Rucker to Daubert to Cutshaw. NO RUNS.

Cutshaw was easy for Seaton and Luderus. Myers walked. Wheat grounded out to Luderus, Myers taking second. Daubert went out, Doolan to Luderus. NO RUNS.

EIGHTH INNING — Seaton singled to right. Paskert struck out. Seaton was out stealing, Miller to Fisher. Knabe walked. Lobert flied to Daubert. NO RUNS.

Smith for the third time fanned. Fisher beat out an infield hit. Miller also beat out a roller to the infield. Callahan batted for Rucker and forced Fisher, Doolan to Lobert. Miller and Callahan advanced a base on a wild pitch. Stengel went out Doolan to Luderus. NO RUNS.

NINTH INNING — Ragan now pitching for Brooklyn. Magee bunted in front of the plate and was out, Miller to Daubert. Smith and Daubert, retired Dolan. Luderus struck out. NO RUNS.

Cutshaw flied to Magee. Erwin batted for Myers and struck out, but Dooin dropped the third one and threw him out at first. Wheat fanned. NO RUNS (*Evening Mail*— April 9, 1913).

B: Play-by-Play and Box Score for the Last Dodger Game at Ebbets Field

Pittsburgh (N.)	*AB*	*R*	*H*	*PO*	*A*	*Brooklyn (N.)*	*AB*	*R*	*H*	*PO*	*A*
Baker, 3b	4	0	0	0	0	Gilliam, 2b	3	1	0	3	4
Mejias, rf	4	0	0	0	0	Cimoli, cf	4	1	1	0	0
Groat, ss	3	0	1	2	3	Valo, rf	4	0	1	2	0
Skinner, lf	4	0	1	2	1	Hodges, 1b	4	0	1	5	1
Fondy, 1b	4	0	0	13	0	Amoros, lf	3	0	0	0	0
Mazeroski, 2b	3	0	1	0	5	Gentile, 1b	2	0	0	4	0
Clemente, cf	3	0	1	0	0	Reese, 3b	1	0	0	0	1
Peterson, c	3	0	1	5	0	Campanella, c	2	0	0	2	0
Daniels, p	2	0	0	1	4	Pignatano, c	1	0	0	7	0
a. Freese	1	0	0	0	0	Zimmer, ss	2	0	2	4	6
Face, p	0	0	0	1	0	McDevitt, p	1	0	0	0	1
Total	31	0	5	24	13	Total	27	2	5	27	13

a. Reached first for Daniels on error in eighth.

Pittsburgh	0	0	0	0	0	0	0	0	0	0
Brooklyn	1	0	1	0	0	0	0	0	x	2

Errors — Daniels, Reese. Runs batted in — Valo, Hodges. Two-base hits — Valo. Clemente. Zimmer. Sacrifice — McDevitt. Double plays — Hodges, Gilliam and Gentile; Mazeroski, Groat and Fondy; Zimmer and Hodges. Left on base — Pittsburgh 5, Brooklyn 5. Struck out — By Daniels 2 Face 2, McDevitt 9. Bases on balls — Off Daniels 3. McDevitt 1. Hits — Off Daniels 5 in 7 innings. Face 0 in 1. McDevitt 5 in 9 innings. Runs and earned runs — Off Daniels 2 and 1. Winning pitcher — McDevitt (7–4) Losing pitcher — Daniels (0–1). Umpires — Donatelli, Delmore, Smith, Conlan and Sudol. Time of game — 2:03 Attendance — 6,702 (*New York Times*—September 25, 1957).

PIRATES 1ST: Baker flied out to right; Mejias grounded out (shortstop to first); Groat grounded out (pitcher to first); 0 R, 0 H, 0 E, 0 LOB. Pirates 0, Dodgers 0.

DODGERS 1ST: Gilliam walked; Gilliam was picked off first but was safe on an error by Daniels (Gilliam to second); Cimoli struck out; Valo doubled to right [Gilliam scored (unearned)]; Hodges grounded out (shortstop to first); Amoros grounded out (shortstop to first); 1 R (0 ER), 1 H, 1 E, 1 LOB. Pirates 0, Dodgers 1.

PIRATES 2ND: Skinner singled to shortstop: Fondy made an out to shortstop; Mazeroski singled to third (Skinner to second); Clemente grounded into a double play (third to second to first) (Mazeroski out at second); 0 R, 2 H, 0 E, 1 LOB. Pirates 0, Dodgers 1.

DODGERS 2ND: Gentile popped to catcher in foul territory; Campanella popped to pitcher; Zimmer walked; McDevitt walked (Zimmer to second); Gilliam grounded out (first unassisted); 0 R, O H, O E, 2 LOB. Pirates 0, Dodgers 1.

PIRATES 3RD: Peterson singled to shortstop; Daniels struck out; Baker forced Peterson (shortstop to second); Mejias grounded out (second to first); 0 R, 1 H, 0 E, 1 LOB. Pirates 0, Dodgers 1.

DODGERS 3RD: Cimoli singled to second; Valo grounded out (first unassisted): (Cimoli to second); Hodges singled to right (Cimoli scored) Amoros grounded into a double play (second to shortstop to first) (Hodges out at second); 1 R, 2 H, 0 E, 0 LOB. Pirates 0, Dodgers 2.

PIRATES 4TH: Groat walked; Skinner struck out; Fondy forced Groat (second to shortstop); Mazeroski forced Fondy (second to shortstop); 0 R, 0 H, 0 E, 1 LOB. Pirates 0, Dodgers 2.

DODGERS 4TH: Gentile flied out to left; Campanella grounded out (pitcher to first); Zimmer doubled to center; McDevitt grounded out (pitcher to first); 0 R, 1 H, 0 E, 1 LOB. Pirates 0, Dodgers 2.

PIRATES 5TH: Pignatano replaced Campanella (playing C); Reese replaced Gentile (playing 3B); Hodges changed positions (playing 1B); Clemente singled to left; Peterson grounded into a double play (shortstop to first) (Clemente out at second); Daniels struck out; 0 R, 1 H, 0 E, 0 LOB. Pirates 0, Dodgers 2.

DODGERS 5TH: Gilliam grounded out (pitcher to first); Cimoli grounded out (second to first); Valo grounded out (pitcher to first); 0 R, 0 H, 0 E, 0 LOB. Pirates 0, Dodgers 2.

PIRATES 6TH: Baker made an out to second; Mejias grounded out (shortstop to first); Groat singled to second; Skinner struck out: 0 R, 1 H, 0 E, 1 LOB. Pirates 0, Dodgers 2

DODGERS 6TH: Hodges flied out to left; Amoros made an out to shortstop; Reese grounded out (shortstop to first); 0 R, 0 H, 0 E, 0 LOB. Pirates 0, Dodgers 2.

PIRATES 7TH: Fondy struck out; Mazeroski struck out; Clemente struck out; 0 R, 0 H, 0 E, 0 LOB. Pirates 0, Dodgers 2.

DODGERS 7TH: Pignatano struck out; Zimmer singled to center; McDevitt out on a sacrifice bunt (second to first) (Zimmer to second); Gilliam grounded out (second to first); 0 R, 1 H, 0 E, 1 LOB. Pirates 0, Dodgers 2.

PIRATES 8TH: Peterson grounded out (third to first); Freese batted for Daniels; Freese reached on an error by Reese (Freese to first); Baker struck out; Mejias popped to first in foul territory; 0 R, 0 H, 1 E, 1 LOB. Pirates 0, Dodgers 2.

DODGERS 8TH: Face replaced Freese (pitching); Cimoli struck out; Valo grounded to first (first to pitcher); Hodges struck out; 0 R, 0 H, 0 E, 0 LOB. Pirates 0, Dodgers 2.

PIRATES 9TH: Groat flied out to right; Skinner struck out: Fondy grounded out (shortstop to first); 0 R, 0 H, 0 E, 0 LOB. Pirates 0 Dodgers 2 (www.retrosheet.org).

C: Music Played at the First and Last Games at Ebbets Field

From Shannon's 23rd Regiment Band to the Brooklyn Sym-Phony and Gladys Goodding, music was an important part of the atmosphere at Ebbets Field. In recognition of that tradition, this appendix lists the music played at the park's first and last Dodgers games.

Music Played by Shannon's 23rd Regiment Band Before April 5, 1913 Opener[1]

1. Grand Inaugural March: "Ebbets Field," inscribed to Charles Ebbets
2. Overture: "All Nations"
3. Excerpts from "The Lady of the Slipper"
4. a. "Killarney"
   b. "Here Comes My Daddy Now," inscribed to E.J. and S.W. McKeever
5. Description: "A Trip Through Dixie," inscribed to Dahlen and his team
6. Gems from "Little Boy Blue"
7. Caprice, "Yankee Patrol"
8. "Broadway Review"

Songs Played by Gladys Goodding on September 24, 1957[2]

"After You're Gone"
"Am I Blue"
"Auld Lang Syne"
"California Here I Come"
"Don't Ask Me Why I Am Leaving"
"How Can You Say We Are Through"
"Give Me the Moon Over Brooklyn"
"If I Had My Way"
"May the Good Lord Bless You and Keep You"
"Memories"
"Mexican Hat Dance"
"Que Sera, Sera"
"So Long, It's Been Good to Know Yuh"
"Thanks for the Memories"
"Vaya Con Dios"
"What Can I Say Dear, After I Say I Am Sorry"
"When I Grow Too Old to Dream"
"When the Blue of the Night Meets the Gold of the Day"

Notes

1. *New York Herald*, April 5, 1913.
2. *New York Times*, September 25, 1957; *New York Herald Tribune*, September 25, 1957; *Newark Evening News*, September 25, 1957; *New York Journal American*, September 25, 1957.

Bibliography

Books

Bevis, Charles. *Sunday Baseball: The Major League's Struggle to Play Baseball on the Lord's Day, 1876–1934*. Jefferson, NC: McFarland, 2003.

Boxerman, Burton A., and Benita W. Boxerman. *Ebbets to Veeck to Busch: Eight Owners Who Shaped Baseball.* Jefferson, NC: McFarland, 2003.

Godin, Roger A. *The Brooklyn Football Dodgers: The Other "Bums."* Haworth, NJ: St. Johann Press, 2003.

Goldstein, Richard. *Superstars and Screwballs: 100 Years of Brooklyn Baseball.* New York: Penguin, 1992.

Golenbock, Peter. *Bums: An Oral History of the Brooklyn Dodgers.* New York: Putnam, 1984.

Graham, Frank. *The Brooklyn Dodgers: An Informal History.* New York: G.P. Putnam's Sons, 1945.

Gunnison, Hebert Foster. *The Realm of Light and Air: Flatbush of Today*. Brooklyn, New York: n.p. 1908.

Jackson, Kenneth T. *The Encyclopedia of New York.* New Haven, CT: Yale University Press, 1995.

Kavanagh, Jack, and Norman Macht. *Uncle Robbie.* Cleveland: Society for American Baseball Research, 1999.

Lowry, Philip. *Green Cathedrals: The Ultimate Celebration of Major League and Negro League Ballparks.* New York: Walker, 2006.

Manley, Effa, and Leon Herbert Hardwick. *Negro Baseball ... Before Integration.* Edited by Robert Cvornyek. Haworth, NJ: St. Johann Press, 2006.

McGee, Bob. *The Greatest Ballpark Ever: Ebbets Field and the Story of the Brooklyn Dodgers.* New Brunswick, NJ: Rutgers University Press, 2005.

Ritter, Lawrence. *Lost Ballparks: A Celebration of Baseball's Legendary Fields.* New York: Viking, 1992.

Selter, Ron. *Ballparks of the Deadball Era: A Comprehensive Study of Their Dimensions, Configurations and Effects on Batting, 1901–1919.* Jefferson, NC: McFarland, 2008.

Seymour, Harold, and Dorothy Seymour Mills. *Baseball: The Early Years.* New York: Oxford University Press, 1960.

Snyder-Grenier, Ellen M. *Brooklyn! An Illustrated History.* Philadelphia: Temple University Press, 1996.

Solomon, Burt. *Where They Ain't: The Fabled Life and Untimely Death of the Original Baltimore Orioles, the Team That Gave Birth to Modern Baseball.* New York: Doubleday, 1999.

Spatz, Lyle. *Bad Bill Dahlen: The Rollicking Life and Times of an Early Baseball Star*, Jefferson, NC: McFarland, 2004.

Zinn, Paul G., and John G. Zinn. *The Major League Pennant Races of 1916: "The Most Maddening Baseball Melee in History."* Jefferson, NC: McFarland, 2009.

Newspapers and Magazines

Brooklyn Citizen
Brooklyn Daily Eagle
Brooklyn Daily Times
[Brooklyn] *Standard Union*

New York Times
Sporting Life
The Sporting News

Articles and Chapters

McCue, Andy. "A History of Dodger Ownership." *The National Pastime: A Review of Baseball History*, no. 13 (1993): 34–42.

Mele, Andrew Paul. "Why Did the Dodgers Leave Brooklyn?" *Brooklyn Eagle Online*, August 6, 2007.

Moses, Robert. "Robert Moses on the Battle of Brooklyn: New York's Outspoken Park Commissioner, Accusing the Dodgers' O'Malley of Bad Faith, Presents a Plan for a National League Site in N.Y." *Sports Illustrated*, July 22, 1957.

Rubin, James. "Why Did the Dodgers Leave Brooklyn?" In *Brooklyn USA: The Fourth Largest City in America*, edited by Rita Seiden Miller. New York: Brooklyn College Press, 1979.

Trumpbour, Robert. "The Brooklyn Dodgers, the Move to Los Angeles, and the Search for Villains: Was Walter O'Malley a Bum, a Victim, or Something Else?" In *Mysteries from Baseball's Past: Investigations of Nine Unsettled Questions*, edited by Angelo J. Louisa and David Cicotello. Jefferson, NC: McFarland, 2010.

Other Sources

August "Garry" Herrmann Papers, BA MSS12. National Baseball Hall of Fame Library, Cooperstown, New York.

Kennedy, Rod, Jr. *Ebbets Field: The Original Plans*. New York: Brooklyn Dodgers Hall of Fame, 1992.

Websites

http://www.ballparksofbaseball.com
http://www.baseball-alamanac.com
http://www.retrosheet.org

About the Contributors

James **Overmyer** is a baseball historian and genealogical researcher from Lenox, Massachusetts. A member of the Society for American Baseball Research, he is the author of *Queen of the Negro Leagues: Effa Manley and the Newark Eagles* and a collaborative author of *Shades of Glory: The Negro Leagues and the Story of African-American Baseball.*

Ronald M. **Selter** is the author of the award-winning book *Ballparks of the Deadball Era: A Comprehensive Study of Their Dimensions, Configurations and Effects on Batting, 1901–1919* (2008), a contributor to *Forbes Field: Essays and Memories of the Pirates' Historic Ballpark, 1909–1971* (2007), and an editor for *Green Cathedrals: The Ultimate Celebration of Major League and Negro League Ballparks* (2006). A member of the Society for American Baseball Research since 1989, he has given presentations at both SABR regional meetings and national conventions.

Ellen M. **Snyder-Grenier** is a public historian, exhibition developer and writer. She has held curatorial positions at the Morris Museum, the New Jersey Historical Society and the Brooklyn Historical Society. The author of *Brooklyn! An Illustrated History*, she has also written books, chapters and articles on a variety of topics relating to American popular and material culture.

John G. **Zinn** is the author of *The Mutinous Regiment: The Thirty-Third New Jersey in the Civil War* (2005) and *The Major League Pennant Races of 1916: "The Most Maddening Baseball Melee in History"* (2009), with Paul G. Zinn. He has also written numerous articles on both 19th century baseball and the Civil War.

Paul G. **Zinn** is a business solutions specialist at Premiere Global Services (NYSE: PGI): an Atlanta-based virtual meetings company. He is the author, with John G. Zinn, of *The Major League Pennant Races of 1916: "The Most Maddening Baseball Melee in History"* and an avid photographer and sports fan.

INDEX

Page numbers in ***bold italics*** indicate illustrations.

Aaron, Hank 215
Abe Stark Sign ***115***, 147, 172, 218
Abell, Ferdinand 9, 11, 12–14
Abrams, Cal 74, 213
Adams, Sparky 67
Adcock, Joe 80, 216
Adler, Marty 176–77
Agar, Nathan 119
Aida 106–07
Albert, Frankie 117
Alexander, Grover Cleveland 59
All America Football Conference 117
All Cubans 88
Allen, Frank 52
Alston, Tom 140
Alston, Walter 57, 149, 163, 167, 169–70, 172, 174, 204
America First Committee 117
American Association 9
American Federation of Musicians 77
American Football League 113
American League 13–14
American Soccer League 118–20
Amoros, Sandy 160, 184
Anderson, Dave 54, 177–79, 207
Anderson, Ferrel 179
Anson, Cap 16
Armstrong, George 98
Army Football 109
Ashburn, Richie 153, 213
Atlantic City (New Jersey) 83–84, 88
Atlantic City Bacharachs-Giants 89, 91

Bacharach, Harry 83–84
Bacharach Giants 83–89, 95
Bailey, Ed 210
Baird, Doug 62
Baker Bowl, Philadelphia 128–29
Baltimore Black Sox 91, 95
Baltimore Orioles (old Orioles) 11–12
Banks, Ernie 200
Barber, Red 146, 185, 200, 202
Barlick, Al 144
Barnie, Bill 10
Barthel, Jack 179–80
Baseball Assistance Team (B.A.T.) 174
Battle of Brooklyn 31, 48
Baugh, Sammy 115, 178
Bavasi, Buzzie 170
Bay Parkways (semi-pro team) 94
Bay Ridge (semi-pro team) 94
Ben Millers Soccer Club 119
Berg, Jackie "Kid" 105
Berlenbach, Paul 104
Bernstein, Harold 181
Bernstein, Sam 180–81
Berra, Yogi 156, 221
Bess, Bill 181
Bessent, Don 184
Bethlehem Steel Soccer 119
Bevens, Bill 73, 185
Black, Joe 79–80, 157
Blades, Ray 66
Bolger, Jim 140
Bond Bread factory 176, 215
Borden's Milk cartons 200, 205
Borkowski, Bob 78, 163
Boston Braves 16, 18, 23, 25, 59, 67, 70–72, 74, 165–67, 179, 185, 201
Boston Celtics 211
Boston Globe 21
Boston Red Sox 24
Boston Yanks 117
Bottomley, Jim 65
Boys High 111–12
Bracken, Herbert "Doc" 98
Bracker, Milton 77
Bradley, Dan 180
Bragan, Bobby 71
Branca, Ralph 74, 78, 150, 161
Braves Field (Boston) 17
Brecheen, Harry 72
Bressoud, Eddie 140
Broadway Sporting Club 102
Bronx Oval (South Bronx) 88–89
Brooklion Horsemen 113
Brooklyn 12–13, 22, 26–28, 31–45, 101, 103, 111, 120–21
Brooklyn Boxing Association 106
Brooklyn Bridge ***34***, 37
Brooklyn Bridge (television show) 216
Brooklyn Brown Dodgers 97–99
Brooklyn Bushwicks 94–95, 207
Brooklyn College 110–11
Brooklyn Cyclones 178
Brooklyn Daily Eagle 9, 48, 101, 178–79
Brooklyn Dodger Hall of Fame 177
Brooklyn Eagles 90–96
Brooklyn Elks 101
Brooklyn Exhibition Company 104
Brooklyn Football Dodgers 113–17
Brooklyn Historical Society 1–2
Brooklyn Horsemen 104, 113
Brooklyn Lions 113
Brooklyn Navy Yard 34, 36
Brooklyn Prep 111, 181
Brooklyn Rapid Transit System 37, 87
Brooklyn Royal Giants 84, 95
Brooklyn Steam Marble Company 37
Brooklyn Sym-Phony Band 41, 69, 76–77, 147, 185, 190, ***203***
Brooklyn Tech 111
Brooklyn Tigers 117
Brooklyn Tip-Tops 22
Brooklyn Union Gas Company 101
Brooklyn Wanderers 119–20
Brotherhood War 13
Brown, Elias "Country" 87–88
Brown, Tommy 71, 201
Brush, John 14–15
Buhl, Bob 196
Burnett, Tex 93
Burr, Harold 110, 178–79
Butler, Edmund 113
Byrne, Charles 9, 13
Byron, Bill "Lord" 59

Cadore, Leon 62
Cagle, Chris 114
Califano, Joseph 181–82
Campanella, Roy 75, 79, 145, 156, 158, 165, 169, 175, 178, 185, 188, 200, 214, 218
Canzoneri, Tony 105
Capitoline Grounds (Brooklyn) 32, 101
Capitti, Pasquale 219
Caro, Robert 182–83
Carollo, Jimmy 106
Casey, Hugh 70, 161
Cashmore, John 77
Castle Brothers 33
Catholic University 110
Cavalleria Rusticana 106
Cawthon, Pete 117
Chadwick, Henry 179
Chance, Frank 15, 48–49, 51
Chapin, Ann Brown 183
Chauncey, George 9
Cheney, Larry 23
Chester, Hilda 42, 172, 178, 190, 205, ***209***

Chicago American Giants 87–88, 95
Chicago Bears 116
Chicago Cardinals 114–15
Chicago Cubs 23, 25, 69–70, 79, 167
Chicago White Sox 21
Cimoli, Gino 56
Cincinnati Reds 1, 14, 19, 21, 25, 43, 62, 67–69, 72, 78, 126, 146, 163, 210, 220
Cincinnati Redstockings 32
Citi Field, New York 183
Citizens' League for Fair Play 91
City College of New York 111
Cividanes, Gil 183–84
Claridge Bar & Grill 199
Clark, George "Potsy" 114
Cleveland Browns 117
Cleveland Indians 24, 63
Cleveland Rams 115
Cleveland Spiders 12
Codner, Ella 107
Cohen, Henry 50
College of the Holy Cross 110
Collins, Joe 79
Columbia University 108, 112
Comiskey, Charles 17, 21
Comiskey Park (Chicago) 17, 172
Commercial Field (Brooklyn) 113
Commodore Hotel 146
Coney Island 39–41, 43
Conlan, Jocko 202
Connor, John R. 84–86, 89
Coombs, Jack 23, 27, 60
Cooper, Mort 177
Cooper, Pat 184
County Stadium (Milwaukee) 54, 152, 167
Cox, Billy 141, 171, 201
Craig, Roger 148, 156, 163–64
Crandall, Del 196
Crawford Grille, Pittsburgh 97
Crosley Field (Cincinnati) 1, 141, 152
Crosson, Jerome 184–85
Crowley, Jim 109
Crystal Motors ***42***
Cummings, Napoleon "Chance" 84
Cunningham, Billy 192
Cunningham, Joe 140–41
Cutshaw, George 24, 52–53, 59–***60***, 133

Dahlen, Bill ***10***, 12, 16–17, 23
Daley, Arthur 72
Daniels, Benny 152
Daniels, Bert 52
Dantonio, Johnny 208
Dark, Alvin 74, 162
Daubert, Jake 17, 27, 52, 59, 132
Davidson, Les 185
Day, Leon 91, 93
Dayton Triangles Football 113
Dean, Jay "Dizzy" ***68***, 211–12
Dean, Paul "Daffy" ***68***, 211–12
Delaney, Hubert T. 92
Delaney, Jack 104
Del Greco, Bob 141
Dempsey, Jack 103–04
Denby, Richard 185
Depler, John 113–14
Detroit Lions 114
Dexter Park 95
Dial, Lewis 91, 95
Diamond, Neil 192
Diering, Chuck 142
DiGiovanni, Charlie 189
DiMaggio, Joe 179
Dixon, Rap 93
Djurgarden (Sweden) Soccer Team 120
Doby, Larry 75
Dodd, Joe 166
Donnelly, Bob 186
Donovan, Patsy 15–16
Dorin, Robert 186–87
Dorinson, Joe 216
Dougherty, Bill 179
Dovey, George 16
Doyle, Joesph 9
Dreamland 40
Dressen, Chuck 146, 170–72
Dreyfuss, Barney 17–19, 21
Driscoll, David 103–04
Dukehart, Mort 187
Durocher, Leo 69, 146, 172–73, 184, 188, 200, 203–04
Duval Giants 83
Dwyer, William V. 113–14
Dyckman Oval (Harlem) 85, 88, 90–91
Dyer, Eddie 142

Eastern Colored League 89
Eastern Park (Brooklyn) 9–10
Ebbets, Charles ***8***, ***49***; Ebbets Field construction 17–19, 21–22, 31–33; finances 9, 12–16, 21–23, 25–26, 101; innovations 8, 26; managers 10–11, 14–17, 23; Sunday baseball 15, 25, 62; syndicate baseball 11
Ebbets, Charles, Jr. 108
Ebbets, Genevieve ***51***–52
Ebbets Field: All Star Game 75, 221; batting 130–37; boxing 102–06; college football 108–11; construction 17–22, 31–33; demolition 33–34, 44–***45***, 127; dimensions and configuration 123–25, 127–30, 141–42; expansion and modification 124–30; fans 140, 142–45, 147–49, 151 153, ***155***, 159–60, 168, 171, 173–74; final game 53–57, 143, 145–46, 152–53, 168–69, 174, 178, 189, 201, 212, 214, 227–29; first games 48–53, 124, 227; high school football 111–12; music 54, 150, 165, 168, 178, 185, 191, 202, 218, 229; no-hitters 65–66, 68–69, 71, 79, 80, 164–65, 179, 202, 211–13; park factors 130–31, 134–36; professional football 113–17; record setting performances 61, 64–65, 68–69, 71–73, 76, 78–82, 140, 163, 216; seating capacity 123, 125–27, 130; site 31–***32***; soccer 118–20; triple plays 64, 66, 69–71, 74; World Series 24, 26, 60, 63, 70, 73, 79, 82, 125, 128–29, 154, 156–57, 160, 163–65, 210, 221
Ebbets Field Apartments 127
Ebbets-McKeever Exhibition Company 103
Ehmke, Howard 79
Eisenhoffer, Joseph 119
Elite Giants 95
Eller, Hod 62
Empey, Arthur Guy 85
Encyclopedia of New York City 202
Enzmann, Johnny 85
Erasmus Hall High School 111–12, 192, 201
Ernest Capelle of Brooklyn 36
Erskine, Carl 76, 79, ***80***, 140, 153, 157, 162, 164–66, 213

Fall River Soccer Club 120
Faust 106–07
Federal League 22
Felton, Happy 143, 151, 153, 157, 168–69, 191
Fenichel, Irwin 187–88
Fenway Park (Boston) 17, 190
Fernandez, Ignacio 105
Fewster, Chick 66–67
Firpo, Louis 103
Fischer, Bobby 192
Fitzsimmons, Freddie 219
Flaherty, Ray 114
Fleischmann, Julius 21
Foiles, Hank 143
Forbes Field (Pittsburgh) 1, 17, 19, 151
Fordham University 108
Fort Greene Meat Market 44
Foster, Andrew "Rube" 87
Four Horsemen of Notre Dame 109–10
Frankhouse, Fred 68
Frawley Act 102
Frederick, Johnny 68
Freedman, Andrew 15
Freese, Gene 144
Freese, George 144
Friedlander, Sid 179
Friedman, Benny 114
Friend, Bob 144–45
Friou, George 117
Fugazy, Humbert 104, 113
Furillo, Carl 56, 77, 141, 143, 145, 147–48, 151, 156, 163, 169, 173–75, 185, 194

Gaffney, James 17–18, 21
Gallagher, Bernard 50

Gallery, Tom 117
Garback, Bob 69
Garbisch, Edgar 109
Gardner, Jim 188–89
Gavin, Mike 179
Genaro, Frankie 104
Gerstein, Ed 189
Getto, Mike 116
Getz, Gus 59
Gilchrest, Dennis 93
Giles, George 92–93
Gilliam, Jim (Junior) 56, 82, 148, 167
Glasgow Rangers Soccer Club 119
Glicksman, Hal 189–90
Godfrey, George 104
Godin, Roger A. 116
Gompers, Samuel 102
Goodding, Gladys 42, 54, 159, 165, 168, 174, 178, 185, 210, 218, 229
Goodwin, Doris Kearns 190–91
Gordon, Sid 165
Goren, Ed 191–92
Gould, Ben 106
Grace Reformed Episcopal Church, Brooklyn 107
Graham, Otto 117
Grande, Adele 192
Grant, Stuart 192–93
Gray, Sid 54
Great Lakes Naval Station Football Team 109
Green, Andrew Haswell 35
Greenlee, William A. "Gus" 96–99
Greenlee Field (Pittsburgh) 97
Gregg, Hal 72
Griffin, John 163, 171, 183
Griffin, Mike 11
Griffith Clark 99
Grimes, Burleigh 24, 63, 68
Groat, Dick 146, 158
Grodenchik, Jane 193
Grossingers 145
Gruber, Ed 193–94

Hafner, Walter 194
Hakoah Soccer Club 119
Hall, Joseph 97
Hallahan, Bill 67
Hamburger, Babe 217
Haney, Fred 144–45
Hanlon, Ned 11–12, 14–16, 23, 27
Hansen, Dave 68
Hapoel Soccer Club (Palestine) 120
Harris, William "Woogie" 97
Harry M. Stevens 187, 217
Hartford Blues 113
Hartnett, Gabby 64
Harvard University 101
Harwell, Ernie 166
Hawthorne Field (Brooklyn) 120
Head, Ed 71, 179
Heagney, Mary Walsh 194–95
Hearn, Jim 162
Hehl, Herman 195
Hehl, Mark 195
Heinrich, Tommy 70
Hennigan, John 54
Henry Miles & Son 37
Herman, Babe 66–***67***, 211
Herman, Billy 165
Herman, Jack 103
Herman, Peter 103
Hermanski, Gene 74, 166
Herrmann, August "Garry" 19, 21, 23
Hewitt, "Tiny" 109
Heydler, John 22
Hickman, Jim 62
Higbe, Kirby 177
Hilldale Baseball Club 87–88
Hirai, George 195–96
Hiss, Alan J. 196
Hodges, Gil 56, ***76***, 78, 80, 144, 152, 165–67, 186, 190–91, 206, 209, 215
Hodges, Joan 186
Hollingworth, Al 202
Holloway, Christopher Columbus "Crush" 93
Holmes, Tommy (player) 213
Holmes, Tommy (sportswriter) 116, 179
Homestead Grays 92, 94–95, 99
Hooks, "Ted" 86
Horace Mann School 182
Hornsby, Rogers 146
Horowitz, Ross 197–98
Horowitz, Susan 196–98
House of David Baseball Team 95
Howard, Elston 156
Hubbell, Carl 177
Hughes, Jim 171
Hurst, Tim 52

Illidge, Eric 94
Impellitteri, Vincent 77
Indianapolis ABCs 87–88
Inlet Park (Atlantic City) 85
International Soccer League 119
International Sporting Club 103
International Stars 85
Irvin, Monte 159
Iverson, John 107

J. G. Carlin Company 37
Jackie Robinson Apartments 127
Jackie Robinson Intermediate School 177
Jackman, Will 93
Jackson, Randy 80, 166–68, 187, 205
Jackson, Thomas 83–84, 89
Jackson, "Tut" 104
James Madison High School 111–12
Jeffcoat, Hal 187
Jenkins, Clarence "Fat" 86, 91, 93
Jennings, Hughie 11
Jiler, John 198–99
Joe F. Carr Trophy 115
John Morton's Sons Company 37
Johnson, Ban 14
Johnson, Rev. John H. 92
Johnson Brothers Company 36
Johnston, Bill 106
Johnston, Jimmy ***64***
Jordan, Tim 14, 16

Kahn, Roger 1, 179
Kansas City Monarchs 91, 99
Kansas State University 110
Kaye, Danny 211
Kaye, Sylvia 211
Keeler, Willie 11
Keenan, James 86
Kelley, Joe 11
Kelly, Bob 147
Kelly, Emmett 140
Kelly, John "Shipwreck" 114
Kid Chocolate 105
Killefer, Bill 175
Kinard, Bruiser 115, 178
Kiner, Ralph 147–48, 216
King, Clyde 168, 172–73
King, Marjorie Burns 199
Kipp, Fred 168–69
Kistner, Ken 199–200
Kitson, Frank 12
Kluszewski, Ted 169, 171, 182, 210
Knothole Gang 168–69, 187, 191, 194, 201–02, 205, 216
Koufax, Sandy 185, 187
Kress, Chuck 169–70
Kurowski, Whitey 142

Labine, Clem 82, 160, 163, 208
La Guardia, Fiorello 92
Lanctot, Neil 98
Landis, Kenesaw Mountain 99
Lang, Jack 179
Larsen, Don 156, 160
Lasorda, Tommy 187
Lavagetto, Cookie 73, 185, 205
Law, Vernon 148, 152
Lawler, Thomas Rev. 107
Layden, Elmer 109
Leavitt, Rev. Horace 107
Leible, Arthur 200
Leible, Mike 200–01
Leonard, William 117
Lesnevich, Gus 106
Lightstone, Ron 201
Lincoln Giants 86–87
Liverpool Soccer Club 120
Livingston, Bud 201–02
Lockman, Whitey 201, 213
Loes, Billy 145
Long, Dale 143
Long Island Railroad 44
Long Island University 217
Lopez, Al 67
Louis Bossert & Sons 36
Louisiana Purchase Exhibition 35
Louisiana State University 110
Lowenfish, Lee 202–03
Luckman, Sid 14, 16

Lucky Strike 169
Lumley, Harry 14, 16
Luna Park (Brooklyn) ***39***–40
Lund, Don 173
Lundy, Dick ***85***–86, 88
Lynch, Joe 103

Mack, Connie 17–19, 21
Mackay, Malcom 203
MacPhail, Larry 117, 177, 213
Maglie, Kay 219
Maglie, Sal 80, 156, 159–60, 162, 204
USS *Maine* 36
Malamud, Bernard 179
Mamakos, Steve 106
Mamaux, Al 24, 62
Manhattan College 110–11
Manley, Abe 89–***96***
Manley, Effa 90–92, 94–***96***, 98
Mantle, Mickey 79, 156, 221
Manual Training High School 111–12, 201
Maraniss, David 107
Maranville, Rabbit 66
Marcantonio, Anthony 203–04
Marcelle, Oliver "Ghost" 86–88
Marchesano, Josephine 204
Markert, William D., Jr. 204–05
Marquard, Rube 23–24, 27, 61, 63–***64***
Martin, Billy 79, 156
Martin, "Pepper" 206
Martinez, Gene 205
Master of the Senate 183
Mauriello, Tami 106
Mays, Willie 158–59, 210
Mazzer, Irving 97
McDaniel, Lindy 148–49
McDaniel, Von 148
McDevitt, Danny ***55***–56, 152, 169
McDonald, Joe 189
McDonald, Webster 97
McEwan, John "Cap" 114
McGinnity, Joe 12
McGowen, Roscoe 165, 179
McGraw, John 14, 16, 23, 60, 67–68
McKeever, Ed 17, 21, 23, 28, ***49***, 51–52, 103
McKeever, Jennie ***49***–52
McKeever, Steve 17, 21, 23, 56, 90, 107
McKelway, St. Clair 35
Medicus, Harry 14
Meehan, Chick (boxing) 106
Meehan, John F. "Chick" (college football) 110–11
Mele, Andy 205
Mercer, Sid 23
Merullo, Lennie 179
Meyer, Russ "Mad Monk" 145, 156, 166, 221
Michigan State University 110
Mickelson, Ed 149–50
Mickens, Glenn 170–71
Miksis, Ed 185, 187, 201
Milk Benefit Game 160
Miller, Bob 150
Miller, Don 109
Miller, Julius "Yellow Charleston" 89
Miller, Rod 171–72
Milwaukee Braves 54, 80–81, 169, 214, 216
Minally, James 205–06
Minarcin, Rudy 151
Mitchko, Peter 206
Montreal Royals 99
Moore, Gene 69
Moran Towing Company 166
Morgan, Bobby 172
Moses, Robert 44, 178, 182, 185
Mulvey, Mrs. Jim 56
Mumford, Louis 42
Munn, Monte 104–***105***
Murphy, Dick 151
Murphy, James J. 112
Murrow, Edward R. 165
Musial, Stan 140, 142, 177, 179, 185, 199, 202, 221
Myers, Hy 17
Myerson, Bess 160

Napolitano, Louis 220
Nathan Strauss Cup 119
Natiello, Robert 206–208
National Challenge Trophy (Soccer) 119–20
National League 8, 9, 12, 15
NBC 69, 114
Neal, Charley 148–49
Negro American League 96
Negro National League 87, 89–90, 93, 95–98
Negro Southern League 89
Nehadoma, Janos 120
Nelson, Johnny 119
Nelson, Rocky 187
New Brighton Theatre 41
New Utrecht High School 111
New York Age 86
New York Black Yankees 91, 94
New York City Board of Alderman 25
New York Cubans 90–91, 94–95
New York Giants (baseball) 12, 14, 23, 25, 48, 58, 60–61, 63–65, 67, 71, 74, 80, 149, 158, 161, 181, 184, 194
New York Giants (football) 113–16
New York Mets 127, 174, 220
New York National Soccer Club 120
New York Oval (Bronx) 89
New York University 108, 218
New York Yankees (baseball) 14, 25, 48, 52–53, 70, 73, 79, 82, 96, 124, 179, 181, 184, 214, 223–25
New York Yankees (football) 117
Newark Bears (football) 113
Newark Dodgers 91, 96
Newcombe, Don 75–76, 81, 152, 158, 184–85, 221
Newport Naval Reserve 108
Niederreiter, Andy 106
Nieman, Butch 70
Niss, Lou 115, 178
Nolan, Tom 208
North Carolina State University 110–11

O'Brien, Eddie 151–52
O'Brien, Johnny 152
O'Connor, Jimmy ***103***
Oliphant, Tom 208–10
Olson, Ivy ***64***
Olympic Field (Harlem) 86
O'Malley, Peter 210–11
O'Malley, Walter 28, 42, ***43***–44, 54–55, 76, 79–80, 160, 178, 182, 185, 194, 221
"On the Banks of the Old Raritan" 108
Owen, Mickey 70–71, 173
Owens, Jesse 68

Pafko, Andy 146, 173, 187, 221
Pagliacci 106
Palica, Erv 187
Palm, Clarence "Spoony" 91, 93
Palmento, Joe 219
Parker, Clarence "Ace" ***113–116***, 178
Parker, Joseph 89
Parrott, Harold 113, 179
Passeau, Claude 70
Pendergast, Bill 110
Perez, Javier 93
Peterson, Harding 153
Pettus, Bill 88
Pfeffer, Jeff 24, 60
Pfund, Lee 172–73
Philadelphia Eagles 114, 116
Philadelphia Phillies 23–25, 48, 54, 58–59, 65, 76, 80, 153, 166–67, 188, 204, 213, 225–27
Philadelphia Stars 91, 93, 95
Pignatano, Joe 57, 169, 173–74
Pittsburgh Crawfords 95, 97
Pittsburgh Pirates 1, 12–13, 23, 25, 54, 61–62, 72, 77, 81, 145, 152, 157, 161, 175, 216, 220, 227–29
Pittsburgh Steelers 116
Players' League 9
Plotz, Charles 211–12
Podres, Johnny 170–71, 185, 210, 221
Poles, Spotswood 86
Pollet, Howard 177
Polo Grounds, (Manhattan) 27, 108–09, 113, 127, 143, 145, 152–53, 167, 190
Poly Prep 111–12
Pompez, Alejandro 90
Posey, Cumberland 97
Pounds, Lewis, H. 41

The Power Broker 182
Pozner, Carol 212

Queen, Mel 77
Queens College 217

Radcliffe, Ted "Double Duty" 91–93
rain check 8, 26–***27***
Ralph, Julian 36
Ramsdell, Willie, 79
Raschi, Vic 165
Real Madrid Soccer 120
Redding, Dick 85–89
Reese, Dottie 194
Reese, Pee Wee 69, 76, 81, 153, 170, 174, 180, 190–91, 194–95, 213–14
Reilly, John 212
Reiser, Pete 71, 127, 143, 177, 185, 188, 194, 201, 211
Repulski, Rip 216
Resker, Edith 212
Rice, Grantland 51, 109–10
Rice, Tom 19, 23, 27, 48, 52, 104, 179
Richardson, Henry "Long Tom" 88
Richmond, Art 145
Richmond, Milt 145
Rickard, Tex 54, 144
Rickey, Branch 98–99, 117, 142, 148, 157, 165, 175
Rigler, Cy 62
Roberti, Roberto 104
Roberts, Curt 144
Roberts, Robin 76, 153
Robeson, Paul ***107***–108
Robinson, Jackie 42, ***71***–72, 74–76, 82, 99, 144, 146–49, 156, 159–60, 165–67, 169–70, 177, 183–85, 187, 190, 194, 199–01, 207, 209–10, 214, 216, 220
Robinson, Rachel 216
Robinson, Wilbert 8, 23–24, 27, 65, 67, ***171***
Robison, Frank 15
Robison Field 131
Rockne, Knute 109
Roe, Preacher 140, 158, 165, 172, 175
Roebuck, Ed 174
Roeder, Bill 54, 178–79
Rojo, Julio 87
Roosevelt, Franklin D. ***118***, 193–94
Roosevelt Stadium (Jersey City) 127
Root, Charlie 69
Rosen, Bob 212–14
Rosenthal, Harold 179
Rosner, Max 95
Rowell, Carvel "Bama" 179
Rucker, Nap 16, 52–53, ***55***
Rudolph, Dick 85
Ruether, "Dutch" 65
Ruffin, Leon 91
Runyan Memorial Cancer Fund 106
Ruppert Stadium (Newark) 96
Rutgers College 108–09
Ruth, Babe 104, 177
Ryan, Mervyn "Red" 87–88

Saffir, Oliver 214
St. Bonaventure 110
St. John's Prep 111
St. John's University 109–111, 113
St. Louis Browns 80
St. Louis Cardinals 1, 25, 62–63, 65–69, 71–72, 99, 140, 149, 168, 174–75, 177
St. Louis Church (Brooklyn) 192
St. Louis Giants 98
St. Louis Soccer League 120
Saltsman, George 214–15
Samiento, Pete 105
San Francisco 49ers 117
Sandlock, Mike 174
Sanford, George Foster 108
Santop, Louis 87
Schissler, Paul 114
Schmidt, Butch 59
Schoendienst, Red 214
Schult, Art 155–56
Schultz, Howard 173, 202
Schwartz, Perry 115
Schweiger, Ron 215–17
Scully, Vin 159, 214
Seattle University 152
Seaver, Tom 65
Seminick, Andy 166
Septoff, Lenny 208
Setaro, Joe 217
Sexton, John 218
Shackelford, John 96–98
Shakespeare, William 58
Shannon's 23rd Regiment Band 52, 229
Shapiro, Michael 28
Sharkey, Jack 104, 106
Sharmon, Bill 211
Sheehan, Joseph M. 44
Sheffield Milk Company 212
Shibe, Ben 17–18, 21
Shibe Park (Philadelphia) 17–18
Shuba, George 174
Siegel, Burt 218–19
Sinatra, Frank 146
Sisler, Dick 76, 153
Skinner, Bob 156
Skowron, Bill 156–57, 164
Slaughter, Enos 156, 160, 174
Smith, Al 25
Smith, J. Carlisle 52
Smith, Paul 157–58
Smith, Sherrod 63
Snider, Duke 55, 80–81, 141, 146, 152, 157–59, 161, 163, 167, 169, 178, 184–85, 190, 196, 200, 210, 212–13
Snyder of Flatbush 37
Soden, Arthur 15
Sollecito, Dan 219
Solomon, Burt 28
Spencer, Billie 219
Spencer, Daryl 158
Spencer, George 158–59
Spooner, Karl 221
Sportsman's Park (St. Louis) 1, 142, 152
Stanky, Eddie 70, 75, 141–42, 179
Stark, Abe 180
Stark, Archie 118–19
Staten Island Stapletons 113
Steeplechase Park, Brooklyn 34, 40–41
Steers, Alfred E. 31–32, 53
Steiger, Gus 56, 179
Stengel, Casey 24, 27, 52, 58–***59***, 62, 156, 165
Stevens, Joseph B. 187
Stone, Ed 91, 93
Stoneham, Horace 70, 219
Streisand, Barbra 192
Strong, Nathaniel C. "Nat" 84–86, 95
Stuhldreher, Harry 109
Sukeforth, Clyde 99, 148
Sunday Baseball 14–15, 25, 62, 125
Sutherland, Jock 115–16
Sutton, Larry 17, 25
syndicate baseball 11

Taylor, Ben 91–92
Taylor, C.I. 88
Taylor, John 17, 19, 21
Tener, John 62
Texas A&M 111
Thomas, Frank 153, 158–60
Thomas, Rex 111, 113
Thompson, Don 171
Thompson, Fred 41
Thompson, Tim 175
Tilyou, George C. 41
Tittle, Y.A. 117
Todd, Al 202
Todd Shipyards Soccer Team 119
Toomey's Diner 194
Toots Shor's Restaurant 166
Topping, Dan 114, 117
Torre, Frank 216
Treat'Em Roughs 85
Trevor, George 109
Tucker, Henry 83–85, 89
Turley, Bob 82, 160–61
Tydol Gas Sign 201
Tyler, Charles 96

UCLA 170
Ulster United Soccer Club of Toronto 119
Union Church of Bay Ridge 107
Union Grounds (Brooklyn) 101
United States Football Association (Soccer) 119–20
United States League (Negro) 96–99
University of Detroit 111
University of Kentucky 111

University of Notre Dame 109–10, 180
University of Pittsburgh 115
Uruguay National Soccer Team 119

Valo, Elmer 56
Van Buskirk, Clarence 7, 18
Vance, Dazzy 25, 64–67
Vander Meer, Johnny 69–***70***, 72, 126
Van Dusen, Fred 204
Vecsey, George 219–221
Vero Beach (Florida) 170
Villa, Pancho 104
Villanova 111
Virdon, Bill 145
von der Horst, Harry 11–12, 14
Voyles, Carl 117

W2XBS Television 43
W.C. Bryant High School, Woodside Queens 203
Wagner, Senator Robert 118
Wait Till Next Year 190
Waitkus, Eddie 213
Walker, Dixie 202, 206–07, 213, 220
Walker, James J. 102, 104
Walker, Mickey 106
Walker, Rube 169, 216
Walker Act 25
Wallabout Bay (Brooklyn) 36
Ward, Robert 22
Washington Park (Brooklyn) 10, 16–17, 22, 26, 53, 101
Washington Redskins (Boston through 1936) 114–16
Washington Senators 99
Watson, James S. 92
Weeghman, Charles 17, 21
Weinrig, Benny 54
Weismantel, Johnny 102
Weiss, Al 202
Western Union 185
Westlake, Wally 161
Whalen, Jim 110
Wheat, Zack 27, 52, 81, 132, 166
When Pride Still Mattered 107
White, Charley 80
Whitehill, John 108
Wilkins, Barron D. 84–86, 89
Williams, Andrew "Stringbean" 86, 88
Williams, Dick 171, 202
Williams, Harry 93
Williams, Joe 86–***87***
Wills, Harry 104
Wilson, Craig 68
Wilson, Hack 68, 211
Wiltse, Hooks 65
Workman, Chuck 71
Worthington, Al 161–62
Wright, Glenn 67–68
Wrigley Field (Chicago) 17, 153, 163, 167, 172, 202
Wyatt, Whitlow 69, 177

Yager, Abe 17, 179
Yale University 101
Yancey, Bill 91
Yankee Stadium (New York) 90, 108–09, 144, 190
York, Barney 19
Young, Dick 179
Young, Fay 99
Young Folks' League of United Israel Zion Hospital 107

Zeidler, Lew 94
Zeinth Sporting Club 106
Zimmer, Don 56, 80, 144, 170, 187, 216
Zuro, Josiah 106